TASTE *of the* MIDWEST

12 States, 101 Recipes, 150 Meals,
8,207 Miles and Millions of Memories

INSIDERS' GUIDE®

Cover photos: Bob Stefko
Cover design: Diana Nuhn
Text layout: Nancy Freeborn

Photographs: Robert Jacobs (p. 161 bottom right, p. 202); Pete Krumhardt (p. 208 top right); Doug Smith (p. 119 bottom left, p. 216 bottom left); Dean Tanner (p. 216 top right). All other photos by Bob Stefko.

Map illustrations: Bill Reynolds, Jeremie Buhler

Editorial credits

Midwest Living® project team: Joan Lynch Luckett, Editorial Project Manager; Sandra Mapes Granseth, Contributing Food Editor; Colleen Weeden, Test Kitchen Food Project Manager; Nancy McClimen, Contributing Copy Editor; Jonathan Morrow, Travel Assistant; Holly Roeske and Matt Bade, Photo Assistants; Karen Ziebarth and Tiffany Cleghorn, Transcriptionists.

 Midwest Living® magazine: Geri Boesen, Creative Director; Greg Philby, Executive Editor; Trevor Meers, Managing Editor; Barbara Morrow, Senior Travel Editor; Diana McMillen, Senior Food Editor; Kathy Roberts, Special Publications Coordinator; Judy Cordle, Brenda Kienast and Merrie Tatman, Administrative Assistants.

 Contributing Editors and Writers: Pam Henderson, George Hendrix, Barbara Humeston, Barbara Klein, Debbie Miller. Fact Checking and Research: Kate Crouse, Christine Feller, Angela Kennebeck, Danielle Sturgis, Tory Thaemert.

Library of Congress Cataloging-in-Publication Data is available.

ISBN-13: 978-0-7627-4071-0 (Hardcover); 978-0-7627-4072-7 (Paperback)
ISBN-10: 0-7627-4071-X (Hardcover); 0-7627-4072-8 (Paperback)

Printed in the United States of America
First Edition/First Printing

TASTE *of the* MIDWEST

12 States, 101 Recipes, 150 Meals,
8,207 Miles and Millions of Memories

A BEST OF THE MIDWEST® BOOK

Written by Dan Kaercher • Photography by Bob Stefko

INSIDERS' GUIDE®

GUILFORD, CONNECTICUT
AN IMPRINT OF THE GLOBE PEQUOT PRESS

Contents

In addition to Dan's essays about the places he visited and the delicious foods he experienced, this book is intended as both a practical travel guide and a cookbook. Please consult the end of each chapter for trip-planning advice, mail-order information for some featured food products, and a listing of food-related events in each state (if you plan to attend an event, call first; dates and particulars may change). All of Dan's recommendations have been thoroughly researched to the best of our ability. The recipes in this book have been carefully tested for flavor and practicality in the *Midwest Living®* Test Kitchen. A recipe index appears on page 215.

Key to Lodgings Prices:

$ $70 or less
$$ $70–$100
$$$ $100–$150
$$$$ more than $150

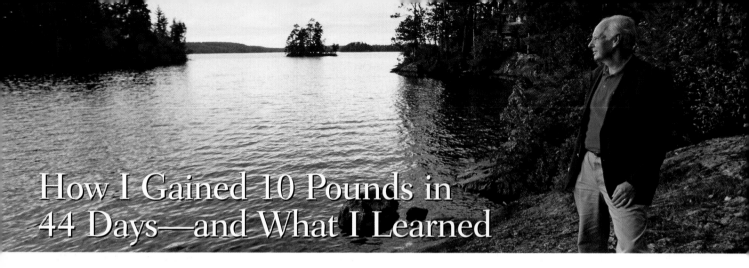

How I Gained 10 Pounds in 44 Days—and What I Learned

No, YOU DIDN'T MISREAD the headline. I know, you're accustomed to books and magazines telling you how to *lose* 10 pounds or more in some ridiculously short period of time. But 10 pounds really is how much weight I put on during my six-week Midwest road-food tour during the summer of 2005. Twelve states, 8,207 miles and untold calories later, I'd moved up a belt notch or two. In this case, the added poundage was anticipated, an affirmation that my remarkable, once-in-a-lifetime food foray on behalf of *Midwest Living®* magazine, Iowa Public Television and the Globe Pequot Press (publisher of this book) was a resounding success.

My culinary mission emerged from a previous book and public television project undertaken during the summer of 2004, entitled *Best of the Midwest: Rediscovering America's Heartland.* At that time, I returned to many places that hold special meaning for me, after 20 years of editing *Midwest Living* and spending almost my entire life in the region. During that sentimental journey of 10,000-plus miles, I became keenly aware of how passionately interested people are in food-travel connections ("culinary tourism").

I also came to the realization that there's a fascinating story to be told about food in the Midwest. That saga encompasses both the delicious foods Midwest cooks prepare with such aplomb (from barbecue, steak and chili to haute cuisine, international specialties and vegetarian alternatives) and the signature crops that thrive here like nowhere else on earth (corn, soybeans and wheat; wild rice, potatoes and asparagus; cherries, blueberries and cranberries; not to mention beef, pork and dairy products).

From that realization, *Taste of the Midwest* was born, thanks in large measure to the indispensable support of my own management at Iowa-based Meredith Corporation (publishers of food- and agriculture-related magazines including *Midwest Living®*, *Better Homes and Gardens®* and *Successful Farming®*, among many other magazine and book titles).

The results of my epicurean inquiry include this book and a series of public television programs and magazine excerpts. To each and every person who traveled with me or facilitated my project in some other way, I thank you from the very bottom of my heart (and, in most instances, my stomach). Each of the individuals listed on the copyright page and featured on the contributors page has earned my deepest appreciation and highest regard—especially Joan Lynch Luckett, who masterminded my daily travel itinerary and coordinated the overall project.

I also want to thank the hundreds of other Midwesterners I met along the way, who broadened my culinary horizons and my waistline so profoundly: leading-edge chefs at gourmet restaurants and self-taught cooks at small-town cafes; master bakers, sausage makers and brewers; ranchers, farmers and growers to whom we owe our region's unrivaled agricultural bounty; the food artisans who create splendid cheeses, breads, wines and confections; the talented inheritors of a rainbow of ethnic cooking legacies; and the innovative processors and retailers who make all those flavors readily accessible to all of us. I would like to make a particular remembrance of a wonderful Indiana Amish cook, Mary J. Miller (1945–2006), and the rewarding conversation and satisfying food we shared one evening during this journey.

I DO NOT REPRESENT MYSELF as a professional "foodie," and I apologize to any gastronomes seeking musings of a more profound and discriminating nature than my palate is equipped to offer. I'm just a very inquisitive guy (to my own detriment at times) who likes to eat—a lot—and has an aversion to almost nothing. I can honestly say I relished almost all of the 500-odd dishes and food products I greedily ingested in one form or another.

My compressed course of study yielded much more than ruminations about the foods set before me. I wanted to explore the cultural and environmental context of food in our region. From Native Americans on reservations in South Dakota and Minnesota, I gained a new reverence for food as a gift of the Creator, never to be taken for granted. A morning with Wes Jackson, president of The Land Institute in Salina, Kansas, heightened my awareness of how farming practices can become more compatible with nurturing our fragile environment. Ambassador Kenneth Quinn, president of the World Food Prize in Des Moines, kindly took the time to inform me about the Midwest's role in feeding a very hungry world.

Others I met enlightened me about trends that can only benefit us all in the long run, ranging from organic growing methods to sustainable agriculture, healthy eating habits and the slow-food movement, as well as consumer behavior and the economics of the food industry.

What else did I learn during my odyssey? A variety of things: It's always wise to carry along in your pocket a toothbrush, toothpick and some dental floss on a mission such as this. Gassy foods are best avoided prior to lengthy drives when traveling with a companion. Limiting portion size is the best way to experience a wide range of dishes without losing your figure (I did my best). For the sake of your fellow diners, it really is only common courtesy to turn off your cell phone and avoid smoking when dining out. There should be more access for disabled diners everywhere. Restaurants that succeed in the long term do so because their owners are obsessed with customer service. Servers who meet your expectations deserve generous gratuities. Chain restaurants are proliferating everywhere—one more step in the homogenization of America, which saddens me as a regionalist. Having a 6-foot-3-inch frame is a definite advantage when you put on extra pounds that need camouflaging.

Finally, I learned that food isn't just about calories, proteins, carbohydrates and fats—it's about culture, community and pure hedonistic pleasure. In the latter regard, I am indebted to the incomparable food writer M.F.K. Fisher (1908–1992), whose works I enthusiastically commend to the uninitiated.

A final indulgence, if you'll permit me: I want to thank my wife, Julie, for her continuing encouragement and steadfast support. At the end of the trail, I was once again reminded, like Dorothy, that proverbial Kansan from *The Wizard of Oz*, that there's no place like home—and no cooking like home cooking. Upon my return, Julie prepared the single most-anticipated meal of my entire journey: homemade meatloaf (slightly soggy and smothered with ketchup, just the way I like it), an unadorned baked potato, fresh green beans cooked with bacon and rhubarb-custard pie. It was heavenly.

Over the years, Julie and the other cooks, past and present, in both our families have taught me a basic truth that I hope you take away if you retain nothing else after reading this book: Regardless of what region you hail from, the one essential ingredient in all good cooking is love.

Dan Kaercher

Dan Kaercher
Editor-in-Chief
Midwest Living® Magazine

Dan's route covered 8,207 miles through 12 Midwest states over 44 days during the summer of 2005.

ILLINOIS
A World of Cultures and Cuisines

THIS PAGE: BEATING THE HEAT AT CROWN FOUNTAIN IN
MILLENNIUM PARK, CHICAGO. OPPOSITE PAGE (ALL TAKEN
IN CHICAGO) FRESH, ORGANIC PRODUCE AT GREEN CITY
MARKET. FAMOUS STUFFED PIZZA AT GIORDANO'S IN THE
LOOP. CEVICHE APPETIZER AT FRONTERA GRILL.

Illinois really should be two states, at least when it comes to food: Chicago and the rest of Illinois. Most of the Prairie State resembles other states in the Midwest Corn Belt in the crops and livestock that spring from its rich farmland, and food processing is the state's top manufacturing activity.

Depending on the year, Illinois vies with Iowa as the nation's top soybean state. In central Illinois, Morton is a Midwest pumpkin-growing and -processing capital. Southern Illinois is known for its orchards, laden with apples and peaches. In Collinsville, near St. Louis, horseradish reigns—along with a 170-foot, ketchup-bottle-shaped water tower that's on the National Register of Historic Places. Hogs seem to be everywhere in Illinois, but various breeders also specialize in goats, elk, ostriches, emus, turkeys, catfish, tilapia and striped bass.

Much of Illinois' bounty ends up in the state's northeast corner, on both the elegant and the humble tables of Chicago's more than 7,000 restaurants. With 9.1 million residents, metro Chicago truly is the Midwest's dining capital. The city is best known for its signature classics: unique Chicago-style pizza and hot dogs and Italian beef sandwiches. But it's also an ethnic dining revelation, with myriad nationalities represented in the city proper alone: Polish, German, African-American, Swedish, Italian, Jewish, Irish, Greek and Chinese, plus lesser-known

Ethiopian, Afghan, Vietnamese, Thai, Guatemalan, Puerto Rican, Ukrainian and Lithuanian enclaves. Proud neighborhoods are identified by their eateries as much as anything: Devon Avenue, Middle Eastern; Pilsen, Mexican; Lincoln Square, German; Andersonville, Swedish; Bridgeport, Irish; Humboldt Park, Puerto Rican; the South Side, African-American; plus Chinatown, Greektown and Little Italy. I plan to probe Chicago's confluence of cultures and cuisines with four days of restaurant hopping.

First, Chicago-style pizza. Thick (at least an inch!), chewy-crusted and layered with tomato sauce and cheese as well as to-order toppings, it's the stuff of dreams. I make a quick stop at Giordano's on Jackson Street in the Loop for my fix. Giordano's was founded in 1974 by Efren and Joe Boglio, two brothers who emigrated to Chicago from northern Italy. They first sold to-go pizzas, but the business didn't take off until Joe talked Efren into christening the restaurant with their mother's maiden name and using her recipe for the gooey pizza she served on holidays back home. Now there are more than 43 Gior-

dano's in the Chicago metro area. Mama Boglio's stuffed-pizza variation is basically one layer of dough, toppings, mozzarella, another layer of dough and tomato sauce on top. It's served piping hot in the pan—pure heaven! Now that I've duly paid my respects to Chicago's No. 1 hometown dish, I'm ready for "Taste."

All in Good "Taste"

Big parties aren't new to Chicago. In 1893, the city hosted the World's Columbian Exposition, which attracted an astounding 26 million visitors over six months. Huge fairs and political gatherings are routine. But one festival—Taste of Chicago—is unique: It's all about food, Chicago-style. Each summer, three city blocks of Chicago's 319-acre Grant Park on Columbus Drive, downtown near Lake Michigan, become the heart of the city, even diverting bumper-to-bumper Michigan Avenue traffic. A total of 3.5 million noshers attend Taste during its 11-day run, which includes a Fourth of July extravaganza. It all began in 1980 with just 35 vendors, and although the idea has been replicated in a score of other Midwest cities, most notably Cincinnati, Madison and Kalamazoo, there's nothing quite like Taste of Chicago.

Near the west entrance, I meet free-lance magazine writer and former *Midwest Living®* staffer Steve Slack, who knows Chicago and the Taste festival like a pizza aficionado knows mozzarella. It's just after lunchtime on a weekday, so the crowds are manageable, but the weather is broiling-hot. "You should have worn shorts, a T-shirt and comfortable shoes," Steve says. "And where are your sunglasses, hat and sunscreen?" Oops. Heed Steve's advice if you plan to attend.

Steve leads us to one of six ticket windows. Although admission is free, 11 tick-ets for food sampling cost $7. At the booths, entrée-size portions require six to nine tickets, but Steve wisely encourages me to limit myself to the smaller "taste" por-tions, which cost just one to three tickets. Where to start? I can stick to Windy City classics or challenge my palate with fried oysters, oxtails, sushi, curried goat, alligator, gumbo, gyros, rice pudding with persim-mons and cranberries, jerk tofu or prime-rib quesadilla. Or seek out local legends, including Eli's Cheesecake, Ditka's pulled-pork sandwich and the Billy Goat Tavern and Grill, with the "cheezborgers" immortal-ized in *Saturday Night Live* sketches.

Between samples, we see cooking demonstrations and food-related exhibits, nary students of Chicago's Kendall College, I pay tribute to another icon, the Chicago dog. I order mine just as Steve advises me to, "dragged through the garden"—an all-beef hot dog served on a poppy seed bun with a tomato slice, fluorescent-looking green pickle relish, fresh cucumber, mus-tard and celery salt. No ketchup allowed!

At Arya Bhavan, an Indian couple from Mumbai (formerly known as Bombay) glee-fully pile my plates with spicy concoctions whose names I can't decipher. But I defi-nitely vote for the various combinations of naan (Indian bread traditionally cooked in a clay oven) and chickpeas, potatoes, cream cheese and, of course, curry and other spices. Around the corner at Jamaica Jerk (referring to the popular Caribbean restau-rant and seasoning), I load up on red beans and rice with fried plantain, jerk chicken and collard greens with ham hocks—even jerk tofu. Where in the Midwest but Taste of Chicago would I be able to experience a world of such incredible flavors?

Shopping with a Master Chef

Have you ever gone produce shopping with a chef? It's not like running to the neighborhood supermarket to pick up a hermetically sealed bag of salad greens and presliced mushrooms! I learn this and more when I meet Bruce Sherman, chef of the upscale North Pond restaurant in Lincoln Park, just north of downtown. We rendezvous early in the morning at Green City Market, on the edge of Lincoln Park a few blocks from North Pond, and I tag along as he shops for his evening diners.

Bruce touts seasonal specialties raised by local growers who believe in organic, sustainable farming. The latter term usu-ally suggests opting for few or no chemi-cal fertilizers or pesticides, employing conservation-friendly farming methods, encouraging more biodiversity in crops

Big parties aren't new to the city, but there's nothing quite like Taste of Chicago. It's all about food.

plus amusement-park rides. At the Gourmet Dining Pavilion, noted Chicago chefs prepare full-course meals. For liba-tions, we can choose from wine at the Wines of the World garden near the park's regal Buckingham Fountain, vodka lemon-ade at the Finlandia booth and a "hurri-cane" at the Southern Comfort counter, plus lots of suds nearly everywhere.

I keep returning to the concourse, where more than 60 vendors lure me with their specialties. First, a rainbow cone from Lynn Sapp-Stenson, the third gener-ation of her family to work at the Original Rainbow Cone in Chicago's Beverly neigh-borhood. A rainbow cone has the same five flavors every time: chocolate, straw-berry, Palmer House (cherry walnut), pis-tachio and orange sherbet. And please note: The ice cream is sliced, not dipped.

At the Kendall Café, operated by culi-

CLOCKWISE, FROM ABOVE: (ALL TAKEN IN CHICAGO) CITY SKYLINE FRAMING TASTE OF CHICAGO REVELERS IN GRANT PARK. FLORAL SELECTIONS AT GREEN CITY MARKET IN LINCOLN PARK. NORTH POND CHEF BRUCE SHERMAN SHOPPING FOR SUPPER, GREEN CITY MARKET. OPPOSITE PAGE: CARIBBEAN SENSATIONS, TASTE OF CHICAGO.

Snapdragons
Lilies
Larkspur
Godetia
$6
local*certified organ

Mixed Bouquets
$8
w/ Sunflowers
local*certified or

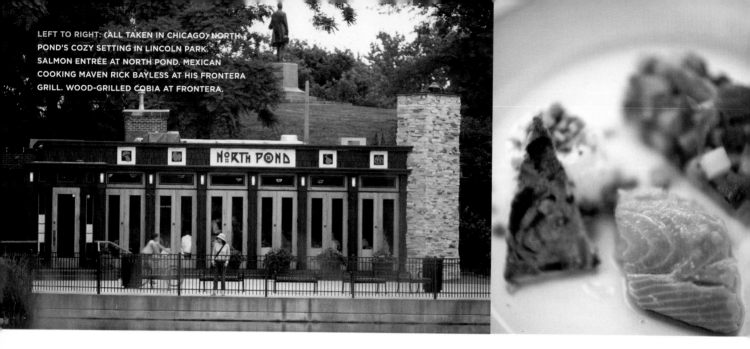

and foods and getting a fair deal in the process. At this market, founded by Chicago cookbook author and food columnist Abby Mandel, Bruce Sherman and others in 1999, about 45 vendors from the greater Chicago area gather in a small "street fair." Stalls are filled with an eclectic collection of fresh fruits, vegetables, herbs and flowers. Chefs, shoppers, growers and browsers mingle and chat at this low-key, friendly gathering place Wednesdays and Saturdays from May through October. I like the intimacy I see here. The concept of connectedness between grower and consumer is apparent, and the market's motto sums it up: "Know your food. Know your farmer."

Bruce and I start a fast tour—touching, crunching and sampling the early-summer vegetable harvest all along the way: arugula, bok choy, rainbow chard, snap peas, baby peas, wheatgrass, dandelion greens, mushrooms, rhubarb, spinach, peas, kohlrabi, wild mushrooms, radishes,

baby carrots, cabbage, garlic, onions, kale, fava beans, squash and squash blossoms, strawberries, vine-ripened tomatoes. And that's just the beginning! There also are fresh-cut flowers, handcrafted candles, dog treats, honey, beeswax lip balm, pussy willows and baked items. One stall offers succulent produce from a cooperative where it's raised by the homeless. Beets alone are a revelation to me here. They come in a variety of shapes, colors and sizes. Radishlike Chiogga beets. Golden beets. Bruce slices open an Italian oblong red beet. "I love beets roasted; we grill them in olive oil mixed with carrots and fresh onions," he says. "We'll do several dishes with beets tonight at dinner."

In the evening I head to North Pond to see what Bruce has wrought from the morning's foraging. Tucked into a lovely and somewhat hidden corner of Lincoln Park, the building originally was a 1912 Arts and Crafts–period warming house for ice-skaters. Later, it became a storage

facility and a park concession stand. The restaurant debuted here in 1997 and got a retooling in 2002. A window wall capitalizes on the pond view and the skyline beyond. Inside, I'm drawn to sayings lettered high on the walls in the Arts and Crafts style: "The lyf so short—the craft so long to lerne" (Chaucer) . . . "To make calm, To feel amidst the city's jar that there abides a peace of thine, Man did not make and will not mar" (Matthew Arnold). No wonder academics particularly like this gem, along with just about everybody else.

Next, another new experience: sitting in on the chef's preopening ruminations about various menu items with the staff, who must be knowledgeable when sophisticated diners inquire about the evening's offerings. Subtle nuances in tonight's dishes are thoroughly discussed—and sampled—around a big table near the kitchen. Techniques and presentation are covered in minute detail. Samples of dishes with ingredients such as fennel, mint, turnips, eggplant, duck, rabbit

and sardines make their way around the table for analysis. My mouth is watering!

Back in the dining room, my tasting menu showcases foods that are at their peak, plus some standards. The feast begins with lobster tail medallions in a sweet-pea mousseline, followed by chilled mushroom soup with rosemary, tomato-poached loin of tuna, middinner sour cherry and apricot sorbets, hickory-wood-smoked beef tenderloin and the finale, a hot lemon soufflé with strawberry-anise hyssop syrup. All through the leisurely meal, I enjoy the chef's wine pairings, which include selections from Burgundy, Bordeaux and the Loire Valley in France as well as from Argentina. Outside, daylight is dimming to twilight. From the Green City Market to North Pond, it's been a long but quite wonderful day.

Chicago's Mexican Frontier

I can't talk about the very with-it Frontera Grill and its upscale, next-door sibling,

Topolobampo, without first introducing their proprietor, Rick Bayless. This culinary juggernaut has authored six cookbooks—his latest book is titled *Mexican Everyday*—can be seen on public television and has won three awards from the world-class James Beard Foundation. Rick is focused on one mission: spreading the word about true contemporary Mexican cuisine. I meet him for a brief interview in the test kitchen-office area above Frontera—my favorite Chicago casual dining spot—on North Clark near the Chicago River and Navy Pier.

Rick Bayless is as close as we come in the Midwest to having our own food media superstar. In person he comes across just as he does on camera: scholarly, articulate and measured in his speech. Yet, his tightly controlled demeanor fairly erupts with passion whenever the conversation turns to such topics as the nuances of mole sauces, exploring the big market in Oaxaca City and his Frontera Farmer Foundation,

which offers grants to help small growers in the greater Chicago area. In sum, this guy probably knows as much about what Mexicans eat and have eaten in the past as anyone on either side of the Rio Grande.

If you're hoping to dine on big, cheesy, hamburger-filled enchiladas smothered in tomato-salsa sauce, don't come to Frontera. The restaurant's very name means "frontier" in Spanish. Rick's cuisine is Authentic-with-a-capital-A Mexican cookery, with a creative edge. First, let's answer the inevitable question: Rick is not Mexican. He's "just a white guy" who grew up in an Oklahoma City family that operated a grocery and a barbecue spot. At 14, he orchestrated a family vacation to Mexico that sealed his career direction. Then came a BA in Spanish at the University of Oklahoma and a master's in linguistics at the University of Michigan.

Rick's wife, Deann, who's from suburban Wheaton, brought him to Chicago, where they now live with daughter Lanie

South-Side Macaroni and Cheese
Army & Lou's Restaurant, Chicago

10   ounces dried elbow macaroni (2½ cups)
 1   8-ounce package shredded sharp
      cheddar cheese (2 cups)
 1   8-ounce package pasteurized prepared
      cheese product, cut up (1 cup)
¼   cup butter, cut into pieces
 3   eggs, slightly beaten
 1   12-ounce can evaporated milk
 1   10¾-ounce can condensed cheddar
      cheese soup
¼   teaspoon seasoned salt
¼   teaspoon ground white pepper

Cook macaroni according to package
directions. Meanwhile, let the cheeses and
butter stand at room temperature. Drain
macaroni; transfer to a very large bowl.
Add 1 cup of the shredded cheddar and the
cheese product to the hot pasta, stirring
until the cheeses start to melt.

In a medium bowl, whisk together eggs,
the softened butter, milk, cheese soup,
seasoned salt and white pepper. Stir egg
mixture into macaroni mixture. Transfer
half of the mixture to a 3-quart rectangular
baking dish. Sprinkle with ½ cup of the
shredded cheddar. Top with remaining
macaroni mixture.

Bake, covered, in a 325° oven for 30 minutes. Uncover; sprinkle with the remaining
½ cup shredded cheddar. Return to oven.
Bake about 15 minutes more or until cheese
is melted and mixture is bubbly and heated
through. Let stand 10 minutes before serving. *Makes 8 to 10 servings*.

in a renovated tavern in the Bucktown
district. In the 1980s, the couple traveled
an incredible 35,000 miles throughout
Mexico; they opened Frontera in 1987
and "Topolo" in 1989. Rick still travels to
Mexico regularly, and the family spends
each Christmas in Oaxaca, an enchanting colonial city in a broad mountain valley in southern Mexico. Beyond the
restaurant, the TV programs, the books
and cooking classes, Rick's Frontera
Foods brand appears on an array of food
products sold in supermarkets, in specialty shops and online.

A line starts forming outside Frontera at
4:30, and the bar is packed right after the
doors open at 5 p.m. Mellow Latin music
complements the restaurant's tropical
color scheme of mustard yellow and
orange. The evening's selection of regional
tamales is like none other I've tasted north
of the border; the flavors are unusual and
intense. I order plantains on the side, fried
and topped with sour cream and fresh
farmer cheese. The tacos are not the
greasy standards; the fillings are deli-
ciously marinated and seasoned skirt
steak, pork and portobello mushroom. I
can't keep all these new sensations
straight in my head, but I know I like what
I'm tasting: aichote, tomatillo, habanero
pepper, citrus marinades, radish, cilantro.
My dessert is the Mexican classic, *pastel
de cuatro leches*: vanilla-almond cake
infused with a four-milk syrup and frosted
with sweetened sour cream.

I ask Rick about his culinary inspirations.
He's informed by his extensive travels and
research, but his eclectic sauces, soups and
desserts and their artful presentations are
triggered by what he *sees*—Mexican paintings, marketplaces and street vendors—as
well as what he *tastes*. Although Chicago is
1,690 miles from Mexico City, it's home to
America's second-largest Mexican popula-

tion (after Los Angeles), a community that's
constantly infusing the city with its rich
culture and cuisine.

Soul of the South Side
One of slavery's innumerable injustices
was that racial inequality also applied to
food: Slaves ate what their masters made
available to them—scraps, offal, wild
greens and lots of beans and rice. Soul
food emerged when they combined these
humble ingredients with their African
cooking traditions and seasonings.
Although I know the term "soul food"
refers to a combination of Southern and
African cookery that evolved on ante-
bellum plantations in the South, I haven't
experienced much of it firsthand.

But people on Chicago's South Side
know what soul food is. Over the years,
this area has been the hub of meatpacking
plants, steel and railroad-car factories,
world-class museums and universities
(and the Chicago White Sox, clean-sweep
winners of the 2005 World Series!). It's
seen waves of Germans, Scandinavians,
Irish, Jews and Eastern Europeans cluster
in tight-knit neighborhoods. Blacks have
had a presence here since before the Civil
War, but South Chicago became the capital of African-American culture in the
early 20th century, when Southern blacks
migrated north seeking factory jobs.
Between 1940 and 1960, Chicago's
African-American population swelled
from 278,000 to 813,000. One legacy of
that culture is legendary music: jazz,
gospel and blues. Another is soul food.

On busy 75th Street in the tidy
Chatham neighborhood, a sign on a small
brick building with a red awning denotes
Army & Lou's Restaurant. Inside, a classy
treasury of Chicago's soul food heritage
awaits. This is a quiet eatery with red-and-
white tablecloths, stained-glass light fix-

tures and artwork by local talents depicting South Side neighborhood scenes and African-American heroes such as Dr. Martin Luther King, Jr. and Malcolm X.

Dolores Reynolds, who has owned the place since 1991, welcomes me warmly with a brief course in soul food classics. My sampling banquet includes smothered pork chops, fried catfish and chicken, and chicken livers and wings; short ribs and baby back ribs, gumbo and ham hocks; peppery mustard and turnip greens, candied sweet potatoes, creamy macaroni and cheese (perhaps the best I've ever tasted) and corn bread dressing with giblet gravy. I even take a deep breath and dive into a side dish of squishy, spicy chitterlings (hog intestines). OK, now I can say I've tried them! The pièce de résistance is a heavenly slice of sweet potato pie with whipped cream.

I check out the kitchen and meet John Watts, who's called the shots here for 25 years. He learned about cooking from his mother back in Kentucky, then honed his skills in the military. When I ask about recipes, John tells me with a grin that most of Army & Lou's secrets are in his head, not on paper. Back in the dining room, a motto on the wall conveys the philosophy here: "The bitterness of poor quality remains long after the sweetness of price has been forgotten."

Dolores, a former food-service manager who studied psychology in college (a great combination of credentials in this business), tells me that Army & Lou's was founded by a husband-wife team in 1945. She's proud to serve many of their original specialties. "We season to taste here; we're not afraid of a little salt and pepper," she says with a discreet wink. The breakfast menu includes standards as well as grits, catfish, fried chicken, wings, pork chops and baby beef liver. On Friday evenings,

CLOCKWISE, FROM ABOVE: (ALL TAKEN AT ARMY & LOU'S, CHICAGO) JOHN WATTS AND DOLORES REYNOLDS AT THE LONG-ESTABLISHED SOUL FOOD RESTAURANT. FRIED CATFISH AND SIDES. DINERS SAVOR THE RELAXED AMBIENCE AND DELICIOUS FOOD.

jazz groups perform and diners are invited to join the jam sessions.

About half of Army & Lou's patrons are from the neighborhood, many of them everyday regulars. "A shift worker can come in for pancakes and eggs at 9 p.m. and we'll fix them," Dolores says. "One gentleman keeps his own special seasonings in our kitchen!" The rest of Army & Lou's patrons hail from all over the Chicago area—and beyond. "I want everyone who comes in to have an experience here, starting with the first bite," Dolores says. I've certainly had a soul food adventure here, every bite a marvelous one at that.

Delightful Asian Dining

Canned chow mein with those crinkly fried noodles was about as exotic as dining got for my family when I was a kid. Luckily my tastes, and the Midwest's, have broadened since those days.

I pay a visit to the once-gritty West Randolph district, formerly the home of Chicago's meat and fish purveyors. Signs indicate that plenty of them are still around, but trendy nightspots and restaurants are now part of the scene here, as well as Oprah Winfrey's TV studio. My destination, Red Light, is appropriately marked by a huge, glowing red light above the entry. (Rumor has it that ladies of the evening used to gather at this corner, hence the risqué restaurant name.) Tonight, I'll be dining on 21st-century pan-Asian, a fusion of flavors and cultures presided over by a gracious Hong Kong native, Executive Chef Jackie Shen.

Inside, Red Light is primarily one large dining room with a red-hued mix of fixtures and decor: sort of Asian, sort of art nouveau, sort of phantasmagoric. The head of a huge, happy Buddha presides in the center of things. One side of the room is a bar; the other is an open grilling area

where huge, steaming woks sizzle with chicken, shrimp and vegetables. It's not long before Jackie, with her glowing smile, sees to it that I have a drink—a colorful mango martini with citrus vodka, mango puree and ginger syrup, garnished with a blackberry—and begins presenting the parade of delights I'll spend the evening sampling. I enter a brave new world of lemongrass, squid, ginger, garlic and curry, all artfully presented.

Thailand is represented by jumbo prawns with curry and a classic phad Thai of pork and shrimp; Indonesia by Mee Gha Ti (stir-fry chicken, chili-mint rice noodles and Kaffir lime-coconut sauce); China by traditional kung pao chicken with peanuts, scallions and pea shoots and by a showstopping whole Shanghai-style fried catfish with a red vinegar sweet-sour sauce; Japan by miso-glazed salmon and paper-wrapped ahi tuna; and Korea by a kimchi salad that includes baby octopus and avocado. Oh, and how could I forget all of the ingenious appetizers: steamed dumplings with foie gras, pork and a cognac sauce (reflecting Jackie's talent for fusing Asian and French influences); a Jonah crab cake; a lobster-mango roll; and pan-seared diver scallops with morel mushroom polenta and coconut sauce.

It all comes together at Red Light. "[Asians] love a variety of flavors, while the French emphasize sauces made with butter and cream," Jackie says. "I think it's a perfect complement to the boldness of Asian cuisine." It's clear her customers are globetrotting more these days and developing more worldly palates. And more Asian communities are appearing in Chicago. That's fine with Jackie: "I ride the bus everywhere," she says. "Here in Chicago, any time I get on a bus, I see at least five different cultures represented among the passengers." Even in such a diverse crowd,

Jackie and the cuisine at Red Light stand apart as something special.

Breakfast Queens

The license plate on Ina Pinkney's car reads "Breakfast." And that says it all. I have many memorable breakfasts on this journey, but I never meet anyone as passionate about starting the day out right, food-wise, as Ina—Chicago's No. 1 champion of the morning board. She's also a pro foodie who writes, develops recipes for corporate clients and teaches cooking classes. But breakfast is her crusade: "I want to change the way people look at breakfast and make it a real treat," she says. "It's a great way to socialize. Let's get beyond scrambled eggs and bacon, please! Let's have some bolder and unexpected flavors."

Ina's is located just outside the Loop on revitalized West Randolph, once known as "the street that feeds Chicago." Ina's building, just down the street from Red Light, once belonged to a potato distributor. As I settle in for my feast, Ina explains the logic of the neighborhood in the old days: Businesses closest to the Chicago River, just a few blocks east of here, dealt in the most perishable foods, such as chicken, fish and meat. The farther from the river you got, the more produce vendors you saw.

I scan the dining room, with plates and platters decorating the walls: homey but classy—just the way Ina likes it. I'm intrigued by the unique salt-and-pepper-shaker sets at every table, each one different. "They were all given to me by my patrons," Ina says, obviously touched by their loyalty. She is an engaging conversationalist. My favorite Ina-ism this morning: "The only two things I don't share: Blame and dessert."

"Now, I'm going to serve you a real breakfast!" she proclaims. Out from the

CLOCKWISE, FROM TOP LEFT: (ALL TAKEN IN CHICAGO) EXECUTIVE CHEF JACKIE SHEN, CREATOR OF RED LIGHT'S ORIENTAL DELIGHTS. MISO-GLAZED SALMON AT RED LIGHT. INIMITABLE INA PINKNEY, CHICAGO'S SELF-PROCLAIMED BREAKFAST QUEEN. HEALTHY FOOD AND CONVERSATION AT INA'S.

Heavenly Hots
Ina's, Chicago

- 4 eggs
- 1 16-ounce carton dairy sour cream
- ¼ cup sifted cake flour or all-purpose flour
- 2 tablespoons potato starch or cornstarch
- 3 tablespoons sugar
- ½ teaspoon baking soda
- ½ teaspoon salt
- Blackberries, raspberries or blueberries (optional)

In a blender, add the eggs, sour cream, cake flour, potato starch, sugar, baking soda and salt. Cover and blend the mixture for 30 seconds. Stop the blender. Scrape down the sides of blender container with a rubber spatula and blend again until the mixture is smooth. Let the batter sit for 2 to 3 minutes.

Pour slightly less than ¼ cup of the pancake batter into a 3-inch circle on a hot, lightly greased griddle or heavy skillet. Cook over medium heat about 2 minutes on each side or until pancakes are golden brown, carefully turning (pancakes are very tender) to second side when pancakes have bubbly surfaces and edges are slightly dry. Serve warm. If you like, serve with berries. *Makes 12 to 13 pancakes.*

kitchen proceeds a series of platters, plates and bowls. My buddies and I dive into the sour cream pancakes Ina calls Heavenly Hots (other specialty pancakes include whole-wheat oatmeal and gingerbread with lemon cream), vegetable hash, steel-cut oatmeal and a pasta frittata. We fairly swoon over the roasted breakfast potatoes with an unmistakable garlic edge and multigrain bread that even includes omega-3-rich flaxseed—Ina likes healthy foods. My standard two eggs, over easy, even get some pizzazz with an assortment of intriguing sausages: veal-chive, chicken and spicy chorizo.

Ina's is a low-key power-breakfast venue for Chicago politicians, businesspeople and doctors. But plenty of regular folks also like Ina's way with breakfast; Sunday brunch is a big deal here. "You would leave your wife for one of my cheese blintzes!" Ina tells me as I depart for my next stop, fully fortified to take on the day. Although that's not likely to happen, I make a note to try one of those blintzes when I return.

The next morning, my Chicago breakfast agenda takes me to Ann Sather and another neighborhood with its own character. As far as I'm concerned, this stretch of Belmont Avenue in Lakeview, north of downtown and not far from DePaul University and Wrigley Field, is the real Chicago. Just down the street, an El train rumbles overhead. Walls of vacant buildings are enlivened with bold artwork created by neighborhood artists. A couple of erotica boutiques and tattoo parlors slip in among a medley of storefront eateries that includes Mexican, Italian, Indian, Thai, Mediterranean, Greek and Chinese. There's also a Starbucks on one corner and Dunkin' Donuts across the street.

So how is it that a Swedish restaurant best known for its breakfasts is thriving here? Easy—the Swedish place was here

first, and it's still the anchor of the neighborhood. This Ann Sather restaurant, one of four in the Chicago area, is the original, founded right after World War II when this was a Swedish neighborhood. Ann Sather was a Swedish-American girl who grew up in North Dakota, joined her brothers here in the city and toiled for years to save $5,000 to purchase a diner. The place grew and expanded, thanks to her no-nonsense cooking and baking skills.

Enter her successor, Tom Tunney. His vita reads a bit differently than Ann's: He was born in Chicago to a South Side Irish family, earned an MA from the Cornell University School of Hotel and Restaurant Management, studied under French chefs, cooked at the Ritz-Carlton in Chicago and then learned Ann Sather's secrets before she sold him the place.

In the dining room, a portrait of Ann hangs above the fireplace mantel, and other walls display photos of longtime employees. I ask Kelly, my bustling, friendly waitress, her nationality: "Half Ukrainian and half German. We also have Italians, Mexicans, Slovenians and Russians working here," she says with a laugh. Later, she returns to tell me one of the cooks is half Swedish and half German.

But the Swedish breakfast delights Kelly balances on a tray are for real: a raspberry-based chilled fruit soup; pleasantly rubbery pancakes topped with cranberrylike Swedish lingonberries; potato sausage with ground pork and veal; potato pancakes that hint of onion, garnished with sour cream and apple slices; and one of Ann Sather's irresistible homemade cinnamon rolls drowning in a sweet, milky glaze. (The rolls are so popular that up to 25,000 are made on a busy Sunday alone!) I scan the lunch and dinner menus and resolve to return next time I'm in town: Homemade chicken potpie, pickled herring, roast duckling with lingonberry glaze, Swedish meatballs and Swedish brown beans are among the specialties.

Tom has been a Chicago alderman since 2002. That's reflected in his passion for the Lakeview neighborhood and Belmont Avenue, and in his efforts to make Ann Sather restaurant a community hub. Upstairs, seniors are gathering for a morning exercise class in a banquet room. Because Tom is the only politician-restaurateur I'll meet on the trip, I have to ask: Who's tougher to please, your constituents or your restaurant patrons? I get a very circumspect answer: "I have the best in both worlds. It's all about service in both cases." Tom is clearly a vote-getter, and so is Ann Sather restaurant.

McDonald's Goes McUptown

Fast food. Just mention the term and most serious gourmets and health nuts sneer— "slow food" is the culinary slogan of choice these days. Me, I'm just a guy who's both hungry and on the go a lot of the time, and I consider myself reasonably fit. So I have no compunction about today's research topic: McDonald's, the world's largest fast-food chain, headquartered in Oak Brook, Illinois.

A brief history lesson: On April 15, 1955, fast-food legend Ray Kroc opened his first McDonald's in nearby Des Plaines. The chain had originated with two brothers in 1948 in San Bernardino, California. In 1954, Kroc was selling six-spindled milk-shake machines (Multimixers) when he learned about the brothers' operation—and success—and later talked them into letting him open a McDonald's franchise in Illinois. A few years later, Kroc purchased the whole caboodle for $2.7 million (today, McDonald's is a publicly held corporation worth an estimated $42 billion). Now there are more than 13,000 McDonald's restau-

CLOCKWISE, FROM ABOVE: (ALL TAKEN IN CHICAGO) LEGENDARY HOMEMADE CINNAMON ROLLS AT ANN SATHER ON BELMONT AVENUE. ANN SATHER, A LAKEVIEW NEIGHBORHOOD ANCHOR FOR DECADES. ELEVATED ART AT A BELMONT AVENUE TRAIN STOP.

rants in the United States and more than 31,000 in over 100 countries around the globe, patronized daily by 50 million customers who are served by 1.6 million employees. No other chain comes close to these numbers.

On North Clark in the trendy River North district downtown, I visit a McDonald's that people want to linger in, not rush out of. The chain bills it as its own 50th-anniversary present. I check it out: two architecturally stunning, glass-encased stories; 23 plasma TV screens tuned to news channels; trash cans that

factor, certainly. Beyond that, Michael points to consistent quality, service, cleanliness and value. Kroc, who died in 1984 at age 82, sold his first burgers for 15 cents apiece (now they average 86 cents). Remember those old signs that tallied how many billions had been served? Well, the company stopped counting and says it's now focusing on one customer at a time.

The core menu still includes the Big Mac, Quarter Pounder with cheese and Chicken McNuggets, but I'm also encouraged to sample Apple Dippers (apple slices with low-fat caramel sauce), breakfast

foods and trays full of fresh salads. As other patrons gape, I do my culinary homework. It's early in the day, so I take a few bites of the ever-popular Egg McMuffin, plus the McGriddle variation, two warm griddle cakes with the syrup baked in that are cleverly embossed with—what else?—the golden arches. I try the new Fruit and Walnut Salad I'll see promoted throughout my journey. Of course, I also indulge in a few bites of burger and sample the fries.

If I were abroad, I'd have even more interesting choices. In India, for example, McDonald's serves Chicken Maharaja Mac sandwiches, made with chicken rather than beef patties. In New Zealand, locals go for the Kiwi Burger, hamburger with fried egg and a slice of pickled beet. In Taiwan, the Rice Burger, a choice of chicken or beef served between two rice patties with tangy sauce, rules. Uruguayans cheer for the McHuevo, a hamburger with mayonnaise and a poached egg. And only Poland claims the McKielbasa, a sausage patty topped with ketchup, mustard and pickles and served on a sesame seed bun.

The Great Pierogi Hunt

If there's one ethnic cuisine that blankets the Midwest more than any other, it's meat-and-potatoes German. Mention German food in the Windy City, and until just recently, people automatically thought of The Berghoff Restaurant, now sadly closed except for a busy cafeteria that survives in the United terminal at O'Hare.

The Berghoff anchored the same block of West Adams in the heart of the Loop for 107 years, operated by the descendants of founder Herman Joseph Berghoff. Herman started out brewing beer in Fort Wayne, Indiana, back in 1887 (that label still is brewed by the Huber Brewing Company of Monroe, Wisconsin—see page 181). I'm thankful for my memories of black-jacketed,

There are more than 13,000 McDonald's restaurants in the United States and more than 31,000 around the globe.

say "thank you" in 10 languages, including Portuguese and Mandarin Chinese; black-onyx tables and brushed-aluminum chairs; escalators leading to an upper level furnished with Barcelona and Le Corbusier chairs. And did I mention the gelato and dessert bar? Overall, there's seating for 300 customers. Out front, twin golden arches stand 60 feet tall and weigh 42 tons each. Lifelike bronze statues depict the corporate patron saint, Ronald McDonald, and assorted McDonald's customers. The dramatic backdrop for all this is North Michigan Avenue's dazzling parade of skyscrapers—awesome!

The artifact-filled "Decades Wall" upstairs displays McDonald's memorabilia, as well as photos of cultural icons, from the Lone Ranger to the Beatles. I chat with Michael Bullington, a historian who manages the company's archives. How did this chain come to dwarf the others? Ray Kroc's entrepreneurial drive is one

bow-tied Berghoff waiters with their white-towel aprons, who seemed to have just stepped off the set of *Hello, Dolly!* They tantalized my German-American palate with delights such as sauerbraten (marinated sirloin of beef), Wiener schnitzel (breaded veal cutlet) and *Kassler Rippchen* (smoked pork loin) and all the "wursts," along with homemade spaetzle (noodles) and sauerkraut, followed by strudel for dessert. My Teutonic taste buds are still quivering! But it's time to try something new, and Polish cookery is a close kitchen cousin to German, despite the two nations' fractious history.

That's why I find myself half lost this morning in the confounding maze of suburbs and highways northwest of Chicago. Signs of the culinary times ring with irony: A place called Le Vichyssois stands practically next door to Buddy's Pub and Pizzeria. Warring fast-food franchise signs pit healthy salads against gargantuan burgers. But I have another objective: the pierogi. It's one of those ethnic foods that can bring tears to the eyes of Poles the way lutefisk stirs Norwegians, albeit perhaps for different reasons. Although I've long known about the pierogi (sort of a Polish pot sticker or ravioli), I've never actually consumed one—until today!

From outside, the restaurant we approach on Front Street in McHenry looks like a typical suburban eatery, until I study its big red sign a bit closer: Zubrzycki's Warsaw Inn Polish American Smorgasbord. In midafternoon, the place is relatively busy, with lots of pleasant-looking older patrons and a sprinkling of younger folks. I suspect that many people drive here from Chicago, which is said to have the largest Polish population of any city outside Warsaw, Poland.

I glimpse the lengthy buffet setup. Regardless of their nationality, there's

CLOCKWISE, FROM ABOVE: **DAN AT THE ULTIMATE MCDONALD'S RESTAURANT ON NORTH CLARK STREET IN DOWNTOWN CHICAGO. SISTER-BROTHER PROPRIETORS BERNICE AND JOE ZUBRZYCKI AT THE WARSAW INN, MCHENRY. A PIEROGI-LOVER'S DREAM AT THE WARSAW INN.** OPPOSITE PAGE: **RONALD MCDONALD DEPICTED IN BRONZE AT MCDONALD'S ON NORTH CLARK, CHICAGO.**

Italian Beef Sandwiches

Inspired by the Launching Pad Drive-In,
Wilmington

- 1 4-pound boneless beef sirloin or rump
  roast, cut into 2- to 3-inch pieces
- ½ cup water
- 1 0.7-ounce envelope Italian dry salad
  dressing mix
- 2 teaspoons Italian seasoning, crushed
- ½ to 1 teaspoon crushed red pepper
- ½ teaspoon garlic powder
- 10 to 12 hoagie buns, kaiser rolls or other
  sandwich rolls, split
  Pickles, chopped onion, pepperoncini
  and/or roasted red sweet pepper
  strips (optional)

Place beef in a 3½-, 4- or 5-quart crockery
cooker. Stir together water, salad dressing
mix, Italian seasoning, crushed red pepper
and garlic powder; pour over beef in crockery cooker. Cover and cook on low-heat
setting for 10 to 12 hours. (Or cover and
cook on high-heat setting for 5 to 6 hours.)

Remove meat with a slotted spoon.
Using two forks, shred the meat. Serve
meat on rolls. Drizzle each sandwich with
some of the juices to moisten.

If you like, top each sandwich with pickles, chopped onion, pepperoncini and/or
roasted red sweet pepper strips. *Makes
10 to 12 sandwiches.*

something about a buffet, smorgasbord or
the magic words "all you can eat" that
brings out the savage in otherwise-civilized
diners. This spread touts 80 items, all of
them prepared on the premises. There are
the usual offerings: fried chicken, roast
beef, fried perch, stew, mashed potatoes,
salad bar standards, green beans, squash
and lots of sumptuous desserts. But duty
calls! I zero in on the Polish fare: creamy
sauerkraut, pork-stuffed cabbage and kielbasa (fresh homemade Polish sausage)
with a wonderful caraway flavor; blintzes
(mini crepes) with various fillings; even
homemade headcheese (made with pork
and pigs' feet).

But back to the main attraction: pierogies. The Warsaw Inn serves three versions,
filled with seasoned ground beef, moist
white baker's cheese or a kraut-cabbage
mixture. All are tender and yummy, especially because they've spent their final
moments bobbing about in a warming tray
filled with melted margarine. I wash everything down with a sampling of two full-
bodied Polish beers, Zywiec and Lomza.

The Slavic-specific dessert selection is
something to write home to Krakow about.
I try Polish-style *kolaczki*—flaky pastry
triangles filled with apricot or raspberry
jam or cream cheese. *Placki ziemniaczane*
are golden crispy potato pancakes you can
top with sour cream and applesauce. As I
depart, I'm also intrigued by the specialty
drinks listed near the entry, especially the
Warsaw Seesaw—three kinds of rum plus
brandy and fruit juice!

Drive-In Kicks on Route 66

Route 66. It's the stuff of legend: a 2,400-
mile ribbon of wanderlust that captivated
Americans for much of the 20th century—and still does. You can drive 85 percent of the road today, although you have
to work at finding it in some areas; it goes

by a number of different names these
days. The last stretch to be purged from
official highway maps was eliminated in
1984, eclipsed by modern four-lane inter-
states. By linking big cities, small towns
and a whole lot of wide-open spaces,
Route 66 reigned as one of America's primary east-west road routes for decades. It
helped nurture automobile-crazed America's newfound appetite for motor courts,
campgrounds, service stations—and highway eateries.

One Route 66 road-food landmark that
still survives is the Launching Pad Drive-
In in Wilmington (population 5,100).
Located near the Kankakee River amid an
endless carpet of green soybean fields,
Wilmington (once an Underground Railroad stop) now knows Route 66 as busy
Illinois-53 running right through the middle of town. Jerry and Sharon Gatties have
owned the Launching Pad for two
decades; Sharon's parents, John and Bernice Korelc, opened it as a Dari-Delite in
1960. The bill of fare is just what I'm looking for, but it's the 500-pound, 28-foot-tall
helmeted spaceman holding a rocket out
front that really puts this place on the
Route 66 map. The Korelcs brought the
giant—once a muffler-chain mascot in
California—home after attending a
restaurant convention in 1963, then had
him retrofitted into "Gemini Giant" in
honor of the U.S. space program.

Europeans in particular seem to be
spellbound by Route 66. Many of them
travel to the United States just to motorcycle all or part of the route. "French,
Germans, Danes, Irish, Swiss . . . we get
them all," Jerry says, bemused. "They even
ask me to sign their Route 66 books." Brits
have ordered crumpets (similar to English
muffins) and Germans want beer; neither
is on the Launching Pad menu. But a teen
working behind the counter tells me

there's one thing most foreign visitors seem to have in common: a fascination with the all-American hot dog.

As if on cue, a young couple from Zurich, Switzerland, pulls up beside the Launching Pad on a motorcycle, guidebook in hand, just starting their 10-day Route 66 journey to New Mexico. I snap their photo in front of the spaceman before they head inside for hot dogs. I notice several people (representing Lithuania and Bulgaria, among other places) doing the same thing during my brief Saturday-morning interlude here. Film crews from Japan and Great Britain have stopped by recently. Jerry says his drive-in also is a popular Route 66 stop for vintage auto clubs and motor coach tours. Back when Jerry was a teen hanging around this place (with his eye on Sharon), the lot was full of Thunderbirds, Corvettes and woody-type station wagons, and gas cost about 25 cents a gallon (ah, for those good old days!).

Inside the Launching Pad, there's a rocket-shaped gum-ball machine and lots of other Route 66 and space-program kitsch. But I'm ready for some road food. The signature sandwich here is the Italian beef, a Chicago-area favorite: juicy, specially seasoned beef served on a hoagie bun with garlic butter, pickles and onion, a hot pepperoncini pepper on the side, cheese optional. Drive-in menus have changed since the heyday of Route 66, when they were all hamburgers, fries, sodas and malts. Jerry points out that now the big menu above the counter includes such items as breaded shrimp, a variety of salads, cappuccino and a slew of ice cream creations. I wonder what the stoic Gemini Giant surveying life along old Route 66 from 28 feet up thinks of all the newfangled stuff they're serving these days at the Launching Pad.

CLOCKWISE, FROM TOP LEFT: (ALL TAKEN AT THE LAUNCHING PAD DRIVE-IN, WILMINGTON) STAFFERS EAGER TO PLEASE THEIR ROUTE 66 PATRONS. WILMINGTON'S TALLEST AND MOST UNUSUAL RESIDENT. ROUTE 66 AND AUTOMOBILE MEMORABILIA DECORATE THE WALLS.

Halibut with Baby Carrots and Snap Pea Puree

North Pond, Chicago

- 4 5- to 6-ounce fresh or frozen skinless halibut steaks
- 8 ounces fresh sugar snap peas or frozen loose-pack sugar snap peas (about 2½ cups)
- ¼ cup kosher salt or 3 teaspoons salt
- 2 cups peeled, organic baby carrots, halved lengthwise
- ¼ cup olive oil or cooking oil
- 1 shallot, thinly sliced
- ½ teaspoon kosher salt or ¼ teaspoon salt
- ¼ teaspoon ground white pepper
- ⅓ cup loosely packed mint leaves (3 sprigs)
- 2 tablespoons vegetable or chicken broth or water
- ¼ cup butter, softened
- 1 tablespoon snipped fresh chives
  Fresh parsley sprigs

Thaw fish, if frozen. Rinse fish; pat dry with paper towels. Set aside. Remove strings and tips from fresh peas. Fill a large bowl half full with cold tap water and 2 cups ice cubes.

In a large saucepan, bring 3 quarts of water to boiling. Add the ¼ cup kosher salt. Add carrots to boiling water; return water to boiling. Cook for 2 minutes. With a strainer or skimmer, remove carrots. Transfer to ice water; chill for 2 minutes. With a strainer, remove carrots; set aside to continue to drain.

Add peas to the boiling water; return water to boiling. Cook fresh peas for 2½ minutes. (If using frozen peas, cook for 4½ minutes.) With a strainer, remove peas. Transfer to ice water; chill for 2 minutes. With a strainer, remove peas; set aside to continue to drain. Reserve ¼ cup of the ice water.

For pea puree: In a small saucepan, heat 2 tablespoons of the oil over medium-high heat. Add shallot. Add ¼ teaspoon of the kosher salt and ⅛ teaspoon of the white pepper. Cook and stir about 2 minutes or until shallot is softened but not brown. Transfer shallot mixture to a blender or food processor. Add mint leaves, drained peas and the reserved ¼ cup ice water. Cover; blend or process for 1 to 2 minutes or until smooth. Press pea puree mixture through a fine strainer; discard solids. Set puree aside.

In a medium saucepan, melt 2 tablespoons of the butter; add drained carrots. Cook and stir over medium-high heat until glazed and hot. Stir in chives. Season to taste; keep warm.

In same small saucepan, combine pea puree and the 2 tablespoons vegetable broth. Bring to boiling; reduce heat. Add the remaining 2 tablespoons butter; heat through. Season to taste; keep warm.

Meanwhile, sprinkle fish fillets with the remaining ¼ teaspoon kosher salt and ⅛ teaspoon white pepper. In large skillet, heat the remaining 2 tablespoons oil over medium-high heat. Add fish; cook 4 minutes. Carefully turn fish. Reduce heat to medium; cook for 2 to 3 minutes more or until fish flakes easily when tested with a fork.

To serve, on 4 heated dinner plates, spoon the warm pea puree in the middle of the each plate. Place a bed of warm carrots on pea puree. Place fish on top of the carrots. Garnish with parsley. Serve immediately. *Makes 4 servings.*

Chicken with Pueblan Green Pumpkin Seed Sauce

Frontera Grill, Chicago

- 2½ to 3 pounds meaty chicken pieces (breast halves, thighs and drumsticks)
- 5 cups water
- 1 large carrot, cut up
- 1 medium white onion, cut up
- 2 cloves garlic, halved
- 1 teaspoon kosher salt or ½ teaspoon salt
- 2 bay leaves
- ¼ teaspoon dried thyme, crushed
- ¼ teaspoon dried marjoram, crushed
- ¼ teaspoon ground black pepper
- 1¼ cups raw pumpkin seeds (pepitas)
- 1 medium white onion, cut up
- 3 small romaine leaves, coarsely chopped (1½ cups)
- ½ cup loosely packed fresh cilantro leaves
- 2 large radish, arugula or sorrel leaves, coarsely chopped
- 3 fresh serrano chile peppers* or 2 small jalapeño chile peppers*, coarsely chopped
- 2 cloves garlic, halved
- 1 tablespoon cooking oil or olive oil
- 1 small zucchini, halved lengthwise and thinly sliced (1 cup)
  Fresh cilantro sprigs (optional)
- 3 cups hot cooked rice

For chicken: Skin chicken. In a 4-quart Dutch oven, combine the chicken, water, carrot, the 1 medium onion, the 2 cloves garlic, salt, bay leaves, thyme, marjoram and black pepper. Bring to boiling; reduce heat. Simmer, covered, for 35 to 40 minutes or until chicken is tender and no longer pink. Remove chicken pieces from broth. Strain broth; discard vegetables and seasonings. Use a large metal spoon to remove fat from hot broth by skimming off the fat that rises to the top. Cover and chill chicken; set broth aside.

For pumpkin seeds: In a 12-inch skillet, evenly spread out pumpkin seeds and, stirring often, heat over medium heat about 5 minutes or until all seeds have popped (from flat to rounded) and turned golden. Remove from heat. To cool, evenly spread out pumpkin seeds in a shallow baking pan.

For sauce: Reserve 1/3 cup of the cooled pumpkin seeds; set aside. In a large food processor or blender, combine the remaining pumpkin seeds, the remaining 1 medium onion, romaine, cilantro, radish leaves, chiles and the remaining 2 cloves garlic. Add 1 1/2 cups of the reserved chicken broth. Cover and process or blend until pureed.

In a large saucepan, heat oil over medium heat. Add the pumpkin seed puree. Cook and stir about 10 minutes or until very thick. Stir in 2 cups of the chicken broth. Simmer, uncovered, about 20 minutes more or until the sauce looks coarse, stirring frequently. Transfer the sauce to a food processor or blender. Cover and process or blend until pureed. (If necessary add a little more chicken broth to give the sauce a medium consistency.)

Return the blended sauce to same saucepan. Season to taste with salt. Add the chicken and zucchini. Heat mixture over medium-low heat about 10 minutes or until heated through (but do not bring to a simmer).

To serve, use a slotted large spoon to transfer the chicken to a warm serving platter. Ladle the sauce over and around it. Sprinkle with the reserved pumpkin seeds. If you like, garnish with cilantro sprigs. Serve with hot cooked rice. *Makes 4 servings.*

*Tip: Because hot chile peppers, such as serranos and jalapeños, contain volatile oils that can burn your skin and eyes, avoid direct contact with chiles as much as possible. When working with chile peppers, wear plastic or rubber gloves. If your bare hands do touch the chile peppers, wash your hands well with soap and water.

Glazed Cinnamon Rolls
Ann Sather, Chicago

- 1 package active dry yeast
- 1 teaspoon granulated sugar
- 1/4 cup warm water (105° to 115°)
- 3/4 cup warm milk (105° to 115°)
- 1/3 cup granulated sugar
- 1/4 cup butter, melted
- 1 1/2 teaspoons salt
- 3 to 3 1/2 cups all-purpose flour
- 1/4 cup butter, melted
- 1/2 cup packed brown sugar
- 1 tablespoon ground cinnamon
  Powdered Sugar Glaze (recipe follows)

In a large mixing bowl, stir yeast and the 1 teaspoon granulated sugar into the warm water. Let stand for 5 minutes to soften yeast.

Stir in warm milk, the 1/3 cup granulated sugar, the 1/4 cup melted butter and salt. Add 1 cup of the flour. Beat with an electric mixer on low to medium speed for 30 seconds, scraping sides of bowl constantly. Beat on high speed for 3 minutes. Using a wooden spoon, stir in as much of the remaining flour as you can.

Turn dough out onto a lightly floured surface. Knead in enough of the remaining flour to make a moderately soft dough that is smooth and elastic (3 to 5 minutes total). Shape dough into a ball. Place in a lightly greased bowl, turning dough once to grease surface of dough. Cover; let rise in a warm place until double in size (about 1 hour).

Punch dough down. Turn dough out onto a lightly floured surface. Divide dough in half. Cover; let rest for 10 minutes. Meanwhile, lightly grease two 9x1 1/2-inch round baking pans; set aside.

Roll each half of dough into a 15x10-inch rectangle. Spread half of the 1/4 cup melted butter over each dough rectangle. In a small bowl, combine brown sugar and cinnamon. Sprinkle half of the mixture over each dough rectangle. Roll up each dough rectangle starting from a long side. Seal seams. Slice each roll into 9 pieces. Place cut sides down in prepared pans. Cover dough loosely with plastic wrap; let rise in a warm place until nearly double, about 45 minutes.

Bake in a 350° oven for 20 to 25 minutes or until light brown (if necessary, cover rolls with foil the last 5 to 10 minutes of baking to prevent overbrowning). Remove from oven. Carefully invert rolls onto wire racks. Cool slightly. Invert again onto a serving platter. Immediately drizzle rolls with Powdered Sugar Glaze. Serve warm. *Makes 18 rolls.*

Powered Sugar Glaze: In a bowl, stir together 2 cups sifted powdered sugar, 3 tablespoons milk and 1/2 teaspoon vanilla. If necessary, add additional milk, a teaspoon at a time, to reach drizzling consistency.

Swedish Fruit Soup
Ann Sather, Chicago

- 1 17-ounce package dried fruit, coarsely snipped
- 3/4 cup raisins
- 1/4 cup dried apricots, coarsely snipped
- 1/4 cup pitted dried plums (prunes), coarsely snipped
- 2 cups water
- 1 tablespoon cornstarch
- 2 tablespoons granulated sugar
- 2 tablespoons packed brown sugar
- 1/4 cup raspberry syrup
- 1 tablespoon lemon juice

In a medium saucepan, combine mixed dried fruit, raisins, apricots and plums. Add the water. Bring to boiling; reduce heat. Simmer, covered, for 8 to 10 minutes or until fruit is tender but not mushy.

Meanwhile, in a small bowl, combine cornstarch, granulated sugar and brown sugar. Stir in syrup and lemon juice. Stir syrup mixture into hot fruit mixture. Cook and stir until thickened and bubbly; reduce heat. Cook and stir for 2 minutes more. Cool about 10 minutes before serving. *Makes 6 servings.*

Travel Journal

More Information

Chicago Office of Tourism (877/244-2246, www.877chicago.com).

Featured Dining

Ann Sather Chicago (773/348-2378), with more locations around the city.
Army & Lou's Restaurant Chicago (773/483-3100).
Frontera Grill Chicago (312/661-1434; same number for sister restaurant Topolobampo).
Giordano's Pizza Chicago (312/583-9400), with many more locations around the city.
Ina's Chicago (312/226-8227).
North Pond Chicago (773/477-5845).
Red Light Chicago (312/733-8880).
Warsaw Inn Polish American Smorgasbord McHenry (815/344-0330).
Launching Pad Drive-In Wilmington (815/476-6535).

More Great Dining

Charlie Trotter's Chicago. An award-winning Lincoln Park restaurant offering a multi-course dining experience with fresh seasonal products (773/248-6228).
Walnut Room Restaurant Chicago. A white-tablecloth dining tradition at the nine-story Marshall Field's department store in the Loop (312/781-3125).

Shaw's Crab House Chicago. Just west of North Michigan Avenue, a premier seafood restaurant serving some 40 fresh entrées in its Oyster Bar and main dining room (312/527-2722).
Spiaggia Chicago. Among the city's top Italian eateries, with a glittery second-floor North Michigan Avenue dining room overlooking Lake Michigan (312/280-2750).
Taste of Chicago eateries: **Arya Bhavan** (773/274-5800), **Billy Goat Tavern and Grill** (312/222-1525), **Eli's Cafe** (773/205-3800, 773/736-3417 for tours), **Jamaica Jerk** (773/764-1546), **Kendall Café** (312/752-2620), **Mike Ditka's Restaurant** (312/587-8989), **Original Rainbow Cone** (773/238-7075).

Featured Stops

50th Anniversary McDonald's Chicago (312/867-0455).
Green City Market Just north of downtown Chicago (847/424-2480).

More Great Stops

The Windy City Chicago claims the honorary title of capital of the Midwest, not only for its nearly 3 million people and stunning Lake Michigan location, but also for a roster of attractions that rival those of any metropolis. The Chicago River divides the city north and south. **To the north:** the North Michigan Avenue Magnificent Mile shopping boulevard, 94th-floor John Hancock Center Observatory, Museum of Contemporary Art, Navy Pier 50-acre entertainment and shopping complex, Lincoln Park and the trendy River North area. **To the south:** the Loop shopping and dining district; 103rd-floor Sears Tower Skydeck; South Michigan Avenue's Millennium Park, with its public art and landscaped gardens; theater district; The Art Institute of Chicago; Museum Campus, including the Field Museum of natural history, John G. Shedd Aquarium and Adler Planetarium & Astronomy Museum; and Museum of Science and Industry.
Blommer Chocolate Store Chicago. Retail shop of a legendary chocolate manufacturer since 1939, when the Windy City was known as the nation's candy capital (312/492-1336).

Garrett Popcorn Shops Chicago. A city favorite since 1949, with four locations: three in the Loop and one along North Michigan Avenue (888/476-7267).

Dan's Lodgings

Fitzpatrick Chicago Hotel Chicago, just east of North Michigan Avenue ($$$$; 800/367-7701).

More Great Lodgings

Best Western Inn of Chicago Chicago. With more than 350 rooms and suites, just steps from North Michigan Avenue ($$$; 312/787-3100).
Congress Plaza Hotel Chicago. A landmark presiding along Michigan Avenue since 1893, overlooking Grant Park ($$$$; 312/427-3800).
Crowne Plaza, Chicago, The Silversmith Hotel Chicago. A Frank Lloyd Wright–inspired design in a historic 1897 Loop building ($$$$; 312/372-7696).
Embassy Suites Downtown Lakefront Chicago. Between North Michigan Avenue's Magnificent Mile and Navy Pier, with family-size suites and full breakfasts ($$$$; 866/866-8094).
Travelodge Chicago For the budget-conscious, with small, serviceable rooms a block from Grant Park near the Loop ($$; 312/427-8000).

Food Events

Rhubarb Fest Aledo, first Friday and Saturday in June—Under the big blue tasting tent, sample rhubarb in foods from ice cream and crisps to wine and barbecue sauce. If you have room for more, stock up at the bake sales around town that offer more than 1,500 homemade rhubarb pies. You can take home free rhubarb seeds or enter the rhubarb recipe contest or the biggest-rhubarb-leaf contest. Also take in a 145-booth crafts sale that encircles the historic courthouse, band shell entertainment, 5K Rhubarb Run and free guided trolley tours (309/582-2751, www.aledo mainstreet.com).
International Horseradish Festival Collinsville, second weekend in June—

TASTE OF CHICAGO AND BUCKINGHAM FOUNTAIN, CHICAGO.

Have a "hot" time in this horseradish capital, which grows nearly 60 percent of the world's horseradish root. In the growers' tent, sample cranberry horseradish and horseradish jelly, buy freshly dug roots and talk to area horseradish farmers. Events include a Bloody Mary–making competition, root-sacking and horseradish-cooking contests, and the Root Derby, featuring derby race cars fashioned from horseradish roots. Live music, a crafts fair and a kids' area round out the fun (618/346-5210, www.horseradishfestival.com).

Taste of Chicago Chicago, late June through early July—Forget counting calories when Chicago-area restaurants dish up their specialties at this annual gastronomic gala. Eat your way from booth to booth in Grant Park, sampling foods from pizza, ribs and Italian beef to grilled alligator, Thai pot stickers and other exotic and ethnic fare. Chefs demonstrate in the Cooking Corner, and a different upscale restaurant serves its specialties each day in the Gourmet Dining Pavilion. Top it all off with free fun in the Family Village and concerts by big-name acts. Tickets sold for food and beverage (312/744-3315, www.cityofchicago.org/specialevents).

Bagelfest Mattoon, third Thursday through Saturday in July—Festgoers crowd around breakfast tables to devour 80,000 free bagels, served with cream cheese, jelly, honey and butter, at the World's Largest Bagel Breakfast (8 a.m. Saturday). Also in the hometown of Lender's Bagel Bakery, you can watch a 1½-hour parade, enter the 5K Run for the Bagel, shop at crafts booths and take a carnival ride. National acts play at nightly concerts. Admission charged to concerts (800/500-6286, www.mattoonillinois.org).

Pierogi Fest Whiting, Indiana (south metro Chicago), last full weekend in July—Celebrate Whiting's Eastern European roots by piling on the pierogies—fried dough stuffed with fruit, potatoes, sauerkraut or meat—at 50 ethnic food booths or at the pierogi-eating contest. Polka bands and Slovak dancers entertain, and the polka parade stars the Precision Lawn Mower Drill Team and the Babushka Brigade. Carousel rides, games and an inflatable play area fill the kids' zone (877/659-0292, www.pierogifest.net).

State Fair Springfield, 10 days starting the second Friday in August—Eat your way through 14 countries at the Ethnic Village, where there's always a line for the Greek gyros (217/782-0770, www.illinoisstatefair.info).

DeKalb Corn Fest DeKalb, last weekend in August—In the heart of corn country, join 200,000 visitors who flock downtown for 30,000 ears of free sweet corn (served Saturday), a carnival, a vintage auto show, a kids' fest and a full lineup of live bands. Work up an appetite at the 3K walk, the 10K run or the bike ride (815/748-2676, www.cornfest.com).

National Sweet Corn Festival Hoopeston, Labor Day weekend—Aw, shucks! This town serves gobs of cobs—24 tons—at its free sweet corn feed, started in 1941. An antique steam engine cooks the corn and blows its horn each afternoon (Saturday through Monday) when the ears are ready. You'll be sweet on the other doings, too: a parade, demolition derby, carnival, 10K race and the National Sweetheart Pageant, with contestants from 30 states (217/283-7873, www.cityofhoopeston.org).

Murphysboro Apple Festival Murphysboro, second weekend after Labor Day—

Southern Illinois' longest-running festival (since 1951) celebrates all things apple with contests centered around eating, peeling and baking the star crop and spitting its seeds. Apple pies are for sale, and area orchards sell just-picked apples and fresh cider. Thirty bands march by in a two-hour parade, and some 60 bands strut their stuff in the Drums at Appletime competition. Admission charged to some events (800/406-8774, www.murphysboro.com).

Pumpkin Festival Morton, second weekend after Labor Day—The community where more than 80 percent of the world's canned pumpkin is processed goes out of its gourd with pumpkin-decorating and -cooking contests, a pumpkin weigh-in and a smorgasbord of pumpkin foods: chili, fudge, pancakes, ice cream and pie. Other fun in the "Pumpkin Capital of the World" includes a 100-unit parade, live entertainment, crafts and art shows, a carnival and a 10K run (888/765-6588, www.pumpkincapital.com).

Mail Order

Frontera Kitchens Award-winning chef Rick Bayless offers a taste of his passion for Mexico with chili mix, organic tortilla chips, salsa, guacamole mix and stone-fired pizza. Frontera gift sets and cookbooks are also available (800/509-4441, ext. 120, www.fronterakitchens.com).

Giordano's Famous for their Chicago-style pizza, which has been voted the best stuffed pizza in the city. The online store offers stuffed cheese pizza with a choice of 10 toppings (no meat; 800/982-1756, www.giordanos.com).

Polana Purveyor of a wide variety of tasty Polish foods: baked breads, including rye; desserts, including kolaches (fruit-filled yeast buns); meats and sausages, including *kiszka;* soups, including beet borscht; and condiments. Gift baskets, special food packages and homemade pierogies are also available, the latter with three fillings: potato and cheese, sauerkraut and mushrooms and sweet cheese (888/765-2621, www.polana.com).

INDIANA
Secrets of Amish Cooks

BUGGIES RULE THE ROAD IN AMISH COUNTRY,
OPPOSITE PAGE, LEFT TO RIGHT: A VIGNETTE AT AMISH
ACRES, NAPPANEE. FRESH FRUIT AT THE BLUEBERRY RANCH,
MISHAWAKA. LIFE ON AN AMISH FARM NEAR NAPPANEE.

The landscape seems to open up almost as soon as I enter Indiana. That's fine with me: I'm a country boy at heart. The farther I travel toward the fertile, flat northern half of the Hoosier State, the more the rumpled terrain relaxes into a pleasant mix of hardwoods and fields of corn and soybeans.

Those towering hardwoods are one of Indiana's crops, winding up in many beautiful furniture pieces made by Hoosier craftsmen. The state's nearly 60,000 farms are leading producers of such diverse edibles as peppermint and spearmint, persimmons, melons, apples, tomatoes and eggs, as well as hogs and sheep. Some huge dairy farms also call Indiana home, one reason the state is a leader in ice cream production (a million gallons annually!). Northern Indiana will tease my palate with three more of the state's signature foods: popcorn, duckling and blueberries.

Indiana's cooking heritage ranges from the heavenly biscuits, ham and gravy of the southern hill country to the hearty, German-influenced farm-style meals served in northern Amish country, my primary destination. I can hardly wait to sample Amish cookery: Fresh apple butter on homemade bread, mashed potatoes, pot roast in rich gravy, green beans slow-cooked with side meat, fried chicken, a pitcher of whole milk to wash down tart, sugary rhubarb pie—if I ate like the Amish every day, I'd be as big as a barn. But I'm not working behind a horse-

drawn plow, throwing hay with a pitchfork or hand-washing the homemade clothing of a big family.

Amish food is based mostly on the ingredients at hand. The season begins in spring with rhubarb; then come strawberries. Summer brings an abundance of tomatoes, corn, beans and other vegetables from big farm gardens. Cabbage and root vegetables are harvested in autumn. The Amish traditionally butcher cattle and hogs in winter and can much of the meat. Most also keep milk cows and hens.

Before my visit to Amish country, a couple of big-city stops beckon me. Both are in the sprawling state capital, which also is the state's culinary capital with an ever-expanding repertoire of cuisines and restaurants. The brawny Indianapolis skyline appears on the central Indiana horizon. I nose my car straight toward those soaring office towers for a midmorning lunch, to be followed by an early-afternoon breakfast (you heard me right).

An Old-Fashioned Deli

I've gorged myself at more than a few old-style New York Jewish delis, but my favorite

all-around classic is Shapiro's Delicatessen and Cafeteria, right in the heart of Indianapolis. Founded by Russian immigrants in 1905, it's housed in a rather featureless one-story building just south of downtown, practically in the shadow of the headquarters of Indy's pharmaceutical giant, Eli Lilly and Company. Shapiro's serves breakfast, lunch and dinner to some 2,000 diners daily here and at their suburban Carmel location.

The word *delicatessen* comes from the German term for delicacies, and you'll find a banquet of them here: nova lox (smoked salmon), kosher salami and franks, chopped liver, smoked tongue, potato pancakes, short ribs, hot German potato salad, stuffed cabbage, matzo ball soup, noodles with sour cream, pickled herring, gefilte fish and sardines. *Oy vey!*

Shapiro's starts serving lunch at 10 a.m. Perfect! I'm in the mood for the mother of all fat, juicy Reuben sandwiches, and here's where I'll find it. New York often gets credit for giving the world this sandwich, but honors actually go to an Omaha, Nebraska, grocer who created it for his poker buddies at the old Blackstone Hotel in Omaha in the 1920s.

Brie and Mushroom Omelets

Café Patachou, Indianapolis

1	tablespoon unsalted butter
1½	cups sliced assorted fresh mushrooms
12	eggs
1	teaspoon kosher salt
¼	teaspoon freshly ground black pepper
¼	cup unsalted butter
1	4½-ounce round Brie or Camembert cheese, cut into thin slices

In a large skillet, heat 1 tablespoon butter over medium heat. Add mushrooms; cook and stir until mushrooms are tender and all moisture has evaporated. Set aside.

In a large bowl, use a whisk to beat eggs, salt and black pepper until well combined and slightly frothy. Heat an 8- or 9-inch nonstick skillet with flared sides over medium-high heat. Add 1 tablespoon of the remaining butter to skillet. When butter has melted, add ⅔ cup of the beaten egg mixture; lower heat to medium.

Immediately begin stirring egg mixture gently but continuously with a plastic spatula. When small pieces of cooked egg are surrounded by liquid egg, stop stirring. Cook for 30 to 60 seconds more or until mixture is set but shiny.

Spoon 2 tablespoons mushrooms and lay ¼ of the cheese slices across center. With a spatula, lift and fold an edge of the omelet about a third of the way toward the center. Remove from heat. Fold opposite edge toward center; transfer omelet to a warm plate. Repeat with remaining butter, egg mixture, mushrooms and Brie cheese. *Makes 4 servings.*

Reuben Kulakofsky was a regular at the hotel, which eventually put his sandwich creation on the menu. (I can vouch for the story because my wife Julie's grandfather, George Lemen, was a friend of the original Reuben.)

The version served at Shapiro's—a huge mound of corned beef, Swiss cheese and sauerkraut with Thousand Island dressing oozing between two perfectly grilled slices of rye bread—deserves a full 21-gun salute. Once again, Shapiro's has claimed my heart, and my stomach, as the best traditional deli in the Heartland.

World-Class Breakfast Fare

Out-of-sequence meals dictated by my driving route are becoming routine on this frenetic trip. So it's no surprise that my next meal is breakfast (at 1 p.m.!) in Indy's Meridian-Kessler residential district, north of the city center. Café Patachou (the word is a French colloquialism for "little cream puff" . . . more about that later) is housed in a small neighborhood shopping center in this pleasantly mixed district of both grand and modest older homes. Inside, it's bright, fresh and contemporary, complete with a busy, toy-filled kids' play corner in back. Ella Fitzgerald standards waft over the sound system—pretty eclectic for an unpretentious neighborhood cafe.

On this, my second visit here, I order a wonderful three-egg omelet stuffed with avocado, tomato, Swiss cheese and fresh herbs. Wow! I've never seen such yellow eggs. Then, there's the world's best cinnamon toast; I choose sourdough bread fresh-sliced and coated with caramelized butter, sugar and cinnamon. The coffee is off the charts too. You serve yourself at the counter, just like at home. I might as well sample the homemade granola: sun-dried cherries, raisins, almonds and toasted oats. Thumbs up. Then I wind up my midday

breakfast with a piece of rich, five-layer chocolate cake. Café Patachou serves lunch as well—soups, salads, breads and desserts, all fresh and delicious, many made with organic ingredients.

Petite Martha Hoover, a county prosecutor who came to Indy from New York and Texas, launched her storefront cafe in 1989 because she wanted a casual neighborhood place where she could escape with her toddlers for healthy food. Her former boss had once made the mistake of calling her a little cream puff, hence the restaurant's name. Martha's toddlers are now in high school and college, but her inspiration still is going strong. She's traveled extensively in Europe and knows exactly what she wants her staff to prepare and how she wants it prepared. That's why Café Patachou recently made epicurean *Bon Appétit* magazine's list of America's top breakfast spots.

Because omelets star here, I ask for Martha's secret. "First, the ingredients: Almost everything here is organic or homemade. Our eggs are outrageously fresh, always laid within the past 24 hours. All our other ingredients have to be equally fresh and delicious. Then, the technique: a French omelet pan, ingredients heated separately and folded into the omelet." What's Martha's favorite? "Brie with fresh mushrooms!" I know what I'm ordering on my next visit, which I hope won't be far off.

A Pace to Embrace

The Amish country of northern Indiana is neat, tidy and mostly flat, with its own unique charm. Farmsteads have red barns and simple, almost austere-looking white frame houses with huge vegetable gardens out front (they're considered less ostentatious than flower gardens). These farms are positioned much closer together than back home in rural Iowa. The typical

Amish spread is just 80 acres. One-room schoolhouses abound. Amish children attend school only through eighth grade before the girls start helping at home full-time and the boys enter Old Order apprenticeships or begin farming.

I see no electrical wires, of course: The area's 20,000 or so Amish don't use electricity or internal combustion engines. The result, as I drive down these lanes past boxy black buggies and rather incongruous-looking Amish bicyclists, strikes me as one big, rural neighborhood. For thousands of tourists like me who descend by the busload, Indiana's Amish country is a Disneyland of festivals, attractions, and crafts and antiques shops—and great eating.

I check in at the big white Inn at Amish Acres in Nappanee, where the tourism slogan is "Embrace the Pace," and head straight to the Vittles Room in a massive, reconstructed 1870s barn. This expansive property also encompasses an 1800s Old Order Amish farmstead that's listed on the National Register of Historic Places; a first-class theater in a towering landmark 1911 round barn, where *Plain and Fancy*, a 1950s Broadway hit, is the perennial favorite; and a cluster of shops proffering a bounty of Amish-themed goods and delectables.

The name Amish Acres is fitting because the primary mission of the founding Pletcher family is to inform visitors about Amish life and traditions. As with several destinations in the area, many Amish actually work here (which demands that visitors show respect: No closeup photos, please).

I've had the privilege of observing the Amish and their lifestyle at various times during my two decades at *Midwest Living*®, and I admire them tremendously. The Amish are frugal and practical; their self-sufficient, God-fearing lifestyle demands it. Yet, they're also very creative and

CLOCKWISE, FROM ABOVE: HISTORIC FARMSTEAD AT AMISH ACRES, NAPPANEE. A STILL LIFE AT AMISH ACRES. MARTHA HOOVER AT CAFÉ PATACHOU, INDIANAPOLIS.

resourceful within the parameters of their beliefs. That's reflected in the hearty and satisfying family-style Threshers Dinner served here: assorted relishes, mashed potatoes and giblet gravy, turkey, roast beef, fried chicken, beef and noodles, sage dressing and vegetables, followed by a selection of pies. Oh, and did I mention the juicy, sweet-cider-baked smoked ham? Or the thick ham-and-bean soup? And I can't get enough of the locally made rich apple butter I slather on slices of homemade bread.

Time to get moving, while I still can! I'm invited into the cavernous, 8,000-square-foot Amish Acres kitchen to make shoofly pie with no-nonsense, Amish Frieda Miller, who bakes a half-dozen or so of them daily, among 50 pies of all kinds. It turns out she's friendly as can be, just a little bemused by the thought of this big, clumsy "English" (read that "not Amish") fellow unleashed in her kitchen.

After placing the piecrust dough in the bottom of the pan, we sprinkle a streusel on the bottom, then a gooey brown mixture of molasses, dark corn syrup, maple syrup, flour, sugar, eggs and water. Frieda offers me a prebaking finger-taste. Wonderful! We top it all off with more streusel and pop our creation into a huge oven for 45 minutes. Voilá! Shoofly pie, christened "shoofly" by the originating Pennsylvania Amish because it's said to be so sweet that it attracts flies on the windowsill while cooling. I ask Frieda if she bakes pies at home. "Are you kidding? After all this? No! But I still like to eat them."

Haystacks and Amish Ways

Dutch Village near Nappanee is another sprawling Amish-oriented tourism complex: Gifts, crafts, antiques and collectibles malls abound, along with a weekly flea market and auction. But I'm not shopping today. I'm headed to the Dutch Kitchen restaurant for a hearty breakfast and conversation with owner Freemon Borkholder, a local "tycoon." With his son, Dwayne,

Freemon has a number of business holdings in the area, including a lumberyard, a furniture factory and a farm.

Freemon, whose grandfatherly appearance reminds me of the late Burl Ives, grew up Amish but now is Mennonite. "I was too entrepreneurial," he says. "I wanted a tractor even when I was a kid working in the fields." His quiet, take-charge Amish sister, Laura Schmucker (oh, those Amish surnames!), who managed the kitchen here for years, has come in today to personally prepare for me their signature breakfast dish: a "haystack" of shredded potatoes, scrambled eggs, and grilled onions and mushrooms, all topped with creamy sausage gravy. Usually, a haystack in Amish country is a layered, one-stop dinner dish of, say, spaghetti or rice, ground beef flavored with taco seasoning, cheese, vegetables, black olives and/or other ingredients. But this satisfying, all-in-one breakfast version works for me. Laura also has prepared some of her cloudlike buttermilk biscuits and the biggest, fluffiest

LEFT TO RIGHT: AMISH-STYLE PARKING. CAREFREE SUMMER DAYS ON AN AMISH FARM. AMISH COUNTRY LANDSCAPE. KING-SIZE DOUGHNUTS AT BORKHOLDER DUTCH KITCHEN, NAPPANEE.

glazed doughnut my eyes—and stomach—have ever beheld.

Freemon's family, which originally emigrated from Switzerland for religious freedom like many of the area's Amish, settled here in the 1850s. He's proud of his roots and the Amish-Mennonite work ethic. "It raises the moral bar for everyone around here." What do Amish families eat? Meat-and-potatoes fare, he says, most of it raised on their farms. Meat and sausage (bologna, bulk pork sausage), cheese (Colby and cheddar are popular), bread, potatoes and gravy, eggs, homegrown vegetables, dairy products and butter from their own herds.

A heavy diet, yes, but remember that manual labor burns calories fast. Freemon says the Amish do love their desserts, especially pies, cakes, cookies and sweet rolls. What crops do they grow on these small, largely self-sufficient farms? Lots of vegetables and fruits, oats and wheat, hay for the horses and cash crops, such as corn and soybeans. Livestock includes hogs, cattle, chickens and dairy cows that supply their families and area dairies.

Thanks to an introduction by Freemon and Dwayne, I get a veiled glimpse of that life soon after I leave the Dutch Kitchen and drive a few miles back in time down Beech Road to the Eli Miller farm. Many Amish are wary of strangers, especially on their own farms, but I chat in the yard with Eli's son, Dennis, and daughter-in-law, Martha, who are raising four children here. Eli and his wife, Edith, don't join us. They live in a small *grossdaddi* or *dawdy,* meaning grandfather, house just steps from the main farmhouse, a typical Amish-country family-compound arrangement.

While Dennis attends to chores, I'm entertained by the three oldest Miller children, ages 2 through 10, who introduce me to their nearly newborn kittens and small dog. They talk about farm life and their nearby school. I, in turn, demonstrate my cellular phone with its e-mail device and even call my wife Julie so they can hear her voice and she theirs. They are among the most unaffected and bright children I've ever encountered. I'm not invited inside, and I didn't expect to be, but I still treasure these priceless moments in my mind's eye.

Flavors of Main Street

Day Two in Indiana Amish land begins with a pastry and coffee on Wakarusa's (population 1,700) picture-perfect main street. It's a bring-your-own breakfast with a rather unconventional setup. You see, several of the local regulars have keys to Cook's Pizza on the corner of Elkhart and Waterford. Cook's isn't officially open for breakfast; the morning patrons just show up around 8 a.m. and start the coffee, solving the world's (and Wakarusa's) problems over doughnuts, rolls and cookies they bring themselves. They leave their coffee money, 50 cents a cup, at the register. Is this Mayberry, RFD? By the time the owners, brothers Steve and Stan Cook, show up around 10 a.m. to prep for lunch and dinner—soups, salads, pizza and *stromboli* rule here—the place is packed and most of the news has been digested, along with breakfast.

On this road-food journey, I'll encounter the same scenario on other main streets and courthouse squares all across the Heartland: the local cafe as community nerve center. I'm told that when the area's *Elkhart Truth* newspaper needs the scoop on what citizens are thinking in Wakarusa, they send a reporter to Cook's at coffee time. Later, Steve Cook tells me: "My brother and I have raised five kids between us and run a good business here ever since we were teenagers. We love this town." And Wakarusa clearly loves its hometown cafe.

What are the flavors here in mainstreet Indiana? At the Wakarusa Bakery a block down the street, a young Mennonite woman busy with customers rings up my whoopee pie—two soft chocolate cookies sandwiching a creamy filling—and a cream cheese–frosted cinnamon

roll, one of the best of my entire journey.

Then, it's next door to Wakarusa's 1902 Dime Store emporium, where I head straight for the massive candy department and jelly beans billed as the world's largest. They're huge, the size of robins' eggs, in assorted fruit, licorice, chocolate-covered-cherry, red-cinnamon and apple-cinnamon flavors. They sell some 20 tons annually! I pick up a bag of the maple-flavored variety (Wakarusa is known for its annual April maple syrup festival).

The owners also stock many vintage candies here, some of which I haven't tasted since I was a kid debating how to spend my nickel at Broadway Drug back home in Council Bluffs, Iowa. Remember the tiny wax "pop bottles" filled with sweet nectar? Those sugary "buttons" you pop off waxed paper? And chocolate Bun candy bars? They're all waiting for you at Wakarusa's Dime Store.

The Glorious Fruits of Summer

Just outside Wakarusa, I'm soon helping an Amish girl unload tomatoes and sweet corn from the back of her buggy to sell at the

Wakarusa Produce Auction. Mennonites started this auction a few years ago so they wouldn't have to haul their crops to city markets in Elkhart and South Bend. Now growers can bring their lovingly cleaned and displayed produce to a big open shed next to a parking lot that's filling up fast with an eclectic mix of pickup trucks, cars and buggies. The customers are Amish and Mennonites purchasing produce for home use or to supplement their own roadside stands, plus individuals and purveyors from as far away as Chicago. (Have you noticed how anything, whether it's a pie, a quilt, a tomato or a rocking chair, is more marketable if it's billed as Amish?)

The men sport straw hats, suspenders and beards; the women, long dresses, aprons and gauzy bonnet-caps. You can tell the difference between Amish and Mennonite women this way: Solid-color dresses are Amish; those with small prints are Mennonite, which is true of the quilts these women make as well. Some of the denizens are speaking the German dialect used by the Amish and Mennonites who live in the area. I can't understand a word and, apparently, most contemporary Germans wouldn't be able to either.

You can pick up farm-fresh eggs here, but the real draw on this July morning is the glory of dozens of midsummer gardens: peppers, cabbages, carrots, tomatoes, apricots, peaches, cucumbers, onions, green beans, beets, eggplant—oh, yes, and zucchini. All are laid out neatly in various containers on the concrete floor, to be auctioned off for the best price the fast-talking auctioneer can fetch. At other times during the spring-to-fall auction season, flowers, melons and pumpkins also abound. Assistants move up and down the rows with the auctioneer, noting the price paid for each lot, with 10 percent going to support the auction.

CLOCKWISE, FROM TOP RIGHT: TALKING BUSINESS AT THE WAKARUSA PRODUCE AUCTION, WAKARUSA. VEGETABLE BOUNTY FROM AN AMISH GROWER. GRAZING IN DOWNTOWN WAKARUSA. OPPOSITE PAGE: GATHERING AT COOK'S PIZZA, WAKARUSA.

Everything but the Quack!

Northern Indiana is one of America's duck-raising centers, along with New York, Pennsylvania and California. Amish farmers raise millions of the fowl, which processors ship around the globe to supermarkets, specialty stores, and gourmet and other restaurants—wherever you find duck on the menu.

I turn off a country road near Middlebury and approach the low-rise buildings atop a knoll at Culver Duck, one of the nation's largest duck processors. They ship 2 million annually, mostly frozen. The Culver family relocated their operation here in 1960 after more than a century at Westhampton, Long Island, New York, once America's duck mecca—remember seeing Long Island duckling

on menus of yore? That's where the white Pekin duck (think: the hapless critter on those Aflac TV commercials) was first raised in this country after being imported from China.

It's been America's favorite breed ever since, accounting for 95 percent of U.S. domesticated duck consumption. Pekin ducks don't fly and they gain weight fast, which is good news or bad news, depending on whether you're the producer or duck. The Culvers moved here to raise Pekins because they wanted to be closer to the food their ducks eat—Midwest corn.

I see where the Culvers' ducks are slaughtered, processed and inspected. I must admit that hundreds of recently deceased ducks unceremoniously parading

by on hooks don't appeal to me nearly as much as a solo bird on a platter, à l'orange. Next comes a taste panel prepared just for me. The surprising marinated duck breast flavors are terrific. Teriyaki is the favorite, they tell me; I also like the Cajun, honey-orange and bacon. Breast is the most popular, meatiest portion of the duck.

Then, utilizing the all-natural leg and breast meat of our late feathered friends, there are duck jerky sticks and duck sausage: cranberry-maple, Italian, sesame-ginger, sun-dried tomato and garlic . . . hey, these Culvers get pretty creative! They also make a popular line of barbecue sauces and herb rubs. And other products, including duck-fat-based facial soap. (Did you know duck fat is supposed to be great for your skin? Well, have you ever seen a duck with

a bad complexion?) Most of the feathers from Culver Duck contributors go to China to be sewn into coat linings.

As I sample, I learn that today's duck is even leaner than chicken, after you remove the fatty but flavorful skin, that is, and tastes a bit like filet mignon (it really does). We're gaining on the duck-loving Europeans and Asians, but Americans still eat only about a half-pound of duck per capita annually. On this trip, I note that duck is gaining popularity as both an appetizer and an entrée on the menus of inventive Midwest chefs.

Duck eggs are hatched here at the home farm hatchery, then the tiny ducklings, about 15,000 per day, ship out to growers for seven weeks at a duck farm. Just so I

get the big picture, we hop in an SUV and head to a nearby farm where a young Amish lad shows me some 9,000 of the guests happily living out their brief existence in a large, sanitary, well-ventilated open shed. The Culvers contract with about 50 such farms in the area and raise ducks on their own property, as well. Friendly Burt Culver, the fifth generation of his family in the business, tells me, "Happy ducks move around a lot. You can also tell [they're happy] by the sound of their chirping." These are happy ducks. Their ephemeral lives seem relatively sweet. I just wish these little balls of fuzz I'm watching weren't so darned cute.

Inn-ovative Cuisine

If there's a picture-perfect country inn anywhere, it has to be the yellow-and-white Checkerberry Inn, on 100 serene acres midway between Middlebury and Goshen. We've featured it several times in *Midwest Living*® magazine. With a grand, wicker-filled porch, croquet lawn, tennis courts and pool, it's the perfect bucolic getaway. Inside, the inn is a hybrid of French provincial and contemporary styles, offering 14 individually decorated rooms.

Whimsically named for the fruit of the wintergreen plant, the Checkerberry was built by John and Susie Graff in 1987. These days, the senior Graffs divide their time between Harbor Springs, Michigan, and a small Caribbean resort hotel on Anguilla, British West Indies, while the inn is operated by their daughter Kelly, executive chef, and partner Karen Kennedy, manager.

I'm here to dine at the Checkerberry's bistro-type restaurant, Citrus. No, they don't grow citrus here in northern Indiana, but the theme influences both the vibrant color scheme and the menu. Karen, a former Chicago nightclub singer

Duck is gaining popularity as both an appetizer and an entrée on the menus of many inventive Midwest chefs.

CLOCKWISE, FROM TOP LEFT: INDIANA DUCKLINGS. DUCKS ON AN AMISH FARM NEAR MIDDLEBURY. THE CHECKERBERRY INN, GOSHEN. ELEGANT FARE AT CITRUS BISTRO, THE CHECKERBERRY INN.

who grew up in Indiana, says people are surprised to find a sophisticated dining spot along these country backroads. "We're an alternative to fried chicken and mashed potatoes. You can have big-city menu selections here while you listen to Amish buggies clip-clopping down the road." What Citrus does share with its location is a bounty of fresh, delicious ingredients in a fusion of Asian, French and Caribbean cuisine.

Bashful Kelly Graff (Karen is the spokesperson for this talented duo) amazingly didn't plan to become executive chef. She took over the kitchen operation when a chef quit just before the busy holiday season in 1999. Without formal training, but with a passion for good food, she's been wowing Citrus diners ever since. The clientele includes knowing area residents as well as guests from as far away as Britain, Denmark, Germany and Switzerland.

In honor of our visit this evening, Kelly has prepared duck with blueberry sauce as my entrée, a worthy tribute to two Indiana specialties. Frankly, I'm sated after just sampling her marvelous appetizers: baked Brie in a puff pastry with apricot preserves, crab cakes with tomato-caper remoulade, chilled cucumber soup and coconut shrimp with passion fruit. My companions feast on pepper steak, a pan-seared rib eye encrusted with black peppercorns and served with wonderful pommes frites you dip in aioli; salmon served with crushed wasabi and a soy-lime glaze; and chicken Florentine made with ricotta cheese and spinach. Every one of Kelly's creations is a winner.

We finish with a departure from the Amish desserts we've been devouring, sharing spoonfuls of a rich chocolate decadence, a light fruit napoleon and a tangy slice of outstanding sweet-tart Key lime pie (we're at Citrus, after all!).

Popping Good Times

In Amish country, the name Yoder, along with the ubiquitous Miller, is as common as Johnson is in Minnesota. So I'm not surprised as I pull into a parking lot surrounded by cornfields near tiny Topeka to see the sign for Yoder Popcorn.

I'm a popcorn-aholic. Put a bowl in front of me and it's gone in five minutes flat. At just 143 calories a serving, it's healthy, if you go easy on the butter and salt, and even has fiber benefits. I'm not alone: A sign on the wall in the big salesroom proclaims that Americans eat 17 billion quarts annually, or about 58 quarts per person. That's a lot of popcorn. (I wonder what percentage is consumed at the movies, a huge value-added idea instituted by Iowa-based theater-chain owner Myron Blank in the 1930s.) This universal snack food dates back thousands of years, to pre-Columbian New World popcorn addicts. It's thought to be the first form of

maize (or corn) the earliest explorers took back to Europe, and it was on the first Thanksgiving menu at Plymouth.

Most of the world's popcorn grows in Indiana (the late Orville Redenbacher hailed from Valparaiso) and Nebraska. The Yoders cultivate 1,200 acres of popcorn, field corn, soybeans and hay and purchase the remainder of their popcorn inventory from other popcorn growers in northern and central Indiana. Besides stocking the shelves here, it winds up in supermarkets and specialty stores and is sold via the Yoder website. Friendly, good-humored Sharon Yoder, who, despite the surname, isn't Amish, capably manages the retail end of this family enterprise, which was founded by a great-uncle in the 1930s.

It turns out I really don't know that much about popcorn, but Sharon cheerily fills me in: Flavors and textures vary. If you're a true popcorn gourmet, you know

that yellow popcorn has a stronger corn taste than white popcorn. Red (yes, red) popcorn can be a bit on the nutty side; black popcorn is sweeter. The smaller ladyfinger variety is appreciated by "mature" fellas like me because it has no hull, which means fewer reminders stuck between teeth.

Sharon prefers Yoder's signature Tiny Tenders, which isn't a variety but the petite kernels at the end of the cob. And she likes her popcorn crisp, not chewy. She tells me the secret to a great batch of popcorn: "Don't seal the popper or pan tightly, because some of the moisture needs to escape or the popcorn will turn out soggy. Use a good, healthy type of oil, such as canola, and make sure it's hot. Then, season to taste and sit down with a bowl while you watch a college basketball game on TV. Preferably IU." Yes, ma'am. Sounds like pure heaven to me.

Back at the Blueberry Ranch . . .

On this sweltering July midmorning, a small, oasislike farm northeast of suburban Mishawaka, just outside South Bend, swarms with "U-pickers" of all ages. They're toting white pails filled with blue fruit. Michigan leads the nation in blueberry production, but the crop also thrives here at the Blueberry Ranch, just across the state line from southwest Michigan's famous fruit-growing Garden of Eden. That's because of the acidic, sandy soil and the climate-moderating effect of Lake Michigan, 30 miles away. Blueberries like it nippy in the spring and early summer, until the berries develop; then, bring on the hot weather.

The ranch, one of the Midwest's largest pick-your-own operations, comprises 65 acres of mostly blueberries, as well as strawberries and raspberries. John Nelson, the owner and my host, is a trim ball

CLOCKWISE, FROM ABOVE: (ALL TAKEN AT THE BLUEBERRY RANCH, MISHAWAKA) SAMPLING THE CROP. RIPE BLUEBERRIES. DAN STEALS A SNACK. U-PICKERS. OPPOSITE PAGE: PRODUCTS ON DISPLAY AT YODER POPCORN, TOPEKA.

JOHN NELSON, THE BLUEBERRY RANCH.

of energy who grew up in a Michigan blueberry-raising family and has operated this farm for 28 years. These days, at the peak of a busy harvest season, he's logging more than 100 hours a week orchestrating the operation.

In the big, no-frills barn, eager pickers hop aboard trams that take them to the fields and bring them back to settle up when they're finished. A variety of blueberry products is on display (blueberry salsa or blueberry barbecue sauce, anyone?). Although the U-pick phenomenon isn't as big these days as it was in the 1970s, you'd never know it here. I see mostly families with young kids who've come from around the immediate area as well as Chicago and Indianapolis. The Amish even hire drivers to bring them here for the picking fun. John tells me it's a wonderful outing, especially for city kids who don't have a clue where their food comes from.

It's been a good year for blueberries hereabouts. As we walk between grass-carpeted, irrigated rows of the leafy, green bushes that resemble lilacs, John explains that blueberries have to be the easiest fruit around: You don't have to slice or pit them, and they last up to two years in a freezer. They're America's second-favorite berry, behind strawberries, cultivated commercially only since the turn of the last century. Need a DIY paint recipe? The early colonists mixed blueberries with milk to make a gray "paint."

Personally, I'd rather eat them, especially the fat, juicy, sweet ones I'm picking and popping into my mouth as I try to keep up with John. These are cultivated highbush blueberries, as opposed to the low-bush varieties that grow wild in the Midwest's north country. The bushes themselves look good enough to be landscape plants, like their botanical cousins, rhododendrons and azaleas. They also attract feathered U-pickers; I see lots of birds here for a snack, to John's dismay. However, because so many people come to experience serenity as well as to harvest blueberries, he's reluctant to set off any loud noisemakers to rattle the unwanted fly-in guests.

John's prolific blueberry bushes typically yield about 4,000 pounds per acre; 20 acres are certified organic. He belongs to a marketing cooperative, so the berries that aren't sold here wind up in food stores across North America and Europe.

Before I leave, I have to ask John his age. He looks like a prematurely gray-haired 30-year-old. But he's 50! He gamely explains that he attributes his youthful appearance to faithfully eating a half-cup of his antioxidant-rich star crop daily. I think I'll sign up for the blueberry fitness plan right away.

Taste of Indiana

Blueberry Buckle Coffee Cake
Inspired by The Blueberry Ranch, Mishawaka

- 1½ cups all-purpose flour
- 1 cup packed brown sugar
- 1 teaspoon baking powder
- ½ teaspoon baking soda
- ½ to ¾ teaspoon ground cinnamon
- ¼ teaspoon salt
- ½ cup butter
- 1 egg, slightly beaten
- ½ cup buttermilk
- 1 teaspoon vanilla
- 1½ cups fresh blueberries, rinsed and drained well
- ¼ cup all-purpose flour
- 2 tablespoons granulated sugar
- 2 tablespoons butter

Grease a 9-inch springform pan. Line the bottom with waxed paper; grease the waxed paper. Flour the pan; set aside.

In a large bowl, stir together 1½ cups flour, brown sugar, baking powder, baking soda, cinnamon and salt. Using a pastry blender, cut in ½ cup butter until mixture resembles coarse crumbs. Make a well in the center of the dry ingredients. In a small bowl, combine egg, buttermilk and vanilla. Add all at once to dry ingredients. Stir just until moistened.

Spread batter in prepared pan. Top with blueberries. In a small bowl, stir together the ¼ cup all-purpose flour and granulated sugar. Cut in 2 tablespoons butter until mixture resembles coarse crumbs. Sprinkle over blueberries.

Bake in a 350° oven for 45 to 50 minutes or until a wooden toothpick inserted near center comes out clean. Cool in pan on a wire rack for 30 minutes. Invert onto a plate and remove waxed paper. Immediately invert the cake again onto a serving plate. Serve warm. *Makes 10 servings.*

Shoofly Pie

Amish Acres, Nappanee

- 1/2 of a 15-ounce package rolled refrigerated unbaked piecrust (1 crust)
- 1 1/2 cups all-purpose flour
- 1/2 cup packed brown sugar
- 1 teaspoon ground cinnamon
- 1/2 cup cold butter, cut into pieces
- 3/4 cup boiling water
- 3/4 teaspoon baking soda
- 1/2 cup mild-flavored molasses
- 1/4 cup pure maple syrup
- 1/4 cup dark corn syrup
- 1/4 teaspoon ground cloves
- 2 eggs, slightly beaten
  Whipped cream (optional)

For pie pastry: Let piecrust stand at room temperature for 15 minutes. Unroll piecrust. Ease into a 9-inch pie plate, being careful not to stretch pastry. Fold under extra pastry. Crimp edge as desired. Do not prick pastry. Set aside.

For topping: In a small bowl, combine flour, brown sugar and cinnamon. Using a pastry blender, cut butter into flour mixture until mixture resembles coarse crumbs. Set aside.

For filling: In a medium bowl, combine boiling water and baking soda. Stir in molasses, maple syrup, corn syrup and cloves. Let mixture cool about 30 minutes or until just warm. Beat in eggs.

Sprinkle 1/2 cup of the topping over the bottom of pie shell. Carefully pour in the filling. Sprinkle remaining topping evenly over pie (make sure to cover entire surface with crumbs to prevent filling from bubbling out during baking). To prevent overbrowning, cover edge of pie with foil.

Bake in a 375° oven for 20 minutes; remove foil. Bake for 20 to 25 minutes more or until mixture appears set when gently shaken. Cool on a wire rack. Serve slightly warm or at room temperature. If you like, serve with whipped cream. Store, covered, in the refrigerator. *Makes 8 servings.*

Amish Breakfast Haystack

Dutch Kitchen, near Nappanee

- Sausage Gravy (recipe follows)
- 1 tablespoon cooking oil
- 3 cups frozen loose-pack diced hash brown potatoes, thawed
- 2 tablespoons butter or margarine
- 2 cups sliced fresh mushrooms
- 1 medium onion, chopped (1/2 cup)
- 6 eggs
- 1/3 cup milk
- 1/4 teaspoon salt
- 1/8 teaspoon ground black pepper

Prepare Sausage Gravy; keep warm.

For potatoes: Heat 1 tablespoon oil in a large skillet over medium-high heat. Add the potatoes. Cook and stir for 8 to 10 minutes or until the potatoes are brown, crispy and tender. Remove potatoes from skillet; keep warm.

For mushrooms: In the same skillet, melt 1 tablespoon of the butter over medium heat. Add mushrooms and onion. Cook and stir until tender but not brown. Remove mushroom mixture and drain; keep warm.

For eggs: In a medium bowl, beat together eggs, milk, salt and black pepper with a whisk or fork until combined but not frothy. In the same skillet, melt the remaining butter over medium heat; pour in egg mixture. Cook over medium heat, without stirring, until mixture begins to set on the bottom and around edges.

With a spatula or large spoon, lift and fold the partially cooked egg mixture so that the uncooked portion flows underneath. Continue cooking over medium heat for 2 to 3 minutes or until egg mixture is cooked through but is still glossy and moist. Remove from heat immediately.

To serve, place hash browns on 4 dinner plates. For each, top with mushroom mixture and scrambled eggs. Spoon the Sausage Gravy over entire dish. Serve immediately. *Makes 4 servings.*

Sausage Gravy: In a heavy large skillet or cast-iron skillet, cook 12 ounces bulk pork sausage and 1 medium onion, chopped (1/2 cup) over medium-high heat until meat is brown and onion is tender, stirring occasionally. Do not drain; leave pan juices in skillet. Sprinkle 2 tablespoons all-purpose flour, 1/4 teaspoon salt and 1/8 teaspoon ground black pepper over meat mixture. Whisk the flour mixture into the meat mixture. Cook and stir over medium heat for 1 minute. While whisking, gradually add 1 1/2 cups milk. Cook and stir until thickened and bubbly. Cook and stir for 1 minute more. *Makes about 3 cups.*

Reuben Sandwiches

Inspired by Shapiro's Delicatessen, Indianapolis

- 3 tablespoons butter or margarine, softened
- 8 slices dark rye or pumpernickel bread
- 3 tablespoons bottled Thousand Island or Russian salad dressing
- 6 ounces thinly sliced cooked corned beef, beef, pork or ham
- 4 slices Swiss cheese (3 ounces)
- 1 cup sauerkraut, well drained

Spread butter on 1 side of each bread slice and salad dressing on the other. With the buttered side down, top 4 slices with meat, cheese and sauerkraut. Top with remaining bread slices, dressing side down.

Preheat a large skillet over medium heat. Reduce heat to medium-low. Cook 2 of the sandwiches at a time over medium-low heat for 4 to 6 minutes or until bread is toasted and cheese is melted, turning once. Repeat with the remaining sandwiches. *Makes 4 sandwiches.*

Travel Journal

More Information

Indianapolis Convention & Visitors Association (800/238-4639, www.indy.org). For Amish country, **Elkhart County Convention & Visitors Bureau** (800/860-5957, www.amishcountry.org) and **LaGrange County Convention & Visitors Bureau** (800/254-8090, www.back roads.org). **South Bend/Mishawaka Convention & Visitors Bureau** (800/519-0594, www.exploresouthbend.org).

Featured Dining

Café Patachou Meridian-Kessler district in Indianapolis (317/925-2823).
Shapiro's Delicatessen and Cafeteria Indianapolis (317/631-4041; also 317/573-3354 in suburban Carmel).
Citrus Bistro At the Checkerberry Inn between Middlebury and Goshen (574/642-0191).
Dutch Kitchen In the Dutch Village west of Nappanee (574/773-2828).
Vittles Room At Amish Acres west of Nappanee (800/800-4942, ext. 2).

More Great Dining

St. Elmo Steak House Indianapolis. A century-old downtown landmark next to Circle Centre, specializing in signature beef and tangy shrimp cocktails that bring tears to your eyes (317/635-0636).
Das Dutchman Essenhaus Southwest of Middlebury. Indiana's largest restaurant, serving hearty Amish-style meals (800/455-9471).
Another delicious stop on Dan's journey was dinner prepared by Ora and Mary Miller, an Amish couple who operated O&M Banquets on their property near Millersburg. Sadly, the Millers were forced to close their business due to illness several months after Dan's visit. A similar rural Amish dining experience is offered by **Yoder's Homestyle Cooking** in Shipshewana. Haystacks, soup, salad and pie are all on the menu (260/499-0552).

Featured Stops

Culver Duck Northwest of Middlebury (574/825-9537).
The Blueberry Ranch Northeast of Mishawaka (574/255-5773).
Yoder Popcorn South of Shipshewana (800/892-2170).
Cook's Pizza Wakarusa (574/862-4425).
Wakarusa Bakery Wakarusa (574/862-2260).
Wakarusa Dime Store Wakarusa (574/862-4690).
Wakarusa Produce Auction Wakarusa (574/862-2740).

More Great Stops

Indianapolis, the state's capital and largest city, best known for its famous speedway, dazzles with other world-class attractions: a revitalized downtown that includes the classy Circle Centre mall; White River State Park, with landscaped pathways leading to the state museum, zoo, NCAA Hall of Champions and Eiteljorg Museum of American Indians and Western Art; and the world's largest children's museum.
City Market East of downtown Indianapolis. A huge building and farmers market area with a 120-year tradition of selling specialty foods and fresh produce (317/634-9266).
Old Bag Factory Goshen. About a dozen artisan-owned and -operated shops in a refurbished, century-old landmark (574/534-2502).

Olympia Candy Kitchen Goshen. Maker and seller of sweet treats on the same corner since 1912 (574/533-5040).
Deutsch Kase Haus Between Middlebury and Shipshewana. Local factory that makes and sells award-winning cheese (574/825-9511).
Menno-Hof Visitors Center South of downtown Shipshewana. Interactive exhibits and multimedia displays about the Amish and Mennonite faiths and cultures, on property resembling an Amish farm (260/768-4117).
Shipshewana Flea Market South of Shipshewana, across from the Menno-Hof Visitors Center. A 1,000-vendor flea market (the Midwest's largest) on 40 acres, selling items from fresh vegetables and baked goods to crafts and collectibles; open Tuesdays and Wednesdays May through October (260/768-4129).

Dan's Lodgings

Inn at Amish Acres West of Nappanee ($$; 800/800-4942).

More Great Lodgings

Canterbury Hotel Indianapolis. An upscale, restored downtown landmark adjacent to Circle Centre ($$$$; 800/538-8186).
Crowne Plaza Hotel Indianapolis. A classy 273-room high-rise in the renovated downtown train station, with rooms that are refurbished Pullman train cars ($$$$; 317/631-2221).
Checkerberry Inn Midway between Middlebury and Goshen. Gracious and luxurious, with French country decor in a rural setting ($$$$; 574/642-4445).
Patchwork Quilt Country Inn North of Middlebury. Fifteen guest rooms in an 1875 white frame house on a farm ($$; 574/825-2417).
Essenhaus Inn and Conference Center West of Shipshewana. A modern motel decorated with country furnishings and quilts ($$$; 574/825-9447).
Standard chain motels in Elkhart, Mishawaka and neighboring South Bend.

Food Events

Parke County Maple Syrup Festival
Parke County, last weekend in February and first weekend in March—Fill up on pancakes drenched in golden maple syrup at the fairgrounds in Rockville, and buy fresh syrup, maple fudge and candies from syrup producers. Then, take a self-guided tour of six maple syrup camps around the county, also home to many famous covered bridges. Fee for pancake breakfast (765/569-5226, www.coveredbridges.com).

Wakarusa Maple Syrup Festival
Wakarusa, fourth weekend in April—What's on tap? Syrup-making demonstrations, a baking contest and an all-you-can-eat pancake breakfast, for starters. Other free-flowing fun: a parade, a crafts and antiques show, quilting and blacksmithing demonstrations and music downtown (574/862-4344, www.wakarusamaplesyrupfestival.com).

Mansfield Village Mushroom Festival
Mansfield, last full weekend in April—On guided hunts, tromp hardwood forests in search of the elusive morel. You'll win $50 if you find the biggest one. You can also bid on a batch of fresh fungi at an auction, buy mushroom sandwiches from vendors or watch more than 300 cars roll into this historic village for a show. Entry fee for hunt (765/653-4026, www.mansfieldvillage.com).

Berne Swiss Days Berne, last Thursday, Friday and Saturday in July—This city revels in its Swiss roots with yodelers, folk dancers, polka bands and a *steintoss* (stone throw) competition. Vendors sell bratwurst, Swiss cheese on a stick, apple dumplings and other treats. You can tour furniture and stove factories, a dairy plant and the Swiss Heritage Village; browse crafts and quilt shows; and enter a bake-off. Fee for some events (260/589-8080, www.berneswissdays.com).

Hot Dog Festival Frankfort, last weekend in July—Frankly, you'll relish the world's only hot dog festival! In the food tent, chow down on Frankfort Dogs topped with sauerkraut or peppers and onions, or enter the Great Wiener Cook-Off. Then, get over to the main-stage entertainment, 200 arts and crafts booths and the kids' games in Puppy Park (765/654-4081, www.accs.net/mainstreet).

Amish Acres Arts & Crafts Festival
Nappanee, second weekend in August—At this restored 80-acre farmstead, Amish Acres staff dish up homemade apple-butter sundaes, roast pork sandwiches, hand-battered onion rings and apple pie, along with the family-style Threshers Dinner. Nearly 400 artisans demonstrate and sell their works, and square dancers, cloggers, bluegrass bands and a medicine show entertain on three stages. Admission charged (800/800-4942, www.amishacres.com).

State Fair Indianapolis, 12 days in mid-August—Follow the herd to the Indiana Beef Cattle Association tent for a juicy Hoosier Rib Eye Steak Sandwich topped off with a milk shake at the American Dairy Association's Dairy Bar (317/927-7500, www.indianastatefair.com).

Marshall County Blueberry Festival
Plymouth, Labor Day weekend—The harvest is finished, so reap rewards such as blueberry doughnuts, sausage and pies at one of the country's biggest blueberry festivals. Runners squish berries piled on the street at the start of 5K and 15K Blueberry Stomps. Also see a bike cruise, a classic-car show, hot-air balloon launches, fireworks and entertainment on three stages. Fee for car show (888/936-5020, www.blueberryfestival.org).

Valparaiso Popcorn Festival Valparaiso, Saturday after Labor Day—Pop into the hometown of Orville Redenbacher for the nation's only popcorn parade. Work up an appetite at the Popcorn Panic 5-mile run or 5K walk, then fill up on the fare that 50 vendors sell. Added attractions: two music stages, 500 crafts booths and hot-air balloon launches (219/464-8332, www.popcornfest.org).

Persimmon Festival Mitchell, last full week of September—The country's oldest persimmon festival (since 1946) honors the tasty fruit with pudding-making and -eating contests, the Persimmon Ball and

CAFÉ PATACHOU, INDIANAPOLIS.

a 5K run. Vendors dish up persimmon ice cream and pudding and traditional fair food. A parade, candlelight tours of Pioneer Village at Spring Mill State Park, an antique-auto show and free entertainment add to the fun (800/580-1985, www.mitchell-indiana.org).

Mail Order

Amish Acres General Store Homemade baked goods (pies, cookies, muffins and yeast breads) and old-fashioned preserves. Dan recommends the award-winning shoofly pie (800/800-4942, www.amishacres.com).

Culver Duck Frozen duck products, including bone-in and boneless breasts, as well as frozen whole ducks and chickens. Also maple-flavored duck jerky and several sauces and savory seasonings (800/825-9225, www.culverduck.com).

Sechler's Pickles Delicious gourmet pickles made by a family-owned and -operated business for more than 75 years. Among the 39 flavors, be sure to try the candied sweet pickles (800/332-5461, www.sechlerspickles.com).

Yoder Popcorn Wide variety of premium popcorn grown in the heart of Amish country. Dan favors Tiny Tender Popcorn for its supreme tenderness (800/892-2170, www.yoderpopcorn.com).

IOWA
America's Agricultural Eden

THIS PAGE: ROWS OF SOYBEANS NEATLY CARPETING FIELDS IN SUMMER. OPPOSITE PAGE: STATE FAIR CONFECTIONS ON A STICK, DES MOINES. TOMORROW'S IOWA HAM AND BACON, SIGOURNEY. SUCCULENT PORK ENTRÉE AT LINCOLN CAFÉ, MOUNT VERNON.

If there's a single state that's most synonymous with American agriculture, it's surely biologically hyperactive Iowa. Envision almost 30 million acres of farmland on growth steroids, and you'll get the picture.

Even though the state ranks 24th in land area, an astounding 25 percent of the nation's Grade-A farmland—and 10 percent of the world's—is loamy, brown-black Iowa soil. Equally amazing, more than 88 percent of the state is cultivated on nearly 90,000 farms, resulting in an annual harvest of more than $12 billion in crisp, green dollar bills for the Hawkeye economy.

Corn is the mother lode here—2.2 billion bushels were grown in 2005 alone. When it comes to the other main cash crop, soybeans, Iowa trades the crown back and forth across the Mississippi River with Illinois (the Hawkeye State reigned in 2005 with 533 million bushels). Iowa also leads the nation in raising hogs, with more than five hogs per person in this state of 3 million people. And just for good measure, beef and dairy cattle abound here, as well as laying hens, which rule the nation's roost in eggs, producing 11.6 billion in 2005.

Ever since the state was first settled in the mid-1800s, farming has been intertwined with its history and culture. Iowa's pastoral landscapes inspired many works of art by native son Grant Wood. The 4-H and FFA (Future Farmers of America) movements began here, and the state's current global outlook is reflected in the fact that the World Food Prize makes its home here. Living History Farms in Urbandale is one of the world's premier farming museums. Generations of media moguls at Des Moines' Meredith Corporation, known for magazine and book publishing and television broadcasting, cut their teeth on *Successful Farming*®, founded in 1902 and still the nation's leading farming magazine. Meredith also publishes yours truly's *Midwest Living*® and the mother of all home and family magazines, *Better Homes and Gardens*®.

Thanks to a morass of economic challenges and the voracious growth of mega farms, the number of Iowans living on midsize farms has declined precipitously in recent decades, threatening the traditional rural way of life. However, a heartening echo is an increase in the number of the state's smallest farms, 50 or fewer acres, where innovative growers are reintroducing biodiversity to a state once renowned for its apples, grapes, squash, melons and many other crops. Chefs, gardeners and consumers are learning to appreciate the quality of Iowa produce, much of which comes from more than 400 certified organic growers. Relative to its population, Iowa has more farmers markets these days than any other state.

Beyond its raw ingredients, Iowa exerts far more influence on what Americans eat than many people realize. In the sleek complex where I work at Meredith Corporation headquarters in downtown Des Moines, a ruthlessly efficient squad of nine home economists rigorously scrutinizes more than 5,600 book and magazine recipes each year in the Meredith Corporation Test Kitchen. This designer-chic facility, recently reoutfitted with the latest in furnishings, appliances and gizmos, also boasts a professional grocery shopper (who spends $120,000 per year!), three food stylists and several assistants.

The concepts popularized by Meredith food editors since the first Test Kitchen opened in 1928 range from tossed salads and backyard barbecues to chiffon cake and untold casseroles. These editors must be doing something right: One Meredith title alone—the iconic red-plaid *Better Homes and Gardens New Cookbook*—has sold more copies than any other hardcover besides the Bible and dictionaries.

Hearty farm cooking, epitomized by the

family-style meals served at the Amana Colonies restaurants in eastern Iowa, still dominates in lots of kitchens. Pig roasts and corn feeds are signature Iowa food gatherings, and many residents love the state's deep-fried breaded pork tenderloin and loose-meat Maid-Rite sandwiches (the latter a steaming heap of fresh ground beef made to order and served on a hamburger bun). In addition, some inventive chefs are doing great things in unexpected places, including the Lincoln Café in Mount Vernon, one of my stops.

My goal in my home state is to explore in more depth what Iowa produces as well as what its cooks serve. Because I-80 is the state's main highway, I make it my culinary thoroughfare as well, choosing stops that are within 30 minutes of the interstate artery.

Sweet Treats and a Truck Stop

I ease into Iowa via ice cream in the Quad Cities. Crossing the Centennial Bridge over the Mississippi River, I head down Locust Street in Davenport for an awesome turtle sundae (hot fudge, butterscotch sauce and pecans atop vanilla ice cream) and a double-fudge Boston (that's a hot-fudge sundae on top of a hot-fudge shake) at red-and-white Whitey's, an eastern Iowa legend founded in 1933. Though my sweet tooth could handle more treats, I have to move on. Just a few miles west of Davenport, near Walcott on I-80, awaits the world's largest truck stop.

My recent road travels have given me a new respect for truckers and for the 4,500 truck plazas and stops that are their homes away from home. The Iowa 80 Truck Stop was opened by Standard Oil in 1965, even before the interstate was completed. Later, it was purchased by the Moon family, which still owns it and a dozen other truck stops in the Midwest and South. This place

is a small city, offering truckers food as well as sleeping quarters, private showers, a surround-sound movie theater, a game room, an embroidery center where they can get their hats and jackets embellished, a barber, a self-service laundry, a chapel, a dentist, postal and Internet services—oh yes, and fuel (an aboveground tank on the premises can store 1 million gallons).

I'm told I just missed the annual two-day trucker-appreciation jamboree, attended by upwards of 50,000 people. The event includes a truck beauty contest, an antique-truck display, a pork chop cook-off and 200 exhibitors. Otherwise, on a typical summer day, about 15,000

brings coffee and expedites my meal: two crispy, deep-fried Iowa pork chops served with mashed potatoes and brown gravy, canned mixed vegetables and a dinner roll with margarine, on a plate nicely garnished with parsley and a tomato slice. It's like a lot of the suppers I had at home when I was a kid, which is the whole idea, according to Bill. The best part of the meal is dessert: a big, piping hot, pleasantly doughy apple dumpling served with cinnamon ice cream.

Honest Food and Happy Pigs

Few people associate Main Street Iowa with gastronomy, but I fantasize about bringing some Epicureans to tiny Lincoln

The Iowa 80 Kitchen specializes in comfort foods—just the kind of fare its patrons would get at home.

truck drivers, business travelers and vacationers mingle here over Wendy's, Dairy Queen and Blimpie fast food. But I want a real trucker's dinner at the adjoining, separately managed Iowa 80 Kitchen, a huge dining hall with room for 300 hungry patrons. "We specialize in comfort foods, just like what these guys would get at home," operator Bill Peel says.

I claim a seat at a U-shaped counter amid several truckers who tell me about their favorite stops in other states. High fuel prices are a big topic. Everybody is friendly, and nobody seems to be in a hurry; this is break time. As for my repast, I skip the monster buffet setup and 50-foot salad bar in favor of the recommended fried pork chops, served with what I would call a classic truck-stop tossed salad of lettuce, cherry tomatoes and cucumbers with a creamy blue cheese dressing. My server promptly

Café in Mount Vernon (population 4,171). I think they'd be pleasantly shocked—as I was. This New England-ish community was first settled in 1836 and now boasts several National Historic Districts: the Cornell College campus, a covey of Victorian homes and the restored downtown shopping district, where I plan to dine.

This quadrant of Iowa bills itself as the Silos & Smokestacks National Heritage Area; the goal is to portray the state's farming and agricultural-manufacturing heritage through a network of attractions. This Saturday evening I'm simply going to dine on some of Iowa's bounty at a highly touted restaurant I've longed to try for some time. Tomorrow I'll visit a bona fide Iowa hog farm that supplies premium pork to discerning establishments across the United States.

Lincoln Café's name derives from the Lincoln Highway, begun in 1912 and better known as US-30 these days. It's not as famous as old Route 66, but it once extended all the way from New York City's Times Square to San Francisco's Lincoln Park—America's first coast-to-coast route, at 3,389 bumpy miles. Today, US-30 serves as a slower-paced alternative to the streams of vehicles racing east and west on I-80 about 18 miles south of Mount Vernon.

In addition to great food, Lincoln Café serves up delightful incongruity. Set in a storefront with a few booths and even fewer tables, the place seats only 50, which is why there'll be a two-hour wait later this evening—no reservations, except for groups of seven or more. No alcohol can be sold thanks to an arcane state law requiring two restrooms (there's only one). So, many diners pick up a bottle of their preferred vintage at DeVine Wine and Beer Cafe on the corner and pay a modest $5 corkage fee at Lincoln Café, where the evening menu

CLOCKWISE, FROM ABOVE: (ALL TAKEN IN MOUNT VERNON) SATISFIED MAIN STREET GOURMETS, LINCOLN CAFÉ. KING CHAPEL, CORNELL COLLEGE CAMPUS. MUSSELS STEEPED IN WINE AND GARLIC, LINCOLN CAFÉ. OPPOSITE PAGE: BUSY IOWA 80 TRUCK STOP TRAFFIC, WALCOTT.

Sunchoke Soup

Lincoln Café, Mount Vernon

- ¾ pound sunchokes (also known as Jerusalem artichokes)
- 1 large baking potato (about 8 ounces)
- 2 tablespoons butter
- 1 medium onion, coarsely chopped
- 2 to 3 cloves garlic, halved
- 1½ teaspoons snipped fresh thyme
- ¼ teaspoon crushed red pepper
- ½ cup dry white wine
- 1 14-ounce can vegetable broth
- 1 tablespoon snipped fresh tarragon
- 1 cup whipping cream
- ¼ cup milk
  Kosher salt or salt
  Freshly ground black pepper
- 2 teaspoons champagne vinegar or white wine vinegar
  Snipped fresh tarragon or truffle oil (optional)

Wash sunchokes and potato. Coarsely chop unpeeled sunchokes. Peel and coarsely chop potato. Set aside.

In a large saucepan, melt butter over medium heat. Add onion and cook for 4 to 5 minutes or until tender, stirring often. Stir garlic, thyme and red pepper into onion mixture; add wine. Bring to boiling; reduce heat. Cook and stir until wine evaporates. Stir in sunchokes and potato. Add broth. Bring to boiling; reduce heat. Simmer, covered, for 15 to 20 minutes or until tender. Stir in tarragon. Remove from heat. Cool slightly (about 20 minutes); do not drain.

Transfer a third of the sunchoke mixture to a food processor or blender. Cover and process or blend until almost smooth. Repeat with remaining portions, one at a time, until all of the mixture is pureed.

Return pureed mixture to the same saucepan. Bring just to boiling; reduce heat. Stir in whipping cream and milk. Cook and stir until heated through (do not boil). Season to taste with salt and black pepper. Stir in vinegar. Check seasoning again as the vinegar will affect the flavor.

To serve, ladle hot soup into bowls. If you like, sprinkle with fresh tarragon or drizzle with a little truffle oil. *Makes 8 (²/₃ cup) side-dish servings.*

is hand-lettered on a big chalkboard set high on the wall by the kitchen.

Although the exposed-brick walls are decorated with a few carefully chosen works by local artists, the ceiling fans, wooden booths, vintage plastic-laminate countertops and red-vinyl kitchen chairs remind me of a hundred other small-town cafes across the state. During the daytime, the menu is humble: burgers, fries, salads—all prepared and served with panache. Come suppertime, owner and chef Matt Steigerwald, who founded the place in 2000, takes things up a notch.

One of the black-garbed waitstaff takes our order: a big, steaming bowl of mussels cooked in wine and garlic and served with grilled bread topped with roasted-garlic-and-basil aioli; an unforgettable sunchoke (also known as Jerusalem artichoke) soup flavored with white truffle oil; a thick, roasted Niman Ranch pork chop with peach-mustard barbecue sauce; superb grilled guinea hen with black truffle risotto; and roasted wild king salmon with lemon polenta. I'm ready to move to Mount Vernon! We share three desserts: a sublime espresso-orange crème brulee, banana-split chocolate waffles (topped with fresh fruit, chocolate and vanilla-caramel sauces and spiced candied peanuts) and blueberry-lemon cake with cinnamon crème fraîche whip.

One of the foods Matt frequently serves is Niman Ranch pork. The brand originated in Marin County, California, in 1994 because founder Bill Niman wanted to offer consumers and restaurateurs better-quality meats raised as humanely and organically as possible. Today, Niman Ranch beef, pork and lamb are served at the best eating establishments and sold at fine meat counters throughout the country. Appropriately, most Niman Ranch pork comes from Iowa producers, including Gary Snakenberg.

Iowa has 8,900 pig farms, which produce a total of 29.6 million hogs annually, more than 23 percent of the U.S. total. But some of the critters have it better than others during their five to six months of life. Oft-criticized "confinement" operations of up to 1,500 hogs restrict the animals to concrete and wood buildings managed with assembly-line precision. It seems like a sad life for the unfairly maligned pig, which actually is quite smart (more trainable than dogs or cats), clean (they wallow because they don't have sweat glands like we do) and naturally lean (we turn them into gluttons to satisfy our own appetites). Iowa's pigs cooperatively gobble up a fourth to a third of the state's enormous corn and soybean crops. All told, it takes about 800 pounds of corn and soybeans to produce a 250-pound hog, which in turn yields 125 pounds of consumable meat cuts.

I'm not qualified to pass judgment on anyone's farming practices, but I do like the approach I see in use at the Snakenberg (SNAHkenberg) farm near Sigourney (population 2,200). Here, it's all about fresh air rather than confinement. Gary and Marie, who grew up in the area, started their operation with 190 acres when they wed in 1973 and now own 700 acres with their sons, Kenny and Andy. Each year, the family raises about 1,200 crossbred hogs, as well as corn, soybeans and about 80 head of cattle.

In a small pasture where pigs loll and root, Gary tells me there are about 400 Niman Ranch pork producers nationally. These producers must meet certain requirements in terms of flavor and using traditional family farming methods that are considered humane and sustainable. Gary explains that his pigs get plenty of fresh air, sunshine and exercise, which results in more lean muscle marbled with fat, which results in superior flavor.

As we stroll the property, he explains how to spot a hog operation like his: Little A-frame sheds dot the pig lot so the outdoor-raised pigs can escape the sun and nap in the shade when they want to. Gary's sows are nursing their piglets in a pen beside a barn. I learn that Kenny has won several awards for his conservation practices, such as building terraces and ponds to conserve soil. Both Kenny and his brother, Andy, are exceptions to the rule nowadays: They want to farm, and they have a family farm to work (farmland hereabouts currently goes for approximately $3,000 per acre).

"We got interested in the Niman Ranch program back in the early 1990s, when the market was tough. Over the years, it's been good for our family," Gary says. Sounds as if the approach has been good for his hogs and for consumers, too.

CLOCKWISE, FROM TOP LEFT: (ALL TAKEN AT THE GARY SNAKENBERG FAMILY FARM, SIGOURNEY) JOHN DEERE HORSEPOWER AT REST. FUTURE NIMAN RANCH PORK PRODUCTS. ANDY, GARY, DAN AND KENNY. OPPOSITE PAGE: SUNCHOKE SOUP, LINCOLN CAFÉ, MOUNT VERNON.

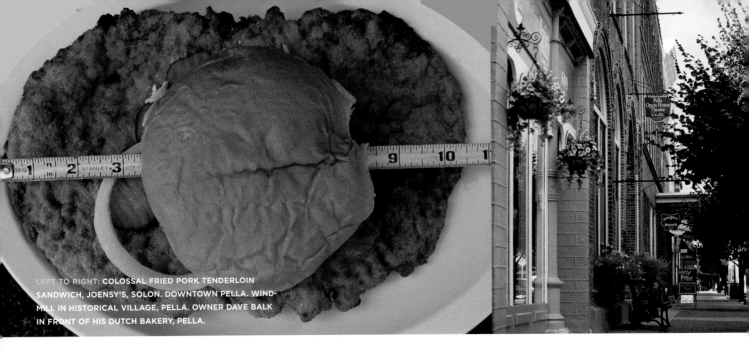

LEFT TO RIGHT: COLOSSAL FRIED PORK TENDERLOIN SANDWICH, JOENSY'S, SOLON. DOWNTOWN PELLA. WINDMILL IN HISTORICAL VILLAGE, PELLA. OWNER DAVE BALK IN FRONT OF HIS DUTCH BAKERY, PELLA.

Loins You Can Count On

Breaded-pork-tenderloin sandwiches are a big deal in Iowa, as anyone who has visited Joensy's, a nothing-fancy bar and restaurant on Main Street in Solon (population 1,200), can tell you. The structure started as an auto-repair garage in the 1920s. But design isn't the point here. The sign above the entry tells the story: "Home of the BIGGEST and BEST Pork Tenderloin in Iowa." Such a claim is not to be taken lightly in this state, where pork producers sponsor an annual competition to anoint Iowa's No. 1 pork tenderloin. The Dairy Sweet in Dunlap claimed the prize in 2005 from a field of 26 entrants. In a town of 1,100, the Dunlap champs sell 8,000 tenderloins a year.

Joensy's is the state's most enduring breaded-tenderloin legend. I claim a booth in the darkish interior and study the menu in a domain of knotty-pine paneling, pool tables, TV screens, video games and a big bar. Hawkeye banners are prevalent (the University of Iowa is just about 10 miles south of here, in Iowa City). I order a whole tenderloin sandwich with the works. A humongous, golden-brown piece of flattened-out fried pork arrives, decorated with big dollops of mustard and ketchup, as well as sliced dill pickles and raw onions. The sandwich weighs a full pound; more than half of that is meat, with the loin measuring almost 7x11 inches! My first bite reveals a crispy masterpiece, not fatty or greasy-tasting at all. The fries and coleslaw seem superfluous —I won't get through even half of the sandwich.

Joensy's serves about 800 tenderloins each week, most of them half-size, some grilled or dolled up. The Texi Melt, for example, is served on Texas toast and smothered with onions and Swiss cheese. Burgers, chicken, catfish, steaks and other specialties appear on Joensy's lunch and dinner menus, but it's the awe-inspiring tenderloins that put this place on the map.

Behind the bar, in the kitchen, owner Brian Joens shows me how he personally hand-cuts his main ingredient from a premium-grade pork loin, runs it through a tenderizing machine three times, then dips it into an egg-and-milk mixture. That's followed by a dredging in cracker crumbs before a trip to the deep fryer for precisely three minutes in soybean oil at 350 degrees (after it's retired from tenderloin duty, the oil eventually winds up in soy diesel fuel!). "Most people just order the half loin, especially after their first visit," Brian tells me with a knowing grin. "But one man came in and ate three full loins in 20 minutes. He was training for a hot-dog-eating contest somewhere." He adds, "We do feed a lot of [University of] Iowa football players." Now, isn't that a surprise.

Baker's Man, Baker's Man

If one category of food rallies ethnic pride more than any other, it must be baked goods and sweets. Just ask a German about strudel, an Italian about cannoli, a Norwegian about krumkake (a large, thin

cookie made from batter poured into an embossed mold) or a Mexican about *tres leches* cake (a butter cake soaked in three kinds of milk)—and watch them well up with tears of joy. That "pat-a-cake" nursery rhyme plays extremely well in Iowa, where Kaffeeklatschers love their treats. Two bakeries on my itinerary stand out among the Hawkeye State's many old-world pastry purveyors. One is Dutch; the other is Czech and Slovak.

Mention Dutch letters—those flaky, S-shaped, almond-paste-filled pastry sensations topped with granulated sugar—to central Iowans, and a grin of satisfaction will likely steal across their faces. Dutch letters come from Pella (population 9,900, located about 45 minutes southeast of Des Moines), founded by Dutch religious refugees in 1845. The town also hosts a huge, three-day Tulip Time festival each May, when hundreds of thousands of spring-drunk Midwesterners gather to watch wooden-shoed street

sweepers, ogle thousands of tulips in bloom (assuming the weather cooperates) and stand outside Jaarsma Bakery on the town square, patiently waiting to purchase Dutch letters.

This is the home of the giant Pella Corporation, which may well have manufactured the windows and doors in your home. Legendary lawman Wyatt Earp spent his boyhood here (you still can visit his home). Pella's religious origins are evidenced by the presence of the Reformed Church in America's Central College and 12 Reformed congregations—and by the fact that virtually everything in town still shuts down on Sunday.

The quaint Pella Historical Village now sprouts America's tallest working windmill (it had to be elevated high enough off the ground—124 feet—to avoid decapitating surrounding structures and to allow the blades to capture the wind). The canal-laced Molengracht Plaza, with its shops, dining and hotel, furthers the Netherlands

theme. Steep-slanting roofs and storybook Dutch stair-step gables abound.

Right on Pella's picture-perfect town square, Herman Jaarsma (YAHRsma) founded a bakery in 1899, using recipes he'd brought from Holland. First he'd bake the day's supply of bread in a brick oven. Then he'd prepare the sweet treats. Four generations and one disastrous fire later, the Jaarsma family is still at it. Dave Balk and his wife, Kristi Jaarsma Balk, are the owners now. Dave is a busy guy who gets to work at 2 a.m. (the staff starts baking at 1 a.m.!). He takes an afternoon nap at home, then heads back to the shop until early evening. Dave tells me he doesn't like coffee, but he is partial to his Dutch letters and pecan rolls (maybe the sugar keeps him going). The bakery sells about 6,000 Dutch letters in an average week, 37,000 during Tulip Time. As I do my sampling, Dave explains that these pastries originated as a Sinterklaas Day (December 6) treat in Holland, hence the

"S" shape. Now they're sold year-round because of popular demand.

Of course, Dutch baking is about more than Dutch letters. It includes *speculaas*, traditional crispy, windmill-shaped Dutch spice cookies with the taste of cinnamon, nutmeg and cloves. *Boter koek* (almond butter cake), a torte with almond filling, butter and honey, topped with slivered almonds and sugar crystals. Dutch apple bread with nuts, apples, brown sugar and cinnamon (the Jaarsmas make 300 loaves daily during Tulip Time). Raspberry-almond tarts. Strudels of various sorts. Dave tells me visitors from Holland sometimes comment that his bakery seems authentic but that Americans like their Dutch treats too sweet. I don't hear anybody complaining . . .

About an hour and a half northeast lies Cedar Rapids, eastern Iowa's largest city

(population 121,000, about 20 minutes north of I-80). It's an attractive city and proud of the fact that—outside of Paris, France—it claims the world's only city hall sited on an island in a river (the Cedar, in this case). It also boasts America's largest cereal manufacturer, Quaker Oats (now owned by PepsiCo), which employs 1,100 people.

Cedar Rapids has a lot of ethnic groups, including one of America's oldest and largest Muslim communities, but the city is best known for its Czech population. A big migration occurred here in the early 1900s, when Czechs came to farm and to work in Cedar Rapids' thriving meatpacking and cereal plants. This is also the home of the handsome National Czech and Slovak Museum and Library, dedicated by presidents Bill Clinton and Vaclav Havel and Michal Kovac a decade ago.

But my main destination is the Sykora (SEEkorah) Bakery, a white-clapboard, general-store sort of building, very authentic, especially with the benches in front that read *Vitame Vas* (that's Czech for "We Welcome You," an inscription you see throughout Czech Village). I step inside and head straight for a certain section of the vintage glass display case. I want a kolache (pronounced KOlahch in the singular and KOlahcheh in the plural).

The Sykora Bakery structure dates back to 1900, when it was built to house a small brewery. The Sykora family of bakers owned it from 1927 to 1991; these days, it's in the loving hands of John and Susan Rocarek. We step into the steaming-hot kitchen, where four bakers (three Czech and one self-proclaimed mongrel) are using special mixers to stir up yeasty dough for the day's kolache output; they'll sell 150 dozen this weekend. Like this building, the venerable Sykora oven is more than a century old, but John says it still

does a better job than most modern ones.

John explains that each batch of kolache dough takes four hours to mix and rise. It gets punched down and rises again five times. The final time, a baker smashes a fist-size opening into the middle, spoons in a glob of a homemade filling and pops the bun into the oven. What comes out 12 minutes later is pure, powdered-sugar-dusted pastry ambrosia: various shapes—round, square, variations of both—of golden-burnished kolaches that resemble fat little inner tubes.

First, I taste-test the classics—poppy seed, prune, cherry, apricot, and cottage cheese and raisin. Then, I sample variations, with fillings that include pineapple, pear, blueberry, rhubarb and strawberry. Poppy seed is the hallmark ingredient in Czech pastries; John says he uses about 50 pounds a month, although most bakeries use that much in a year.

Czechs also are big on fungus variations, mushrooms, specifically. In fact, Houby Days each May is a big festival here, when thousands celebrate the spring's crop of wild morel mushrooms, so we taste *hobove satecky*, mushroom tarts made with cream cheese. John shares other Czech specialties with me: *slany housky*, salted braids; *ovocne rezy*, molasses and raisin cookies; *rohliky*, crescent-shaped rolls made of a sweet dough; *zelniky,* pastry-dough pockets filled with cabbage and onions (like a pastie if you're from Michigan); *kremove trubicky*, cream horns; apple, cherry and poppy seed strudel; *houska,* a five-strand braided bread filled with fruit and raisins and drizzled with white frosting; and Sykora's famous Bohemian caraway rye bread (the bread and kolaches account for 80 percent of John's sales). I can't pronounce the names of half of what I'm sampling, but fortunately that doesn't matter here at the Sykora Bakery.

CLOCKWISE, FROM TOP LEFT: (ALL TAKEN AT CZECH VILLAGE, CEDAR RAPIDS) A YOUNG CZECH FOLK DANCER IN COSTUME. VILLAGE STREET SIGNS. "VITAME VAS" AT THE CIRCA 1900 SYKORA BAKERY. MAKING PASTRIES AT THE SYKORA BAKERY. OPPOSITE PAGE: DUTCH TREATS, JAARSMA BAKERY, PELLA.

Iowa Steak and Tomato Salad with Maytag Blue Cheese

Inspired by Maytag Dairy Farms, Newton

- 1 pound boneless beef sirloin steak, cut 1 inch thick
- 3 tablespoons salad oil
- 3 tablespoons white balsamic vinegar
- 2 teaspoons Dijon-style mustard
- 1 teaspoon dried oregano, crushed
- 6 cups torn Boston or Bibb lettuce
- 1½ cups chopped, seeded tomatoes
- ¾ cup crumbled Maytag Blue cheese or other blue cheese (3 ounces)
- 6 slices bacon, crisp-cooked, drained and crumbled
- 3 hard-cooked eggs, coarsely chopped
- ½ small cantaloupe, peeled and cut into thin slices or 1 medium avocado, halved, seeded, peeled and cut into wedges
  Dijon Vinaigrette (recipe follows)

Slash fat edges of steak at 1-inch intervals, being careful not to cut into the meat. Place steak on the rack of an unheated broiler pan. Broil 3 inches from heat for 12 to 15 minutes for medium doneness, turning once. Cool slightly and cut into thin slices. Place steak slices in a plastic bag. Set aside.

For marinade: In a screw-top jar, combine oil, vinegar, mustard and oregano. Cover; shake well. Pour marinade over steak slices; seal bag. Marinate in refrigerator for 6 hours or overnight, turning bag occasionally. Drain off any excess marinade.

To serve, arrange lettuce on 6 chilled salad plates. Evenly divide steak slices, tomatoes, cheese, bacon and eggs among the plates, arranging overlapping on top of the lettuce. Top each salad with thin cantaloupe slices. Drizzle with vinaigrette and pass remaining. *Makes 6 main-dish servings.*

Dijon Vinaigrette: In a small bowl, combine ⅓ cup white balsamic or white wine vinegar; 1 teaspoon Dijon-style mustard; 1 clove garlic, minced; ½ teaspoon sugar; ¼ teaspoon salt and ¼ teaspoon ground black pepper. Using a wire whisk, in a slow, steady stream, whisking constantly, add ⅓ cup olive oil. *Makes about ⅔ cup.*

Penicillin Never Tasted So Good!

Under bright blue skies, I'm on my way to Maytag Dairy Farms, just north of Newton (population 15,600), to research cheese at a historic farmstead with the Maytag cheese makers. Although the appliance and cheese companies share the same name, the infinitely smaller cheese-making operation (with about 85 employees) is run independently by a group of 12 third- and fourth-generation Maytags.

Back in 1919, E.H. Maytag, a quiet man and son of the wash-day magnate, established what became a renowned herd of black-and-white Holstein dairy cows on an Iowa farm—partly as an avocation, primarily to ensure a supply of pure milk for his family and Maytag employees. In 1941, E.H.'s son, Fred Maytag II, a well-traveled man with an educated palate, partnered a project with Iowa State University (in Ames, just 58 miles northwest of Newton). He wanted to develop a new use for the milk those Holsteins were producing, in the form of a blue cheese that would become an alternative to French Roquefort (made with sheep's milk).

Roquefort, a truffle among the mushrooms of the cheese world, if you will, is said to have originated more than 500 years ago when a French shepherd left behind bread and cheese in a damp cave. He returned months later to find his repast moldy, but was either hungry or adventurous enough to eat it anyway. Humankind has been savoring Roquefort's moldy glory ever since. Today, the wide range of variations includes Stilton in England, Gorgonzola in Italy, a Danish blue cheese—and Maytag Blue.

Maybe it's home-state pride, but I don't think there's a finer cheese than Maytag Blue. In my travels, I've noted the Maytag brand proudly touted on menus from New York to San Francisco. I've savored it as a salad accompaniment, a snack dip, a quiche ingredient and in a dozen other forms, but I love Maytag Blue best all by itself. It's uniquely creamy, tangy, a bit salty and spicy and distinguished by a marblelike, blue-green veining.

No Maytag Holsteins contentedly graze here these days, so the cheese makers' main ingredient comes from about 400 dairy cows whose owners belong to a local cooperative. Maytag Dairy Farms' president, Myrna Ver Ploeg, oversees the manufacture of almost 1 million pounds of Maytag Blue annually (1 pound of cheese requires 10 pounds of milk). We start our tour near what once was the farm manager's home, now part of an above- and underground complex that includes four "caves" where cheese is aged and stored at just the right temperature and humidity.

Rules are rules, so I wear a hairnet. As with the other cheese-making operations I visit on this tour, Maytag Blue starts in a spotless workroom where milk is heated. Then rennet is added to help create the custardlike curd, which is cut into cubes to further separate it from the whey. From there, it's a matter of continuing to drain off the whey and hand-packing the curds into dozens of stainless-steel hoops. Somewhere along the way (it's a trade secret, Myrna tells me), *Penicillin roqueforti* mold is added to create Maytag Blue's distinctive taste, texture and appearance. (Yes, I said penicillin, but this isn't the antibacterium you get in shot form at a doctor's office to treat infections.)

The 4-pound cheese wheels are punched with needles so air can circulate during the aging process, creating the veins that give Maytag Blue its unique flavor and color. Then, the salted rounds are inspected and hand-turned weekly for a total of four to six months (exact details are another delicious Maytag trade secret). Finally, Myrna personally approves each batch: "It has to have that creamy texture, but it also has to be crumbly. We look for a slightly pungent flavor and just a hint of saltiness."

Robert Wadzinski, the plant manager, is from a Wisconsin cheese-making family and has been in this occupation since he was 12. He and his white-attired associates produce about four batches of Maytag Blue per workday. Because each batch requires roughly five hours to complete, this is a 24-hour operation, six days a week. Workers wearing high-top rubber boots bustle about, performing their tasks with precision. The plant and equipment are hosed down constantly. We enter one of the "caves"—actually a whitewashed, pleasantly musky-smelling underground room—where endless rows of cheese rounds repose during the gestation period before being washed, waxed and further aged.

Back up the hill, I purchase several 2-pound, hand-wrapped wheels, all shiny in the distinctive Maytag foil imprinted with a familiar Holstein's head. The price is much less if you buy here, well worth a few minutes' detour off I-80, but you also can get Maytag Blue via mail order or at finer markets or food specialty stores. The company shop also offers Maytag-branded white cheddar, brick, Edam, baby Swiss and other cheese products that are manufactured in Wisconsin and Illinois and aged and packaged here.

Interestingly, Maytag Blue isn't the appliance family's only culinary claim to fame. Back in the 1960s, Fred Maytag II's son, Fritz, a graduate of Stanford University in Palo Alto, California, launched the microbrewery revolution when he acquired Anchor Steam Beer in San Francisco. Hmmm . . . wouldn't a nice microbrew taste good with some of this Maytag Blue I just purchased?

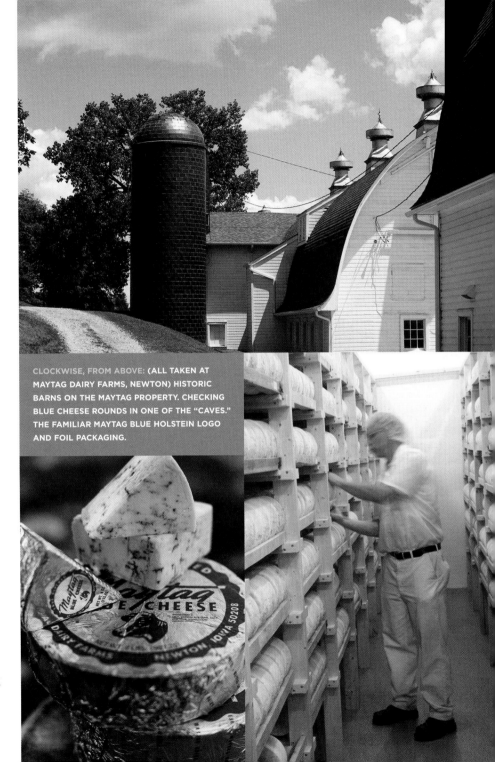

CLOCKWISE, FROM ABOVE: (ALL TAKEN AT MAYTAG DAIRY FARMS, NEWTON) HISTORIC BARNS ON THE MAYTAG PROPERTY. CHECKING BLUE CHEESE ROUNDS IN ONE OF THE "CAVES." THE FAMILIAR MAYTAG BLUE HOLSTEIN LOGO AND FOIL PACKAGING.

Land of Giants

We're from Ioway, Ioway;
State of all the land,
Joy on every hand.
We're from Ioway, Ioway.
That's where the tall corn grows.

Almost every loyal Iowan knows the tune to the rousing "Iowa Corn Song," penned in 1912 by the secretary of the Des Moines Chamber of Commerce for a Shriners' conclave. Corn remains the state's botanical icon, just as wheat defines Kansas and potatoes denote Idaho. Americans depend on corn more than any other single field crop, for products that include animal feed, fructose sweetener and even bioplastics and the ethanol fuel that helps propel our vehicles. Iowa proudly stars as the nation's top corn-producing state, even though most Iowans hardly ever set foot in a field these days.

Still, the crop dominates our collective psyche and newspaper headlines as few other topics do—especially in the dog days of summer, when high temperatures threaten the yield. Thanks to today's enlightened water- and soil-conservation practices, the potent chemical fertilizers farmers use and ever-higher-yielding corn hybrids (the latter being my primary focus today), the harvest rarely disappoints: Incredibly productive hybridized strains yield more than 200 bushels per acre on many Iowa farms.

Bring up corn in Iowa, and agri-historians usually refer to two men: brilliant, idealistic and politically progressive Henry A. Wallace, who served as secretary of agriculture and vice president during the F.D.R. administration, and Roswell Garst, an ebullient, blustery farmer-salesman from Coon Rapids in the rolling hills of west-central Iowa. One of Wallace's many contributions to agriculture and society at large was the advancement of hybrid seed corn technology through his own experiments and his family's Iowa-based Pioneer Hi-Bred (now owned by DuPont). Today, it's Roswell Garst's life story—one day of it in particular—that I want to know more about. I learn the details firsthand from his granddaughter, Elizabeth (Liz), manager of Garst Farm Resorts and the related Whiterock nature conservancy, dedicated to preserving more than 4,000 acres of Iowa wetlands, prairies and woodlands.

I ease the car along winding, scenic State-141 toward tiny Coon Rapids (population 1,300), crossing the tree-banked Middle Raccoon River about an hour northwest of Des Moines. (That's the *Middle* Raccoon, not to be confused with the South Raccoon or the West Branch of the Middle Nodaway or the North Skunk or the just-plain North River or the Middle River!) Soon, I pull into the drive of a cozy, well-kept bed and breakfast that is part of an extensive, 4,500-acre farm "eco-resort." Liz Garst ushers me to a big dining table in the red-papered Russian Room (you'll understand that name shortly) and serves a simple farm-style lunch: Garst Farms–raised buffalo meat loaf, creamed corn casserole, cucumber-and-onion salad and red cabbage with bacon.

The Garst family has been a towering presence in Coon Rapids since 1869. In fact, two of the maple trees among the resort's beautiful flowerbeds arrived on the first train that stopped in Coon Rapids back in 1886. The original Garst brothers ran a general store and got into the seed business. Roswell was born in 1898 and married a cultivated, gracious schoolteacher named Elizabeth Garst in 1916. After some rocky business ventures, Roswell and Elizabeth came home to Coon Rapids and the Garst homestead, now this five-bedroom farmhouse, in 1929.

Thanks in part to what he learned from his friend Henry A. Wallace, Roswell began selling the newfangled notion of hybrid seed corn to flinty Iowa farmers. First, he'd convince a leading farmer to just try the stuff, and soon that farmer would be selling hybrid seed corn to his neighbors. By 1940, almost all corn planted in the United States was a hybrid variety, resulting in bigger yields that transformed the lives of many poor Midwest farm fam-

Impulsive, shoe-thumping Nikita Khrushchev once had a backyard picnic lunch just outside this dining room window.

ilies (indeed, regulating overabundance is one of the primary challenges facing Midwest agricultural economists today).

Garst's success at championing hybrid corn and many other agricultural innovations internationally took him several times to the Soviet Union and won him the attention of Nikita Khrushchev, the post-Stalin-era leader who desperately wanted to modernize Russian agriculture. Through a complex series of contacts and events (initiated in part by Elizabeth Garst and Mrs. Khrushchev, who had met in the Soviet Union), the impulsive, shoe-thumping Khrushchev and his entourage wound up having a backyard picnic lunch just outside the dining room window I gaze out right now. The date: September 23, 1959, at the terrifying height of the Cold War.

"Khrushchev and my grandfather had very similar personalities; they liked each other a lot," Liz says. "The same was true of Nina Khrushchev and my grandmother. Both couples remained good friends even after Khrushchev was deposed in 1964." She goes on to explain her grandfather's fundamental belief that "hungry people are dangerous people." Helping Russians learn how to grow more food would only contribute to global understanding, he reasoned. I ask Liz what she thinks was her grandfather's ultimate legacy to Iowa, the Midwest and the world. She doesn't hesitate: "Showing the world how to grow more food. First he learned how to do it himself, then he sold his ideas to the nation and the world. He was a fabulous salesman."

One of Roswell Garst's causes was promoting cow-calf herds (rather than just corn-fattening, or "finishing," of adult cattle) in western Iowa. I may be biased, but I'll attest: Iowa corn-fed beef makes the best steaks you'll ever taste. So, it's fitting that my next Iowa stop is to pay my

CLOCKWISE, FROM TOP LEFT: (ALL TAKEN AT GARST FARM RESORTS, COON RAPIDS) TIMELESS RURAL CHARM. LIZ GARST AND DAN ENJOYING A NOONDAY FEAST. HARVEST TIME. OPPOSITE PAGE: VINTAGE PHOTO OF FARMER-PROMOTER ROSWELL GARST AND NIKITA KHRUSHCHEV (UPPER RIGHT AND LOWER RIGHT, RESPECTIVELY).

respects to another Iowa "giant": Albert the Bull. I drive about 25 miles over roller-coaster western Iowa hills from the Garst property to Audubon (population 2,300), named for the famed artist and naturalist.

On the south side of town, Albert, a brownish-red-and-white Hereford leviathan, has presided since 1964. He's the brainchild of a promotion-minded local banker, the late Albert Kruse (hence the name). It all started in 1951 with Operation T-Bone, an effort to promote Iowa corn-fed beef in the Chicago market. Audubon still hosts a weekend T-Bone Days festival each August (during which, curiously, they serve hamburgers but not T-bones). Herefords like Albert have largely been supplanted by meatier breeds such as Angus, Charolais and Simmental, but Albert still reigns here.

Other food-related icons evince more local Iowa pride. The world's largest Cheeto, almost the size of a tennis ball, is on display at Sister Sarah's Bar and

Restaurant in Algona in north-central Iowa, where the local citizenry raised $180 to purchase it from its discoverer. Strawberry Point in northeastern Iowa claims the world's largest strawberry (at 15 feet tall), tethered atop a pole in front of city hall. In southwestern Iowa, Swedish Stanton (the home of the late Virginia Christine, Mrs. Olson of coffee-commercial fame) decorated its water tower to create the world's largest coffeepot. I'm learning that, like Roswell Garst, rural Iowans aren't all that reticent when it comes to their agricultural prowess or their small-town pride.

My Favorite Fair—on a Stick!

It's time for one of my favorite events anywhere, the Iowa State Fair in Des Moines. There's probably been more written about this event than any other Iowa topic outside of how the weather is affecting a given year's corn crop. Much of the credit begins with *State Fair*, the enormously popular 1932 novel by *Des Moines Register* reporter and editorial writer Philip Duffield Stong (1899–1957), which fueled three films.

The 1945 celluloid version (my favorite) was the only movie Rodgers and Hammerstein ever graced with original lyrics and music. Who can forget tunes such as "It Might As Well Be Spring," "Our State Fair" and "It's a Grand Night for Singing"? The Iowa-wholesome plot just makes you feel good, like the Iowa State Fair itself still does today.

Iowa held its first state (actually, territory) fair in aptly named Fairfield way back in 1854. The event moved to Des Moines in 1879, and the current fairgrounds was dedicated in 1886. Julie and I attended our first Iowa State Fair on a date during our college years back in the 1960s, and it became an annual August family ritual for us, and later, for our children. Nowadays, we take our eager

6-year-old grandson, Luis, along. In a typical year, fair attendance averages about 1 million during 11 days.

Much of what we cherish about our state fair is the food—from cotton candy and funnel cakes to corn dogs, pork chops, fresh-made lemonade and chocolaty ice cream bars. Nearly every fairgoer has a favorite. Today I'm going to concentrate my grazing on one category: foods on a stick. There are about 25 such options, with the format making it easier to simultaneously stroll and nosh your way past the exhibits—with less cleanup for all concerned.

I start at the Midway, with 80 rides, shows and games in a carnival atmosphere. Nearby are 20 acres of farm machinery exhibits plus dozens of buildings devoted to livestock, produce—and cooking! In the latter department, 820 hopefuls submitted more than 11,500 entries to 893 judging classes covering categories from appetizers to cakes and pies, other desserts and snacks. The winners will take home more than $54,711 in premiums and other prizes. One fair exhibit at the Agriculture Building doesn't get sampled: a refrigerated, life-size butter cow, sculpted annually by Norma Duffield Lyons, niece of Philip Stong. It's often accompanied by a companion work such as *The Last Supper* or Elvis, Garth Brooks or Tiger Woods rendered in butter.

With more than $200 in hand (fairgoers spend $125 per day here on average, so I want to be prepared!), I pick up a Food Concessions Directory and check off my targets. The absolutely awesome list includes barbecue, funnel cakes, cotton candy, gyros, hot dogs, ice cream, kettle corn, lemonade, pork rinds, sausages, and on and on. As I peruse the many technicolor stands festooned with signs, pennants and lightbulbs, I keep my focus on foods on a stick.

CLOCKWISE, FROM ABOVE: (ALL TAKEN AT THE IOWA STATE FAIR, DES MOINES) DEBATING WHAT TO TRY NEXT FROM FOOD VENDORS. FRIED TWINKIE ON A STICK. FOUR IOWA FAIR BEAUTIES. RISING ABOVE IT ALL ON THE SKYGLIDER. OPPOSITE PAGE: AUDUBON'S MOST FAMOUS— AND SIZABLE—RESIDENT, ALBERT THE BULL.

DAN'S FAIR FEAST.

First on my list: a golden corn dog, the juicy, batter-dipped and deep-fried sausage that has to be the fair's No. 1 food on a stick. I always eat mine with a single line of yellow mustard. Yummy, but I keep moving with my "stick list": Dill pickle. Grilled pork chop. Fried pepper-jack cheese. Caramel apples—both green- and red-apple varieties, with and without the peanut coating (I recommend the tartness of the green apple with the crunchiness of the nutty coating). Nutty bar (ice cream dipped in chocolate, then nuts). Hickory-smoked turkey drumstick (on its own "stick," of course). German sausage. Teriyaki beef. Corn on the cob. Dutch bologna. Chocolate-covered banana.

One vendor near the Midway dazzles me with her Cajun chicken and shrimp kabobs and fat Italian meatballs, each served on a stick (fantastic, and well worth the $22 I spend for all three). Lamb kabob. Hard-boiled egg (free!). Veggie dog (a nod to healthy stick-eating). Smoked pork sausage. To wash it all down, I need four lemon shake-ups, made fresh. Oh, and another non-stick item I couldn't resist: a deep-fried whole onion, artistically sliced to resemble an exotic blossom.

I've always avoided the most blatantly fattening-sounding of fair foods on a stick: deep-fried Snickers, Twinkies and Ho Hos—but not today. And they're wonderful! In the dessert department, I also give five stars to the Fudge Puppy (a waffle drenched in chocolate syrup and topped with whipped cream). Was that one served on a stick? Frankly, I'm on such a sugar high, I can't tell! I follow up with a chocolate-dipped cheesecake wedge and nougat-filled peanut roll.

About five hours into this eating frenzy, my sun-scorched skin matches that of this year's Iowa State Fair big boar champion (Tooter, weighing in at 1,080 pounds), and I feel just as bloated. In retrospect, I'll attribute most of the 10½ pounds I gained on my trip to this single state fair binge. I hop the tram back up the hill. My stick-y purchases averaged $5 per serving. Somehow, my morning ATM transaction has dwindled to just a few dollars.

Heading toward my car, I claim a bench in Pioneer Hall and study the exhibit directly before me. Back in 1915 you could pay 50 cents for an all-you-can-eat state fair meal at Mary Hardenbrook's Dining Hall in this building. In the 1940s, parking-lot picnics became the rage, and those corn dogs arrived on the scene from the Texas fair. Deep-fried Twinkies made their debut in 2003.

Enough! I don't need any more reminders. Although my stomach is a bit queasy, I wouldn't trade a moment of this day or any day I've spent at the Iowa State Fair. I look at a sign that proclaims this year's theme: "America's Favorite Fair." Indeed, it is—mine, too.

Taste of Iowa

Czech Kolaches
Sykora Bakery, Cedar Rapids

3³/₄ to 4¹/₄ cups all-purpose flour
1 package active dry yeast
1 cup milk
³/₄ cup unsalted butter
¹/₂ cup sugar
1 teaspoon salt
4 egg yolks
1¹/₂ teaspoons vanilla
2 tablespoons unsalted butter, melted
Cherry Filling, Dried Plum Filling or Apricot Filling (recipes follow)

In a large bowl, stir together 2 cups of the flour and the yeast. Set aside.

In a medium saucepan, heat and stir milk, the ³/₄ cup butter, sugar and salt just until warm (120° to 130°) and butter almost melts. Add to the flour mixture. Add egg yolks and vanilla. Beat with an electric mixer on low to medium speed for 30 seconds, scraping bowl constantly. Beat on high speed for 3 minutes. Using a wooden spoon, stir in as much of the remaining flour as you can.

Turn dough out onto a lightly floured surface. Knead in enough of the remaining flour to make a moderately soft dough that is smooth and elastic (3 to 5 minutes total). Place dough in a greased bowl, turning once to grease the surface. Cover and let rise in a warm place until double in size (1¹/₂ to 2 hours).

Punch down dough. Turn dough out onto a lightly floured surface. Divide dough in half. Cover; let rest for 10 minutes. Grease baking sheets; set aside.

Shape each half of dough into 12 balls, pulling the edges under to make smooth tops. Place the balls 3 inches apart on the prepared baking sheets. Flatten each ball to 3 inches in diameter. Cover; let rise until nearly double in size (about 45 minutes).

Using your thumb or 2 fingers, make a

deep indentation in the center of each dough circle. Spoon about 2 teaspoons of the filling into each indentation. Lightly brush the 2 tablespoons melted butter around edges of rolls.

Bake in a 375° oven for 10 to 12 minutes or until rolls are golden. Remove from baking sheets. Cool on wire racks. *Makes 24 rolls.*

Cherry Filling: In a small bowl, stir together 1 cup canned cherry pie filling, 1/8 teaspoon ground cardamom or allspice and 1/4 teaspoon rum extract.

Dried Plum Filling: In a medium saucepan, combine 8 ounces (1 1/3 cups) pitted dried plums (prunes) and 3/4 cup water. Bring to boiling; reduce heat. Simmer, covered, for 10 minutes. Cool for 20 minutes; drain, reserving liquid. Place dried plums and 2 tablespoons cooking liquid in a food processor. Cover and process until smooth. Stir in 1/4 cup sugar, 1/2 teaspoon vanilla, 1/8 teaspoon salt and 1/8 teaspoon ground cinnamon. Set aside to cool.

Apricot Filling: In a small saucepan, combine 1 cup snipped dried apricots and enough water to come 1 inch above the apricots. Bring to boiling; reduce heat. Simmer, covered, for 10 to 15 minutes or until apricots are very soft. Drain, reserving 2 tablespoons cooking liquid. In a blender or food processor, combine apricots, the reserved cooking liquid, 1/4 cup sugar, 1 teaspoon lemon juice and 1/8 teaspoon ground nutmeg. Cover and blend or process until smooth, stopping to scrape side as necessary. Set aside to cool.

Iowa Creamed Corn Casserole
Garst Farm Resorts, Coon Rapids

- 2 cups frozen whole kernel corn, thawed
- 1 cup finely chopped onion
- 1/2 cup finely chopped red sweet pepper
- 1/2 cup finely chopped green sweet pepper
- 1 tablespoon sugar
- 1/2 teaspoon salt
- 1/4 teaspoon ground black pepper
- 2 cups crushed saltine crackers (about 40 crackers)
- 1 1/4 cups half-and-half or light cream
- 1/4 cup butter, melted

Grease a 2-quart baking dish. Set aside. If necessary, drain thawed corn.

In a medium bowl, combine corn, onion, sweet peppers, sugar, salt and black pepper; mix well. Stir in 1 cup of the crushed crackers and half-and-half. Transfer corn mixture to prepared baking dish.

In a small bowl, combine the remaining 1 cup crushed crackers and melted butter; sprinkle over the corn mixture.

Bake in a 350° oven for 35 to 40 minutes or until knife inserted near center comes out clean. Let stand 10 minutes before serving. *Makes 6 servings.*

Truck Stop Apple Dumplings
Iowa 80 Kitchen, Walcott

- 1 15-ounce package rolled refrigerated unbaked piecrust (2 crusts)
- 3 cups thinly sliced, peeled Granny Smith and/or Braeburn apples (about 3/4 pound)
- 2 teaspoons lemon juice
- 4 teaspoons sugar
- 1 teaspoon ground cinnamon
- 1/2 cup apple juice
- 2 tablespoons light-colored corn syrup
- 1 tablespoon butter
- 1 teaspoon cornstarch
- 1/2 teaspoon vanilla
  Milk
  Sugar
  Ground cinnamon
  Cinnamon or vanilla ice cream

For pastry shells: Let piecrusts stand at room temperature for 15 minutes. Unroll piecrusts.

Cut eight 4- to 4 1/2-inch pastry rounds from piecrusts. Press half of the pastry rounds lightly into bottom and up sides of four 3 1/2- to 4-inch individual tart pans with removable bottoms. Set aside.

For filling: In a large bowl, sprinkle apples with lemon juice. Sprinkle apples with the 4 teaspoons sugar and the 1 teaspoon cinnamon; gently toss until coated. Set aside.

For syrup: In a small saucepan, combine apple juice, corn syrup, butter and cornstarch. Cook until thickened and bubbly. Remove from heat. Stir in vanilla. Set aside.

Evenly divide apple mixture among the 4 pastry-lined pans. Spoon syrup over apples. Cut 3 slits in each remaining pastry round. Place pastry rounds on top of the filling. Use a small knife or thin spatula to tuck extra pastry down inside the edges of the pans. If you like, cut decorative trimmings from pastry scraps and arrange on top crusts; brush top pastry with milk. Lightly sprinkle with additional sugar and cinnamon.

Place dumplings directly in the center of an oven rack. Place a baking sheet on the oven rack below them. Bake in a 375° oven for 45 to 50 minutes or until the fruit is tender and the filling is bubbly. Cool slightly on a wire rack.

Before serving, remove dumplings from pans; arrange each in a shallow dessert plate. Serve warm with ice cream. *Makes 4 servings.*

Travel Journal

More Information

Amana Colonies Convention and Visitors Bureau (800/579-2294, www.amana colonies.com). **Cedar Rapids Area Convention & Visitors Bureau** (800/735-5557, www.cedar-rapids.com). **Greater Des Moines Convention and Visitors Bureau** (800/451-2625, www.SeeDesMoines.com). **Mount Vernon Area Chamber of Commerce** (877/895-8214, www.mountvernon iowa .org). **Pella Convention & Visitors Bureau** (888/746-3882, www.pella.org). **Quad Cities Convention & Visitors Bureau** (800/747-7800, www.visitquad cities.com).

Featured Dining

Lincoln Café Downtown Mount Vernon (319/895-4041).
Joensy's Solon (319/624-2914).
Iowa 80 Truck Stop Near Walcott (563/284-6961).

More Great Dining

Colony Inn and **Ox Yoke Inn** Amana Colonies. Among a half-dozen restaurants, primarily in the villages of Amana and Homestead, specializing in hearty German and American meals served family style (319/622-3030 and 800/233-3441, respectively).
801 Steak and Chop House Des Moines. In the state's tallest building, a clublike restaurant where celebrities and local dignitaries go for prime beef (515/288-6000).
Maid-Rite Des Moines. Seventy-plus locations, more than 40 in Iowa (515/276-5448 for locations).

Palmer's Des Moines. Dine in or carry out at this big deli and market just west of downtown, with food-court-type "stations" for traditional and specialty sandwiches, salads, soups and baked goods (515/274-4004; also locations in downtown, suburban West Des Moines and Urbandale).
Sam & Gabe's Des Moines. A full-menu restaurant west of downtown, specializing in northern Italian cuisine with a welcoming, bistrolike atmosphere (515/271-9200).
Tursi's Latin King Des Moines. Just west of the Iowa State Fairgrounds, outstanding Italian-American fare for nearly 60 years in a friendly setting that resembles an Italian villa (515/266-4466).
Strawtown Inn Restaurant Pella. Listed on the National Register of Historic Places and featuring Dutch dishes such as traditional spiced beef. Also 17 guest rooms decorated in Dutch style (641/621-9500).

Featured Stops

Sykora Bakery Cedar Rapids (319/364-5271).
Garst Farm Resorts At Whiterock Conservancy in Coon Rapids (712/684-2964).
Whitey's Three locations in Davenport (888/594-4839).
Iowa State Fair Des Moines, mid-August (800/545-3247).
DeVine Wine and Beer Cafe Mount Vernon (319/895-9463).
Maytag Dairy Farms Newton (800/247-2458), with a cheese shop and tours.
Jaarsma Bakery Pella (641/628-2940).
Pella Historical Village and Dutch Windmill Pella (641/628-4311).

More Great Stops

Amana Colonies Amid the east-central Iowa hills just north of I-80, Germans seeking religious freedom founded these seven villages in the mid-1800s. Designated a National Historic Landmark, the colonies' attractions include the two listings below, as well as restaurants, bakeries, a smokehouse, a microbrewery, a woolen mill, general stores, galleries, museums and furniture, crafts, antiques and gift shops.
Ackerman Winery Amana Colonies. Six-level winery with tours, tastings and wine sales (319/622-3379).
Communal Kitchen and Cooper Shop

Museum Amana Colonies. Authentic 1932 communal kitchen house, including a dining room, with a barrel-making shop across the street (319/622-3567).
Czech Village Cedar Rapids. Featuring ethnic and specialty shops, a bakery and restaurants, plus the National Czech and Slovak Museum and Library (319/362-2846 and 319/362-8500, respectively).
Des Moines The golden-domed state capitol crowns the funky establishments of the newly reborn East Village district and looks west toward the skyline of downtown, which has blossomed with a botanical center, historical museum, science center and new arena for sporting events and entertainment productions. Visitors venture farther west to the art center, designed by three internationally known architects; specialty stores and galleries in historic Valley Junction; the Living History Farms, which span 300 years in exhibits (515/278-5286); and Jordan Creek Town Center, the area's newest shopping destination.
In't Veld Meat Market Pella. Owned by Dutchman Stan Bogaard, with three smokehouses out back, featuring specialties such as Pella bologna, summer sausage, jerky and Dutch cheeses (641/628-3440).
World's largest coffeepot Stanton (877/329-2840 or 888/623-4232).
World's largest strawberry Strawberry Point (563/933-4400).

Dan's Lodgings

Holiday Inn Express Cedar Rapids ($$; 319/294-9407).
AmeriHost Inn Pella ($$; 641/628-0085).

More Great Lodgings

Die Heimat Country Inn Homestead. The oldest of the Amana Colonies' half-dozen bed and breakfasts, a converted 1854 stagecoach stop with 18 rooms ($$, with full breakfast; 888/613-5463).
Garst Farm Resorts at Whiterock Conservancy Coon Rapids. A five-bedroom bed and breakfast in a 1940s-era farmhouse, plus cottages and campsites on a 4,500-acre river valley preserve, with fishing, hiking, trail rides, canoe floats and other outdoor activities ($; 712/684-2964).

Embassy Suites Hotel Des Moines. Beside the Des Moines River and just down the hill from the state capitol, where shuttle buses run to the state fairgrounds ($$, with full breakfast; 515/244-1700).

Food Events

Tulip Time Festival Pella, first Thursday, Friday and Saturday in May—Indulge in authentic Dutch treats, such as almond-filled Dutch letter pastries, Pella's famous bolognas and cheeses, and Windmill bread and flour ground by the country's tallest working Dutch windmill, located here. Costumed dancers clomp in wooden shoes and street scrubbers join in the parades. Twenty-five thousand tulips, an antique street organ, wooden-shoe makers and Dutch folk dancers greet visitors at the town's Historical Village. Admission charged to some events (641/628-4311, www.pellatuliptime.com).

Houby Days Cedar Rapids, weekend after Mother's Day—"Czech" out the ethnic foods, such as sauerkraut, dumplings, pork, kolaches (fruit-filled yeast buns), goulash and poppy seed cake, at the Taste of Czech. Also at these Houby (Czech for "mushroom") Days, win a prize for the smallest or largest morel and start your day at the mushroom-and-egg breakfast. The Czech Village hosts Maypole dancing, music in the bandstand, crafts and food vendors, and a parade. Fee for Taste of Czech (319/364-0001, www.ncsml.org).

Truckers Jamboree Walcott, second Thursday and Friday in July—Keep on truckin' to the world's largest truck stop for this annual gig for big rigs. Fuel up with Iowa pork chop dinners grilled in the parking lot. Then, watch the Trucker Olympics, the Super Truck Beauty Contest and the Trucker's Best Friend Pet Contest, and shop for items from motor oil to trucking T-shirts and memorabilia. More than 250 rigs line up for the antique-truck display, and live country music plays on the main stage (563/468-5519, www.walcotttruckersjamboree.com).

T-Bone Days Audubon, first weekend in

CZECH DANCERS, CEDAR RAPIDS.

August—The town known for Albert, a 30-foot-tall, 45-ton concrete bull, beefs up for this tribute to its livestock industry. Operation T-Bone started in the 1950s as an elaborate send-off for the annual shipping of cattle to the Chicago stockyards. "Steak" out these festivities: a hamburger feed, parade, crafts show, fun run, kids' games and free stage entertainment (712/563-3780, www.auduboniowa.org).

Sweet Corn Festival West Point, second weekend in August—At Iowa's largest sweet-corn festival, nibble on free samples of the featured crop, compete in the sweet-corn-eating contest and enjoy a dinner of barbecued pork chops, chicken and sweet corn, of course. More fun includes 5K and 10K runs, a carnival, a parade and free stage entertainment. Townsfolk gear up for the festival by shucking more than 17 tons of sweet corn (319/837-6313, www.westpointcornfestival.com).

State Fair Des Moines, 11 days starting the second Thursday in August—The life-size butter cow sculpture, corralled inside an ice-cold compartment at the Agriculture Building, has been a beloved tradition at the fair since 1911 (800/545-3247, www.iowastatefair.org).

World Food Festival Des Moines, mid-October—Sample culinary traditions from around the world at this festival held in conjunction with the World Food Prize Harvest Festival. Vendors dish up jambalaya, baklava, egg rolls, tamales and more than 100 other foods at the ethnic cafe, and the international beer tent offers suds from around the world. Also on the down-

town streets surrounding the capitol and its grounds: West African drummers, Scottish bagpipers and other global entertainment, plus shopping opportunities at the international market (515/286-4906, www.downtowneventsgroup.org).

Mail Order

Amana Meat Shop & Smokehouse Succulent meats cured the old-world way. Order the famous Amana ham, bacon, steaks, sausage and cheeses. Also available: jams and jellies (800/373-6328, www.amanameatshop.com).

Iowa Pork Producers Association Juicy, flavorful cuts of Iowa pork packaged in special gift cartons. Stock up on chops, loin roasts, grilling fillets, chop on a stick (rib chop) or the smoked sampler, which includes chops, boneless pit ham, pepper-smoked bacon and apple double-smoked bacon (800/372-7675, www.iowapork.org).

Jaarsma Bakery Luscious Dutch pastries made in Pella by a family-owned and -operated bakery since 1899. Gift packages include the famous Dutch letters (S-shaped flaky puff pastry wrapped around almond-paste filling) and other specialties, including *speculaas* (spice cookies) and *boter koek* (almond butter cake) (641/628-2940, www.jaarsmabakery.com).

Maytag Dairy Farms Located north of Newton in central Iowa and acclaimed internationally for premium blue cheese. You can purchase Maytag Blue wheels and wedges and other cheeses, including white cheddar, brick, Swiss, and Edam (800/247-2458, www.maytagblue.com).

Pella Bologna Robust, peppery bologna that has been hickory-smoked and shaped into a ring; made in Pella, a touch of Holland in Heartland America, since 1868. Ulrich Meat Market ships its own brand (641/628-2771, www.dutchmall.com).

Whitey's Super-premium ice cream made in the Quad Cities since 1933. More than 36 fantastic flavors available online, where you can order a combo of ice cream and extra-thick shakes or malts (888/594-4839, www.whiteysicecream.com).

KANSAS
Great Plains Granary

THIS PAGE: CLASSIC KANSAS SILHOUETTE IN THE SALINA AREA.
OPPOSITE PAGE, LEFT TO RIGHT: LONGHORN AT PRAIRIE ROSE
CHUCKWAGON SUPPER, BENTON. AN ICONIC KANSAS WINDMILL AT
PRAIRIE ROSE. WINTER WHEAT, THE STATE'S BUMPER GRAIN CROP.

Kansas and the other "rectangular" states I'll visit (Nebraska, South Dakota and North Dakota) all begin on their green eastern flanks looking typical of the Midwest Corn Belt—lots of farm fields lush with corn and soybeans. Then come the infinite horizons of the Great Plains.

In eastern Kansas, there's also a profusion of truck farms, apple orchards and even nascent vineyards in the fertile river valleys. Roadside markets and "U-pick" farms offer ample opportunities to enjoy the abundance.

Thank a Kansan for discovering the once-ubiquitous Winesap apple near Leavenworth in eastern Kansas back in 1866. In central Kansas, Hutchinson sits atop mines that yield much of the salt Americans consume. Spinach once ruled in Lenexa, where during an annual festival they still toss the world's largest spinach salad with pitchforks in a huge plastic pool. Of course, Kansas also is known indelibly as the Sunflower State, even though North Dakota actually is the nation's No. 1 producer of those platter-size yellow blossoms.

Kansans keep their eyes on the skies: Disastrous spring cyclones and calamitous summer thunderstorms are legendary here in Tornado Alley (remember Dorothy, Toto and their farmhouse spiraling skyward in *The Wizard of Oz*?). One example of the state's climatic diversity: The growing season in this 14th-largest state is 50 days longer in its southeastern

corner than in its northwestern corner!

The east-west transition begins in the Flint Hills, North America's largest unplowed grassland, where each summer some 1 million cattle graze on huge ranches. Beef cattle—Black Angus, Charolais, Hereford and other breeds—are the state's top agricultural moneymakers ($5.6 billion in 2004), as evidenced by the expansive feedlots that line the approaches to Dodge City and Garden City in southwestern Kansas. All told, almost 9 million head of cattle are brought to market in Kansas each year, many finished on another top Kansas crop, cornlike grain sorghum, also known as milo.

Although beef and sunflowers claim part of the Kansas spotlight, the state's star commodity is a protein-rich grass consumed almost the world over: wheat. Nearly 10 million acres of Kansas is planted in wheat, yielding 420 million bushels of the nutty brown grain (almost a $1 billion harvest in 2004). Towering, white grain elevators sprout throughout the generally level state. One of those elevators alone is a half-mile long and holds 46 million tons of grain! Kansas winter

wheat—as opposed to the spring wheat grown farther north—typically is planted in fall, grazed by cattle in the dormant winter months and harvested by huge combine crews in June. Most Kansas wheat goes into baking flour—one bushel of wheat yields 42 pounds of flour. The state leads the nation in both wheat production and flour milling.

All that Kansas bounty translates into some "mighty good eatin'," served up at friendly small-town cafes. Kansas wheat is transformed into satisfying loaves of bread and tempting, sweet cinnamon rolls—and into crisp, dry wheat lagers. Kansas beef shows up in juicy steaks and the near-universal Kansas tenderized-and-breaded chicken-fried steak, liberally doused with creamy country gravy. Speaking of fried, Kansans fancy juicy breasts, golden thighs and well-turned legs—all of the fried-chicken variety, served crispy on the outside and juicy on the inside. That's not to say I haven't savored foie gras and lobster in my share of sophisticated Kansas eateries, clustered in cities such as Overland Park (40 Sardines), Lawrence (Teller's) and Topeka (New City Café).

Setting the stage for my visit, I pull off humming I-70 in Bonner Springs just west of metro Kansas City for an introduction to Kansas' rural heritage. Here, the National Agricultural Center and Hall of Fame opened in 1965 to celebrate farmers and farming on a 172-acre site now surrounded by suburban development. It's a U.S. Congress–chartered center, funded largely by donations from corporate agribusiness organizations. Thousands of Kansas City–area schoolchildren, who come here for a glimpse of a bygone way of life, are among the primary beneficiaries. Inside the main building, the Hall of Fame exhibit celebrates 36 Americans who shaped American agriculture.

I hop aboard a hayrack pulled by a 1950s John Deere tractor for a brief ride down the hill to a cluster of vintage structures and reproductions called Farm Town U.S.A., dominated, appropriately enough, by a whirring windmill. A miniature Union Pacific Railroad train circles the grounds; stops include a blacksmith shop, poultry hatchery and one-room schoolhouse. Back up the hill is a 20,000-square-foot museum packed with farm machinery, tools and other treasures. As I leave to resume my Kansas sojourn, I pause at the impressive, domed National Farmers' Memorial out front, a monument dedicated to the people who produce the crops that feed America and much of the globe. Big bronze relief panels depict farmers of the past, present and future. This tribute sets the perfect tone for my visit to one of America's leading agricultural states.

Amber Waves of Grain

Over millions of years in the snail's pace of geologic time, Kansas and most of the rest of the Great Plains lay submerged at the bottom of giant oceans that ebbed and flowed, leaving behind the limestone and shale that underlie most of the state today. Now, waves of a different type riffle in the prairie winds—golden wheat. Kansas is America's No. 1 wheat state, producing more than 40 percent of the protein-rich, hard red winter wheat flour we consume at the rate of 136 pounds per person annually in yeast breads and baked treats.

The cycle on a Kansas wheat farm is this: Seeds are sown in autumn. They sprout and sometimes are grazed by cattle before going dormant. In spring, the wheat comes back to life, weaving a golden carpet that can reach a height of 4 feet. In June, combines begin munching their way northward, reaping by the billions the 50 or so kernels, or berries, that form in each head of wheat; about half will stay in the United States and half will be exported. Then, most of the fields are left fallow for several months, waiting for the cycle to begin anew.

Ethnic German Mennonites fleeing persecution in their temporary homeland on the Russian steppes introduced protein- and gluten-rich Turkey Red hard winter wheat to Kansas in 1874—just after the family farming operation I'm visiting today

was founded near Oxford (population 1,200), about 30 miles south of Wichita. The wheat harvest is finished here, with only telltale stubble left behind.

I pull into the driveway of the Morton farm and, inside their up-to-date, ranch-style home, join Tom and his wife, Mary, over coffee and hearty, warm bread made with flour ground from their own wheat. I'm here to get a feel for life on a wheat farm. Tom and Mary, both natives of this community and graduates of Kansas State University, raised two children on their 2,500 tillable acres. That's a medium-large farm hereabouts, but it wouldn't be in western Kansas, where it takes a 10,000-acre spread to impress. "My great-grandfather founded this farm after he emigrated to Kansas from Scotland," Tom says. "It was a 160-acre homestead back then. He expanded to 500 acres. A man could make a good living on 500 acres back then; now you need 2,000 acres and a wife who works in town!"

What changes has Tom noted through the years? Most of the classmates he attended high school with have left farming for other occupations, but technology helps Tom stay in the family business. With a virtual heavy-equipment dealership of trucks, tractors, combines and other contraptions, he can manage the entire farm himself, with only the assistance of a high-school student in summer.

One legacy of the Great Dust Bowl years is an increased emphasis on soil conservation throughout the plains: less tilling, more crop rotation. Another change is globalization. "Our wheat can wind up anywhere from South America to China to Nigeria—anywhere people eat bread," Tom says. "And there's more competition these days, from areas like the Black Sea region of Russia." Tom isn't getting rich as a wheat farmer, but he knows what he's doing is important. "Wheat is the bread of life. My crop helps feed the world. That makes me feel good," he says. Bravo!

Of course, my journey is as much about what Midwesterners *eat* as about what they *grow*. Next stop is Yoder, a prosperous west-central Kansas community just off busy State-96 about 45 minutes northwest of Wichita and 20 minutes southeast of Hutchinson. Like many tourism-oriented communities across the Midwest, Yoder thrives because it's at the heart of an Amish-Mennonite district of livestock and dairy farms. The village teems with shops that purvey handcrafted furniture, antiques, meats and sausages, candles, hardware, quilts, crafts—and hearty Amish food at the Carriage Crossing restaurant.

My hosts for a midmorning breakfast here are Dawnita and Mike Miller, a go-getting couple who dress in contemporary garb and are descended from those German-Russians who brought Turkey Red hard winter wheat to Kansas. In addition to their very popular restaurant (which offers parking for Amish buggies as well as autos), Mike operates a nearby sporting-

Sour Cream Raisin Pie

Carriage Crossing Restaurant, Yoder

- 4 cups water
- 1½ cups raisins
- 1 16-ounce carton dairy sour cream
- 1½ cups sugar
- ½ cup cornstarch
- 4 egg yolks, lightly beaten
- ½ teaspoon salt
- 1½ teaspoons vanilla
  Pastry for 10-inch Pie (recipe follows)
- 1 8-ounce carton frozen whipped dessert
  topping, thawed

In a medium saucepan, bring water to boiling. Remove from heat; stir in raisins. Set aside.

For filling: In a heavy large saucepan or Dutch oven, stir together sour cream, sugar, cornstarch, egg yolks and salt; mix well. Stir in the water and raisin mixture. Cook and stir over medium heat until thickened and bubbly. Cook and stir for 2 minutes more. Remove saucepan from heat. Stir in vanilla. Pour the filling into a large bowl. Cover surface of filling with plastic wrap. Chill for at least 4 to 6 hours.

To serve, pour filling into Pastry for 10-inch Pie. Spread dessert topping over filling; seal to edge of crust. Serve immediately. Store any remaining pie, covered, in refrigerator. *Makes 10 servings.*

Pastry for 10-inch Pie: In a medium bowl, combine 1½ cups all-purpose flour and ½ teaspoon salt. Using a pastry blender, cut in ½ cup shortening until mixture resembles crumbs that are pea-size. Add 2 to 4 tablespoons ice water and stir until dough is just moistened. Form dough into a ball; cover with plastic wrap and let stand for 1 hour. On a lightly floured surface, slightly flatten dough. Roll dough from center to edges into a circle 13 inches in diameter. Ease pastry into pie plate without stretching it. Trim pastry to ½ inch beyond edge of pie plate. Fold under the extra pastry. Crimp edge as desired. Line pastry with a double thickness of foil. Bake in a 450° oven for 8 minutes. Remove foil. Bake about 7 minutes more or until golden. Cool on a wire rack. *Makes one 10-inch pie shell.*

goods store and Dawnita manages the restaurant's boutique, filled with Amish-themed crafts and keepsakes.

Looking around from my seat in the big dining room, I see platter-size, 99-cent cinnamon rolls oozing a brown-sugar-and-butter frosting (they bake about 16 dozen each day here), and people enjoying selections from among 30 kinds of pie. I sample the sour cream raisin, coconut cream, peanut butter cream and chocolate peanut butter cream. And, on the side, fried mush; I recall my mother made these stick-to-your-ribs cornmeal strips occasionally on cold winter mornings when I was growing up. For dinner, the menu is pure Kansas: fried chicken, chicken-fried steak, grilled pork chops and grilled smoked ham—plus those pies, of course.

The Millers' wonderful cinnamon rolls are made with Hudson Cream flour, which comes from a mill about 60 miles west of Yoder in an even smaller community, Hudson (population 145). I cruise west, off the main highway, toward the 110-foot-tall grain elevator that marks this and a hundred other Kansas towns. At the Stafford County Flour Mill, I'm greeted by Al Brensing, spry, witty—and 88 years

"old." He's worked at the mill since 1937, taking only two years off to serve with the armed forces during World War II. Not surprisingly, Al attributes much of his longevity to eating his own product, a premium baking flour with a cultlike following around the United States. The Stafford mill is the last of Kansas' independently run large flour mills, still owned by shareholders from the area. These days, most of the state's wheat gets processed by corporate giants such as ConAgra, Archer Daniels Midland and Cargill. As we tour the facility, Al shares some history, most of which he's witnessed firsthand.

Hudson's mill was founded by a German immigrant, Gustav Krug, whose original wooden mill burned in 1913. This successor was built in 1914. Al points out the basic steps from grain to flour: cleaning, grinding, sifting and sacking. The wheat and flour are moved from point to point by pneumatic tubes and bagged by machine—3,000 five-pound sacks per hour—before being whisked off to supermarkets in an average of 25 truckloads per week. (Hudson Cream also is sold through the mail.) Here, 100 pounds of wheat wind up as 62 pounds of vitamin-enriched Hudson Cream flour—bleached and unbleached, white and whole wheat, in a variety of products including self-rising flour (with salt, baking powder and soda added). The remainder goes into lower-quality flour and animal feed.

In 2004, Hudson's mill processed 2 million bushels of Kansas wheat, most purchased by home bakers. Why have these cooks remained so loyal to the Hudson Cream brand for decades? "It's just the best there is," Al says. "One woman wrote us her husband was going to take a job in Tennessee, and she told him she wouldn't move unless they could find Hudson Cream there—and they did."

CLOCKWISE, FROM TOP LEFT: RURAL KANSAS SCENE IN THE SALINA AREA. WHEAT FARMER TOM MORTON, OXFORD. GRAIN AT VARIOUS STAGES OF MILLING, STAFFORD COUNTY FLOUR MILL, HUDSON. AL BRENSING, LONGTIME EMPLOYEE AND PRESIDENT OF THE STAFFORD MILL. OPPOSITE PAGE: CARRIAGE CROSSING EXTERIOR, YODER.

Beef Brisket

Inspired by Prairie Rose Chuckwagon, Benton

- 1 5- to 6-pound beef brisket
- 1 tablespoon cooking oil
- 2 tablespoons seasoned salt
- 1 cup cider vinegar
- 1 cup liquid smoke
- 4 to 6 cups mesquite wood chips
- ½ cup water
-   Favorite bottled barbecue sauce

Brush both sides of meat with oil (do not trim fat). Sprinkle seasoned salt evenly over both sides of meat; rub in with your fingers. Place the meat in a large resealable plastic bag set in a shallow dish. Pour vinegar and liquid smoke over meat; seal bag. Marinate in the refrigerator for 12 hours or overnight, turning bag occasionally.

At least 1 hour before grilling, soak wood chips in enough water to cover. Drain meat, discarding marinade. Drain wood chips.

For a charcoal grill, arrange medium-low coals around a drip pan. Test for low heat above pan. Sprinkle half of the drained wood chips over the coals. Place meat, fat side up, on grill rack over drip pan. Cover and grill for 3½ to 3¾ hours or until meat is tender. Add more wood chips about every 45 minutes. (For a gas grill, preheat grill. Reduce heat to low. Adjust for indirect cooking. Add wood chips according to manufacturer's directions. Place meat on a rack in a roasting pan; place on grill rack. Grill as above.)

Remove the meat from grill. Cool for 20 minutes. Place meat in a foil-lined 13x9x2-inch baking pan. Cover and chill for 12 to 24 hours. Slice meat thinly across the grain. Place meat back into the baking pan. Add water.

Bake, covered, in a 350° oven about 45 minutes or until meat is heated through and very tender. Meanwhile, in a medium saucepan, warm barbecue sauce over low heat. Serve meat with barbecue sauce. *Makes 14 to 16 servings.*

Eat Like a Cowboy—Sort Of

Kansas is the Midwest's rootin' tootin' cowhand state. The tradition dates back to the years immediately following the Civil War, when somebody figured out that folks back East and an ever-swelling tide of hungry European immigrants might enjoy the excess longhorn beef then roaming wild in Texas, thanks to neglect during the war.

Enterprising ranchers began branding the ornery critters and funneling 5 million longhorns to railheads in Abilene and other Kansas frontier outposts—an arduous journey that took up to nine months at a mile an hour. The ranchers engaged Civil War veterans and teenage boys alike to herd up to 5,000 cattle at a time on the 900-mile Chisholm Trail, with hot baths and saloons waiting at the end of the trip. Many noble cowboys still work the vast ranches of the Great Plains region, but the real heyday of the American cowboy didn't last more than a couple decades in the late 1800s; its end was brought about by the expansion of railroads and the introduction of barbed-wire fences that cordoned off the open range forever.

Kansans continue to revel in their cowboy past at rodeos, roundups, trail rides, guest ranches, historic attractions—and chuckwagon meals. I relish the latter at the Prairie Rose Chuckwagon Supper, which annually attracts about 70,000 visitors. Its setting is part of a 700-acre working ranch on the open prairie in Benton, about 15 miles northwest of modern, aviation-oriented Wichita (population 580,000).

In a dining and entertainment hall called the Opera House, the dinner bell rings each night at 6:30; guests at long tables chow down on a cumulative 1 ton of beef each week, followed by live Western music and stage banter. Because I can't attend an evening performance and still make my next date, Thomas Etheredge, who owns this spread with his wife, Cheryl, has agreed to stage a chuckwagon lunch and live performance by the very talented Prairie Rose Wranglers—just for me. Yippee!

I'm served the standard, all-you-can-eat supper menu of slow-barbecued beef brisket, smoked beef sausage, warm buttermilk biscuits, red beans, potato salad and hot peach cobbler. Very satisfying, although I'll soon learn this wasn't a typical meal on the Chisholm Trail. Then comes that mini performance by the Prairie Rose Wranglers. Thomas calls the music of the award-winning group a "water and weeds" repertoire because the characteristically doleful, lovelorn cowboy classics include "Cool, Clear Water" and "Tumbling Tumbleweed." By the time they harmonize "Ghost Riders in the Sky" and "Rose of San Antone," I'm waaaay gone, tapping my foot and basking in fond memories of Roy Rogers and the Sons of the Pioneers.

Time for my tour and some cowhand history. Thomas, courtly in an old-fashioned way and gifted with a resonant speaking voice, is garbed in classic cowboy attire. Raised on a Texas ranch, he pursued a banking career here and overseas before settling down at this ranch his wife's family has called home for more than 120 years. Then came hard times for beef ranchers in the mid-1990s. "We had to think outside the box," Thomas recalls. The result: The Etheredges kept the ranch (they still raise about 300 head of cattle), and Thomas became a Kansas tourism legend.

From the first chuckwagon suppers back in 1999, the Etheredges' complex has grown to a dozen buildings, and they're about to launch America's first cowboy theme park in Park City, a Wichita suburb (at a cost of $20 million!). We end my visit at the 10,000-square-foot Hopalong Cas-

CLOCKWISE, FROM ABOVE: MODERN-DAY DESCEN-
DANTS OF YESTERDAY'S LONGHORNS GRAZING
NEAR SALINA. PRAIRIE ROSE CHUCKWAGON SUPPER,
BENTON. SATISFYING COWBOY FARE AT PRAIRIE
ROSE. RANCHER AND ENTREPRENEUR THOMAS
ETHEREDGE OF PRAIRIE ROSE.

sidy museum, packed with ephemera from the glory days of the late "King of Cowboy Merchandisers."

As for what those Chisholm Trail cowboys really ate, Thomas sets the record straight for me: "Most of the time, it was navy and pinto beans (frijoles) and biscuits (referred to as "sinkers"). If a longhorn got sick or got killed on the trail, they had fresh beef, but that was a treat." If the cook was feeling merciful, dessert was a cobbler made with dried fruit.

Thomas tells me he's hosted guests from all 50 states and 80 foreign countries. "Whether it's Europe, Russia, China or India, when people hear about America, they want to hear about cowboys. They're the American icon around the globe."

Fried-Chicken Dramas

Panfried, deep-fried, pressure-fried or oven-fried. Cooked in vegetable oil, butter, bacon grease or lard. Skin intact or scalped. Bone-in or deboned. Single- or double-dipped in flour or crumbs, with or without seasonings beyond the de rigueur salt and pepper. However you prefer yours, crispy, golden fried chicken is one of America's classic dinnertime and convenience-food favorites. The dish usually is associated with rural Southern cooks, but the preparation method actually arrived with Scottish immigrants. African-American slaves added their zesty seasonings, and a legend was born. But Midwest cooks have their own claim on the poultry crown, and I've never met people who take their fried chicken more seriously than Kansans.

The Sunflower State's most vaunted and enduring fried-chicken establishment is the Brookville Hotel—which is neither a hotel nor located in Brookville (population 260 on a good day). Here's the story: The enormously popular restaurant was indeed set in a railroad hotel in tiny Brookville from 1870 until 1999, when it finally overtaxed the town's limited municipal water and sewer systems. In 2000, descendants of founders Mae and Gus Magnuson moved their enterprise about 45 miles northwest to Abilene (population 7,000) and a brand-new replica of the frontier-Victorian original structure. These days, I-70 travelers and locals savor the Brookville Hotel's succulent chicken, skillet-fried in lard, plus family-style side dishes served in Blue Willow china bowls: cream-style corn, silky mashed potatoes with creamy gravy, biscuits and what I consider the world's best coleslaw, bathed in whipping cream, vinegar and sugar.

If you want a saga of tragedy, conflict and romance along with your fried chicken, I suggest you head to the state's southeastern corner, just across the state line from Missouri and the hilly Ozarks.

family or a Chicken Mary's clan. No shilly-shallying in this town!

It's a story I've heard several times, even though this is my first visit here. Back in 1934, Chicken Annie (real name: Annie Pichler) faced a crisis. Her husband, Charlie, had been maimed in a mining accident. How could she support a family of five? Feisty Annie started selling veal-cutlet and ham sandwiches to hungry miners. Soon, she was cooking fried-chicken dinners in her home on weekends. The kids helped her raise and slaughter chickens, which were considered a delicacy for many nonfarm families at the time. She hosted Saturday-night dances, and a little moonshine was drunk—that is, until the revenuers raided the place and put Annie in the slammer! But the business thrived and was passed on to Annie's children after she retired in 1961.

If you want a saga of tragedy, conflict and romance along with your fried chicken, I suggest you head to Pittsburg.

Pittsburg, Kansas, is the largest community hereabouts (population 20,000), resting atop a labyrinth of now-abandoned coal-mine tunnels. The mines once drew Slavic and Italian immigrants, as well as the ever-present Midwest Germans.

One aspect of the mining legacy lives on in a settlement called Yale, right across the road from the old Yale Camp 13 coal mine. Here, two rival fried-chicken eateries preside just a block apart on a leafy lane several miles north of town. Five thousand diners find their way to these establishments most every weekend, choosing sides in the ultimate poultry brouhaha: You're either a Chicken Annie's

About a decade after Annie's misfortune, Mary Zerngast confronted a similar catastrophe: Her husband, Joe, also a miner, had developed a heart condition—especially bad news because he was a dynamiter. Mary followed in Annie's footsteps and opened her own successful fried-chicken enterprise in the rural neighborhood. Hours weren't posted; miners just showed up, and Mary put the chicken in the frying pan. Later, Mary set up shop in a renovated pool hall she moved to a spot near the restaurant's current location. A culinary feud festered between Mary and Annie. Mary passed in 1980, but her offspring (like Annie's) guard the chicken legacy.

Today, both places, built in the 1970s, are pleasant eateries with distinctive chicken-themed road signs outside. The fare at each is uncannily similar, from the star attraction right down to unremarkable side-dish options that still reflect the area's immigrant heritage, including German- or Italian-style potato salad and slaw and Italian spaghetti. At both restaurants, the chicken itself is deep-fried to bronze perfection, and that's all that really counts.

Now, here's the kicker to my Kansas fried-chicken saga, a postscript worthy of Shakespeare's Montagues and Capulets. Chicken Annie's grandson, Anthony Pichler, married Chicken Mary's granddaughter, Donna Zerngast, in 1965. This Romeo and Juliet relationship survived, and indeed flourished. The union produced three children, who with their parents now operate their own fried-chicken restaurant—called Pichler's Chicken Annie's—six miles south of Pittsburg. Not so surprisingly, the menu is similar to that at both Chicken Mary's and Chicken Annie's. I call Anthony Pichler to ask whose chicken is best. "I can't say which I prefer, and I don't think it would be smart of me to answer that, anyway," he says with a chuckle. My sentiments, exactly!

Chile Peppers on the Prairie

Kansas is one of several Midwest states swimming in a bright-red sea of spicy salsa these days. The number of Hispanic residents, mostly from Mexico, has more than doubled to almost 200,000 in recent years. While the proportion still is relatively small—7 percent of Kansans—Hispanics now constitute the largest ethnic minority in the state.

In 1540 and 1541 an explorer named Francisco Vasquez de Coronado ventured north into what's now Kansas, searching for the fabled seven cities of Cibola and

CLOCKWISE, FROM ABOVE: (ALL PHOTOS TAKEN NEAR PITTSBURG) CHICKEN MARY'S, KNOWN FOR FRIED-CHICKEN DINNERS. THE BILL-OF-FARE AT CHICKEN ANNIE'S. JANICE AND LONNIE LIPOGLAV, PROPRIETORS OF CHICKEN ANNIE'S, FRIENDLY RIVAL TO CHICKEN MARY'S.

the province of Quivira. He was looking for gold, but all he found was prairie grass. After that, Spain and France traded control of the region until 1803, when what's now Kansas became part of the United States, along with the rest of the Louisiana Purchase.

Since then, and beginning in earnest at the turn of the 20th century, Hispanics have streamed into Kansas with far humbler aspirations: employment and a better life for their families—first with the state's railroad lines, then working the sugar-beet fields, now in the meatpacking industry. Today, towns such as Garden City in western Kansas, Emporia in the east-central part of the state, and the urban centers of Kansas City, Wichita and Topeka all are home to thriving Mexican communities. In food terms, the influx has resulted in a hybrid cuisine, half American, half Mexican.

I'll dine in two Mexican restaurants: The first is just off Wichita's 21st Street

barrio district; the other is on the outskirts of Salina (population 46,000), not far from a busy nexus of interstate highways. Both are highly successful enterprises that serve honest food.

From the outside, adobe-style Taqueria El Paisa (*paisa* means "countryman" or "-woman" in English) looks like a touch of Santa Fe, New Mexico, tucked into a Wichita neighborhood of modest bungalows and storefront businesses with Spanish signage. Inside, the restaurant is a rustic mix of ceiling timbers, colorful Mexican tiles, carved wooden benches, mariachis and Mexican flags and banners. Taqueria El Paisa is run by Concepcion "Connie" Acosta, a determined businesswoman, and her younger brother, Martin Acosta, both from Chihuahua, a desert state in northern Mexico. Connie opened the original Taqueria El Paisa in 1997 as a two-table eatery in a former hamburger and ice cream stand. The current Taqueria El Paisa, opened in 2003, boasts 34 tables.

My colleagues and I order a Mexican smorgasbord of Connie's Midwest-Mexican classics: salsa, guacamole, ceviche, fajitas, enchiladas, tacos, chile rellenos, tamales, *pastor* (seasoned, slow-roasted pork) and *carne asada* (grilled steak served with tortillas). It's a fiesta of aromas and flavors, redolent of garlic, chile peppers, cilantro and lime.

The atmosphere is more upscale at my second Mexican restaurant stop. It's near busy I-135 in central Kansas, on the outskirts of Salina. My sights are set on Gutierrez, a newer, bright-pink building housing a large, classy dining room with a burbling fountain at its heart. It's another Hispanic success story, related to me by the articulate husband-wife owners, Jerry and Amanda Gutierrez. Jerry and his brothers grew up in a large Mexican-American family that emigrated over the years from several Mexican cities to the Rio Grande Valley in Texas, and then to Russell, Kansas, about 70 miles west of

here. Jerry tells me his mother, Elida, opened a small restaurant to help pay the bills for her eight children—a familiar story. In the early 1970s, several of the Gutierrez brothers opened a restaurant here in Salina, and Jerry stuck with it (another brother now owns a restaurant in Hays).

Because Jerry's approach demands fresh, locally grown, often organic ingredients, he works with a local growers' consortium, the Prairieland Food Cooperative. "We serve a fresh take on Mexican," he says. "We don't deep-fry here, we saute. I like to use leaner cuts of beef and lots of chicken." Jerry orders my meal. The *fondido de champinones* is a vegetarian triumph containing portobello mushrooms, tomatoes, onions, red bell peppers, fresh jalapeño and garlic, all rolled into a flour tortilla and topped with green chile-tomatillo sauce. Another colorful dish sums up Jerry's approach: a kicky Mexican stir-fry with chicken, fresh asparagus, spinach, summer squash, zucchini, onion and lots of chipotle sauce made with smoked chile peppers. For dessert, it's a refreshingly tart Key lime pie. I leave the table feeling satisfied that I've had a very healthful, flavorful dinner.

Roadside Treasures

Today I'm cruising around two fertile north-central Kansas river valleys: the Smoky Hill and the Republican. (For the record: The Republican in Republican River Valley was taken from the Native American Pawnee Republic once based here.) I speed past some huge beef feed-lots on my way to Courtland (population 350), where I strike gold at Pinky's, almost in the shadow of the local grain elevator.

A legend in these parts, Pinky's serves its renowned chicken-fried steak only on Wednesdays—and it's Wednesday! The restaurant usually sells out of its star menu item by 12:30 p.m., which explains why an army of sunburned ranchers and farmers are already seated when I arrive just before noon. JoAnne Kenyon, the current owner and cook, doesn't have much time to talk. When my hand-breaded chicken-fried steak arrives, I understand what the fuss is all about. It's thick, juicy-tender, a little peppery, and served with mashed potatoes and brown gravy, plus spinach (my choice) and a dinner roll on the side—all for just $6.17, including my coffee! I screw up my courage and ask JoAnne if she'll share her recipe. "I could, but then I'd have to kill you," she says with a chortle.

My post-lunch meandering takes me about a mile north of Courtland on US-36 to the Depot Market, operated by enterprising Dan Kuhn. This vintage blue-and-white structure resembles a country store inside, packed with fresh fruits and vegetables from Dan's fields and other area growers, plus locally made candy, salsa, honey, jam, jelly and whole wheat flour. The building itself is housed in Courtland's century-old former train station, which Dan purchased for $3,500 and

WATERMELON HARVEST, COURTLAND.

Red Chipotle Chicken

Gutierrez Restaurant & Bar, Salina

　　Red Chipotle Sauce (recipe follows)
4　skinless, boneless chicken breast
　　halves
2　tablespoons olive oil
2　cloves garlic, minced
1　small red onion, cut into very thin
　　wedges
2　cups broccoli florets
1½　cups bias-sliced zucchini
1½　cups bias-sliced yellow summer squash
½　of a 12-ounce jar roasted red sweet
　　peppers, drained and cut into
　　bite-size strips (½ cup)
¾　cup shredded Monterey Jack cheese or
　　queso fresco (3 ounces)
2　tablespoons snipped fresh cilantro
4　cups hot cooked rice (optional)

Prepare the Red Chipotle Sauce; set aside. Cut chicken into bite-size strips; set aside.

　　Pour oil into a 12-inch skillet or wok. (If necessary, add more oil during cooking.) Heat over medium-high heat. Add garlic. Cook and stir for 30 seconds. Add onion to skillet; cook and stir for 1 minute. Add broccoli; cook and stir for 2 minutes. Add zucchini and summer squash; cook and stir for 2 to 4 minutes more or until vegetables are crisp-tender. Remove vegetables from skillet.

　　Add chicken to skillet. Cook and stir about 5 minutes or until no longer pink. Push chicken from center of skillet. Add 1 cup of the Red Chipotle Sauce to center of skillet. Cook and stir until bubbly. Return vegetables to skillet. Stir in sweet peppers. Cook and stir about 2 minutes or until heated through.

　　To serve, transfer to a large, shallow serving bowl or rimmed platter. Sprinkle with cheese and top with cilantro. If you like, serve with hot cooked rice. Pass some of the remaining sauce. *Makes 6 servings.*

moved to this site in 1989. I hadn't expected to find a produce farm on the dry, windswept Kansas plains, but Dan explains that it's possible because his farm's aquifer is the floodplain of the Republican River.

In season, Depot Market bins overflow with Kansas bounty: Apples. Twenty-five varieties of pumpkins. Gourds. Tomatoes. Potatoes. Green beans. Sweet corn. Onions. Cucumbers. Zucchini. Cantaloupe. And watermelon. Dan and I hop into a truck for a visit to his 12-acre watermelon patch. A shirtless cadre of migrant workers and strapping college students, including several of Dan's own offspring, are heaving huge melons to a coworker standing atop a slow-moving truck.

The melons are a variety known as Sangria and weigh about 17 pounds on average, some double that. However, it's not about size these days in the watermelon world; customers actually prefer smaller,

seedless melons they can store in a refrigerator. Seedless melons are more of a challenge for Dan to grow. "They're fussy," he says. "We have to start the plants inside. They like it hot. They're more expensive, but people seem to love them."

I want to learn how to pick a ripe melon, so Dan shares the secrets. In the field, look for a dull finish. Check for a dried "curl" that resembles a pig's tail, the remainder of the stem on the end of the melon. Thump the melon and listen for a dull sound. And roll the melon over to see if there's a yellowish "butter belly"—the surest indicator of good quality if you're buying a watermelon at the supermarket.

Dan, a devout Roman Catholic, is clearly a man of the land and a man of faith. When I ask what led a city boy to this life, he speaks in biblical terms. "You're in God's will when you're doing this. You're in sync." What a beautiful thought . . .

Red Chipotle Sauce: For grilled onion, slice 1 small onion into 1/2-inch-thick slices. For a charcoal grill, grill onion slices on the rack of an uncovered grill directly over medium heat for 8 to 10 minutes, turning once. (For a gas grill, preheat grill. Reduce heat to medium. Place onion slices on grill rack over heat. Cover and grill as above.) Coarsely chop onion slices.

In a food processor or blender, combine onion, one 12-ounce can chipotle peppers in adobo sauce and 1 1/2 cups water. Cover and process or blend until almost smooth. Transfer to a covered container. Store, covered, in refrigerator for up to 1 week. If you like, freeze any remaining sauce. *Makes about 3 1/2 cups.*

Creamy Peaches & Cream Coffee Cake

Stafford County Flour Mills Company, Hudson

- 1/2 cup butter or margarine
- 2 eggs
- 1/2 cup Hudson Cream Short Patent Flour or all-purpose flour
- 1/2 cup sugar
- 1/4 cup cold butter or margarine
- 1/4 cup sliced almonds
- 2 cups Hudson Cream Short Patent Flour or all-purpose flour
- 1 teaspoon baking powder
- 1 teaspoon baking soda
- 1 cup sugar
- 1 teaspoon vanilla
- 1 cup dairy sour cream
- 1 egg yolk, slightly beaten
- 1 8-ounce package cream cheese, softened
- 1 teaspoon vanilla
- 1/2 cup sugar
- 1 cup peach preserves

Allow the 1/2 cup butter and the 2 eggs to stand at room temperature for 30 minutes. Meanwhile, grease and lightly flour a 9-inch springform pan; set aside.

For topping: In a small bowl, combine the 1/2 cup flour and the 1/2 cup sugar. Using a pastry blender, cut in the 1/4 cup cold butter until mixture resembles coarse crumbs. Stir in almonds. Set aside.

For cake: In a medium bowl, stir together the 2 cups flour, baking powder, baking soda and 1/4 teaspoon salt. In a large mixing bowl, beat the 1/2 cup softened butter with an electric mixer on medium to high speed for 30 seconds. Add the 1 cup sugar and 1 teaspoon vanilla; beat until well combined. Add room-temperature eggs, 1 at a time, beating well after each addition. Alternately add flour mixture and sour cream to butter mixture, beating on low speed after each addition just until combined. Set aside.

For filling: In another mixing bowl, beat the egg yolk, cream cheese and the remaining 1 teaspoon vanilla until light and fluffy. Gradually add the 1/2 cup sugar, beating well. Set aside.

Spread half of the cake batter into prepared pan. Spread filling over cake batter. Spread peach preserves over the filling. Spread the remaining cake batter over the preserves. Sprinkle with topping. Place cake pan on baking rack with a baking sheet positioned on a lower rack to catch any spills.

Bake in a 325° oven for 55 to 60 minutes or until a wooden toothpick inserted near center comes out clean. Cool coffee cake on a wire rack for 20 minutes. Remove sides of the pan. Serve warm. *Makes 10 to 12 servings.*

Kansas Chicken-Fried Steak

Inspired by Pinky's Bar and Grill, Courtland

- 1 pound boneless beef top round steak, cut 1/2 inch thick
- 3/4 cup fine dry bread crumbs
- 1/2 teaspoon salt
- 1/2 teaspoon dried basil or oregano, crushed
- 1/4 teaspoon ground black pepper
- 1 beaten egg
- 1 tablespoon milk
- 2 tablespoons cooking oil
- 1 small onion, sliced and separated into rings
- 2 tablespoons all-purpose flour
- 1 1/3 cups milk
  Salt and ground black pepper (optional)

Trim fat from meat. Cut meat into 4 serving-size pieces. Place each piece of beef

between 2 sheets of plastic wrap. Working from center to edges, pound meat lightly with the flat side of a meat mallet to 1/4-inch thickness. Remove plastic wrap.

In a shallow dish or on waxed paper, combine bread crumbs, the 1/2 teaspoon salt, basil and the 1/4 teaspoon black pepper. In another shallow dish, combine egg and the 1 tablespoon milk. Dip meat pieces into egg mixture, then coat with the bread crumb mixture.

In a 12-inch skillet, cook meat, half at a time, in hot oil over medium heat about 6 minutes or until brown, turning once. (Add more oil, if necessary.) Return all meat to skillet. Reduce heat to medium-low. Cover and cook for 45 to 60 minutes more or until meat is tender. Transfer meat to a serving platter, reserving drippings in skillet. Keep meat warm.

For gravy: Cook onion in the reserved drippings until tender but not brown. (Add more oil, if necessary.) Stir in flour. Gradually stir in the 1 1/3 cups milk. Cook and stir over medium heat until thickened and bubbly. Cook and stir for 1 minute more. If you like, season to taste with additional salt and black pepper. Serve gravy with meat. *Makes 4 servings.*

Travel Journal

More Information

Abilene Convention & Visitors Bureau (800/569-5915, www.abilenekansas.org). **Greater Hutchinson Convention/Visitors Bureau** (800/691-4282, www.visithutch .com). **Greater Wichita Convention & Visitors Bureau** (800/288-9424, www.visitwichita.com). **Kansas City, Kansas/Wyandotte County Convention and Visitors Bureau** (800/264-1563, www.visitthedot.com). **Lawrence Convention & Visitors Bureau** (888/529-5267, www.visitlawrence.com). **Overland Park Convention & Visitors Bureau** (800/262-7275, www.visitoverlandpark.com). For Pittsburg, **Crawford County Convention & Visitors Bureau** (800/879-1112, www.crawfordcountycvb.com). **Salina Area Chamber of Commerce** (877/725-4625, www.salinakansas.org). **Topeka Convention & Visitors Bureau** (800/235-1030, www.topekacvb.org).

Featured Dining

Prairie Rose Chuckwagon Supper Benton (316/778-2121).
Pinky's Courtland (785/374-4200).
Chicken Annie's Pittsburg area (620/231-9460).
Chicken Mary's Pittsburg area (620/231-9510).
Pichler's Chicken Annie's Pittsburg area (620/232-9260).
Gutierrez Restaurant West side of Salina (785/825-1649).
Taqueria El Paisa Wichita (316/838-0337).
Carriage Crossing Yoder (620/465-3612).

More Great Dining

Brookville Hotel Abilene (785/263-2244).
Teller's Restaurant Lawrence. Upscale fare in a renovated, historic downtown bank (785/843-4111).
40 Sardines Overland Park. Sophisticated dining in a modern American bistro (913/451-1040).
KC Masterpiece Barbecue & Grill Overland Park. Suburban restaurant featuring barbecue favorites (913/345-1199).
Jim's Steak House Pittsburg. A casual restaurant operated by the Castagno family since 1938 and known for its beef, onion rings and great prices (620/231-5770).
New City Café Topeka. Eclectic Mediterranean and Caribbean cuisine in a hip atmosphere (785/271-8646).
Olive Tree Bistro Wichita. Nationally acclaimed restaurant northeast of downtown featuring American and Mediterranean cuisine (316/636-1100).
Stroud's Wichita. Panfried chicken dinners served family-style in a country setting north of downtown (316/838-2454).

Featured Stops

National Agricultural Center and Hall of Fame Bonner Springs (913/721-1075).
Depot Market & Cider Mill Courtland (888/243-3764).
Stafford County Flour Mills Hudson, tours offered (800/530-5640).

More Great Stops

Kansas City, Kansas, Metro Area South and west of Kansas City in Wyandotte and Johnson counties, crisscrossing highways link a collection of suburban communities, including Bonner Springs, Leawood, Lenexa, Mission, Olathe, Overland Park and Shawnee. Attractions include the Kansas Speedway and the surrounding Village West for dining, lodging and shopping; Olathe's Mahaffie Stagecoach Stop and Farm; Shawnee Town and Museum and the Johnson County Museum of History in Shawnee; and the 300-acre Overland Park Arboretum and Botanical Gardens. Shopping malls and plazas seem to pop up around almost every corner.

Overland Park Farmers Market Overland Park. One of the largest markets of its kind in Kansas. Open seasonally on Wednesday and Saturday mornings downtown (913/642-2222).
Salina A busy small city with a historic downtown district that includes a cluster of antiques and specialty shops, galleries and theaters, plus the Smoky Hill Museum, where exhibits salute the region's heritage. Don't miss the Land Institute, a private, nonprofit research and educational organization dedicated to reducing the impact of agriculture on the ecosystem (785/823-5376, tours by appointment).
Wichita The state's largest city combines its Western heritage with modern attractions, including an art museum featuring works by noted frontier artist Charles Russell; the Mid-America All-Indian Center; Exploration Place hands-on learning center; and the Old Cowtown Museum, a 17-acre living-history enclave of 1870s buildings and costumed interpreters. Other Wichita highlights include Botanica, The Wichita Gardens; Delano, a historic 10-block shopping and dining district once dominated by brothels and saloons; and Old Town, a revitalized historic warehouse district, now the city's hub for dining and entertainment, with a seasonal Saturday morning farmers market.
Kansas Originals Market Wilson. Selling food items and Kansas arts and crafts from its headquarters store 50 miles west of Salina (877/457-6233); second store east of Topeka (785/379-0200).

Dan's Lodgings

Hampton Inn Salina ($$; 800/426-7866).
Hilton Garden Inn Northeastern Wichita ($$; 316/219-4444).

More Great Lodgings

Moore Ranch Bucklin. A working longhorn cattle spread 40 miles southeast of Dodge City, welcoming guests for spring and fall trail drives and ranch vacations, with stays in renovated ranch cabins or camping along the trail (cabins $$$; 620/826-3649).
Sun Rock Ranch Resort Junction City. A 3,000-acre working horse and cattle ranch with three guest rooms 45 miles east of

Salina in the Flint Hills ($$; 800/710-2728).
Great Wolf Lodge Kansas City, in the Village West area. A sprawling, four-story structure with the look of the North Woods, including an indoor water park and 281 all-suite guest rooms ($$$$; 913/299-7001).
The Hotel at Old Town Wichita. A handsomely refurbished 1906 warehouse furnished in Victorian style just east of downtown ($$$; 877/265-3869).

Food Events

Mennonite Relief Sale Hutchinson, early April—Congregations of 70-plus Kansas churches pitch in for this annual benefit for worldwide relief. Crowds flock to the home-cooked fare, especially the *verenika* (cottage cheese dumplings served with ham gravy), *bohne beroggi* (buns filled with sweetened mashed pinto beans) and borscht (beet soup) served at the German buffet. Bid on furniture, handcrafted items and more than 250 quilts at auctions, or shop for crafts, plants and more in seven buildings on the state fairgrounds (620/665-7406, www.kansas.mccsale.org).
Beef Empire Days Garden City, first two weekends in June—Hoof it to this beef empire, home of the world's largest beef-packing plant, for more than 30 events. Of course, beef is on the menu at the chuck-wagon feed and chuckwagon breakfast, and buses take you to five restaurants for beef entrées during the Cattle Crawl progressive dinner. The roundup also includes professional rodeo performances, carnival rides, 5K and 10K races and a grand parade. Admission charged to some events (620/275-6807, www.beefempiredays.com).
Great Lenexa Barbeque Battle Lenexa, fourth Saturday in June—Follow the savory smells to Sar-Ko-Par Trails Park, where 185 barbecue teams from across the nation compete for the title of Kansas State Champion. It's the third-largest barbecue cook-off in the country, so big it takes 240 judges to select winners in various categories. Vendors sell barbecued fare, and live music and kids' activities add to the fun. Admission charged (913/541-8592, www.lenexabbq.org).

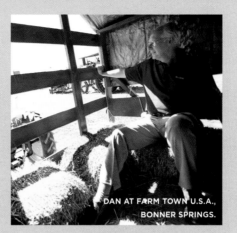
DAN AT FARM TOWN U.S.A., BONNER SPRINGS.

Farm Heritage Day Bonner Springs, second Saturday in July—Spend a down-home day on the farm watching threshing, harvesting and baling demonstrations in the fields at the 172-acre National Agricultural Center and Hall of Fame. Other doings include miniature train rides, old-time tractor and equipment displays, living-history programs and an antique-tractor pull. Admission charged (913/721-1075, www.aghalloffame.com).
Fiesta Mexicana Topeka, early to mid-July—For more than 70 years, crowds have flocked to the festival grounds outside Our Lady of Guadalupe Church for homemade tacos, enchiladas, tamales, burritos and tostadas. Three stages of free entertainment star award-winning Tejano, mariachi, banda and salsa groups and other top Latino musical acts. Additional activities at this weeklong fiesta include a 5K run and walk, carnival rides and a coronation ball (785/232-5088, www.olg-parish.org).
Flint Hills Beef Fest Emporia, third weekend in August—Drive your herd to Flint Hills for this weekend roundup of beefy meals, cattle shows, ranch rodeos and country dancing. Listen to live music at the Blues and Barbecue competition, and beef up at a steak dinner. Other activities: a cow-chip toss, a team-roping contest, a pedal-tractor pull and pony-wagon rides for kids. Admission charged to some events (620/343-4741, www.beeffest.com).
Harvest-Wine Festival Salina, weekend before Labor Day—Smoky Hill Vineyards

and Winery entertains visitors with tours, tastings and an authentic Mediterranean dinner featuring kabobs, dolmas (stuffed grape leaves), baklava and more. A German band keeps participants hopping during the grape stomp, and a priest performs the solemn Blessing of the Grapes in the vineyard. Kids can participate in face painting and games. Admission charged (866/225-2515, www.kansaswine.com).
State Fair Hutchinson, 10 days starting the first Friday after Labor Day—Devour homemade chicken and noodles and sour cream-raisin pie, fair favorites cooked at the South Hutchinson United Methodist Church food stand since 1948 (620/669-3600, www.kansasstatefair.com).

Mail Order

Kansas Originals Market A multitude of Kansas foodstuffs, including bread and muffin mixes, pancake flour, wheat snacks, sunflower-seed cookies, apple butter, honey, homemade mustard, beef strips, ice cream toppings, fruit jams and jellies (877/457-6233, www.kansasoriginals.com).
Kansas Sampler Delicious medley of Kansas-made food products packed in gift baskets with clever themes. Individual items are also available, including barbecue sauces, sunflower cookies, quick-bread mixes, fruit spreads and many more treats (800/645-5409, www.kansassampler.com).
Kansas Wheat House Excellent source for tasty wheat products, including wheat for baking and grinding; the gourmet Kansas Cow Patti, an "udderly" delicious combo of wheat grains, soy nuts and sunflower seeds mixed with caramel and coated in chocolate; and S'Wheat Grain Cookies (800/261-6251, www.kansasgrown.com).
Stafford County Flour Mills Renowned for Hudson Cream, a premium flour produced from a "short patent" process that results in a smooth texture, making baked goods light and fluffy. Along with this mill's signature bleached and unbleached flours, you can order self-rising, whole-wheat and bread flours and cornmeal. Also available: corn bread, biscuit and gravy mixes (800/530-5640, www.hudsoncream.com).

MICHIGAN
Fruits of the North

THIS PAGE: CHATEAU GRAND TRAVERSE, TRAVERSE CITY. OPPOSITE PAGE, LEFT TO RIGHT: CHERRIES, SUTTONS BAY AREA. GELATO DEVOTEES AT AMERICAN SPOON FOODS, PETOSKEY. RELAXED DINERS AND SOPHISTI-CATED FARE IN THE NORTH WOODS AT TAPAWINGO, ELLSWORTH.

Trying to characterize Michigan food with one broad brushstroke is rather like coming up with a single word to describe the flavor of a tantalizing stew: No ingredient dominates—they all simply blend into a savory delight.

The Great Lakes State encompasses a variety of microclimates that sustain a remarkable 200 food and farm products. Its significant commercial crops include cherries, grapes, peaches, apples, blueberries, melons, wheat, sugar beets, asparagus, celery, carrots, potatoes (the state's leading produce commodity), green beans and navy beans. Plus, there are the fruits of the state's seemingly endless forests, such as morel mushrooms, ramps (wild leeks) and maple syrup. Whew!

In addition to a huge dairy industry and the other livestock found in most Midwest states, Michigan adds lamb and domesticated elk, plus whitefish, trout, salmon and yellow perch from its Great Lakes waters and fish farms. And I used to think this was an industrial state consumed solely with making autos and everything that goes into them!

You even can thank Michigan, specifically Battle Creek, for the ubiquitous boxes of breakfast cereal arrayed in our kitchen cupboards. Mr. Kellogg and his upstart rival, Mr. Post, both health fanatics, struck gold here in the form of cornflakes, puffed oats and shredded wheat.

Michiganians are culinary artists when it comes to preparing their bounty. You know what I mean if you've ever dined at one of their top resort-area restaurants or traveled home from a beach vacation laden with boxes of creamy Michigan fudge, cherry pies and preserves or a pastie (meat pie) to nosh in the car. These lake-studded woodlands are home to one of the highest concentrations of fine restaurants in the Heartland, certainly the highest outside a major city—places the caliber of Andante in Petoskey, Windows near Traverse City, Samuel's (formerly Hattie's) in Suttons Bay, La Bécasse in Burdickville, Walloon Lake Inn in Walloon Lake and the Rowe Inn and Tapawingo in Ellsworth.

On this journey, I visit two contrasting areas of the state: the varied growers and expert cooks clustered around Grand Traverse and Little Traverse bays in breathtakingly beautiful northwestern Michigan, and the vast greater Detroit area in the state's southeastern corner, with its rich, sometimes even exotic, ethnic traditions.

Back to (Culinary) School

On the way to my first Michigan destination in the Traverse City area, I can't resist stopping at the renowned Cherry Hut restaurant and store in tiny Beulah for, you guessed it, a slice of the world's greatest cherry pie à la mode. Cherry pie was one of my mother's claims to fame, and the Cherry Hut's juicy rendition comes closer to her sweet-tart version than any other I've tasted. They bake an amazing 400 pies a day here during the peak summer season and should know what they're doing: They've been at it since 1922! Blissfully sated, I'm back onto US-31.

I head toward Traverse City, the bustling hub of the region, with 15,000 year-round residents. Signs here promote two festivals: Traverse City's huge National Cherry Festival held in July and a September coho salmon festival in the small nearby community of Honor. Both these indigenous foods are indeed worth celebrating, even more so when combined into one dish, as I'll soon learn at my destination—the Great Lakes Culinary Institute, perched right along the bay.

Cooking classes are the focus here for 140 students seeking restaurant careers, local gourmets and the summer-cottager set. Why would a culinary institute operate in a relatively small community like this? Two main reasons: This is one of the Midwest's premier resort areas, and its dozens of top-drawer dining establishments are hungry for well-trained personnel. Many gourmet-cooking ingredients are raised and processed in the region, further enhancing its stature as a culinary hotbed.

Visitors are welcome to sign up for special classes on such topics as grilling, morels, pairing wine with food, Asian cuisine and vegetarian cooking. The institute even offers hands-on cooking classes for kids. My teacher today is Chef Fred Laughlin, C.C.E. (that stands for Certified Culinary Educator). He tosses me an apron and starts setting up for my special two-hour lesson on making grilled-salmon salad with cherry sauce and a cherry-vinaigrette dressing.

As we chop vegetables to add to the marinade for our salmon fillet, I ask a lot of questions: Is it true an additive is used to color the flesh of domesticated salmon to resemble wild? "Yes, but they're only feeding them beets to do it. Beets are good for you." We warm up olive oil, garlic and shallots on a saucepan, "just until the flavors are released," Fred cautions, taking care not to overcook.

Because it's also important not to over-marinate the fish (it can quickly turn mushy), we call the process quits at a half hour, then dab off the excess sauce with a paper towel. Flaky, pink salmon is the goal, grilling just five minutes to a side or until the fish is opaque. What kind of cherries are we using for our sauce? I ask. "Pureed red tart cherries, the ones used most often in pies and for baking. They're also known as sour cherries," Fred says. We puree our little ruby gems, then add cherry-juice concentrate (a great source of antioxidants, Fred tells me), honey, red-wine vinegar, olive oil, salt and pepper—plus a pinch of clove, which Fred says will bring out the other natural flavors nicely.

What's the best olive oil? "Extra-virgin, cold-pressed. No heat or chemicals used in the process."

We finish off my mini class by mixing balsamic vinegar, cherry brandy, cherry-juice concentrate, Dijon-style mustard and dark brown sugar for the salad dressing. Then, we assemble our perfectly grilled salmon and the delectable sauce atop a mix of fresh, organic field greens. Fred invites me to join him in the adjacent world-class dining room with a glass of Pinot Noir to experience the result. Gladly!

Pledge Allegiance to Cherries

Glen Arbor (year-round population 788), just down the road from The Homestead, a beach and golf resort, is one of those Michigan villages that cast a spell you can't forget. A sort of North Woods Shangri-la, it nestles under huge beech, oak and pine trees between the gigantic sand dunes of

Lake Michigan's Sleeping Bear Bay and inland Glen Lake. Settings such as this are one reason this corner of northwestern Michigan swells with 1.3 million summer residents and visitors who come for boating and other water sports, camping and hiking, golf—and food. When their usually all-too-brief respite is over, they want a piece of it to take home.

"It really is about making memories," Bob Sutherland tells me. "What we try to do is give visitors some of the essence of northern Michigan in a product they can take home to their parents or dog sitter or just for themselves. When they open that box of chocolate-covered cherries, they recall this place."

Bob should know. His fantasy Cherry Republic domain on the edge of Glen Arbor has been fueling vacationers' memories since he established the mythical nation back in 1988. This cherry-blanketed region has always been Michigan's version of a Central American "banana republic"—after all, this is America's tart-cherry capital. In a good year, and this is one, growers harvest 175 million pounds, three-quarters of the nation's total, in this five-county area. They also produce about 45 million pounds of sweet cherries, the kind you just pop into your mouth or that wind up brined as maraschinos.

During his college years at Northern Michigan University in Marquette (an English and speech major, he never took a single business course), Bob created a whimsical T-shirt. Now a northern Michigan icon, it depicts a stealthy raccoon snitching cherries from a tree, with the slogan "Life, Liberty, Beaches and Pie." He sold 3,500 of the shirts out of the trunk of an old Toyota, then branched out into food products such as dried cherries, chocolate-covered cherries, cherry salsa and cookies, notably his famous Boom-

CLOCKWISE, FROM ABOVE: TART-CHERRY TREES IN AN ORCHARD. MERRY VACATIONERS AND TYPICAL SIGNAGE AT CHERRY REPUBLIC, GLEN ARBOR. MICHIGAN'S FINEST AWAITING HARVEST. OPPOSITE PAGE: CHEF FRED LAUGHLIN AT THE GREAT LAKES CULINARY INSTITUTE, TRAVERSE BAY.

Artichoke Canapé
Café Bliss, Suttons Bay

1	14-ounce can artichoke hearts, drained and coarsely chopped
1/3	cup grated Romano cheese
1/4	cup mayonnaise
1/4	cup dairy sour cream
1/4	teaspoon onion powder
1/4	teaspoon garlic powder
1/4	teaspoon dried marjoram, crushed
1/4	teaspoon ground black pepper
2	tablespoons grated Romano cheese
1/8	teaspoon paprika
	Crostini, toast points, assorted crackers or bagel chips

In a medium bowl, combine artichokes, the 1/3 cup Romano cheese, the mayonnaise, sour cream, onion powder, garlic powder, marjoram and black pepper; mix well.

Transfer artichoke mixture to an ungreased 9-inch pie plate. Sprinkle the top with the 2 tablespoons Romano cheese and paprika. Bake, uncovered, in a 350° oven for 15 to 20 minutes or until bubbly around the edges. Serve warm with crostini, toast points, crackers or bagel chips. *Makes about 1 1/2 cups (eight 3-tablespoon servings).*

chunka cookie made with rolled oats, dried cherries and white chocolate. Soon, Cherry Republic was born in a 10x10-foot Glen Arbor shop. The business now encompasses three North Woods–style retail buildings totaling 4,500 square feet centered among dazzling, English-style floral gardens with cozy benches. In addition to the main retail structure, there's a bakery and cafe, a winery, and a thriving mail-order and Internet business.

Bob offers almost 150 cherry food products, many of them available for sampling: biscotti, caramel corn, granola, barbecue sauce, fudge sauce, candy, tea, mustard, ketchup, vinegar, jam, salad dressing and syrup—all made with cherries. Even chocolate-covered cherry pits! Not into eating cherries? Then how about a cherry-themed T-shirt or beach towel or cherry lip balm, hand lotion, candles, soap or bath salts?

At the cafe and bakery, every time someone purchases a Boomchunka cherry cookie, a clerk beats a big drum (Bob sells more than 100,000 of them annually, some 50,000 through mail order alone). The number of cherry pies sold is tallied on a large abacus featuring, you guessed it, rows of bright red wooden cherries. Customers choose from 12 cherry ice cream flavors that clerks pile onto cones.

I order a pulled-pork sandwich with cherry barbecue sauce, a cherry chicken salad and a cherry hamburger (turns out ground cherries make a great low-fat, low-cholesterol filler for ground beef)—along with cherry pie à la mode and one of those famous cookies. The pork sandwich wins me over, heart and stomach. In the winery building, which also offers nonalcoholic wines, juices and soda, I sip a cherry dessert wine, a cherry sparkling wine, a cherry sangria, an all-cherry white wine and a cherry Merlot, all worth trying.

Bliss-ful Dining

I confess that the phrases "health food" and "vegetarian menu" carry certain negative epicurean connotations for those of us who prefer more eclectic, carnivorous dining experiences. Café Bliss in Suttons Bay, another of those enchanting waterside resort towns on the Leelanau Peninsula north of Traverse City, has changed my mind about all that for good.

On a balmy evening I approach a building resembling a cozy, forest-green Victorian cottage, with ivy climbing up the chimney. I step inside and meet the owners of vegetarian- and organic-oriented Café Bliss: Ewa Einhorn; her husband, Tim Johnson; and his sister, Sarah Jane Johnson. The latter two grew up near here. Ewa came to the United States from Poland and met Tim when both were in the restaurant business in New York; they're veterans of the Rainbow Room and the late, great Russian Tea Room.

All three are friendly but also dead serious about their culinary mission. These days, Ewa manages the dining end of the business, while Tim and Sarah Jane handle the kitchen. Sarah Jane's specialty is designing the menu offerings, especially the desserts, while Tim creates the daily specials and soups. Tim and Sarah Jane are educators, so this summers-only enterprise suits them perfectly.

Over a glass of wine, I learn that this trio has traveled the globe extensively, as reflected in their menu featuring low-fat, natural ingredients and many ethnic traditions: East Indian, Chinese, Mexican, Thai, Italian, Brazilian, Polish and Greek. Flowers are another signature at Café Bliss, from Tim's lush beds outside to the edible blossoms garnishing the artfully styled dishes that emerge from the kitchen to the blossomy Café Bliss signage.

I ask Tim how he characterizes the cuisine here. "Healthy food that tastes really good. We don't label it vegetarian or non-vegetarian. Much of our food comes from growers in Michigan and elsewhere in the region. That's important to us." Some ingredients, such as organic peas, tomatoes, squash and peppers, are even grown on Sarah Jane's five-acre farm. At Café Bliss, higher consciousness governs more than the healthy menu items. Absolutely everything here, from tin cans to organic waste, gets recycled.

My companions and I start with appetizers, including a garlicky artichoke canapé with herbs and Romano cheese, skewered strips of Thai-style chicken *satay,* and thick portobello mushrooms sauteed in garlic butter. My favorite among this banquet of delights? Tofu Gahn—slices of marinated, custardlike soybean tofu stuffed with garlic and peanut tahini sauce, served with sauteed veggies. I also dive into the vegetarian enchiladas, a gingery chicken stir-fry, Lake Michigan whitefish, fat sea scallops, grilled salmon and a four-cheese lasagna.

The crowning glories are two of Sarah Jane's simple, flavorful desserts: raspberries Romanov and a delectable rhubarb crisp. "Desserts should be comforting first and foremost, not overly designed," she tells me. At Café Bliss, that means lots of fresh Michigan fruits combined with natural sweeteners such as maple syrup, molasses and honey. Hear! Hear!

Diverse Crops and Flavors

Although cherries are perhaps the best-known flavor associated with northwestern Michigan, others abound as well. I learn more about two of them while traveling down tree-canopied lanes in the Empire area, right next to popular Sleeping Bear Dunes National Lakeshore.

Ever been to an asparagus farm? Neither had I. But this is the asparagus-

CLOCKWISE, FROM TOP LEFT: (ALL TAKEN AT CAFÉ BLISS, SUTTONS BAY) THE BEGINNINGS OF A GREAT DISH. FRESH VEGETABLES NEVER TASTED SO GOOD. THE CHARMING, COTTAGELIKE EXTERIOR.

consciousness-raising day of my journey. Asparagus, like many other Great Lakes crops, thrives in well-drained, sandy-loam soil, and in this cool but lake-tempered climate. Michigan grows a lot of the apple-green spears, mostly south of here in Oceana County. Harry Norconk, a pioneer of sorts, grew up on this 160-acre farm, lived in Oceana County for a few years and then returned to the family homestead determined to make a living growing asparagus. He has 40 acres, all told; the rest of his land is hayfields and woodlands. From what I can see, he is succeeding splendidly.

We hop into Harry's pickup and survey a huge field of plants that resemble bamboo from a distance. It's midsummer, and this year's harvest is over. Harry's Jersey

gus" poetry reading and an asparagus-spear-throwing contest!

I always thought smaller stalks were more tender and bigger stalks tougher and stringier. Not so, Harry tells me. It all hinges on growing conditions and when the crop is harvested (asparagus spears are happy when it's 70 degrees outside). Harry also shares his preferred way of preparing asparagus, a purist's approach: Snap it in half-inch pieces and put it into a small amount of water, then boil or steam it. Add butter, salt and pepper and start drooling.

A few minutes up the highway and it's time for another northwestern Michigan delight: maple syrup, one of my favorite sweeteners. I love the smoky-sweet flavor —twice as sweet as granulated sugar—on

liquid gold, making Tom a mid- to large-scale producer for this area.

Maple syrup making began with the Native Americans and continues in abundance hereabouts, as well as in New England. "It's all about tapping, filtering, boiling and bottling," Tom explains. As we tramp into shady woods crowded with towering sugar maples, I wonder about the white tubes running here and there, draining into a big tank. You mean a weathered man in a red-plaid jacket and Scotch hunter's cap doesn't come out with a hand-brace drill and a galvanized pail and tap each maple tree individually? "Nope. I use a gas-powered drill," Tom says.

Sap collection takes up to two weeks, depending on the weather. Then comes the distilling process, back at the "shack," where Tom spends his days—and nights— for two to three weeks. When the trees start budding with leaves, the season is over. "What's good for cherries around here is usually bad for maple syrup," Tom says. "We need it cold." When the job is finished, the syrup is sold in almost 30 stores and by mail order. And Tom can enjoy his favorite maple treat: his sister's maple syrup cookies.

A weathered man in a red-plaid jacket doesn't tap each maple tree individually? Nope. Tom uses a gas-powered drill.

Knight and Jersey Giant asparagus plants have grown up to 8 feet tall, replenishing the root systems that will send up succulent shoots for harvesting next May and June. The plants will be mowed down in November, and a freshly seeded crop of rye will flourish as a winter blanket over their heads.

As a small-scale producer of a specialty crop, Harry is on the right side of a big trend, supplying half his high-quality, fresh asparagus directly to local restaurants, groceries and farmers markets; the rest goes to processors for freezing and canning. He's so enthusiastic about his main crop that he instigated an annual asparagus festival, held each May in Empire, complete with an "Ode to Aspara-

or in just about anything from ice cream to pancakes. So does another affable area producer, Tom Casier, proprietor of Casier Maple Syrup, hidden off a quiet lane just east of Empire.

While Tom's 30x60-foot, insulated metal pole barn isn't exactly the romantic wooden "sugar shack" I'd expected, it is much more efficient. A reverse-osmosis device removes up to 75 percent of the water in the sap. Then, a stainless-steel evaporator boils an average of 10 gallons of maple sap down to 1 gallon of syrup, which can range from light amber (the early sap, more delicate in flavor) to dark amber (the later sap, stronger in flavor). In a good year, Tom, his dad and their assistants will bottle 500-plus gallons of this

On a Vineyard "Mission"

First, an admission: Although the ranks of wine connoisseurs in the Heartland are swelling rapidly, I'm shockingly uninformed when it comes to wines. But I'm having a lovely time sipping a glass of award-winning late-harvest Riesling this evening at Chateau Grand Traverse, as the setting sun kisses the golden waters of the west arm of Grand Traverse Bay in the distance. Riesling is the signature premium wine of the area, and of this winery. I'm in the company of three vintners from the pioneering O'Keefe family, which founded Chateau Grand Traverse on this spot about midway along the 18-mile Old Mission Peninsula that snakes northward from Traverse City.

In a *Midwest Living*® article featuring Michigan wines, one of our more flowery writers described the locale this way: "A heavenly convergence of natural factors makes the grapes here very happy due to the deep bay waters" (up to 750 feet!). Those waters "act as a hot water bottle for tender grapevines during the long Northern winters." Chateau Grand Traverse, offering as many as 35 different kinds of wine at any given time, is one of the largest and most respected wineries among the 16 within a 20-mile radius of Traverse City (one even has a celebrity connection; the Ciccone Vineyard and Winery is operated by Detroit native and Madonna's dad, Tony). Five are on this still-pastoral orchard- and vineyard-filled peninsula.

These days, wineries are proliferating across our region; I'm among some of the best here in the Traverse Bay area. At one time, southwest Michigan dominated the state's premium wine industry, and it's still a hub for wines as well as grapes for juice. Nobody thought premium wines vinted from fragile European vinifera grape varieties could survive the winters here, even though this peninsula lies near the same 45th latitude as some of Europe's great vineyards and the loamy soils are conducive to grape-growing. Frigid northern Michigan isn't exactly Provence in the wintertime, but the Traverse City region shares center stage now, too, thanks to risk takers such as Ed O'Keefe, Sr.

Back in 1974, this former federal narcotics agent and management consultant for the health-care community looked at his family's vacation playground and thought, *Cherries, peaches and native-American grape varieties seem to thrive here, why not European vinifera grapes?* All

CLOCKWISE, FROM ABOVE: **DAN AND HARRY NORCONK AT NORCONK ASPARAGUS, EMPIRE. POST MARKER IN CHATEAU GRAND TRAVERSE VINEYARDS, OLD MISSION PENINSULA. MAPLE AND CHERRY SYRUPS, EMPIRE.**

that lake-effect snow—up to 200 inches on the peninsula—would act as a natural winter blanket from howling Canadian winds. Like a determined ant, Ed Sr. and crew moved a million cubic yards of dirt on his 80 acres of paradise to create the precise southwest exposure he wanted here at the highest point on the peninsula, then planted vines and waited seven years for the results. Now, he's semiretired, and his two sons, Ed Jr., the business guy in the family, and Sean, the wine-making guy (he studied wine making at Geisenheim University in Germany), are reaping the harvest of their father's vision. It's a story I've heard from vintners elsewhere in the Midwest, which now boasts vineyards and wineries in every state, including frosty North Dakota and northern Minnesota.

The sun has just about disappeared now. It's a rich moment for the senses. I note a pink-and-red rosebush planted at the end of each row of vines. What's that about? I ask Ed Jr. He tells me that at one

time roses were the "canaries in the coal mine" in vineyards such as this: They alerted vintners to problems before they affected the sensitive vines. These roses look happy. So am I.

A Town with Very Good Taste

I love the magical character of Michigan's Grand and Little Traverse bays, especially the lake-skirting stretch of US-31 between Charlevoix and Petoskey, with its surf-and-turf vistas of turquoise waters. In many respects, this compact area is also one of the Midwest's and the nation's culinary hotbeds. I start the day right, with a wonderful breakfast in the Roselawn Porch dining room at the turreted Victorian Stafford's Bay View Inn, just outside Petoskey (population 7,000).

I'm greeted by the owner, Stafford Smith. Nattily attired in a tie and blue seersucker sports jacket, he seems to mesh perfectly with the 1886-vintage inn. Over breakfast in the dining room with its breathtaking

view of Little Traverse Bay, Stafford regales me with the area's history. This community, on the National Register of Historic Places, was established by Methodists in 1875, when rail companies promoted pollen-free northern Michigan as a summer escape for sniffling hay fever sufferers. The founders created a Chautauqua-type summer-home association dedicated to religion, education, and arts and culture—oh yes, and recreation, too. Notables such as Helen Keller and William Jennings Bryan spoke here. Today, Bay View is going stronger than ever, with 430 gingerbread-style summer cottages lovingly tended primarily by descendants of the founders.

Just across US-31 from all those cottages is the Bay View Inn, to my mind a mini version of the regal Mackinac Grand Hotel just about an hour northeast of here. After various expansions and renovations over the years, many of the inn's 31 rooms feature spas, fireplaces, private baths and closets—amenities not standard in the

19th century! Stafford's family had vacationed here since 1913; he worked here during summers as a college student and even met his future bride here. At just 22, he made a bold purchase and found himself the youngest resort proprietor in Michigan. Things have turned out well for him. He now also owns a distinguished 80-room historic hotel in Petoskey, along with The Weathervane Restaurant in Charlevoix and The Pier Restaurant in Harbor Springs.

My only regret this morning is that it's not Sunday, when Stafford's legendary brunches draw long lines of diners eager for his tomato pudding, whitefish, turkey, ham and desserts that include a famous bread pudding. Still, I'm wowed by the breakfast spread before me: a malted waffle with strawberries and cream on the side, homemade cherry-cinnamon-bread French toast and a sweet-potato pancake with apple butter, all served with maple syrup; plus a three-egg omelet, applewood-smoked bacon and a glass of cherry juice.

A few curves down the highway, I meet another Michigan food legend in Petoskey, American Spoon Foods founder Justin Rashid. Beloved across the nation by epicureans and home cooks alike for championing the fresh, intense flavors of Michigan's fields and forests, this guy is a big shot in the food world, with seven stores in Michigan and products sold to giants such as Williams-Sonoma and Whole Foods as well as through the Internet. On the way to his plant at the edge of town, we talk about how this all got started.

Justin's father, a Lebanese-American grocer from the Detroit area, bought a northern Michigan farm as a summer getaway for the family back in the 1950s. Justin's parents shared a passion for fresh, natural foods, so part of their fun was foraging for wild berries and fruits and selling them at a family summer produce stand. In 1978, after Justin and his wife, Kate Mar-

shall, had settled here and begun their own family, Justin began supplying morel mushrooms to Larry Forgione, an up-and-coming New York chef. Soon, the two men forged a partnership that blossomed into American Spoon Foods.

"We're perched at the top of one of the most superb fruit-growing regions of the country," Justin says. He is obsessed with authentic, honest flavors in all his products. His motto: "We capture and preserve what nature makes perfect." That applies to just about anything that can be preserved in a bottle or jar: colorful preserves, butters, spoon fruits, condiments, grilling sauces and dressings—150 in all, most made from locally grown strawberries, plums, apples, wild blackberries, wild thimbleberries, blueberries and, of course, cherries.

At the plant, I see and smell those ingredients coming together in huge copper kettles. What's that aroma? "Pineapple-chili grilling sauce!" It's just one of the dozens of intense taste sensations that await when we return to the small but busy flagship shop back in Petoskey's Gaslight District. I sample from all the open jars, tasting delicacies from pumpkin butter to a surprising ginger-plum grilling sauce. Justin is right; it's all about flavor—the more intense, the better.

Justin has something new up his sleeve—gelato, that soft, dense and intensely flavorful Italian frozen dessert. Behind a big glass window in the shop, culinary director and chef Chris Chickering mixes a batch of strawberry, made with American Spoon Foods Early Glow strawberries, and explains that gelato is only 6–8 percent butterfat, less than half the amount in ice cream. That fact, he says, allows those intense flavors to shine.

I watch Chris mix milk, cream, sugar and skim-milk powder, along with strawberries, in a special imported gelato-making machine; then I sample the result. Wow. The flavor definitely rules. I'm adding gelato to my growing list of new taste experiences worth repeating, especially after testing spoonfuls of wild blueberry, maple pecan, wildflower honey, pumpkin, burnt caramel and hazelnut.

Now, a final stop, just a couple blocks away. Anyone who knows Petoskey will tell you that you shouldn't leave town without having pie at Jesperson's on Howard Street. The place has been here since the grandfather of Bobbe Kroll, the current owner, started it back in 1903. Bobbe, a lively Dane who's the grandmother of 14, and her business partner, Bill Fraser, carry on the tradition. In fact, Bobbe has been running the show here for 43 years. Ever since I've known her, she's threatened to sell the place, sending chills down the spines of local pie lovers and sentimental summer vacationers, me included.

As usual, the place is packed. At the lunch counter, Bobbe takes my order.

First, some of Jesperson's superb homemade chicken-noodle soup and a salad, then down to business! Bill, who bakes about 150 pies a day at the peak of summer season, offers me a belt-busting sampler: strawberry-rhubarb, peach-raspberry, coconut cream, banana cream, caramel-apple-walnut and the pie that made Jesperson's a legend: cherry-berry.

As I studiously devour the pie selections, Bobbe leans over the counter and retells the cherry-berry story: She was baking a cherry pie at home for her kids, ran out of cherries and threw in some raspberries to finish it off. At that moment, world pie history was made. I ask my usual question about the possibility of her retirement. "Yes, I'm thinking about it. But what would I do?" And what would the rest of us do, Bobbe and Bill, without Jesperson's and that cherry-berry pie?

Place of Peace and Joy

A winding 25-mile drive southwest of Petoskey takes me to the village of Ellsworth to renew my acquaintance with a restaurant we've featured many times over the years in *Midwest Living*® publications: Tapawingo. On this epicurean odyssey, two or three dining experiences are in a league of their own. This is one of them. The word *tapawingo* means "place of peace" in the native Ojibwa language. Or is it "place of joy"? To me, it's both and more. *The New York Times* once called Tapawingo the greatest American restaurant more than four hours' drive from a major city.

Except for his monogrammed white chef's jacket, Harlan "Pete" Peterson looks like he could be a Scandinavian farmer: close-cropped hair, thick mustache, deep-set eyes. He is indeed Scandinavian and grew up on a North Dakota farm, studied industrial design in California and wound up as an automotive designer in Detroit. But a passion that began as a hobby started to consume him, inspiring him to sign up for a weeklong cooking class in Paris. Then he took a working vacation in the North Woods, cooking and learning for two weeks at a restaurant near here. The proprietors liked him and he liked what he was doing. So he made the Big Life-Altering Career Change most of us cower away from facing. Then, just over two decades ago, he focused his dreams on Tapawingo.

The gray-shingle, cottage-style house on seven wooded and landscaped lakeside acres was built in the 1920s as a summer home. Before the dining room fills up, I chat with Harlan for a few moments on the terrace. Over a glass of a local Michigan sparkling wine, I ask the basic question I ask every chef: How do you describe your cuisine? "At first, I was frankly naive; simple provincial food. Then I got more adventurous." What an

CLOCKWISE, FROM TOP LEFT: (ALL TAKEN AT TAPAWINGO, ELLSWORTH) CHEF HARLAN "PETE" PETERSON. ENTRANCE TO THE RESTAURANT. AN UNDERSTATED, ELEGANT TABLE SETTING. OFFERINGS FROM THE WINE CELLAR. CHILLED CANTALOUPE SOUP. OPPOSITE PAGE: JESPERSON'S, PETOSKEY.

understatement, when you consider the influence this man has had on innovative American cooking. "I like exquisite presentation. Lots of surprises. Local seasonal ingredients, yet also fish and specialties from other regions. Comfortable, friendly ingredients infused with other fresh flavors. I call it fancy comfort food, flavors that make your taste buds come alive in new ways."

I ask if the place is open year-round, as if this were a remote Arctic outpost in winter. "Of course! I can't believe how many times I still get asked that." Harlan goes on to describe how the seasons influence his ever-changing menu: more hearty soups and stews that "stick with you when you head out in the snow" in winter, more fresh salad ingredients and chilled dishes in summer. "But we definitely are far busier during the summer vacation season. During the winter, we have time to host special tasting events and cooking classes with top chefs."

We go back to Harlan's background as an industrial designer. What are the parallels? "Food presentation takes a lot of styling. And there's the logic of simply getting it prepared and on the table." I see what he means in the small, highly organized kitchen presided over by executive chef Jeremy Kittelson, another Scandinavian, who hails from Norwegian-to-the-core Decorah, Iowa.

In the dining room, now filled with vacationers in classy casual attire, my companions and I embark on the evening's epicurean journey: a crab- and shrimp-stuffed squash blossom tempura appetizer, golden-raisin-and-fennel wheat bread, chilled cantaloupe soup with delightful lemon and mint flavors. Main dishes of black-truffle polenta with roasted peppers and figs; rack of lamb with squash, eggplant, fava beans and cannelloni in a port

wine sauce; and grilled sturgeon with clams, mushrooms, fennel and roasted garlic.

Our wines include a Falanginah from Italy and a Craggy Range Pinot Noir from New Zealand, both from a global cellar that includes 500 selections and 6,000 bottles! And the desserts: a bittersweet-chocolate terrine with caramel sauce, Strawberry Neapolitan and a trio of sorbets: apricot, raspberry and lime. A blueberry–lemon curd tart completes the triumph. Each dish has been prepared and presented in the most artful way, fulfilling my basic appetite for good food along with my aesthetic spirit. That's what Tapawingo's "fancy comfort food" is all about.

College of Flavors

Angling southeast toward Ann Arbor from the Traverse Bay region, I marvel at Michigan's contrasts: lakeside resorts, small towns and farms, as well as factories and teeming urban areas. It's the same with food: Cherry pies, forest finds and fresh-

modest building. Both were working at an Ann Arbor restaurant and had loved the delis in their hometowns (Paul hailed from Detroit, Ari from Chicago). What to name the operation? Saginaw and Weinzweig? Saginaw's? Weinzweig's? Nothing sounded right until the two contrived something Jewish-sounding yet contemporary that became a legend in the food world: Zingerman's. Now, the organization that started with a humble corner deli employs 400 people in seven operating units that also include a huge mail-order business, a bakery, a restaurant, a catering operation, a coffee shop, a creamery (gelato and cheese) and consulting.

I'm mesmerized by the atmosphere—sort of like a grandmother's attic, only packed ceiling-high with cheese and bread, pasta and seasonings waiting to be discovered. Salamis hang from the ceiling. Whatever you buy here, it's special, simply the best: unbleached, unbromated flour; extra-virgin olive oil; Indonesian cinna-

> I'm mesmerized by the atmosphere—sort of like a grandmother's attic, only packed ceiling-high with cheese and bread, pasta and seasonings waiting to be discovered.

caught fish yield to urban ethnic fare. In its historic brick-storefront quarters, Zingerman's Delicatessen fits like Swiss cheese and ham with Ann Arbor and the endless ivy-covered halls of the vaunted University of Michigan. If I were a student in this city, Zingerman's would be my classroom when it comes to the world of flavors.

Zingerman's began in 1982 when two former university students, Paul Saginaw and Ari Weinzweig, decided to pursue their hearts' desire and open a deli in this

mon; sea salt; fresh-roasted coffee; pure vanilla. Forty kinds of olive oil alone crowd the shelves!

The deli case teases me with salads, soups and sandwiches I've never seen before. Curried root vegetables, whitefish salad, maple syrup sweet potatoes, lamb potpie. I never knew there were so many kinds of honey, salt, pepper or vinegar. My confreres and I fill a tray (well, actually two and then a third) and retire to a picnic table in the courtyard for a tasting frenzy. Among the spoils: a latke (potato pancake) with applesauce, chilled Bulgarian cucumber soup served with pumpernickel rye, matzo ball soup, a knish (potato-and-onion-filled pastry) and blintzes (Jewish crepes with a filling of cream cheese, chestnut honey and vanilla). Plus a Reuben sandwich and a perfect chewy, crusty bagel with cream cheese and smoked salmon. Oh, and then banana cream pie, hummingbird cake (a traditional Southern layer cake made with crushed pineapple and bananas), gelato, sour-cream coffee cake and chocolate cheesecake from the coffee and dessert shop next door. And all that was just for starters!

Today my host at this avant-garde food emporium is managing partner Grace Singleton. "Our focus is on full-flavored, traditionally made foods, often regional and from small producers. We travel all over the world to find the best of everything and to see how it's made." She lovingly talks about Zingerman's salamis, their 100-year-old vinegar and a farm bread that's made from a natural starter and no yeast. I can attest it's bread to build a meal around, hearty and crusty. Here's a job to die for: Every month, Grace and her fellow Zingerman's managing partners gather for a tasting of 50-plus products, from cheese to chocolate, just to keep up with the latest and greatest in the food world.

Food and Understanding

In a Midwest once dominated by German, Scandinavian and Irish Americans, the shop signs along Dearborn's Warren Avenue, many in Arabic, say it all: Hallal Amish Chickens and Fresh Fish, Hallab Bakery, Holy Land Market, Yum-Yum Doughnuts (hey, how did that one get in there?). This is the heart of America's largest Middle Eastern community.

CLOCKWISE, FROM ABOVE: (ALL TAKEN AT ZINGERMAN'S DELICATESSEN, ANN ARBOR) BREADS OF EVERY TYPE. A WELL-DOCUMENTED SLICE OF CHEESE. THE ANNEX, WHICH PROFFERS SWEETS AND COFFEE.

The big, spiffy New Yasmeen bakery and cafe seems the perfect spot to begin my day of exploring new ethnic flavors. I step inside and admire the landscape mural high on the wall. Manager Tarek Seblini, a Lebanese American, helps me fill up a breakfast tray, explaining that this establishment traces its roots back to a village bakery in Lebanon. Founder Mohamed Seblini, his uncle, emigrated to the United States and opened the first New Yasmeen in Dearborn in 1985, then moved to this 15,000-square-foot facility in 1991. The young men behind the counter all seem to be Arab American, and many of the customers are, too. The TV is even tuned to an Arab network.

I sample savory pastries filled with cheese, yogurt, spinach and parsley, as well as sweet, flaky ones oozing with honey, nuts, cinnamon and other spices. It's the perfect exotic introduction to Dearborn.

Fortified, I'm off to the Michigan Avenue location of La Shish, the area's top Middle Eastern restaurant chain, where I'll observe the morning food preparation and experience a lunch I won't soon forget. La Shish means "the skewer," as in kabobs, but there's a lot more to the menu here than those. My host is Charlie Saad, an executive with the 14-restaurant chain based in Dearborn. La Shish has 500 employees who hail from Lebanon, Egypt, Syria and Jordan, even Romania and Mexico, among other lands. Founded as a single small eatery by Talal Chahine in 1989, La Shish definitely feels Middle Eastern: the music, the decor, the fashion—and the food!

Charlie tells me the La Shish chain is Michigan's No. 1 purveyor of lamb, and judging by what I see and smell, it must be right up there when it comes to chickpeas, yogurt, olive oil, tomatoes, garlic and seasonings such as oregano, cumin, basil, cilantro, pepper and sumac. I watch two cooks who wear the traditional modest long dress and head scarf of a Muslim woman: Mohammed Ali, a young woman from Jor-

dan, prepares traditional crispy *saj* bread on a metal heating plate, much the way I've seen tortillas made in Mexico. In the open kitchen area, I banter with good-natured Fatima Sareini as she makes a Lebanese stir-fry called chicken *ghallaba* with carrots, tomato, onion, green pepper, chicken and a zesty sauce made from garlic, sumac, oregano, lemon juice and fresh herbs. Juices are popular in Lebanon and here at La Shish, so I try a Cobra; the name is an acronym for its fresh-blended carrot, orange, beet, radish and apple juices.

Charlie introduces me to the top chef in the La Shish organization, Jamil Eid. Jamil grew up in Lebanon, became a chef by graduating in Continental cooking, then lived in Liberia for 28 years before coming to the United States in 1990. Assistants spread a feast before us. I feel like a sultan! Tabbouleh, the classic salad of parsley, mint, scallions, lemon and cracked wheat. Hummus, ground chickpeas seasoned with garlic, olive oil and herbs, served with sauteed pine nuts. Lightly marinated lamb chops and grape leaves stuffed with rice, lamb, tomatoes and spices. An eggplant dip with a name I can't spell, let alone pronounce (but I do remember it means "my father loves me"). Spinach *fattoush* (salad) served with pita bread. The chicken *ghallaba*. And dessert: Baklava (which the Lebanese insist they, not the Greeks, invented), rice pudding and strong Turkish coffee flavored with cardamom and sugar. All in all, a very healthy feast, with lots of fresh vegetables, light on sauces, not much fat.

Who eats here? I'm surprised to learn only 15 percent are Middle Easterners; the rest are primarily Detroit-area Midwesterners. Time for a turnabout: I ask Jamil what American foods he's learned to enjoy most. His reply: Roast beef, turkey and hamburgers. Hamburgers? Yes, he says, with "the works" and French fries!

Opa! Gifts from the Greeks

When Greeks first came to Detroit in the late 1800s, they congregated with others who spoke their native language. Soon, Albanians, Turks and Macedonians joined them. That was the beginning of Detroit's Greektown along a now-shrinking stretch of Monroe Avenue. This area, once packed with restaurants, groceries, bakeries and coffeehouses, is now home to a giant casino.

One of those Greektown restaurants, founded more than a century ago at the corner of Monroe and St. Antoine, is New Hellas, meaning new Greece. Amazingly, it's still in the same family. Its current proprietor, Gus Anton, a man of gentle demeanor and good humor, has run the place for more than 58 years. This Mount Olympus of historic Detroit ethnic eateries has fed the likes of entertainers Zero Mostel, Debbie Reynolds, Bea Arthur and

CLOCKWISE, FROM ABOVE: (ALL TAKEN IN DETROIT) GREEKTOWN STREET SCENE. GREEK SALAD AT NEW HELLAS CAFE. GUS ANTON, LONGTIME PROPRIETOR. OPPOSITE PAGE: SAVORY MIDDLE EASTERN FARE AND A *SAJ*-MAKING DEMONSTRATION AT LA SHISH WEST, DEARBORN.

SPINACH PIE, NEW HELLAS CAFE, DETROIT.

Bob Hope. But Gus tells customers who ask about celebrities to look in the mirror near the big carved entry door. "You're looking at the most important celebrity here! You're my customer!"

"Bring this guy something to eat," Gus instructs our waiter, one of many longtime employees; people stick with this place, customers and employees alike. I see many similarities between this and the Middle Eastern fare I enjoyed in nearby Dearborn, and yet some differences. Lots of onion, garlic, lemon and oregano. Those heavenly Greek Kalamata black olives. Vegetables including eggplant, zucchini and artichoke. And lamb. "I serve only American lamb!" Gus declares.

My feast comes out of the kitchen in waves: Lamb, stewed with rice and vegetables. Spinach pie made with spinach, feta cheese, eggs, onions and dill set in so-flaky phyllo pastry. Two classic Greek casserole dishes, moussaka (layers of ground lamb, eggplant, zucchini and potatoes with a béchamel sauce) and pastitsio (a sort of Greek macaroni lasagna with

ground beef, onions, tomato, a hint of cinnamon and béchamel sauce). A crusty Greek bread. A shish kabob of marinated lamb chunks and vegetables. Greek salad. Stuffed grape leaves. Oh, and the main event: a flaming *saganaki* appetizer of breaded and fried *kasseri*, a mozzarellalike cheese set ablaze with brandy by a competent waiter, then slathered onto bread in all its stringy, gooey goodness. Opa! says the waiter. Opa! say I.

Just blocks away along Detroit's Michigan Avenue, I'm looking for a flatiron-shaped building at Michigan and Lafayette—American Coney Island, right next door to archrival Lafayette Coney Island. Detroit is loaded with coney joints, the city's fast-food trademark. Basically, a Coney in this town is a hot dog with chili sauce, almost always served with onion and mustard. American was founded on this corner by immigrant Gus Keros in 1917. Inside, historic photos show what this neighborhood looked like in Detroit's heyday, during the years when Henry Ford's assembly lines were busy cranking out a total of 15 million Model Ts.

Dan Keros, the late Gus Keros' grandson and the general manager here, tells me his grandfather thought downtown Detroit resembled Coney Island in New York, thanks to all the streetlights and theater-district marquees. Gus brought his little brother over from Greece in 1927 and set him up in the place next door, which became today's Lafayette Coney Island (it's been out of the Keros family for a decade, hence the friendly rivalry). Just for the record, I try a coney from each establishment, and think they're both pretty terrific. Dan tells me this really is fast food—he even has it timed: The average transaction takes 22 seconds, from placing an order to heading for the door. But who's hurrying?

Taste of Michigan

Fresh Blueberry and Lemon Tarts

Tapawingo, Ellsworth

Pastry Tarts (recipe follows)
6 tablespoons unsalted butter, cut into pieces
5 slightly beaten egg yolks
1 cup sugar
1 tablespoon finely shredded lemon peel
1/2 cup lemon juice
2 cups fresh blueberries
1/2 cup dry white wine or water
1 teaspoon finely shredded lemon peel
1 tablespoon lemon juice
2 teaspoons cornstarch
Shredded lemon peel
Fresh mint sprigs (optional)
Fresh edible violets and violas (pansies) (optional)

Prepare the Pastry Tarts; set aside. Allow butter to stand at room temperature for 30 minutes.

For lemon curd: In the top of a double boiler, combine egg yolks, sugar, the 1 tablespoon lemon peel and the 1/2 cup lemon juice. Place over gently boiling water (upper pan should not touch water). Cook, stirring frequently with a whisk, about 15 minutes or until sauce is thickened (it should thinly coat a metal spoon). Immediately remove from heat.

If you like, pour hot mixture through a fine sieve to remove the small pieces of lemon zest. Cover surface of the curd with plastic wrap to prevent a "skin" from forming while the curd is cooling. Chill at least 1 hour or for up to 1 week. (Or, transfer to a freezer container; freeze for up to 2 months. Thaw in the refrigerator before serving.)

For blueberry sauce: In a medium saucepan, combine 1 cup of the blueberries, the wine, the 1 teaspoon lemon peel, the 1 tablespoon lemon juice and 2 teaspoons cornstarch. Cook and stir over medium heat until the mixture is slightly thickened and

the blueberries have "popped." Remove from heat. Force the mixture through a fine sieve; discard the skins. Cool the puree to room temperature. When the puree is cool, fold in the remaining 1 cup blueberries. Cover and chill at least 1 hour or for up to 48 hours.

To serve, remove sides of tart pans. Transfer tart shells to 8 dessert plates. Divide the chilled lemon curd among the tart shells. Top with enough of the chilled blueberry sauce to cover the lemon curd. Spoon additional blueberry sauce onto the plate. Sprinkle additional lemon peel over the blueberry sauce. If you like, garnish each with a fresh mint sprig and violas. *Makes 8 servings.*

Pastry Tarts

1³/₄ cups all-purpose flour
³/₄ cup cold unsalted butter, cut into
   ¹/₄-inch cubes and frozen
¹/₂ cup powdered sugar
2 teaspoons finely shredded lemon peel
¹/₂ teaspoon kosher salt or ¹/₄ teaspoon salt
5 to 6 tablespoons ice water

In a food processor, combine flour, butter, powdered sugar, lemon peel and salt. Cover and process with a few quick on/off turns until most of the mixture resembles cornmeal but a few large pieces remain. (You should be able to feel the small pieces of butter with your fingers.)

Pour 5 tablespoons ice water through the feed tube. Process with 2 quick on/off turns. Scrape down sides. Process with 2 more quick on/off turns (mixture may not all be moistened). Remove the dough from bowl; shape into a ball by gently pushing down with the heel of your hand so that the mix-

ture will come together. (Add only as much water as needed. Too much water or mixing will make the dough tough.) Cover dough with plastic wrap or put the dough in a plastic bag and seal; chill for 30 to 60 minutes or until dough is easy to handle.

Unwrap; equally divide dough into 8 portions. On a lightly floured surface, use your hands to slightly flatten 1 portion. Roll dough from center to edges into a circle about 5 inches in diameter. Line a 4- to 4¹/₄-inch tart pan with a removable bottom with pastry. Press pastry into fluted sides of tart pan; trim edges. Prick bottom and sides of pastry. Repeat with the remaining 7 portions of pastry.

Line pastry with a small sheet of double thickness of foil or a single layer of heavy foil. If you like, fill with pie weights. (The foil prevents the crust from shrinking.) Place the tart pans on a large baking sheet.

Bake in a 350° oven for 15 minutes. Remove baking sheet from oven. Carefully remove the pie weights, if using, and the foil sheets. Return baking sheet to oven. Bake for 8 to 10 minutes more or until pastry shells are firm and just beginning to brown around the edges. Remove from oven. Cool pastry shells on a wire rack. *Makes eight 4-inch tart shells.*

Spanish Garlic Potato Salad

Zingerman's Delicatessen, Ann Arbor

6 medium round red potatoes (about 2 pounds)
3 tablespoons sherry vinegar or white wine vinegar
1 teaspoon sea salt or kosher salt or ¹/₂ teaspoon salt
¹/₄ teaspoon freshly ground black pepper
1¹/₄ cups mayonnaise
¹/₃ cup snipped fresh Italian (flat-leaf) parsley
2 cloves garlic, minced
1 to 2 tablespoons milk (optional)

In a large saucepan or 4-quart Dutch oven, place unpeeled potatoes and enough lightly salted water to cover. Bring to boiling; reduce heat. Simmer, covered, for 20 to 25 minutes or just until tender. Drain; cool slightly. Peel, halve and cut potatoes into ¹/₄-inch slices.

In a large bowl, place potato slices. Sprinkle with vinegar, salt and black pepper. In a small bowl, combine mayonnaise, parsley and garlic. Spoon over potatoes; toss lightly to coat. Cover and chill for 4 to 24 hours. Just before serving, if necessary, stir in 1 to 2 tablespoons milk to make creamy. *Makes 6 to 8 servings.*

Lamb Chops with Greek Lemon-Garlic Marinade

New Hellas Cafe, Detroit

¹/₄ cup olive oil
1 teaspoon finely shredded lemon peel
¹/₄ cup lemon juice
1 tablespoon snipped fresh oregano or 1 teaspoon dried oregano, crushed
2 teaspoons minced garlic
¹/₂ teaspoon coarsely ground black pepper
8 lamb rib or loin chops, cut 1 inch thick

For marinade: In a small bowl, combine oil, lemon peel, lemon juice, oregano, garlic and black pepper.

Trim fat from chops. Place chops in a self-sealing plastic bag set in a shallow dish. Pour marinade over chops; seal bag. Marinate in the refrigerator for 2 to 4 hours, turning bag occasionally.

Drain chops, discarding marinade. Preheat broiler. Place chops on the unheated rack of a broiler pan. Broil 3 to 4 inches from heat for 10 to 15 minutes for medium (160°), turning meat over after half of the broiling time. Transfer to a serving platter. *Makes 4 servings.*

Travel Journal

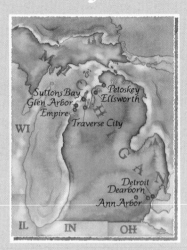

More Information

Ann Arbor Area Convention & Visitors Bureau (800/888-9487, www.annarbor .org). **Charlevoix Convention & Visitors Bureau** (800/367-8557, www.charlevoix lodging.com). **Detroit Metro Convention & Visitors Bureau** (800/338-7648, www.visitdetroit.com). **Petoskey-Harbor Springs-Boyne Country Visitors Bureau** (800/845-2828, www.boynecountry.com). **Sleeping Bear Dunes National Lakeshore** (231/326-5134, www.nps.gov/slbe). **Traverse City Convention & Visitors Bureau** (800/940-1120, www.mytraversecity.com).

Featured Dining

Zingerman's Delicatessen Ann Arbor (734/663-3354).
Stafford's Bay View Inn Bay View (800/258-1886).
La Shish West Dearborn (313/562-7200), with 13 other locations in the Dearborn/Detroit area.
New Yasmeen Bakery Dearborn (313/582-6035).
American Coney Island Detroit (313/961-7758).
Lafayette Coney Island Detroit (313/964-8198).
New Hellas Cafe Detroit (313/961-5544).
Tapawingo Ellsworth (231/588-7971).

Cherry Republic, Inc. Glen Arbor (800/206-6949).
Jesperson's Petoskey (231/347-3601).
Café Bliss Suttons Bay (231/271-5000).

More Great Dining

Terry's Place Charlevoix. Featuring whitefish prepared by a local chef trained in French cooking (231/547-2799).
The Whitney Detroit. Elegantly prepared American dishes and fine wines served in a 52-room downtown Romanesque mansion built in 1894 (313/832-5700).
Tribute Farmington Hills, just northwest of Detroit. Classical French cuisine with innovative touches and an award-winning wine list (248/848-9393).
Grand Traverse/Little Traverse Bay area This region's collection of intimate, finedining restaurants, many off the beaten path, includes: **Andante** in Petoskey (231/348-3321); **Samuel's** in Suttons Bay (231/271-6222); **La Bécasse** in Burdickville (231/334-3944); **Rowe Inn** in Ellsworth (231/588-7351); **Walloon Lake Inn** in Walloon Lake (800/956-4665); and **Windows,** halfway between Traverse City and Suttons Bay (231/941-0100).
The Bluebird Leland, on the Leelanau Peninsula. Family-owned restaurant since 1927, specializing in fresh fish and local ingredients (231/256-9081).

Featured Stops

Cherry Hut Beulah (231/882-4431).
Greektown Detroit (800/338-7648).
Casier Maple Syrup Two miles east of Empire (tours in season; 231/995-9336).
Norconk Asparagus Three miles south of Empire (in-season sales; 231/326-3540).
American Spoon Foods Petoskey (231/347-9030).
Chateau Grand Traverse Eight miles north of Traverse City on the Old Mission Peninsula (231/223-7355).
Great Lakes Culinary Institute at Northwestern Michigan College Traverse City. Serving lunch at Lobdell's, a teaching restaurant, Tuesday–Thursday when school is in session (231/995-3120 for reservations).

More Great Stops

Ann Arbor This city of 114,000 is home to the University of Michigan, as well as shopping, galleries and varied restaurants along the Huron River 45 miles west of Detroit.
Janice Bluestein Longone Culinary Archive at the William L. Clements Library On the University of Michigan Ann Arbor campus. Books, menus, magazines, manuscripts and thousands of other works relating to culinary history are available for public viewing weekdays (734/764-2347).
Dearborn This suburban community of 97,000 is home to The Henry Ford, the nation's largest indoor-outdoor historical complex, encompassing The Henry Ford Museum, Greenfield Village and Ford Rouge Factory Tour. Dearborn also boasts the Arab-American National Museum, the only one of its kind in the United States.
Detroit Amid a continuing downtown revitalization, this super-size city is home to The Charles H. Wright Museum of African American History; the Motown Historical Museum; the Detroit Institute of Arts (undergoing renovation/expansion to be completed in 2007); the General Motors Renaissance Center shopping and office complex; and Hart Plaza, site of a riverfront ethnic and music festival in May.
Grand Traverse/Little Traverse Bay area Each of the communities that anchor this 100-mile-long corridor has its own attractions, from distinctive shopping in the Gaslight District of Petoskey to the fanciful Victorian cottages of Bay View. Strike out on winding roads inland; through vineyards, orchards and small towns on the Leelanau and Old Mission peninsulas; and through 70,000-acre Sleeping Bear Dunes National Lakeshore.
Amon's Orchards Ten miles northwest of Traverse City. Half-century-old cherry orchards, farm market and bakery (800/298-3409).
Ciccone Vineyard and Winery Eight miles north of Traverse City on the Leelanau Peninsula (231/271-5553).

Dan's Lodgings

Grand Traverse Resort and Spa Acme. Just north around the curve of Grand Traverse Bay from Traverse City ($$$$; 800/236-1578).
AmeriHost Inn Dundee, southwest of Detroit ($$; 734/529-5240).

More Great Lodgings

Bell Tower Inn Ann Arbor. A distinctive, 66-room European-style hotel downtown ($$$$; 734/769-3010).

Stafford's Bay View Inn Bay View. Victorian-style lodgings in an 1886 inn that's on the National Register of Historic Places ($$$; 800/258-1886).

The Dearborn Inn Dearborn, two blocks south of The Henry Ford. A gracious, Georgian-style hotel on 23 acres ($$$; 313/271-2700).

The Inn on Ferry Street Detroit. With individually decorated guest rooms in four meticulously restored Victorian homes and two carriage houses in the university Cultural District ($$$; 313/871-6000).

Grand Beach and **Sugar Beach** Grand Traverse Bay. Family-friendly sister hotels among high-rises along the sand ($$$$; 800/968-1992 and 800/509-1995, respectively).

The Homestead At the foot of the Leelanau Peninsula. Sprawling, upscale resort surrounded by Sleeping Bear Dunes National Lakeshore ($$$$; 231/334-5000).

Stafford's Perry Hotel Petoskey. A sunny-yellow 1899 landmark ($$; 800/737-1899).

Food Events

Vermontville Maple Syrup Festival Vermontville, last full weekend in April—Michigan's oldest maple syrup festival (since 1940) is sweet, indeed, when you watch syrup-making demonstrations, devour syrup-drenched pancakes and shop for syrup, candies and maple cream (517/726-0394).

Empire Asparagus Festival Empire, third weekend in May—Asparagus goes wild along the shores of Lake Michigan. You will, too, at the asparagus-spear-throwing contest, the "Ode to Asparagus" poetry reading and the 5K Kick-Assparagus Run/Walk. Enter your creation in the cook-off, and sup on cream of asparagus soup. Admission charged to some events (231/326-5922, www.empirechamber.com).

National Morel Mushroom Festival Boyne City, weekend after Mother's Day—Hone your mushroom-hunting skills at a practice

hunt Friday, then win prizes for bagging the most morels in the national hunt Saturday. You also can sample mushroom dishes, wild leeks and other specialties at the Taste of Boyne. More fun at this fungi fest: a carnival, a crafts fair, live music and a Mardi Gras North party. Admission charged to some events (231/582-6222, www.boynechamber.com).

National Asparagus Festival Hart and Shelby (alternating sites each year), second weekend in June—Oceana County, the "Asparagus Capital of the Nation," salutes its shoots with bus tours to asparagus farms and a food show, where you can sample everything from meat loaf to cake and salsa, all made from the versatile veggie. Work up an appetite at the parade, 5K run, crafts fair and rodeo. Admission charged to some events (231/861-8110, www.hartsilverlakemears.com).

National Cherry Festival Traverse City, eight days starting the first Saturday in July—A bumper crop of cherry delights, orchard tours, pie-eating contests and more than 150 other events abounds in the "Cherry Capital of the World." Eat your fill at the Taste of Cherries and Grand Cherry Buffet, then take home products from the farmers market tent. Also at this jubilee: big-name concerts, air shows, children's festivities, three parades and a fireworks finale. Admission charged to some events (800/968-3380, www.cherryfestival.org).

State Fair Detroit, 13 days in late August—Each day spotlights a different Michigan agricultural product—honey, asparagus, cherries, corn, apples and more—with

special events, such as an apple-pie-baking contest, a cherry-pit-spitting contest and samples of jams, candy and other foods made with state commodities (313/369-8250, www.michiganstatefair.com).

Traverse Epicurean Classic Traverse City, mid-September—Celebrity chefs from across the nation join Michigan chefs for this three-day food and wine marathon at the Great Lakes Culinary Institute and other venues. Visitors can sip at the international wine tastings, take winery tours, attend cooking classes and enjoy Great Chefs Great Wines dinners in top area restaurants. Admission charged (231/933-9688, www.epicureanclassic.com).

Mail Order

American Spoon Foods Nationally recognized for their premier products, including jams and jellies, dried fruits, vinaigrettes, grilling and roasting sauces, relishes and more (888/735-6700, www.spoon.com).

Cherry Hut Products Offerings include cherry preserves, chocolate-covered dried cherries and cherry vinaigrette. The famed cherry pie is available only May through October (888/882-4431, www.cherry hutproducts.com).

Cherry Republic More than 150 gourmet cherry foodstuffs, including the signature Boomchunka cherry cookies, chocolate cherries, nut mixes, jams and jellies, sauces and toppings, salsa and baked goods. Gift boxes available (800/206-6949, www.cherryrepublic.com).

Michigan Gold Delightfully sweet pure maple syrup made by family-owned Casier Maple Syrup (231/995-9336, www.michigangold.com).

Michigan Grape and Wine Industry Council Excellent resource for locating state wineries with mail-order capabilities (517/241-4468, www.michiganwines.com).

Zingerman's Delicatessen Legendary with patrons in Ann Arbor and across the country. Products include farmhouse cheeses, estate-bottled olive oils, vinegars, mustards, pastries and sweets, coffee and tea, chocolates, sea salts and much more (888/636-8162, www.zingermans.com).

MINNESOTA
Land of Lakes, Loons
and Lutefisk

THIS PAGE: INDIAN ISLAND IN BURNTSIDE LAKE, NEAR ELY. OPPOSITE PAGE,
LEFT TO RIGHT: WINNOWING WILD RICE, PERCH LAKE. A FREIGHTER PASSING
BY CANAL PARK, DULUTH. LOU'S SMOKED FISH DELICACIES, TWO HARBORS.

To my mind, Minnesota is the Upper Midwest's Valhalla, where the mythical chieftain-god Odin rules his huge celestial banquet hall. But in this case, his guest is a flannel- and overalls-clad Ole, who's feasting on a platter of lutefisk, the rubbery reconstituted cod Minnesota Norwegians seem to love to hate.

Our hero Ole quaffs a flagon of mead served by a Rubenesque Valkyrie named Lena, her hair done up in flaxen braids. It's a scene worthy of Wagner.

Of course, Minnesota is more than Scandinavian Oles and Lenas; it's also a mixture of Germans, Irish, Poles, African Americans, Southeast Asians and Native Americans, among others. Much of the North Star State is pristine and prosperous, spangled with shimmering lakes and dense woodlands, basking in the riches derived from its agricultural, mining, forestry and manufacturing enterprises. It does well in the food department, too, as I can attest from past ventures into the North Country.

Elongated Minnesota, the second-largest state in the Heartland (after Kansas), extends 410 miles from north to south. Forget that business about there being 10,000 lakes; the figure really is more like 20,000 lakes, ponds and marshes of five acres or more. Approximately 6,000 of those waters are fishable, which is why sportfishing is a $1.6 billion industry here. Two great rivers—the mighty Mississippi and the Red River

of the North—begin their journeys to the sea in Minnesota. The state also is home to Duluth, America's busiest inland ocean port, perched at the southwestern tip of the world's largest freshwater sea, tempestuous Lake Superior.

Pioneers plowed southern and western Minnesota prairies into some of the nation's most fertile farmlands, dominated by the Corn Belt troika of corn, soybeans and hogs. The state leads or nearly leads the nation in the production of sugar beets, green peas, turkeys, dairy products, spring wheat, canola and cultivated wild rice, the state's official grain. Minnesota boasts other agricultural all-stars: potatoes, oats, flax, barley and cattle. The Jolly Green Giant of the once-famed "Ho, Ho, Ho" commercials inhabited the Minnesota River Valley around the town of Le Sueur, just southwest of the Twin Cities, and a 55-foot-tall statue of the nature boy still presides near I-90 at Blue Earth.

I'll have to pay my respects to the Giant another time, because I have only four days in the state. On past visits, I've reveled in the varied cuisines of the Twin

Cities of Minneapolis–Saint Paul (metro population 3.4 million, a remarkable two-thirds of the state's 5 million residents). My favorite restaurant on the Saint Paul side of the Mississippi is the classic, clubby St. Paul Grill in the historic Saint Paul Hotel downtown. In downtown Minneapolis, I vote for a somewhat kitschy and improbable survivor of an earlier dining era: the circa-1946 Murray's restaurant and cocktail lounge, "Home of the Silver Butter Knife Steak." Brit's Pub also deserves a mention, for the fun of enjoying bangers and mash and a pint of ale in a very British setting.

The Brainerd area of west-central Minnesota also beckons, with its upscale resort restaurants. But my appetite is luring me still farther north, away from farm country to the forests of birch, pine and spruce and the deep, dark lakes of northeastern Minnesota, where the growing season is a brief 100 days and rocks rule the landscape. My itinerary includes a stop just outside the Boundary Waters Canoe Area Wilderness to sample resort fare in a wilderness setting; Hibbing, to explore the food traditions of the area's

Lemon Verbena Ice Cream
Burntside Lodge, Ely

- 2 cups half-and-half or light cream
- 1½ cups whipping cream
- ½ cup lightly packed fresh lemon verbena leaves or long strips of peel from 1 lemon* plus 2 sprigs fresh lemon thyme or thyme
- 7 egg yolks
- ¾ cup sugar

In a large saucepan, combine half-and-half, whipping cream and lemon verbena leaves. Cook and stir over medium heat until tiny bubbles just form around the edge. Remove from heat; let stand for 15 minutes.

Place the egg yolks in a medium bowl; slightly beat with a fork. Gradually whisk about 1 cup of the hot cream into the egg yolks. Add egg yolk mixture to cream in saucepan. Stir in sugar. Cook and stir over medium heat until mixture thickens slightly and coats the back of a clean metal spoon (about 170°). Quickly chill the mixture by placing the saucepan in a large bowl of ice water and stirring the custard for 1 to 2 minutes.

Pour the cream mixture through a fine mesh sieve into a large bowl. Discard lemon verbena leaves. Cover and chill the cream mixture in the refrigerator for 6 to 24 hours.

Freeze the custard mixture in a 4-quart ice cream freezer according to the manufacturer's directions. If you like, ripen for 4 hours. (To store, transfer ice cream to a freezer container; cover and freeze. Before serving, let ice cream stand at room temperature about 10 minutes to soften.) If you like, serve with berry sorbet and fresh berries. *Makes about 1 quart (8 servings).*

iron-mining families; and the Lake Superior shoreline, where I'll indulge in a 50-mile eating spree from Beaver Bay to Duluth. Along the way, I'll learn how authentic wild rice is harvested; then I'll head to the Austin area to find out what's really inside a can of Spam and why Minnesota Norwegians are so conflicted when it comes to traditional lutefisk.

In the Singing Wilderness

If I were simply dining at Burntside Lodge, part of a vintage cabin resort hidden in a remote corner of Minnesota six miles northwest of Ely (population 3,700), I'd feel richly rewarded for seeking out the first-rate restaurant. But it's more than the food that inspires me here. It's viewing the most spectacular sunset of my entire journey as it paints a coral, orange and amber canopy over an island-dotted lake; hearing the eerie, haunting call of a black-and-white loon (Minnesota's state bird, the mosquito notwithstanding); and rediscovering the essays of Sigurd Olson, the conservationist largely responsible for preserving the 1-million-acre Boundary Waters Canoe Area Wilderness within Superior National Forest. *The Singing Wilderness* and several of Olson's other essay collections eloquently articulate why the human spirit soars in wild places such as this.

I start my tour of the resort, which is on the National Register of Historic Places, at Cabin No. 26, perhaps the most photographed resort cottage in Minnesota. Like its neighbors in the compound, the cabin clings to a mossy shelf of Canadian Shield bedrock, the source of this region's mineral riches. At its doorstep is the 9-mile-long, 200-foot-deep Burntside Lake, named by the Chippewa for a long-ago conflagration that consumed its shoreline. The lake is dotted with more than 125 islands rimmed with conifers.

I hike up a path to the main lodge for my real purpose here: to eat. Convivial clusters of guests are gathering in the lounge area, awaiting the 6 p.m. opening of the big, porchlike dining room. Lonnie LaMontagne, the gracious host who operates Burntside Lodge with her husband, Lou, and their two grown children, Nicole and Jacques, tells me that the most-ordered entrée is Walleye à la Burntside: flaky white fillets served with a mushroom-walnut cream sauce.

My traveling companions and I are ravenous, so we start with appetizers—a summer-vegetable tart and a smoked-duck risotto topped with leeks. Then we share that walleye dish, as well as free-range chicken with a wild rice salad and lamb chops accompanied by a wild rice cake, currants and spinach. Other specialties appear from the selection of pastas, steaks and barbecued ribs.

An inquiry about dessert brings forth Nicole's artful creations: berry sorbets served with a delicate ice cream (flavored with a lemon verbena herb she grows on the property), and pastries such as blueberry scones, cinnamon rolls and biscotti, as well as Burntside's crème brulee and tiramisu. Nancy LaMontagne, Nicole's late grandmother, also is represented on the dessert menu. "We still serve some of her specialties, like her calypso pie, which is our most popular dessert," Nicole says. It's frozen coffee ice cream with a chocolate cookie crust, topped with a fudge sauce.

Nicole has managed the Burntside dining room since 1997. She encourages the staff to use local ingredients whenever possible: herbs and vegetables; all sorts of berries, including blueberries, raspberries and currants; and wild rice. She also has developed an impressive wine cellar that's received *Wine Spectator* magazine's top award for seven years running, beginning in 1998. The beer offerings here are equally inclusive: I count 33 labels. "Our guests are always surprised to find a menu and wine list like this way up North. We've always had fine dining and great chefs in our kitchen," Lonnie says.

Gazing out the window over my coffee, I glimpse several returning canoeists as they near the dock. The summer season is short at Burntside Lodge, and the restaurant is open only from Memorial Day through September. Perhaps that's part of what makes dinner in this "singing wilderness" so very magical.

Mining the Iron Range—for Food

They call them "the three Ps" here in Hibbing (population 17,100), capital of northeastern Minnesota's fabled Iron Range: *potica* (poTEETsa), a delectable, usually nut-filled sweet bread attributed to the area's Slavic bakers; *porketta* (por-KETTa), an Italian variation of pork roast that's seasoned with garlic, salt, pepper and fennel; and pasties (PAHstees or PASStees), the famous Cornish miners' pocket pies stuffed with beef and pork, potatoes, onions, carrots and rutabagas. To me, each is a worthy food representative of a hardworking region with a diverse culinary heritage.

Iron-ore mining rules in Hibbing, and it has ever since the town's founding back in 1893. In fact, open-pit iron mines grew so rapidly in the early 20th century that they threatened to swallow up a good share of Hibbing. Beginning in 1918, almost 200 buildings were relocated several miles south to an area now known as the North Park section of town. One such structure on Third Avenue houses part of the Sunrise Bakery, where I meet Mona Meittunen Abel, a guide who knows Hibbing's food story intimately. A Finnish-

CLOCKWISE, FROM ABOVE: (ALL TAKEN AT BURNTSIDE LODGE, NEAR ELY) LAKESIDE CABINS. THE PORCHLIKE DINING ROOM. A SIGNATURE WILD RICE CREATION.

English grandmother of four, Mona is a self-described recipe diva who's authored two cookbooks that include hundreds of dishes and anecdotes from Iron Range cooks. She and I are greeted enthusiastically by Ginny Forti, whose grandfather, Julio Forti, founded the Sunrise Bakery back in 1913. The business consists of two side-by-side white frame buildings: One is the shop, constructed on this site; the other is the bakery kitchen, which made that move so long ago.

Like a power shopper at a grand-opening sale, Ginny starts grabbing samples from her shelves and cases. Of course, there's *potica*. It's made from a sweet yeast dough rolled paper-thin and spread with melted butter, brown sugar and nuts or cream cheese, then rolled into a fat loaf—sort of a Slavic strudel. Walnut *potica* is traditional, Ginny tells me, but pecan has become her best seller.

Then, there are the flatter, pastrylike German strudels: apple, cream cheese and a hearty Jewish variation that's filled with apples, raisins, walnuts and coconut. The walnut swirl, ginger and moist ricotta cheese cookies are standouts. There's also an amazing confection called *frutti e chocolato* (fruitcake bits dipped in dark chocolate), plus fruitcakes, muffins, buttery-almond and amaretto-soaked polenta cakes, banana and date breads, bars and brownies, biscotti and perfectly textured hard rolls. "My family may be Italian, but we bake everybody's specialties here," Ginny says. The Sunrise Bakery is more successful than ever, thanks to Internet and catalog mail-order sales.

Just a few blocks away on First Avenue, Ginny's baker brother, Tom, and his wife, Mary, operate the Sunrise Deli in the former Lybba Theater, a movie house operated for years by the Edelstein brothers, whose mother's name was Lybba. Perhaps you've heard of her folksinger great-grandson, Bob Dylan, who hails from Hibbing.

These days, the stars here are the deli foods. The variety of meats, sausages, cheeses and specialty items recalls the delicatessens I've seen in large cities. Mona and I claim a small table up front, and I dive into the second "class" of my Iron Range food course: herby *porketta* served with a hard roll; Italian *stromboli*, pizza dough rolled up with ham, salami and cheese; *sarma*, cabbage leaves topped with tomato sauce and filled with beef, pork and ham ground up with rice; and that miner's mainstay—a pastie pocket pie. "Never put gravy on a pastie," Mona declares. "It's a sin!"

Soon she and I are off to the north side of town and the Fraboni Sausage Company, founded in 1968 by Leo Fraboni and his wife and operated for the past few years by Norwegian brothers Mark and Wayne Thune. About 30 people work here, churning out an array of meat products—including 15 varieties of sausages, many locally inspired (potato, wild rice, hot Italian, *porketta*). In all, the company sells 10,000 pounds of meat products each week in Hibbing and northeastern Minnesota.

It's Fraboni's *porkettas* that I'm here to learn more about. They're made with the usual seasonings, plus fresh fennel. "If we have a bad fennel year, we don't make *porketta*," Mark says as he shows me the large fennel patch in back of the plant. In 2005 he and Wayne sold 3,000 of the 4- to 5-pound netted pork shoulder roasts with their mild anise flavor. "You can eat your *porketta* hot or cold; it tastes totally different either way," Mona says. "Of course, the miners had theirs cold. I like to fix mine in a slow cooker all day, then serve it hot on Sunrise Bakery hard rolls."

As we depart, Mona points out a boccie ball court across the street from Fraboni's. It's witness to the ethnic traditions of 44 nations still kept alive here by Italians, Finns, Norwegians, Swedes and Slavic descendants. "Everybody had their own neighborhood at first—Finn Town, the Italian neighborhood and so forth," Mona says. "Then they started to mix, and so did their foods. That's what makes it so interesting here."

Feasting on the "Riviera"

Myriad dining spots beckon along the busy stretch of State-61 that hugs the north shore of vast Lake Superior—Minnesotans call it the Scandinavian Riviera. Craning my neck, I drive southwest toward Duluth, covering about a third of the 150-mile-long Lake Superior scenic byway, with cliffs, beaches and that vast, mysterious inland sea on one side and Superior National Forest on the other.

Nordic types crowd resorts and cabins up and down the shore for a hint of the fjords their ancestors left behind, and that Viking affinity applies in the food realm as well: Scandinavians eat a lot of fish! At one time there were 400 commercial fishermen on Lake Superior who netted millions of pounds of herring, lake trout, chub and cisco. Today, the number of commercial fishing operations has dwindled to about 25 because of overfishing and environmental issues. But you still can reel in a great fish dinner just about anywhere in these parts.

The spread at my first stop is exceptional. From the highway, the only thing remarkable about Northern Lights Roadhouse in the tiny settlement of Beaver Bay (population 175) is the red double-decker bus parked beside it. Inside, the decor is what I call northern-Minnesota Adirondack: mounted fish and other stuffed critters on the walls, along with canoes, vintage fishing gear and snowshoes.

My host, affable Tom Porter, steers me to a screened, porchlike dining room at the rear. About 250 feet down a rocky path, gunflint-blue Lake Superior reposes serenely; I can just make out Wisconsin's Apostle Islands on the far shore. It's the perfect setting for a lunch I'll long remember.

The specialty is planked walleye. My golden fish fillet, artfully wreathed in piped mashed potatoes, has been baked for 15 minutes at 420 degrees on a slab of sugar maple (oak or cedar also can be used). Apparently, the planking tradition started with the native Ojibwa; the resulting superb, smoky flavor makes Tom's walleye dish a perennial favorite. It's accompanied by sweet and savory wild rice specialties: creamy soup, quiche and wild rice–cranberry bread.

The menu's Scandinavian offerings include *lefse* (Norwegian flatbread made with potatoes) served with a tangy-sweet lingonberry-and-orange spread, hot fruit soup redolent with clove and nutmeg, and Swedish meatballs and gravy seasoned with caraway, nutmeg and dill. For dessert, there's "fruits of the forest" pie with rhubarb, apples, blueberries, blackberries and raspberries.

CLOCKWISE, FROM ABOVE: (ALL TAKEN AT HIBBING) MINING TACONITE ORE AT THE HUGE OPEN PIT. DAN AT THE SUNRISE BAKERY. VARIATIONS OF SLAVIC *POTICA* SWEET BREAD. OPPOSITE PAGE: A PASTIE POCKET MEAT PIE.

Before Tom and his wife, Margy, opened this place in 1993, Tom had a business acquiring used double-decker buses in London and reselling them in the United States. But he liked cooking more, and he loves it here. "Especially in the winter and when it's stormy," he says. "We can see 20-, 30-foot waves crashing on the shore."

He also loves the wildlife: moose, timber wolves, raccoon, foxes and bald eagles. Tom's menu includes wild game such as pheasant, reindeer, caribou and elk from Minnesota and other states, as well as steaks, prime rib and hearty sandwiches. "Still good?" a hungry vacationer asks me as he enters Northern Lights and I walk out the front door to resume my journey. "Still good," I affirm.

About 30 miles down the highway just north of Two Harbors (population 3,600), the big parking lot is jam-packed at Betty's Pies, and would-be diners wait on benches outside. This North Shore legend was founded in a tiny shack in 1956 as a smoked-fish shop, but the pie-making skills of the establishment's eponymous Betty Lessard soon outdistanced that enterprise. Breakfast, lunch and dinner are served here, but they're really just a prelude to the main attraction. After Betty (now 81) retired in 1984, business declined; thankfully, the restaurant was reborn when Twin Citians Carl Ehlenz and Marti Sieber purchased the place in 1998 and reinstated many of the original pies. I ask Carl what makes Betty's recipes so special. "Lard piecrusts—absolutely. Everything made from scratch. And the best ingredients," he replies.

In the blue-and-white dining room decorated with Betty's rolling pin collection, I claim my share of the 350 pies the staff turn out on a busy summer day, from a repertoire of 45 flavors all told: blueberry-peach crunch, spicy apple crunch,

strawberry-rhubarb, wild blueberry. . . . As I put my fork to work, Carl offers more tips: "The less you handle the crust, the better. Use just the right combination of fruit and sugar. Go with real, heavy whipping cream in your cream pies."

A fellow diner looks up in disbelief from the book he's reading as more slices appear: banana cream, fresh strawberry cream, toffee cream. They're all terrific, but my picks are the five-layer chocolate and the raspberry-rhubarb crunch. Betty's legacy is secure.

What could taste better on top of all that pie than—smoked fish? Just down the road a piece is Lou's Fish House, in a faux-log-sided former motel. Owner JoAnn Sjoberg greets me at the door of the retail shop with a platter of delicacies and a

Breakfast, lunch and dinner are served at Betty's Pies, but they're really just a prelude to the main attraction.

scrapbook of newspaper and magazine articles—including a *Gourmet* feature—about this place and her late husband, Lou. As a teen in Duluth, Lou started selling fresh fish out of his mother's basement; then he learned to smoke fish and opened the original Lou's in 1975. He went on to become a plumber, a pipe fitter and a star on the pro wrestling circuit. It's obvious that both Lou's memory (he passed in 2003) and his fish-smoking secrets are revered here.

JoAnn introduces me to Scott Beck, who's finishing a batch of salmon in one of Lou's two smokers, each the size of a roomy walk-in closet. There's something painterly about the huge, bronzed sides of salmon and silvery racks of whole lake trout hanging near the fire; Scott says the secret lies in closely regulating the fire with

the amount of wood used. Today, he's burning his favorite, sugar maple. Scott uses up to five cords of wood to smoke 600 pounds of salmon and 400 pounds of trout each week during the busy summer vacation season. Before smoking the fish, he brines the catch for about 12 hours in salt water; salmon and trout also get a sweetening dose of brown sugar. Then, it's time for the smoking: four to seven hours at 180–200 degrees.

Besides the top-selling salmon and trout, Lou's also smokes whitefish, cisco, herring, shrimp and scallops, as well as turkey and beef jerky. Back in the retail shop, JoAnn generously plies me with samples of all, plus her popular salmon spread and some of the tasty cheeses she sells. (I later learn that JoAnn has moved on to a well-deserved retirement in Arizona and that Lou's has new ownership—but there are no plans to change its wonderful smoked-fish products.)

On to Duluth (population 87,000), a hardworking port that has become a top summer tourism destination as well as a TV and film stand-in for San Francisco. It's easy to see why: Streets spill down impossibly steep hillsides past ornate Victorian houses, and there's a huge, oceanlike harbor filled with gargantuan cargo ships, creating an unusual—for the Midwest—nautical atmosphere. In Canal Park, the hub of the city's harbor-front district, I head toward Grandma's Saloon & Grill.

Funky Grandma's is a Duluth institution, having opened in 1976, and the Grandma's chain is No. 1 nationally

CLOCKWISE, FROM TOP LEFT: VICE BY THE SLICE AT BETTY'S PIES, TWO HARBORS. NORTH WOODS AMBIANCE AT NORTHERN LIGHTS, BEAVER BAY. CANAL PARK, DULUTH HARBOR. SMOKED SENSATIONS AT LOU'S FISH HOUSE, TWO HARBORS.

when it comes to wild rice soups and entrées, which include shrimp and chicken dishes made with the local delicacy. I nestle into one of the green booths in the circa-1869 two-story brick structure and study the vintage photos, signs, advertisements and other antiques and collectibles decorating the walls.

This seems to be the perfect spot for vacationing families looking for great food in a fun setting. Part of that fun is in the fictitious Victorian "Grandma" herself, whose bemused-looking, bonneted image is practically everywhere you turn. Many folks know the restaurant because of Grandma's Marathon, an event it launched in 1977 and still cosponsors, attracting 15,000 runners and 50,000 spectators to Canal Park each June.

Grandma's is known for its overstuffed sandwiches, huge salads and pasta dishes. I feast on chicken–wild rice soup; handmade onion rings; a salad of fresh greens served with a tasty ginger-rice vinaigrette dressing and two wild rice–walleye cakes; and a big, juicy Bicycle Burger—two beef patties topped with grilled onions, sauteed mushrooms, and mozzarella, cheddar and American cheese. As I leave, dozens of shorts-clad would-be diners mill about near the entrance waiting for their tables; they're among the 10,000 who will pack Grandma's this week alone.

My final Lake Superior dining destination, Pickwick, lies at the north end of the downtown Duluth lakeshore. It's right next to a castlelike 19th-century building of rough-cut brownstone that once housed Fitger's Brewery, a longtime establishment that closed in 1972 and was later reborn as Fitger's Brewhouse. Pickwick began life as a saloon inside the original Fitger's Brewery in 1914, and that's exactly how it seems when you step inside—especially in the Dutch (as in German) Room, one of three dining rooms overlooking the lake, with its dark-stained oak paneling, huge fireplace, high-backed chairs, beamed ceilings, murals of German village scenes and lots of stuffed critters. There's even a buzzer in the wall beside every table that diners once pushed to request the next course.

Up front, the Pickwick bar looks as if it was transported intact from the brewery all those years ago, and most of it was. I pause to study the ornate woodwork, a divider that once separated men from women (customary at the time), an elaborate cashier's cage that's still used, a big collection of beer steins and decorated mugs, and a barrelhead from the original Fitger's. Even the Pickwick management has been around seemingly forever: Chris Wisocki is the fourth generation of his family to run the place. The bartender offers me a trendy pineapple-infused vodka martini, but I order a brown ale on tap—it just seems more fitting.

Some people consider this a steak house, and charcoal-broiled meats are indeed what Pickwick is known for. But I'm in the mood

for a farewell taste of golden, broiled Lake Superior trout, served with sides of creamy coleslaw and bacon wild rice. Although Chris still serves the classic Pickwick steaks, prime rib, seafood and chops, he's introduced new items, including stuffed halibut, ahi tuna, elk tenderloin and broiled, marinated duck breast. I sample some from my companions' plates. The entrées are all terrific, as is the signature bananas Foster, swimming in a buttery homemade caramel sauce. What a delightful finale to this memorable day of feasting on the Scandinavian Riviera.

Ricing on the Rez

Next I'm on the Fond du Lac Indian Reservation, about 20 miles southwest of Duluth—a white-knuckle passenger in a speeding, top-down 1964 Corvette Stingray convertible with a license plate that reads REZ CAR. The driver is Jim Northrup, an Anishinaabe Renaissance man who's taking me to a shallow lake where wild rice—called *manoomin* in his native language—flourishes.

Jim is one of about 3,200 members of the Fond du Lac band of the Lake Superior Chippewa, as the Anishinaabe also are known, half of whom live on this checkerboard-configured, 24,000-acre reservation. He counts himself an author, playwright, poet, newspaper columnist, Vietnam veteran, former police officer, storyteller, basket maker, hunter, fisherman—and wild-ricer. "My people have been harvesting wild rice for 400 years," Jim says. "They followed the rice as they moved westward from the St. Lawrence Valley in Canada." In Minnesota and Wisconsin, wild rice is the signature "grain" of the North Woods. Signs offering it for sale are posted throughout the area, and it appears on almost every restaurant menu.

Wild rice is prized for its nutty flavor, high protein and carbohydrate content, and unusual texture and color. True wild rice is an aquatic, biannual grass that matures in about 100 days and can grow up to 6 feet tall; it's found only in Canada and the northernmost United States. Although most wild rice these days is cultivated in paddylike fields that are artificially submerged and mechanically harvested, it still grows truly wild on reservations such as this one, where only Anishinaabe may harvest it, as well as in other lakes, rivers and streams, where anyone can harvest it.

Cultivated wild rice, developed in the 1960s and grown primarily in Minnesota and California, is often mixed with white, long-grain rice. Jim is adamant that it's not the same dietary staple his Anishinaabe ancestors and the Dakota depended upon for sustenance, the one that thrives in the nutrient-rich mud of our destination: shallow Perch Lake, just 3 feet deep on average. As for "the real thing," it's costly and a gourmet delicacy.

Near the shore, we survey a "lake" that looks more like a grass-filled marsh. Jim says the crop looks good, but he doesn't keep track of whether he'll harvest 100 pounds or 200 pounds in a given year. "It's about more than that; this is a gift from the Creator," he tells me reverently. I ask how the rice is harvested. "Two of us go out in a canoe that's propelled by someone pushing a Y-shaped, 12-foot-long spruce-and-willow pole," Jim explains. "The other person uses two rice-beater sticks, or knockers, made of white cedar, that literally knock the seeds into the boat." What doesn't fall into the boat goes back into the lake as seed.

We return to the reservation so Jim can show me some of the handcrafted tools of the ricer's trade. "When wild rice is harvested, it's green; at that point, we spread it out on a tarp to dry in the sun," he says. "Then we parch it for several hours in this big cast-iron kettle, stirring it with a canoe paddle." That's when it darkens and many of the grains turn black (much commercial wild rice has been bred to appear similar in color). "Then, we winnow the rice like this," Jim says, tossing the kernels in the air repeatedly so the chaff blows away. He's using a winnowing basket made from birch bark over a willow frame with basswood stitching.

Next, Jim shows me a canvas-lined pit where he dons moccasins and dances on the rice to remove the hulls. I'm amazed at all the time-consuming steps involved in this harvesting procedure. But to Jim and his fellow Anishinaabe, it's a sacred ritual, not a manufacturing process. "This is a spiritual food for us," Jim says, adding that rather than sell the rice, his family uses it ceremonially at feasts and funerals and as a frequent item on their dinner table. "I probably eat it three times a week," he says.

Staples of Humor and Cuisine

As part of my brief visit to the Austin area, about 100 miles south of the Twin Cities, I get the rare opportunity to eat my fill of two Minnesota folk-humor icons—lutefisk and Spam—in a single day.

My first stop is sleepy Oslo (population 50), about 26 miles of serene farmland northeast of Austin. I'm meeting a pair of lutefisk aficionados in the heart of town at Tiegen's Oslo Store, a spartan white frame structure down the road from Evanger Lutheran Church. One expert is Dale Tiegen, who operates the store with his wife, JoAnn. The other is Mike Field of Mike's Fish and Seafood in Glenwood, Minnesota, who's honored me by driving 240 miles with his wife, Priscilla, and a precious cargo of lutefisk intended expressly for this get-together.

Dale is proud to be 100 percent Norwegian; Mike confesses he's just about everything but, at least in genetic terms. Yet both are here to fulfill a decades-old ambition of mine: to partake of lutefisk in all its glory, a Nordic culinary experience I've somehow dodged despite living almost all my years in the Upper Midwest.

Mike is one of America's largest purveyors of ready-to-cook lutefisk, marketing about 250,000 pounds annually, and Dale is one of Mike's leading retail customers. As they and their wives set to preparing my midday banquet, I stroll through Tiegen's, a real old-fashioned general store selling items from shoes and farm equipment to food and Norwegian knickknacks.

But my lutefisk calls. If you're Norwegian, you say "LOOTfisk." If you're Swedish, you say "LOOTAfisk." Either way, it's a big deal around here, especially in the fall and winter, when would-be lutefisk feeders fairly stampede small-town Lutheran church basements to get their annual fix. Lutefisk dates back to the untamed Vikings, who may or may not have used it to plug leaks in their ships as well as to sustain sailors on their lengthy voyages to pillage and plunder Europe.

It starts as something called *lingcod,* which is netted from Norwegian fjords, then dressed and air-dried in kilns for about 30 days (Mike says the cod once was dried on fjord beaches). The paper-thin dried fish subsequently gets an all-expenses-paid trip to Minnesota, where Mike springs into action at his plant on the outskirts of Glenwood (it's on the outskirts because lutefisk processing can be a very stinky undertaking). There, he has 50 tanks that can hold up to 1 ton of lutefisk each.

First the cargo is reconstituted in water and the skin is removed. Then, the fish is soaked in caustic lye for five days (*lute* means "lye" in Norwegian). After that, it's off to the hydrogen peroxide tank for another five-day beauty bath to turn the now-brown fish white again. Finally, restored to its original 2½-inch thickness, the lutefisk luxuriates five more days in fresh water before it's ready for home cooks, who only have to boil it in water for a few minutes before serving.

So, how does it taste? I have no complaints. The appearance is rather translucent-white and flaky. There is no odor. I find the texture pleasantly rubbery, like lobster tail. As for the flavor, lutefisk is served with copious amounts of melted butter, so any true flavor is either masked by the butter or dissipated by all that lye, hydrogen peroxide and water.

I actually like lutefisk, especially with the traditional church-supper accompaniments Priscilla and JoAnn also have prepared: *lefse* (to which I add butter and brown sugar), mashed potatoes and Swedish meatballs with brown gravy. Oh, and there's aquavit: Mike and Dale make sure I down some of the potato-based Norwegian vodka liquor. With an alcohol content of 40 percent, caraway-flavored aquavit is said to make lutefisk go down easier.

CLOCKWISE, FROM TOP LEFT: BOILING LUTEFISK IN AN OUTDOOR COOKER, OSLO. A LUTEFISK FEAST, TIEGEN'S OSLO STORE. THE SPAM MUSEUM, AUSTIN. AN INTERACTIVE EXHIBIT AT THE SPAM MUSEUM.

My lutefisk mission accomplished, I head to Austin (population about 23,000) for my last Minnesota culinary revelation: Spam. I stop for a brisk walk around geese-filled Mill Pond, in a lovely park in the heart of Austin. On one side of the trail is the municipal pool and tidy downtown. On the other sits the enormous Hormel Foods plant, which covers 1.27 million square feet and employs 1,800 workers (nationally, the $5.4-billion food-processing giant has 17,600 employees).

Mill Pond is part of the reason Hormel located here: Huge blocks of ice cut from the pond in winter helped refrigerate founder George Hormel's sanitary, high-quality meat products in an era when deplorable conditions in the meatpacking industry were a national scandal. Farmers raise a lot of hogs here in southeastern Minnesota and just 12 miles away in Iowa. Each day, 20,000 of them arrive at the plant and come out as bacon, ham, sausage—and Spam, at the rate of 21,000 cans per hour!

I head up North Main Street to the red-brick Spam Museum, which celebrates Hormel's best-known product with a wink and a smile. Introduced in 1937, Spam was christened by a contest entrant who decided to condense the words "spiced ham." It's made entirely of high-quality pork shoulder and ham, despite folklore to the contrary. Exhibits at the museum high-light Hormel history, its wide-ranging product roster and the story of the World War II era, when Spam became a staple in America's kitchens and on the battle-field—and grist for jokes that Hormel wisely plays along with. At Chez Spam, videotaped chefs from around the globe prepare Spam dishes: fried Spam fritters and gourmet salad from an Englishman, barbecued Spam with steak and fruit from an Australian, Spam and rice wrapped in seaweed and seasoned with a garlic-ginger sauce from a Hawaiian. (Hawaiians are the nation's leading per capita consumers of Spam, which is sold in 47 countries.) Early Spam ads feature bygone stars such as George Burns and Gracie Allen. A Monty Python exhibit plays the classic Spam TV skit.

Time to get serious—and try a couple of Spam creations. There are two restaurants within a block of the museum. At Jerry's Other Place, I sample the very respectable Spam Museum Special sandwich, which combines a grilled slab of Spam with melted cheese, onion, tomato, pickle slices, lettuce and mayonnaise on a kaiser roll. Nearby, rival Johnny's Main Event goes a bit further with its "Spama-rama Menu." I try the Spam eggs Benedict; the Western Spam melt, a winner with sauteed onions and peppers, bacon, Swiss and American cheese and barbecue sauce, served on grilled potato bread; and a Spam chef's salad (a healthy way to eat your Spam).

"I probably go through 100 cans of Spam a week here in the summertime," owner Johnny Clark says. "People come in here after visiting the museum and want to try it. It's been great for business. Can you believe some people never heard of Spam before?" No, I can't, Johnny. But that's certainly not because Austin isn't doing its part to spread the word!

Taste of Minnesota

Potica
Sunrise Bakery, Hibbing

2	packages active dry yeast
1/4	cup warm milk (105° to 115°)
3	tablespoons all-purpose flour
1	tablespoon sugar
4 1/4 to 4 3/4	cups all-purpose flour
1	teaspoon salt
1/2	cup butter, softened
1/4	cup sugar
5	egg yolks
1 1/4	cups milk
6	cups ground walnuts (about 1 1/2 pounds)
1 1/2	cups half-and-half or light cream
1/2	cup sugar
1/4	cup honey
1	tablespoon butter
2	eggs, slightly beaten
2	teaspoons ground cinnamon
2	teaspoons finely shredded lemon peel

In a small bowl or glass measuring cup, sprinkle yeast over the 1/4 cup warm milk. Stir in the 3 tablespoons flour and the 1 tablespoon sugar. Let stand about 10 minutes or until foamy. In a medium bowl, combine 2 1/2 cups of the flour and the salt; set aside.

In a large mixing bowl, beat butter with an electric mixer on medium to high speed for 30 seconds. Gradually add the 1/4 cup sugar, beating on medium speed until well combined, scraping sides of bowl often. Add egg yolks, 1 at a time, beating after each addition. Add yeast mixture. Alternately add flour mixture and the 1 1/4 cups milk to butter mixture, beating on low speed after each addition just until combined. Using a wooden spoon, stir in as much of the remaining flour as you can. Dough will be soft.

On a lightly floured surface, knead in enough of the remaining flour to make a moderately soft dough that is smooth and elastic (about 5 minutes total). Shape into a ball. Place dough in a greased bowl, turning once to grease surface. Cover and let rise in a warm place until double in size (1 to 1¼ hours).

For filling: In a large saucepan, combine ground walnuts, half-and-half and ½ cup sugar. Cook and stir until mixture begins to simmer gently (plop). Remove from heat; stir in honey and the 1 tablespoon butter. Cool slightly; stir in the 2 eggs, cinnamon and lemon peel; set aside.

Punch dough down. Turn dough out onto a lightly floured surface. Cover; let rest for 10 minutes. Meanwhile, grease 2 very large or 4 smaller baking sheets. Divide dough into 4 portions. Roll each portion into an 18x12-inch rectangle. Spread each with one-fourth of the filling to within ¼ inch of edges. Tightly roll up each rectangle, starting from a short side. Pinch dough to seal seams and ends. Place, seam side down, on prepared baking sheets. Cover dough with lightly greased waxed paper, leaving room for dough to rise. Let rise in a warm place until nearly double in size (45 to 60 minutes).

Bake in a 325° oven for 40 to 45 minutes or until bread sounds hollow when lightly tapped (if necessary, cover loosely with foil the last 10 minutes of baking to prevent overbrowning). If using 4 smaller baking sheets, bake on 2 oven shelves and rotate halfway through baking. While 2 of the loaves are baking, refrigerate the remaining 2 risen loaves. Remove bread from baking sheets. Cool on wire racks. *Makes 4 loaves (36 servings).*

Minnesota Planked Walleye

Inspired by Northern Lights, Beaver Bay

- 4 6- to 8-ounce fresh or frozen boneless walleye fillets with skin
- 4 individual or 2 medium (15x 7 x ½-inch) maple, cherry or cedar grilling planks Mashed Potatoes (recipe follows)
- ½ teaspoon salt
- 3 tablespoons lemon juice
- 3 tablespoons garlic-infused olive oil or olive oil
- 2 tablespoons snipped fresh dill or 1 teaspoon dried dillweed
- 4 teaspoons garlic-pepper seasoning

- 1 tablespoon packed brown sugar
- 2 teaspoons lemon-pepper seasoning
- ½ teaspoon paprika
- 2 tablespoons butter, melted

Thaw fish, if frozen. At least 2 hours before grilling, soak planks in enough water to cover. (Place weights on the planks so they stay submerged during soaking.) Prepare the Mashed Potatoes; set aside.

Rinse fish; pat dry with paper towels. Sprinkle fish with salt. In a small bowl, combine the lemon juice, oil, dill, garlic-pepper, brown sugar, lemon-pepper and paprika. Brush the flesh side of each fillet with lemon-oil mixture. Drain planks.

For a charcoal grill, place the planks on the rack of an uncovered grill directly over medium coals about 5 minutes or until planks begin to crackle and smoke. Carefully arrange each fillet, skin side down, on a board. Spoon or pipe about ¾ cup of the Mashed Potatoes around each fillet. Lightly drizzle potatoes with melted butter. Cover; grill for 18 to 22 minutes or until fish flakes easily when tested with a fork. (For a gas grill, preheat grill. Reduce heat to medium. Place planks with fish and potatoes on grill rack over heat. Cover and grill as above.)

To serve, bring planks to table and set each on a large plate. Serve immediately. *Makes 4 servings.*

Mashed Potatoes: In a medium saucepan, cook 3 medium peeled and quartered baking potatoes (about 1½ pounds) and ½ teaspoon salt, covered, in enough boiling water to cover for 20 to 25 minutes or until tender; drain. Mash with a potato masher or beat with an electric mixer on low speed. Add 2 tablespoons butter, ½ teaspoon salt and ¼ teaspoon ground black pepper (or

to taste). Gradually beat in 1 to 2 tablespoons milk to make mixture light and fluffy. Let cool for 5 minutes. If you like, spoon mixture into a pastry bag with a large star tip.

Spam Benedict

Johnny's Main Event, Austin

- 1 12-ounce can Spam
- 4 English muffins, split
- ½ teaspoon cornstarch
- ½ teaspoon dry mustard
- ¼ teaspoon salt
- ¼ teaspoon garlic powder
- ¼ teaspoon ground white pepper
- ½ cup unsalted butter, cut up
- ¾ cup half-and-half or light cream
- 4 egg yolks
- 1 teaspoon lemon juice Paprika (optional) Hot cooked hash brown potatoes

Slice Spam lengthwise into 8 equal pieces; set aside. Place muffin halves, cut sides up, on a baking sheet; set aside.

For sauce: In a small bowl, combine cornstarch, dry mustard, salt, garlic powder and white pepper. In a small saucepan, melt butter; stir in cornstarch mixture. Add half-and-half. Cook and stir over medium heat until thickened and bubbly; reduce heat. Cook and stir for 2 minutes more. Remove from heat.

In a small bowl, slightly beat eggs with a fork. Gradually stir about ½ cup of the hot mixture into the egg yolks. Add egg yolk mixture to sauce mixture in saucepan. Cook and stir over medium heat until mixture is thickened and bubbly. Cook and stir for 2 minutes more. Remove from heat. Stir in lemon juice. Keep sauce warm.

Broil muffin halves 3 to 4 inches from heat about 2 minutes or until toasted. Top each muffin half with 1 slice of the Spam. Broil about 1 minute more or until meat is heated through.

To serve, spoon sauce over each Spam-topped muffin half. If you like, sprinkle with paprika. Serve with hash brown potatoes. *Makes 4 servings.*

Travel Journal

More Information

Austin Convention and Visitors Bureau (800/444-5713, www.austincvb.com). For Beaver Bay and Two Harbors: **Two Harbors Area Chamber of Commerce** (800/777-7384, www.twoharborschamber.com). **Boundary Waters Canoe Area Wilderness** (877/550-6777, www.bwcaw.org). For Duluth: **Visit Duluth** (800/438-5884, www.visitduluth.com). **Ely Chamber of Commerce** (800/777-7281, www.ely.org). **Glenwood Chamber of Commerce** (866/634-3636, www.glenwood-lakes-area.info). **Hibbing Area Chamber of Commerce** (218/262-3895, www.hibbing.org). **Iron Trail Convention & Visitors Bureau** (800/777-8497, www.irontrail.org). **Lake Superior North Shore Association** (www.lakesuperiordrive.com). **Superior National Forest** (218/626-4300, www.fs.fed.us/r9/forests/superior/).

Featured Dining

Jerry's Other Place Austin (507/433-2331). **Johnny's Main Event** Downtown Austin (507/433-8875). **Northern Lights Roadhouse** Beaver Bay (218/226-3012). **Grandma's Saloon & Grill** Duluth (218/727-4192); two other Grandma's locations in the Duluth area (218/722-9313 and 218/628-7010), plus Grandma's Sports Garden Bar & Grill (218/722-4724).

Pickwick Duluth (218/727-8901). **Burntside Lodge** Ely (218/365-3894). **Sunrise Deli** Hibbing (218/263-5713). **Betty's Pies** Two Harbors (877/269-7494).

More Great Dining

The Old Mill Austin. Just north of downtown in a converted flour mill that overlooks the Cedar River, serving a full menu of steaks, seafood and chicken, plus home-made soups and desserts (507/437-2076). **Fitger's Brewhouse Brewery and Grille** Duluth. Featuring 31 seasonal microbrews, along with a menu of sandwiches, salads and vegetarian dishes, in the renovated lakeside Fitger's Brewery complex. Live music five nights a week (218/279-2739). **New Scenic Cafe** Eight miles northeast of Duluth along the North Shore. Paneled dining rooms with Scandinavian touches in a cafe serving an innovative menu of beef, fish and vegetarian dishes (218/525-6274). **Brit's Pub** Minneapolis. Along Nicollet Mall downtown, classic English pub atmosphere and menu, including shepherd's pie and bangers and mash (612/332-3908). **Murray's** Minneapolis. Family-owned since 1946, the city's original downtown steak house, nicknamed the "Home of the Silver Butter Knife Steak" (612/339-0909). **The St. Paul Grill** Saint Paul. Serving a menu of prime steaks, thick-cut chops and seafood in an upscale setting of polished-wood booths and tables at the historic Saint Paul Hotel downtown (651/224-7455).

Featured Stops

Spam Museum Austin (800/588-7726). **Fraboni Sausage Company** Hibbing (218/263-8991). **Sunrise Bakery** Hibbing (800/782-6736). **Tiegen's Oslo Store** Oslo (800/972-0419). **Lou's Fish House** State-61 in Two Harbors (218/834-5254).

More Great Stops

Austin Just 12 miles from the Iowa state line, this southeastern Minnesota county seat has been nicknamed "Spam Town USA." Besides the Spam Museum, attractions include the historic Hormel Mansion, renovated Paramount Theatre and Hormel Nature Center.

Duluth Nearly two decades of revitalization have energized this port city, which traces the Lake Superior shore for 17 miles and extends inland. Freighters glide into the harbor beneath the landmark Aerial Lift Bridge, steps from the Lake Superior Maritime Visitors Center. Part of the Lakewalk skirts historic Canal Park, a dining, lodgings, shopping and entertainment district at the foot of downtown. Other attractions include an iron-ore freighter open for tours; harbor excursions; the Great Lakes Aquarium; an Omnimax theater; and the renovated 1892 depot, housing four museums and headquarters of the North Shore Scenic Railroad. **Ely** Superior National Forest surrounds this community, the major western gateway to the Boundary Waters Canoe Area Wilderness (BWCAW). Outfitters and secluded resorts provide getaway experiences. Other area attractions include arts and crafts shops downtown; the International Wolf Center, with its resident wolf pack and exhibits; and the Dorothy Molter Heritage Museum, a tribute to the last resident of the BWCAW. Hungry? Stop by the Chapman Street Market, a downtown gourmet food shop that serves lunch (218/365-6466). **Iron Range** About 60 miles northwest of Duluth, a collection of communities (including Hibbing, Chisholm, Mountain Iron, Eveleth and Virginia) forms the backbone of the Mesabi Range iron-ore mining region. In Chisholm, visit the Ironworld Discovery Center and the Minnesota Museum of Mining. Other area attractions include mine tours and overlooks, the 90-mile Mesabi Trail for hiking and biking, state parks and the U.S. Hockey Hall of Fame. **North Shore** Lake Superior complements a dramatic landscape of craggy shore, forested ridges and tumbling rivers along the eastern edge of a 150-mile-long arrowhead of land between Duluth and Canada. Old Highway-61 leads to lakeside resorts, seven state parks, a re-created 1700s fur-trading post and cozy towns such as Two Harbors, which claims the shore's first lighthouse; Tofte, site of the North Shore Commercial Fishing Museum; and Grand Marais, home to a thriving artists' colony. Hiking the Superior and Gunflint trails and kayaking the Lake Superior Water Trail are popular activities along the way.

Dan's Lodgings

Holiday Inn Austin ($$$; 800/985-8850).
Radisson Hotel Duluth Harborview Duluth ($$$$; 800/333-3333).
Burntside Lodge Northwest of Ely ($$$$; 218/365-3894).
Hibbing Park Hotel & Suites Hibbing ($$; 800/262-3481).

More Great Lodgings

AmericInn Austin. With 53 motel rooms and suites just northwest of downtown ($$; 800/634-3444).
Fitger's Inn Duluth. In a renovated brewery on a cliff above Lake Superior, with Georgian-style furnishings in 62 rooms and suites ($$$; 888/348-4377).
Grand Ely Lodge Ely. A 61-room lakeside resort, including a restaurant, indoor pool, marina and activities such as biking and hiking; located a mile north of town on a 10-acre site ($$$$; 800/365-5070).
River Point Resort Ely. About nine miles southeast of town on a wilderness peninsula adjacent to the BWCAW, with secluded housekeeping cabins, vacation homes and villas, plus canoe-outfitting service ($$$$; 800/456-5580).
Cove Point Lodge Just south of Beaver Bay. A handsome three-story inn with a Scandinavian flavor; includes 45 rooms and suites, plus a restaurant, on 150 acres beside Lake Superior ($$$; 800/598-3221).

Food Events

Twin Cities Food & Wine Experience Minneapolis, held in February—During this sprawling spread at the Minneapolis Convention Center, more than 300 exhibitors serve samplings of their gourmet foods, fine wines and beers, along with the latest in culinary tools and gadgets. Learn cooking secrets from top chefs or sit in on wine seminars with celebrated wine makers. Admission charged (612/371-5800, www.foodwineshow.com).
A Taste of Minnesota Saint Paul, Fourth of July weekend—All ashore at Harriet Island,

where more than 50 area restaurants and pubs serve samples of their walleye strips, turkey drumsticks, egg rolls, cheese curds, cheesecake and more. Also at Minnesota's largest free festival, musical acts play on five riverfront stages, and fireworks blast nightly over the Mississippi River. Fee for food (800/627-6101, www.tasteofmn.org).
State Fair Saint Paul, 12 days ending on Labor Day—Choose from 450 different foods served at 300 booths. Start with Tom Thumb Mini Donuts, then wash them down at the Midwest Dairy Association's All The Milk You Can Drink stand (651/288-4400, www.mnstatefair.org).
Norsefest Madison, second weekend in November—In the "Lutefisk Capital of the World," locals dish up the underappreciated fish (cod soaked in lye) at a lutefisk supper and lutefisk-eating contest (the record consumed is 8¼ pounds). Work up an appetite at the outhouse race, and shop for *hardanger* (embroidery) and rosemaling at the arts fair (320/598-7301, www.madisonmn.info).

Mail Order

Betty's Pies Homemade pies shipped overnight. Fruit pies include apple, strawberry, cherry, a signature bumbleberry and more. Cream pies include coconut cream, Key lime, a signature five-layer chocolate and many others. Also available: chicken or beef pasties, rye bread and coffee (877/269-7494, www.bettyspies.com).
Bineshii Hand-harvested, wood-parched wild rice gathered the traditional Ojibwa way at the Leech Lake Ojibwa Reservation in northern Minnesota. Also available: hominy, made from sun-dried corn slow-roasted over oak ashes; fry bread mix; corn bread mix; all-natural fruit jams; and maple syrup (800/484-2347, ext. 7580, www.bineshiiwildrice.com).
Fraboni Sausage Company A wide variety of award-winning sausages, including potato sausage, snack sticks, hot Italian sausage, bratwurst and garlic sausage. Also known for *porketta*, a seasoned, rolled pork roast (218/263-8991, www.frabonis.com).
Lou's Fish House Famous for its wood-smoked fish, including Lake Superior white-

fish, cisco, herring and lake trout, as well as Alaska salmon. Fully smoked, cooked and ready to eat cold. Salmon spread also available (218/834-5254, www.lousfish.com).
Mike's Lutefisk Fresh or frozen lutefisk from one of the largest lutefisk-processing companies in the United States. Also available: potato *lefse* (flatbread), pickled herring and lutefisk TV dinners (800/950-4755, www.lutefiskmike.com).
Mona's Cookbooks Delightful books written by Mona Meittunen Abel that showcase ethnic dishes and home-style recipes complemented by historical photographs and humorous stories about the northern Minnesota Iron Range (218/254-7239, www.cookbooksbymona.com).
Spam Gifts Online store offers 15 Spam choices, including Spam Spread Snack Kits and the Spam Variety 12 Pack. Packaged in 12-ounce cans, this renowned luncheon meat requires no refrigeration (800/588-7726, option 4, www.spamgift.com).
Sunrise Bakery High-quality gourmet foods such as *potica* (European-style sweet bread), strudels, buttery almond cakes, biscotti, homemade cookies, polenta cakes and much more. Meat products—*porketta* and pasties—are shipped overnight (800/782-6736, www.sunrisegourmet.com).
Tiegen's Oslo Store Scandinavian foodstuffs, including lutefisk, extra-sweet herring, creamed or smoked herring, lingonberry sauce, *lefse* and a selection of mixes for *lefse*, fruit soup and potato dumplings. To ensure freshness, lutefisk, herring and *lefse* are shipped October through April. Also available: Scandinavian fortune cookies with Ole and Lena jokes inside (800/972-0419, www.tiegens.com).

MISSOURI
Down-Home Ozark Cookery

THIS PAGE: BIG CEDAR LODGE, RIDGEDALE. OPPOSITE
PAGE: BLACK WALNUTS AT HAMMONS PRODUCTS,
STOCKTON. ROLLER-COASTER THRILLS AT SILVER
DOLLAR CITY, BRANSON. WOOD-BURNING STOVE COOK-
ERY IN A HISTORIC LOG CABIN, SILVER DOLLAR CITY.

Envision a colorful calico patchwork quilt, hand-stitched by a bonneted Ozark woman's gnarled hands, and you'll have an analogy in fabric for Missouri's food traditions. This large, populous state boasts rugged rural areas and two great cities, each with distinctive culinary icons.

In older St. Louis on the Mississippi River, The Hill neighborhood is packed with Italian restaurants and bakeries founded in the 1800s by aspiring Italian immigrants. Here, I've devoured more than my share of memorable pasta creations (fried ravioli, anyone?) and old-world pastries, plus the locally famous gooey butter cake. Across the state, where the Missouri River hooks northward, a much younger Kansas City displays Western influences with its juicy K.C. strip steaks and, in my opinion, the world's absolute best barbecue. The city's vibrant African-American community deserves credit for the latter, a miraculous marriage of Southern and Southwestern smoking techniques and secret sauces.

In those sprawling metropolises and elsewhere around the state, centuries-old ethnic influences live on in Missouri cookery, from the French enclave of tiny Ste. Genevieve on the Mississippi to Hermann in the Missouri River Valley, where Germans revel in their sausage, wine and beer.

Crop-wise, Missouri is a transition state from its prolific Midwest Corn Belt neighbors. The soil ranges from rich river val-leys to rocky, shallow grazing land. You find more rural Missourians raising beef and dairy cattle—and the hay, sorghum and alfalfa that feed them—than hogs, more soybeans than corn. Orchards laden with peaches and apples dot the state. At Stark Brothers, in the soaring Mississippi River bluffs south of Hannibal in Mark Twain country, orchardists developed the renowned Golden Delicious and Gala varieties of apples. There's even a small rice-growing region in far-southeastern Missouri's corner Bootheel, a reminder of the state's Southern surprises.

Food-wise and in many other respects, the imagery of a single region—the Ozark Mountains in the south-central and south-western parts of the state—unites Missourians. Actually a gigantic, eroded limestone plateau, the region is America's most diverse in biological and botanical terms. Because of its postcard-pretty, rumpled topography, the forested Ozark hills and valleys were settled late and remained isolated from the outside world even longer. The settlers who built their rustic log cab-ins here eked out a flinty existence. Most of them migrated from the Appalachian states, from one pocket of poverty to another—until resorts and retirees transformed the region decades later.

Throw Me Another Roll, Please

One of my stops perfectly encapsulates Missouri's tourism-friendly, just-for-fun hillbilly personality and humor: Lambert's Café in Ozark (population 15,000), on US-65—the gateway to the Branson area, famed for its live-performance theaters.

Just off the highway I thread through a parking lot packed with cars and charter buses. Hundreds of people crowd the shady front porch, waiting for a turn to step inside a world of pure Ozark merri-ment. My friends and I are lucky: A booth is waiting for us. We pass vintage advertis-ing signs, old photos, license plates and other assorted country kitsch adorning the rough-hewn-timber walls and floors. Fifties rock-and-roll tunes blare on the sound system. I don't see a single person among the ocean of vacationing families who isn't smiling broadly.

Part of the atmosphere has to do with the anticipation of the "throwed roll" cart approaching. These rolls got their name from the serving style. According to legend, the original Lambert's (in Sikeston) was a quiet cafe until the day a customer requested a dinner roll from a cart. When owner Norman Lambert couldn't quite reach, his guest said, "Just throw the thing." The tradition continues today: A server with a superb arm simply fires your dinner roll at you from across the dining room. Grandmothers and grandkids alike wave gleefully, vying to be the pitcher's next target. Most rolls land securely in the hands of their intended recipients. Some don't, but nobody seems to care. Backhand, overhand, fast-pitch, lofty lobs—this guy should be in the majors!

I catch my prize and welcome the young server who follows with a pot of golden, slow-moving sweet sorghum molasses for me to drizzle over the roll. Shortly, a server in a red bow tie and suspenders shows up with tasty, cornmeal-fried okra that he spoons onto a paper towel. I order a mostly vegetarian assortment of side dishes that reflect the Ozark heritage: candied yams, turnip greens, white beans, corn bread, black-eyed peas,

fried potatoes and macaroni with stewed tomatoes. Simple fare, served in abundance. On the decidedly nonvegetarian side, I request fried hog jowl—the cheek of the animal, which resembles a thick slab of bacon. Next time, I'll dive into the meatier side of Lambert's menu: pork steaks, fried catfish fillets, barbecued ribs, country-fried steak. For dessert, I choose the blackberry cobbler.

I visit the expansive, totally modern kitchen filled with mile-high pots bubbling or simmering on low-set burners. This kitchen is the largest I'll see on my entire journey. In a side area, two young men are preparing throwed rolls. I learn that they'll bake 1,000 dozen to sell the day before Thanksgiving (they're closed Thanksgiving Day), including many for to-go orders. The arsenal of prospective dining room missiles rises a total of about three hours before they're baked to perfection for precisely 13 minutes in a huge oven.

Today, three busy Lambert's Cafés (one in Alabama) pride themselves on such mind-boggling statistics as serving up 40,800 pounds of white beans and

335,400 eggs in a recent year—not to mention 73,440 pounds of fried okra. As I step back out into the midafternoon sunlight, hundreds of would-be diners of various ages still mill about, waiting to fulfill the restaurant's motto: "Come hungry, leave full and hopefully have a laugh or two!"

Ozark Folklore and Food Lore

Ozark specialties and the kindhearted cooks who prepare them rate among the most heartwarming memories of my journey. Simple. Honest. Homespun. Genuine. Straightforward. Rustic. Those words describe the denizens who inhabit this magical domain of fiddlers, clog dancers, corncob pipes, quilts and ramshackle cabins. I appreciate the humanity they dispense along with my entrées. And there's more to it than that. The real inspiration I draw from my Ozarks sojourn is how the impoverished but resourceful settlers of these remote hills and hollers transformed the make-do ingredients they had at hand into classic country feasts. Mix these foods with tales of outlaws, vigilantes, trappers, preachers, mountaineers and moonshiners, and you have fascinating food lore as well as folklore.

Nowadays, most people travel to Branson for the 100-plus sometimes rambunctious, always patriotic and God-fearing musical shows. I wish I could have visited here when the town was founded back in 1882, before the RVs, motels and mega theaters. *The Shepherd of the Hills*, Harold Bell Wright's inspiring 1907 story of a country preacher (now the nation's longest-running outdoor drama, still performed in Branson), recalls those days. It's precisely that yearning for simpler times that draws tourists to this city of 7,000 just 40 miles south of Springfield. The area's sweeping mountain vistas, man-made

CLOCKWISE, FROM TOP LEFT: "THROWED" YEAST ROLLS AND SORGHUM MOLASSES AT LAMBERT'S CAFÉ, OZARK. ROLLS IN FLIGHT AT LAMBERT'S. A CANDY SHOP AT SILVER DOLLAR CITY. TRADITIONALLY GARBED OZARK ENTERTAINERS, SILVER DOLLAR CITY. OPPOSITE PAGE: THRONGS AWAITING THEIR TURN TO BE PELTED AT LAMBERT'S.

LEFT TO RIGHT: (ALL TAKEN AT SILVER DOLLAR CITY) SERVING UP BUCKSHOT ANNIE'S SUCCOTASH. ONE OF MANY OZARK-THEMED AMUSEMENT PARK RIDES. JUNE WARD'S BRITTLE AT BROWN'S CANDY FACTORY. SHIRLEY CLARK PREPARING DINNER ON HER WOOD-BURNING STOVE.

lakes and family resorts also have spelled surefire success for area developers.

One other ingredient in Branson's evolution as a tourism mecca has been Silver Dollar City, a theme park unlike any other I've visited. To my mind, it is absolved of any culpability in Branson's traffic problems because of its improbable cultural impact: preserving for hordes of otherwise unknowing vacationers a sense of what the Ozarks were like more than a century ago.

Inspired by a tiny mining town once located atop Marvel Cave, Mary Herschend and her sons, Jack and Peter, founded the theme park in 1960. The idea was to celebrate the Ozark heritage in myriad ways—through folklore, storytelling, crafts, dance, music and food—while inflicting minimal aesthetic damage on the surrounding shady glades filled with oak and hickory. (The family still designs rides and attractions around trees rather than removing them; even roller coasters are cleverly folded into the ter-

rain.) The Herschend's wholesome Bible Belt formula still works, to the tune of 1,500 employees and 2 million-plus visitors each year.

But I'm here for some Ozark food fun at Silver Dollar City's 12 restaurants and 24 food concessions: ham and beans, catfish fillets, corn on the cob, barbecued ribs, fresh-squeezed lemonade, funnel cakes, kettle corn, saltwater taffy and peaches and cream. They also serve (surprise!) rosemary-scented pork loin on focaccia bread at an Italian place. I decide to focus on three delights in particular: succotash, peanut brittle and an Ozark dinner prepared entirely on a wood-burning stove.

Succotash is one of the many specialties that reflect the Ozarks' Southern inclination. Usually, it's a mix of lima beans, sweet-corn kernels and chopped peppers. At Silver Dollar City, the preparation and the ingredient list are a bit more interesting than that. Costumed interpreters and their rollicking banter are a hallmark at the

park, as I learn firsthand from spunky Buckshot Annie, my first Ozark cooking teacher. To her stadium-size skillet (5 feet across!), we add ingredients one gigantic scoop at a time: corn, breaded okra, peppers, squash, diced chicken and onions, seasoned with salt, pepper and garlic. Oh, and lots of melted butter.

The aroma is so enticing that parkgoers gather to watch Annie blend all 200 pounds of this colorful Ozark stir-fry. Annie (who's actually Shirley Tolar, a 25-year employee, also a Silver Dollar City baker) uses so much okra in her succotash—20 pounds per batch and 15 tons per year—that she's earned the nickname "The Okra Queen" from grateful area growers.

Down another Silver Dollar City lane, opposite a re-created smithy, I open the door to Brown's Candy Factory, where June Ward (who's been a candy maker since 1968) is waiting to teach me all about brittle making. As the story goes, the original Brown's was founded in 1882, and the

owners' descendants helped set up this replica. June puts me to work stirring approximately 4 pounds of corn syrup, 8 pounds of sugar and 6 pounds of raw peanuts in a copper cauldron that soon reaches a temperature of about 280 degrees (June doesn't require any measuring cups or thermometers). We add salt and baking soda before eventually turning out the molten brittle onto a table to cool.

"First, we put some wampus-cat slab oil on the counter so our brittle won't stick. That's vegetable oil to you, feller," June instructs. Uh-huh. At just the right moment, we use a dough scraper to break the confection into crunchy shards of nutty ambrosia. Other brittles at Brown's include black walnut, cashew, almond and a coconut-pecan variation. But the crunchy-good peanut brittle rules: June and her calico-costumed assistants make 180 pounds daily each summer.

My final food stop here is an 1843 Ozark log cabin where I enjoy dinner cooked entirely on a wood-burning stove. Before it was rescued by Silver Dollar City, this rough-hewn abode was occupied by the same Forsyth, Missouri, family for more than a century. Aunt Shirley (who's actually interpreter Shirley Clark but has the chiseled features of a true Ozark pioneer woman) puts me to snapping green beans in the kitchen as she expertly manipulates the 1890s Majestic brand stove to produce a sumptuous feast: skillet corn bread, chicken and homemade noodles on mashed potatoes, green beans with shallots and ham, and cinnamony peach cobbler for dessert. In our age of high-tech kitchens, I'm amazed that all this came from a contraption fueled by oak logs.

As we tour the place after dinner, I realize this log home is actually two cabins under one roof: the cooler living and sleeping quarters on one side, the sometimes broiling-hot kitchen on the other, connected by long front and back porches. Shirley tells me the logging family who lived here would have had a dairy cow and a couple of pigs, goats and turkeys, along with the output from a vegetable garden. Other foodstuffs might have been bartered from neighbors, and the woman of the house would have spent about six hours a day cooking.

Beyond Beans and Biscuits

In addition to all the showbiz hillbilly fare and honest country cooking, there's an elegant side to Ozark cuisine. That's apparent at the 800-acre Big Cedar Lodge about 10 miles south of Branson, where Chef Robert Stricklin presides over four restaurants that offer inventive creations—nouvelle Ozark, if you will.

Big Cedar is a sprawling, upscale wilderness resort that hugs the impossibly pretty cove of Table Rock (formerly the White River), the largest of the area's constructed lakes. This is pretty civilized wilderness, if you ask me. The resort's 243 rooms range from cozy cottages and log cabins to several large, modern lodges showcasing native stone, rough timbers and lots of antlers, courtesy of Bass Pro Shops. Here, guests can unwind by boating, waterskiing, fishing, hiking, bicycling, viewing wildlife and riding horseback. They also can relish the comforts of the spa or lounge around one of three pools. For good measure, there's access nearby to a 10,000-acre nature park and a designer golf course, plus those rousing Branson shows in the evenings.

Although Top of the Rock is the best known of the restaurants on the property, I dine at Devil's Pool, housed in a handsome former retreat built by a Roaring Twenties type. Chef Robert and his staff are classically trained, with varied backgrounds. Robert is serious about basing much of his cuisine on authentic Ozark themes—and he's researched the topic extensively. "I want to go beyond beans and biscuits," he declares. I'm surprised to learn that many ethnic cultures abound in these hollers and in Springfield, the "Queen City of the Ozarks." Osage and

other American Indian tribes, Scots, Irish, English, French, Swedes, Germans, Dutch and Swiss—all have feasted on the region's famed wild bounty, from buffalo, venison, bear, wild turkey, wild boar and trout to corn, beans, pumpkins, squash, nuts, herbs, and wild greens and fruits.

How does Robert blend all those ingredients and influences into his unique brand of Ozark cuisine? I find out first-hand with a glorious spread: Hickory-smoked trout cakes made with scallions and capers. Rosemary herb biscuits. A salad of field greens with blueberry–poppy seed dressing. Tender beef short ribs glazed with bourbon and sorghum molasses. A meat loaf like none other—smoked chicken and mushrooms combined with the expected beef and pork. And, on the side, heavenly grits starring sun-dried tomatoes, boursin and cheddar cheese; green beans with pecans; and sauteed sweet corn. For dessert, an individual streusel-topped blackberry–sour cream cobbler. It's a vibrant mix of flavors, textures and colors.

Sunday Brunch at Hard Work U

My Sunday brunch at the College of the Ozarks, just south of country-glitzy Branson, is the equal of many I've had at big-city hotels and first-class resorts. Yet, my meal is all the sweeter when I learn the story of this inspiring four-year liberal arts school founded in 1906. The 1,500 students and their faculty form not only an academic community, but also a self-sufficient town named Point Lookout. But what's really unique here is the guiding philosophy: Nobody pays tuition; instead, students earn their way at what's known as Hard Work U. The Christian-oriented (originally Presbyterian) college was founded in nearby Forsyth to give youth from impoverished Ozark families a chance at a higher education. After a disastrous fire in 1915, it was relocated to Point Lookout—named for the bluff-top view of Lake Taneycomo on the White River, as seen from a campus promontory.

I park my car outside the massive (almost 100,000 square feet) log-style Keeter Center, which houses the Center for Character Education; 15 guest rooms and suites that I consider the best lodging deal in the Branson area; and the Dobyns Dining Room, where I plan to dine. About 200 College of the Ozarks students studying hospitality management work at the Center, guided by 15 faculty. Before I'm seated by a white-jacketed, solicitous student host, I step out onto the expansive veranda for a splendid view of the campus, with Branson and the Ozark hills beyond.

I can see the cottage industries, most of them food-oriented, that make this college tick economically: greenhouses that supply landscape plants to many Branson theaters, a dairy with 150 Holstein and Jersey cattle that students milk twice daily, a gristmill where students formulate pancake and biscuit mixes, a kitchen

CLOCKWISE, FROM ABOVE: GROUNDS AT BIG CEDAR LODGE, RIDGEDALE. TROUT CAKES AT DEVIL'S POOL RESTAURANT, BIG CEDAR LODGE. KEETER CENTER, COLLEGE OF THE OZARKS, POINT LOOKOUT. STUDENT WAITER SERVING DAN BRUNCH, KEETER CENTER. OPPOSITE PAGE: RUSTIC-ELEGANT DEVIL'S POOL DINING ROOM, BIG CEDAR LODGE.

Hummingbird Cake

Inspired by Hammons Products Company,
Stockton

1½ cups sugar
1½ cups all-purpose flour
1 teaspoon baking soda
¼ teaspoon salt
¼ teaspoon ground cinnamon
1 8-ounce can crushed pineapple (juice
   pack), drained
½ cup cooking oil
4 eggs, lightly beaten
1 teaspoon vanilla
1 cup chopped bananas
1 cup chunky-style applesauce
⅔ cup toasted, chopped black walnuts
   or pecans
   Cream Cheese Frosting (recipe follows)
1½ cups toasted, chopped black walnuts
   or pecans
2 tablespoons toasted, chopped black
   walnuts or pecans

Grease and lightly flour two 9x1½-inch
round cake pans. Set aside.

In a large mixing bowl, combine the sugar,
flour, baking soda, salt and cinnamon. Add
drained pineapple, oil, eggs and vanilla. Beat
with an electric mixer until combined, scraping the sides of the bowl occasionally. Stir in
bananas, applesauce and the ⅔ cup walnuts. Divide batter between prepared pans.

Bake in a 350° oven about 35 minutes or
until top springs back when lightly touched.
Cool cake layers on wire racks for 10 minutes. Remove from pans; cool thoroughly
on wire racks.

Prepare the Cream Cheese Frosting.
Frost cake. Lightly press the 1½ cups walnuts into sides of cake. Sprinkle the 2 tablespoons finely chopped walnuts on top of
cake. Cover and store in the refrigerator.
Makes 12 to 16 servings.

Cream Cheese Frosting: In a large mixing
bowl, beat one 8-ounce package cream
cheese, softened; ½ cup butter, softened
and 1 teaspoon vanilla with electric mixer
until light and fluffy. Gradually add 5 cups
sifted powdered sugar, beating until
smooth and of spreading consistency.
Makes about 3½ cups.

building where student cooks prepare
jams, jellies and the famous fruitcakes
(40,000 per year) they ship all around the
globe. The college also has its own water
system, power plant, post office, radio station, fire department, hospital and meat-
processing plant. I'm told they even make
their own concrete here, and that most of
the buildings were constructed with student labor. I learn that about 75 percent
of the students come from the Ozark
region (which also includes parts of
Arkansas, Oklahoma and Kansas). But
some of the students I banter with in the
dining room and big, modern kitchen are
from much farther away—other regions of
the United States as well as Indonesia,
Ukraine, Russia and the Philippines.

Plate in hand, I begin the first of several
visits to the extensive brunch buffet.
Chicken and dumplings and tender, melt-
in-your-mouth pot roast with gravy are
among the specialties, but there's also the
famous College of the Ozarks ham (juicy
and tender), smoked salmon, Thai
chicken salad, sesame chicken and a
parade of homemade potato-bread rolls,
salads, pastries and delectable desserts,
including fruit tortes, mousses, cheese-
cakes and homemade chocolates. The
cranberry–cream cheese bread pudding is
a revelation. Students working at the buffet and waiting on tables are just as professional as other restaurant staffs I've
encountered on my journey and more
eager to please than most.

Missouri in a Nutshell

My next touring day begins with a shim-
meringly beautiful Missouri sunrise at the
Orleans Trail Resort on a cove of Stockton
Lake, an Ozark boating and fishing para-
dise with almost 300 miles of shoreline.
(Add this body of water to Lake of the
Ozarks, Harry Truman Reservoir, Mark

Twain Lake and Table Rock Lake, and
Missouri has to be the best-dammed state
in the Midwest!)

Today I aim to learn all about black walnuts, but my first order of business is
breakfast. I heed a local's advice and head
to the Train Station Café in Stockton
(population 2,000). This isn't a train station, and it never was—the owner just
likes trains, according to my server. She
soon brings two buttery eggs, fixed sunny-
side up and runny; a nest of nongreasy,
golden hash browns; a gargantuan fluffy
biscuit; and a juicy, 1-pound (you heard
right) bone-in ham slice, accompanied by
lots of black coffee. I won't be eating again
until, well, um, noon—but I'm very well
satisfied with my first Missouri breakfast.

I'm also blown away by the story of a
monster tornado that literally shredded
Stockton at precisely 6:30 p.m. on May 4,
2003. Although things are cleaned up
now, the dearth of trees and the high proportion of new buildings in town should
have clued me in when I first arrived. My
waitress tells me almost every building in
Stockton was destroyed or damaged. On
the square, only the Art Deco Cedar
County Courthouse survived. But Missourians are plucky, and most of the town
has been rebuilt.

That includes the Hammons Products
facility, a supplier of black walnuts, just a
few blocks north of the square. Nuts,
mainly black walnuts, are a big crop in
woodsy Missouri. There are an estimated
73 million black walnut trees in the state,
which named that variety its official nut
tree. Most Americans prefer the milder
taste of thinner-shelled English walnuts,
which are grown primarily in California
groves, but I love the more robust, earthy
flavor of the black walnut. From Kansas to
Ohio in the Heartland, black walnut trees
pop up just about everywhere as volunteer

plants in pastures or coexisting with row crops in fields.

Brian Hammons, grandson of the local grocer who founded the Hammons company in 1946, greets me at the offices. Brian grew up here, studied law, practiced in Kansas City and returned to run the family business. Between calls and e-mails, he explains the nut-harvesting process: Each October or November, people gather fallen nuts from farm pastures or from their own yards—a tradition in many Midwest households—and deposit them at one of 250 Hammons collection stations in 16 states. The nuts' green outer hulls are removed on the spot; then the walnuts are trucked to Stockton, where about 120 Hammons employees use steel rollers to crack and sawlike teeth to separate the thick, furrowed shells and retrieve the meats from 25 million pounds of walnuts each season. Only about 7 percent of a black walnut is edible meat; the rest gets pulverized into a variety of natural industrial abrasive products.

After a quick tour and a visit to a walnut grove on the property, we head to Hammons Black Walnut Emporium back in the heart of Stockton for some product sampling. The shop is a squirrel's paradise: native black walnuts, pecans, cashews, macadamias, peanuts and almonds—all sold under the Hammons Pantry label. Brian explains that most black walnuts wind up in ice cream, followed by baked goods and candy. But more cooks these days are adding them to salads, main dishes and vegetables. I zero in on the ice cream counter for a tasting of Brian's exclusively made, 16-percent-butterfat creations: plain black walnut, caramelized black walnut, peach black walnut, black walnut turtle (with caramel and chocolate) and double-chocolate black walnut. I also can't resist a black

CLOCKWISE, FROM ABOVE: (ALL PHOTOS TAKEN IN STOCKTON) BLACK WALNUT CREATIONS FILL HAMMONS EMPORIUM. A STATELY BLACK WALNUT TREE ON THE HAMMONS PROPERTY. CREAMY BLACK WALNUT ICE CREAM SERVED WITH OTHER NUTTY TREATS AT HAMMONS EMPORIUM.

Smokin' Grilled Jumbo Shrimp with Sauce Remoulade

Fiorella's Jack Stack Barbecue, Kansas City

- 2 cups hickory wood chips (optional)
- 12 6-inch wooden skewers
  Sauce Remoulade (recipe follows)
- 12 fresh or frozen jumbo shrimp
  (1¼ to 1½ pounds)
- 2 tablespoons butter
- 2 tablespoons snipped fresh parsley
- 2 teaspoons Cajun seasoning, steak rub seasoning or seafood seasoning, such as Old Bay
- 1 to 2 cloves garlic, minced

If you like, use wood chips. Soak chips in enough water to cover for at least 1 hour before grilling. Soak wooden skewers in water for 30 minutes before grilling. Meanwhile, prepare Sauce Remoulade; cover and chill until needed. Thaw shrimp, if frozen. Peel and devein shrimp; set aside.

Drain skewers. Thread shrimp lengthwise onto each skewer beginning at tail end until they are straight. In a small skillet or saucepan, melt butter over medium heat; remove from heat. Stir in parsley, Cajun seasoning and garlic. Brush butter mixture on all sides of shrimp.

For charcoal grill, drain wood chips, if using. Sprinkle chips over hot coals. Grill shrimp on the greased rack of an uncovered grill directly over medium coals for 7 to 9 minutes or until shrimp turn opaque, turning several times during grilling. (For a gas grill, preheat grill. Follow manufacturer's directions for using wood chips, if using. Reduce heat to medium. Place shrimp on greased grill rack over heat, and grill as above.)

To serve, transfer skewers to a serving plate. Serve with Sauce Remoulade. *Makes 12 appetizers.*

Sauce Remoulade: In a small bowl, combine ⅔ cup tartar sauce; 1 tablespoon lemon juice; 1 tablespoon capers, drained; 1 tablespoon Dijon-style mustard and 1 teaspoon Cajun seasoning, steak rub seasoning or seafood seasoning (such as Old Bay). Cover and chill until ready to use. *Makes about ¾ cup.*

walnut–blueberry muffin and a black walnut–oatmeal cookie, a Missouri State Fair prizewinner.

I feel guilty about all the goodies I'm scarfing down until Brian explains that black walnuts are really good for you. They're high in protein, minerals and fiber. They contain no cholesterol but have lots of monounsaturated fats (the good ones) and omega-3 fatty acids, like those found in olive oil. Brian says black walnuts also have a high satiety effect, which means they fill you up fast. I don't think that's true in my case. But how often do I get to hang out in a black walnut shop, anyway?

Always Room for Barbecue!

Although Ozark cookery is my focus in Missouri, I'd be guilty of a food felony if I didn't detour for a barbecue binge in Kansas City (metro population about 2 million), the hilly, friendly metropolis that straddles a big chunk of northwestern Missouri and northeastern Kansas.

On the pages of *Midwest Living*® magazine, we've probed the secrets of K.C. barbecue many times. It's one of those local specialties that claim a loyal national following, like Chicago pizza and Sheboygan brats. I consider this the best barbecue anywhere, and believe me, I've sampled my share, from Louisiana to North Carolina, Texas to Tennessee. The primary ingredient—pork or beef—has long been raised on area farms and ranches. Kansas City's large African-American community added their Southern techniques for making less expensive cuts of meat irresistible with tangy-sweet sauces.

Barbecue is serious business here, available in establishments ranging from elegant restaurants to humble roadside stands. If you ask for a recommendation, be prepared for a discourse on why so-

and-so's is the best, bar none. I start my binge with what's historically been the national media darling of the K.C. barbecue scene: Arthur Bryant's on Brooklyn Avenue, just east of downtown, near the handsomely restored 18th & Vine Historic Jazz District. Back in the 1920s, Charlie Bryant, Arthur's brother, fine-tuned his skills over an outdoor pit under the tutelage of Henry Perry, who's considered the father of K.C. barbecue. Arthur came on the scene after Charlie died and lent his name to the place in 1946. He and his barbecue became a legend in the 1960s, when Calvin Trillin, a K.C. native and a writer for *The New Yorker* magazine, proclaimed this the "single best restaurant in the world." Arthur passed from the scene in 1982, but the current owners haven't changed a thing.

It's a rather spartan place, with laminate tabletops, vinyl-covered chairs and a cafeteria-style ordering setup. Jazz music plays on the sound system—very appropriate, because some of the genre's greats got started in clubs just blocks from here. Arthur Bryant's to-go meals still are wrapped in butcher-paper bundles. But I'm dining in this evening, feasting on burnt ends—the well-done side of the beef brisket, loaded with flavor—served on sauce-absorbing slices of plain white bread. I sample all the sauce variations (original, sweet heat, rich and spicy), with fries, baked beans and coleslaw on the side. The legend lives on—humble Arthur Bryant's is still worthy of all its acclaim.

Next, I head east of downtown Kansas City's Art Deco skyscrapers to an industrial and warehouse district just over the Kansas line on Southwest Boulevard. Marisha Brown-Smith and her family have been smoking ribs at Rosedale ever since her grandfather, Anthony Rieke, opened the place on July 4, 1934. One old-timer, here for a nostalgic meal with several children, and grandchildren, recalls when Rosedale was a post-Prohibition "bucket shop": Customers came with pails to be filled with beer and root beer. Back home, they'd use a hot poker to raise a head of foam on the brew!

It wasn't long before Marisha's grand-dad installed a rotisserie oven to hickory-smoke his meats and developed his own sauce. Sauce is sacred here. "Our philosophy is that the sauce has to complement the meat perfectly; ours is spicy and has a kick," Marisha tells me. "We don't overdo the ketchup and molasses like others do."

As I tuck in a napkin, bib-style, and begin the feast ordered just for lucky me, I ask what has changed over the years. Marisha says more people are fat-conscious these days, ordering barbecued turkey, chicken and leaner cuts of beef and pork. Pulled pork, long a Southern barbecue signature, has won a following here as well. Bill Smith, Marisha's husband, shows me around the kitchen with its enormous smokers. They've obviously had lots of use. The best seller here? Pork ribs, to the tune of some 400 pounds on a typical business day.

My final stop on the barbecue trail is an old railroad yard just south of downtown. Here, two culinary legends share space in a former freight house near Kansas City's splendidly restored Union Station. I'll have to try Lidia's Italy—an Italian restaurant run by TV cooking star Lidia Bastianich—another time, as my destination is Fiorella's Jack Stack Barbecue, the upscale K.C. barbecue restaurant next door. Founded by an Italian grocer whose business suffered when supermarkets exploded on the scene in the 1950s, Jack Stack is barbecue corporate style: In addition to three dine-in restaurants (the other two are in Martin City, Missouri, and

CLOCKWISE, FROM TOP LEFT: (ALL SHOTS TAKEN IN THE KANSAS CITY AREA) A FAMILIAR SIGN TO K.C. BARBECUE LOVERS. MARISHA BROWN-SMITH, ROSEDALE BARBECUE PURVEYOR. SAUCE-SLATHERED BURNT ENDS AND FRIES AT ROSEDALE. JACK FIORELLA AT WORK, FIORELLA'S JACK STACK BARBECUE NEAR UNION STATION DOWNTOWN.

BRANSON FROM POINT LOOKOUT

Ozark Mountain Succotash
Silver Dollar City, Branson

- 12 ounces skinless, boneless chicken breast halves
- 1/3 cup all-purpose flour
- 1/3 cup yellow cornmeal
- 1/4 teaspoon salt
- 1/8 teaspoon ground black pepper
- 1 egg, slightly beaten
- 1 tablespoon milk
- 8 ounces whole okra, cut into 1/2-inch-thick pieces (2 cups)
- 1/3 cup cooking oil
- 1 medium green sweet pepper, chopped (3/4 cup)
- 1 medium onion, chopped (1/2 cup)
- 2 cloves garlic, minced
- 1 small yellow summer squash or zucchini, cut into thin, bite-size strips (1 cup)
- 1 cup frozen whole kernel corn, thawed

Cut chicken into bite-size strips. Set aside.

For okra: In a plastic bag, combine the flour, cornmeal, salt and black pepper. In a mixing bowl, combine egg and milk. Toss okra pieces in egg mixture. Add one-fourth of the okra to plastic bag; close bag and shake to coat okra well. Remove coated okra. Repeat with remaining okra, egg mixture and flour mixture. Set aside.

For vegetables: In a large skillet, heat 1 tablespoon of the oil over medium-high heat. Add green pepper, onion and garlic. Cook and stir over medium heat in hot oil for 3 to 4 minutes or until onion is tender but not brown. Add summer squash and corn to skillet. Cook and stir for 2 to 3 minutes more or until corn is tender. Remove from skillet. Drain vegetables on paper towels. Set aside.

Carefully add another 1 tablespoon oil to skillet. Add chicken. Cook and stir over medium-high heat for 2 to 3 minutes or until tender and no longer pink. Add to vegetables. Set aside.

Overland Park, Kansas), the franchise is one of the nation's busiest restaurant-caterers. Chain-wide, they prepare 1.5 million pounds of beef brisket and 250,000 gallons of sauce per year! A mail-order operation ships various combinations of 30 precooked barbecue meats, side dishes, rubs, sauces and other products to aficionados around the globe.

Both the barbecue and the surroundings rate four stars in my book. Located on the edge of the lively, loft-filled Crossroads Arts District (Kansas City's answer to New York's SoHo), the former freight house still sports exposed-brick walls and dark-stained ceiling beams with suspended wrought-iron fixtures. Huge prints and relief works portray farm animals and bygone farm and railroading scenes. A U-shape bar up front is the place where local lawyers, government officials and business executives hatch deals as they wait for a table.

On a tour of the modern kitchen, I learn a few of the Fiorella family's secrets. Pit master Ronnie Holloway explains that the approach is to first sear in juices and impart that distinctive hickory-and-oak

flavor (I note a huge woodpile just outside the back door), then to transfer the meat to a rotisserie oven to create a slow smoked finish. There's no sauce at first—just a dry rub on most of the cuts, which are graded choice or higher. I ask Ronnie if he eats much barbecue at home. "There's *always* room for barbecue!" he replies enthusiastically.

I claim a booth and begin my final barbecue banquet, the third in a matter of hours. This time, avuncular Jack Fiorella and his son-in-law, Case Dorman, scrutinize my reactions as I sample huge portions of barbecued beef, pork ribs and butt, ham, sausage, chicken and lamb. The meat is obviously of excellent quality, not overcooked or overpowered by the smoking or saucing. There's no escaping the fact that fat is what gives much barbecue its heavenly flavor, Jack says.

I wolf down my last morsels of this K.C. specialty like a sailor anticipating months at sea. Meanwhile, Case nibbles at a salad and a bowl of soup, saying, "You can't live on barbecue every day, especially when you're in this business." But wouldn't it be nice to try?

In the same skillet, heat the remaining oil. Test oil by adding 1 piece of okra; if okra sizzles, fat is hot enough. Fry okra, half at a time, over medium-high heat for 3 to 4 minutes or until golden, turning once. Using a slotted spoon, remove okra from skillet, reserving 2 tablespoons oil in the skillet.

Return okra, chicken and vegetables to skillet. Stir gently until heated through. Serve immediately. *Makes 4 servings.*

Bourbon-Glazed Beef Short Ribs

Big Cedar Lodge, Ridgedale

    4   pounds beef short ribs
  1/2   cup all-purpose flour
    1   teaspoon kosher salt or 1/2 teaspoon salt
  1/2   teaspoon ground black pepper
    2   tablespoons cooking oil
    3   medium carrots, coarsely chopped
    1   medium onion, coarsely chopped
    1   celery stalk, coarsely chopped
    2   tablespoons tomato paste
        Bourbon Glaze (recipe follows)

Trim fat from meat. In a shallow dish, stir together flour, salt and black pepper. Dip meat into flour mixture, coating well on all sides. In an ovenproof 6- to 8-quart Dutch oven, brown meat, half at a time, in hot oil over medium-high heat.

Add carrots, onion, celery and tomato paste to Dutch oven. Add enough water to cover meat (about 4 cups). Bring to boiling. Transfer Dutch oven to the oven. Bake,

covered, in a 350° oven for 1 1/2 to 2 hours or until the meat is very tender.

Remove Dutch oven from the oven; cool about 10 minutes. Using a slotted spoon, remove short ribs from the cooking liquid. When cool enough to handle, remove meat from bones; discard bones. Place meat and cooking liquid in separate storage containers. Cover and chill in the refrigerator for at least 4 hours or up to 24 hours.

For sauce: Spoon fat from the surface of the cooking liquid; discard fat. In a medium saucepan, bring cooking liquid to boiling; reduce heat. Simmer, uncovered, about 20 minutes or until mixture is reduced by half. Transfer to a food processor or blender. Cover and process or blend until smooth. Season to taste with additional salt and ground black pepper. Keep sauce warm until ready to serve.

For ribs: Dip meat into Bourbon Glaze, coating well on all sides. For a charcoal grill, grill meat on rack of an uncovered grill directly over medium coals about 10 minutes or until heated through and edges are crisp, turning once halfway through grilling time and brushing again with glaze. (For a gas grill, preheat grill. Reduce heat to medium. Place meat on grill rack over heat. Cover and grill as above.) Pass sauce with meat. *Makes 4 to 5 servings.*

Bourbon Glaze: In a small bowl, stir together 1/2 cup molasses, 1/4 cup bourbon and 1 tablespoon coarse stone-ground mustard. *Makes about 2/3 cup.*

Dinner Rolls

Inspired by Lambert's Café, "Home of the Throwed Rolls," Ozark

  3 1/4   to 3 3/4 cups all-purpose flour
      1   package active dry yeast
      1   cup milk
    1/3   cup butter, margarine or shortening
    1/4   cup sugar
    3/4   teaspoon salt
      1   beaten egg

In a large mixing bowl, stir together 1 1/4 cups of the flour and the yeast. In a medium saucepan, heat and stir milk, butter, sugar and salt just until warm (120° to 130°) and butter almost melts. Add milk mixture to flour mixture along with egg. Beat with an electric mixer on low speed for 30 seconds, scraping side of bowl constantly. Beat on high speed for 3 minutes. Using a wooden spoon, stir in as much of the remaining flour as you can.

Turn dough out onto a lightly floured surface. Knead in enough of the remaining flour to make a moderately stiff dough that is smooth and elastic (6 to 8 minutes total). Shape dough into a ball. Place in a lightly greased bowl, turning once to grease surface. Cover; let rise in a warm place until double in size (about 1 hour).

Punch down dough. Turn the dough out onto a lightly floured surface. Divide the dough in half. Cover; let rest for 10 minutes. Meanwhile, lightly grease a 13x9x2-inch baking pan.

Shape the dough into 24 balls. Place balls in prepared baking pan. Cover and let rise in a warm place until nearly double in size (about 30 minutes).

Bake in a 375° oven for 15 to 18 minutes or until rolls sound hollow when lightly tapped. Immediately remove rolls from pan. Cool on wire racks. *Makes 24 rolls.*

Tip: For a soft and shiny crust, brush the baked rolls with butter when you take them out of the oven. If you prefer a glossy, crisp crust, brush the shaped dough with milk or a beaten egg before baking.

Travel Journal

More Information

Branson/Lakes Area Chamber of Commerce and Convention & Visitors Bureau (800/214-3661, www.explorebranson.com). **Kansas City Convention & Visitors Association** (800/767-7700, www.visitkc.com). **Hermann Chamber of Commerce** (800/932-8687, www.hermannmo.info). **Lake of the Ozarks Convention & Visitor Bureau** (800/386-5253, www.funlake .com). **Ozark Chamber of Commerce** (417/581-6139, www.ozarkchamber.com). **St. Louis Convention & Visitors Commission** (800/916-0092, www.explorestlouis .com). **Ste. Genevieve Chamber of Commerce** (573/883-3686, www.sainte genevieve.org). **Stockton Area Chamber of Commerce** (417/276-5213, www.stocktonmochamber.com).

Featured Dining

Devil's Pool Big Cedar Lodge, 10 miles south of Branson (417/335-5141). **Arthur Bryant's Barbeque** Kansas City, (816/231-1123); also in the Ameristar Casino northeast of downtown (816/414-7474) and in Kansas City, Kansas (913/788-7500). **Fiorella's Jack Stack Barbecue** Kansas City (816/472-7427); also in suburban Martin City (816/942-9141) and Overland Park, Kansas (913/385-7427). **Rosedale Barbecue** Kansas City (913/262-0343).

Lambert's Café Ozark (417/581-7655) and Sikeston (573/471-4261). **Dobyns Dining Room** College of the Ozarks, Point Lookout (417/239-1900). **Buckshot Annie's** Silver Dollar City (800/831-4386). **Train Station Café** Stockton (417/276-2534).

More Great Dining

The Baldknobbers Country Restaurant Branson, next door to the Baldknobbers Theatre. A full menu of home-style dishes, including chicken-fried steak and catfish, plus belt-stretching breakfast, lunch and dinner buffets (417/334-7202). **Showboat Branson Belle** Branson. An 1880s paddle wheeler with a 700-seat dining theater for lunch and dinner cruise shows (800/831-4386). **Top of the Rock** Big Cedar Lodge, 10 miles south of Branson. Bistro-type dining and a casual atmosphere with inspiring lake views (417/339-5320). **Gates Bar-B-Q** Kansas City. A family-owned barbecue tradition since 1946 at three Kansas City, Missouri, locations (816/483-3880 downtown, plus 816/753-0828 and 816/531-7522); also in neighboring Independence, Missouri (816/353-5880), and in Kansas City and Leawood, Kansas (913/621-1134 and 913/383-1752, respectively). **Lidia's Italy** Kansas City. TV cooking star Lidia Bastianich's popular Italian restaurant, just south of downtown near Union Station (816/221-3722). **The Majestic Steakhouse** Kansas City. Dry-aged prime steaks, seafood and jazz in a historic landmark building just west of downtown (816/471-8484). **Stroud's** Kansas City. A longstanding restaurant known for its panfried chicken dinners served family-style, northeast of downtown (816/454-9600).

Featured Stops

College of the Ozarks Point Lookout (417/334-6411). **Silver Dollar City** (800/831-4386). **Brown's Candy Factory** Silver Dollar City (800/831-4386). **McHaffie's Homestead** Silver Dollar City (800/831-4386).

Hammons Products/Black Walnut Emporium Stockton (888/429-6887).

More Great Stops

Branson Forty miles south of Springfield, green hills and valleys surround this historic mountain town and three serpentine lakes that serve as a backdrop for south-central Missouri's live family-entertainment capital. Attractions include more than 100 shows in nearly 50 theaters; Silver Dollar City's renowned 1880s Ozark Mountain theme park, along with the Grand Exposition of 1882 area, opening in 2006; a variety of museums; shopping at Branson Landing and three outlet malls; and outdoor activities such as boating, fishing, hiking and golf. **Stone Hill Winery** Hermann. Offering a tasting room, gift shop and tours of the winery, which produces cream sherry and spumante (888/926-9463). The on-site restaurant specializes in German fare (800/909-9463). **Kansas City** Transformed from a rough-and-rowdy Old West outpost, this city of parks, boulevards, statues and fountains takes pride in attractions such as The Nelson-Atkins Museum of Art, with its 17-acre sculpture park; Kemper Museum of Contemporary Art; historic jazz district; restored beaux arts Union Station, including its Science City complex; and shopping, dining and entertainment in the historic Westport district, the high-rise Crown Center complex and amid the Spanish-style architecture of The Country Club Plaza. At the City Market just north of downtown, some 30 merchants sell produce, specialty foods and gift items (816/842-1271). This is one of the Midwest's largest farmers markets on Saturdays.

Dan's Lodgings

Chateau on the Lake Resort Southwest of Branson ($$$$; 888/333-5253). **Orleans Trail Resort & Marina** Along Stockton Lake, just southeast of Stockton ($ for cabinlike fourplexes, $$$$ for modern motel units with kitchenettes; 877/525-3886).

More Great Lodgings

Big Cedar Lodge Ten miles south of Branson, with restaurants, resort-style amenities and activities. Accommodations include lodge rooms ($$) and classy log cabins and suites ($$$$; 417/335-2777).

The Raphael Kansas City. A landmark hotel with 123 traditionally furnished rooms and suites, a restaurant and an old-world atmosphere on The Country Club Plaza ($$$; 800/821-5343).

Southmoreland Kansas City. A 1913 Colonial-style bed and breakfast with 12 rooms and one suite two blocks from The Country Club Plaza ($$$$; 816/531-7979).

Keeter Center College of the Ozarks, Point Lookout. Fifteen guest rooms and suites ($$$$) and 15 motel-style rooms nearby on campus ($; 417/239-1900).

Still Waters Resort Along Table Rock Lake just south of Silver Dollar City. A full marina for boating and fishing, plus seasonal motel rooms ($$) and condominiums ($$$; 800/777-2320).

Food Events

Wurstfest Hermann, fourth weekend in March (one week earlier if Easter falls on that weekend)—This sausage-making competition boasts the best of Missouri's wurst. Sample and buy bratwurst, *leberwurst, schwartenmagen* and *sommer* sausage made in Missouri. In the Wiener Dog Derby, dachshunds enter a fashion show, a longest-dog contest and races. German music and dancers entertain (800/932-8687, www.hermannmo.info).

Silver Dollar City Festivals Branson, April–December—Silver Dollar City theme park kicks off its festival season in April with World-Fest, starring international performers and foods. From mid-May through early June, the Bluegrass & BBQ festival pairs music acts with a saucy barbecue spread. Everybody sings "hallelujah" for the fried chicken and gospel music at the Southern Gospel Picnic in early September. Other festivals: National Kids' Fest (early June through mid-August), Festival of American Music & Crafts (mid-September

SILVER DOLLAR CITY.

through October) and An Old Time Christmas (November through December) (800/831-4386, www.silverdollarcity.com).

State Fair Sedalia, 11 days starting the second Thursday in August—At the historic Beef House, the Missouri Cattlemen's Association wrangles up its popular 10-ounce, Missouri-grown rib eye steak dinner (800/422-3247, www.mostatefair.com).

Ethnic Enrichment Festival Kansas City, third full weekend in August—"Taste the World" when more than 55 ethnic cultures come together in Swope Park to showcase their native foods and culture. Dozens of booths serve entrées such as American Indian fry bread, Lithuanian apricot torte, Jamaican jerk chicken, Japanese shrimp tempura and French crepes. You also can shop for authentic crafts from around the world (816/513-7553, www.eeckc.org).

Black Walnut Festival Stockton, last full weekend in September—Nutty about walnuts? Tour the plant of the world's largest black walnut processor (Hammons Products Co.), enter a walnut-cooking contest and buy black walnut candy and ice cream at this festival in the city park. Other attractions include a parade, live music, carriage rides through the park, and crafts demonstrations and sales (417/276-5213, www.stocktonmochamber.com).

American Royal Barbecue Kansas City, first weekend in October—At this contest, dubbed the "World Series of Barbecue," more than 500 teams cover 20 acres in the historic stockyards district to compete for $80,000 in prize money. Come hungry to the Barbecuelooza section to sample the fare from some of the city's finest barbecue joints at Restaurant Row. Concerts and fireworks light up both nights. The event is the opening competition at the American Royal livestock show, horse show and rodeo, which continues through mid-November. Admission charged (816/221-9800, www.americanroyal.com).

Mail Order

Arthur Bryant's Barbeque Legendary sauces and rubs from the "King of Ribs." Enjoy secret recipes at home by ordering Arthur Bryant's Original, Rich & Spicy or Sweet Heat Sauce and their Meat & Rib or Poultry & Fish Rub (816/231-1123, www.arthurbryantsbbq.com).

College of the Ozarks, Keeter Center Famous for fruitcakes produced on the Point Lookout campus since 1934. Student workers, along with supervisors, bake more than 40,000 cakes a year. Also available: a variety of jellies and preserves (417/334-6411, ext. 3395, www.cofo.edu).

Fiorella's Jack Stack Barbecue Award-winning hickory-barbecued meats originated in 1957 by the Fiorella family. Pork spareribs, pork burnt ends, beef brisket, barbecued sausage and legendary Hickory Pit Beans or KC Original BBQ Sauce all can be delivered to your door (877/419-7427, www.jackstackbbq.com).

Hammons Products Company Premier supplier of American Eastern black walnuts. Besides shelled and unshelled nuts, you can buy a variety of delectable black walnut specialties: fudge, brittle, pancake mix, syrup, pound cake, preserves and more. *Cooking with Black Walnuts* cookbook and gift tins are also available (800/872-6879, www.black-walnuts.com).

Wolferman's Legendary supersize English muffins and other irresistible bakery products from a specialty foods company started in 1888. Online store sells English muffins, crumpets and scones and offers delicious toppings, elegant desserts, premium teas and specially blended coffees. Gourmet gift boxes available (800/999-0169, www.wolfermans.com).

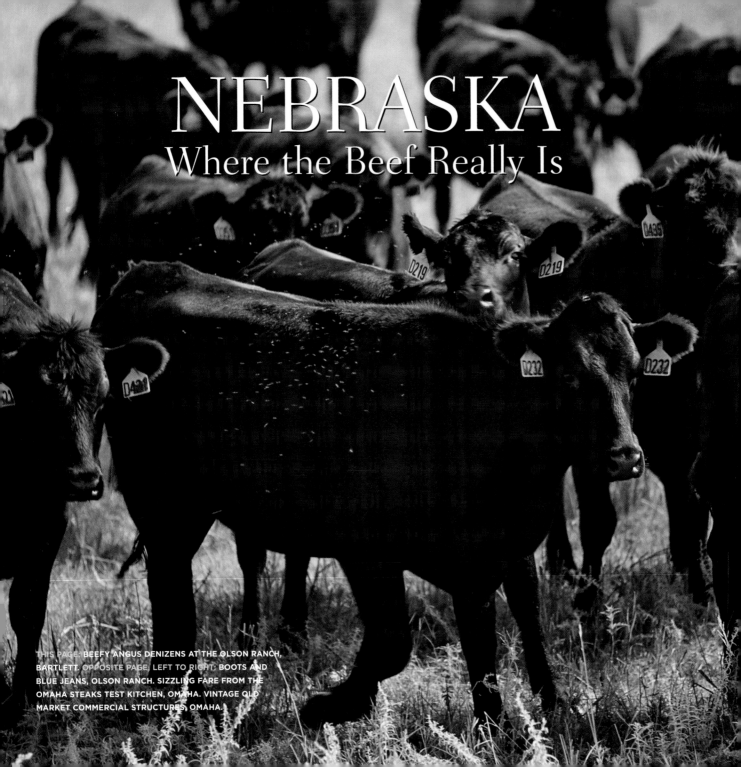

NEBRASKA
Where the Beef Really Is

THIS PAGE: BEEFY ANGUS DENIZENS AT THE OLSON RANCH, BARTLETT. OPPOSITE PAGE, LEFT TO RIGHT: BOOTS AND BLUE JEANS, OLSON RANCH. SIZZLING FARE FROM THE OMAHA STEAKS TEST KITCHEN, OMAHA. VINTAGE OLD MARKET COMMERCIAL STRUCTURES, OMAHA.

Nebraska has fed me well over the years. I spent most of my growing-up days in the Omaha area, so it was Nebraska cooks who stuffed me at holiday tables and carefree family-reunion picnics. It's time for a return visit.

Omaha also introduced me to the sublime satisfaction of a perfectly grilled Nebraska corn-fed steak, as well as my first "authentic" French dining experience. My wife, Julie, and I even attended our high-school senior prom in a ballroom atop the Livestock Exchange Building, a formidable 1926 office tower that for decades presided like a castle over South Omaha's huge warren of cattle pens. These days, the stockyards the city once proudly touted as the nation's largest are long gone, supplanted by vast green lawns.

I bivouac in downtown Omaha, the "Gateway to the West" (St. Louis' claim to the same title notwithstanding), several blocks from the swift-flowing Missouri River and just a few miles north of where it absorbs the lazy, shallow Platte River. That junction is one reason Omaha exists where it does, dating back to sites once occupied by native tribes, fur traders and even the Lewis and Clark Expedition.

An early-evening stroll is a revelation to me. Once wasted by urban renewal run amok, downtown Omaha has blossomed. In addition to sleek office towers and newer civic venues, it teems with restaurants that feed an urbane clientele of food-processing, telecommunications, biotechnology and insurance executives, as well as an impressive cadre of homegrown financiers that includes multibillionaire Warren Buffet (whose local steak-house hangout is Gorat's on Center Street).

When I was growing up, license plates proclaimed Nebraska's preeminence as the Beef State, and it's still that to me. Though sparsely populated, Nebraska is the nation's largest meat processor and exporter, ranking behind only much larger Texas when it comes to total cattle receipts. The state's ranchers raise almost 2 million head of cattle and corn-fatten or "finish" an additional 4.8 million for a total of about 7 million cattle slaughtered here each year. The overall impact of beef on the state's comparatively modest economy is enormous: almost $12 billion annually. Juicy and tender, rich with protein and iron, Nebraska corn-fed beef is savored throughout the nation and around the globe.

Although carnivores rule here, Nebraska also is known as the Cornhusker State (a name beloved by the state university's football fans). Corn, soybean and hog farms in eastern Nebraska gradually yield to a flat, polka-dot landscape of huge pivot-irrigated fields in the state's drier western reaches. The immense underground Ogallala Aquifer flows under more of Nebraska than any other state, with 2 billion acre-feet of water enabling semiarid counties to irrigate nearly 8 million acres of corn, wheat, grain sorghum, alfalfa hay, sugar beets and edible dry beans. Like ranchers and farmers everywhere these days, Nebraska growers aim to diversify even more with new, sometimes unexpected specialties such as grapes, buffalo, elk, ostriches and fish.

So, dear reader, please divest yourself of any stereotypes about this robustly contrasting state. In two discrete segments of my food journey, I'll roam both lofty urban canyons and sun-baked plains to assess Nebraska's topographical as well as culinary diversity. From steaks to snails, European-style pastries to mega cookies, sausage gravy to sauce béchamel, Nebraska warrants a second look.

A Feast of Apples—and Trees

Orchard crops (apples, peaches and cherries) are one of the "new" commodities Nebraska farmers are exploring these days. How quickly they forget: Back in the early 1900s, southeastern Nebraska's windblown loessial soil produced more apples than all the Pacific Northwest states combined. But during a deadly Armistice Day storm in 1940, trees still green with sap froze and some even exploded when the temperature dropped as much as 70 degrees. The industry never recovered here, but its memory is kept alive at the 1925 Kimmel Orchard, a demonstration farm, educational center and retail shop just north of charming, historic Nebraska City (population 7,500) and 45 minutes south of Omaha in the verdant Missouri River Valley.

I stop briefly to inspect 60 ripening acres of traditional Lodi, Delicious and Winesap apples, as well as the newer Gala, Braeburn and Honeycrisp varieties (among the 21 types grown at the Kimmel farm and 7,500 cultivars grown worldwide,

At Nebraska City's annual AppleJack Festival in September, visitors dig into a banquet of tasty apple delights.

2,500 in the United States alone!). For years, the orchard was operated by William Oberdieck, a German who'd worked here as a prisoner of war and returned after World War II to eventually purchase the place from his former overseer, Mr. Kimmel. With permission, I preview this year's crop and revel in the satisfaction of plucking an almost-ripe apple straight from the tree and savoring that first flavorful, tart and juicy crunch. (Do eat the peel: It's loaded with fiber and antioxidants.)

The Kimmel Orchard, owned by the Kimmel Charitable Foundation, is managed by the National Arbor Day Foundation in collaboration with the University of Nebraska and Nebraska City's Arbor Day

Farm, a legacy of leading citizen J. Sterling Morton, who died in 1902 (Morton Salt was founded by his son, Joy). Morton's passion was planting trees on the windswept Nebraska prairies. Here in Nebraska City, the newspaperman and former U.S. Secretary of Agriculture founded Arbor Day and left behind Arbor Lodge, a stately, white-columned home you still can visit.

The Nebraska-based National Arbor Day Foundation carries on Morton's mission and operates one of my favorite places in the state to stay and dine: the woodsy-feeling, Arts and Crafts–inspired Lied Lodge and Conference Center, perched like a Tibetan monastery on a hilltop beside 260 acres of beautifully wooded parks and preserves. A fun, albeit busy, time to visit is during Nebraska City's AppleJack Festival in September.

Local cooks tempt some 50,000 visitors with a banquet of apple delights: doughnuts, pie, wine, cider, caramel apples, apple butter—and much more.

Pioneers, Then and Now

Omaha dominates Nebraska, but in most respects, including cuisine, it's an urban anomaly in a wide-open Plains state. The "other" Nebraska is the fought-for pioneer land captured in prose decades ago by Willa Cather, one of the Midwest's most celebrated authors.

Cather grew up in Red Cloud (population 1,100) in south-central Nebraska and attended the state university in Lincoln. The brave settlers in Cather classics such as *My Antonia* and *O Pioneers!* brought with them a legacy of old-world food traditions—Czech, Swedish, German, Irish, French—that they resourcefully married with the harsh scarcities of life on the prairie. Cather's works often portray how the unforgiving Nebraska plains resisted the settlers' early attempts at farming, and she writes of struggling families eating mush, corn cakes and rabbit stew. Cather spent her later years in New York as a literary lioness until she died in 1947.

I have no culinary reason to stop in the author's hometown, but I long to visit the Cather Center, housed in a former small "opera house" on Main Street, and Cather's childhood home on Cedar Street. Then, sated in the literary sense, I'm off through the gentle Republican and Blue river valleys the author so hauntingly described to Hastings (population 24,000), about 40 miles north. This tidy former railroad hub now churns out a lot of the irrigation equipment that waters Nebraska crops.

My supper hour is spent in the convivial atmosphere of a classic tavern downtown, Murphy's Wagon Wheel. My meal is fan-

CLOCKWISE, FROM ABOVE: TRANSPORTATION AND COMMERCE, DOWNTOWN OMAHA. CLASSIC APPLE PIE, NEBRASKA CITY. ARBOR DAY FARM ADMONITION, NEBRASKA CITY. SOARING ARTS AND CRAFTS LOBBY, LIED LODGE, NEBRASKA CITY. OPPOSITE PAGE: WILLA CATHER'S CHILDHOOD HOME, RED CLOUD.

PLANT TREES

Awesome Peanut Butter Chocolate Chip Cookies

Inspired by Eileen's Colossal Cookies, Hastings

- 1 cup peanut butter
- 1/2 cup granulated sugar
- 1/2 cup packed brown sugar
- 1 teaspoon baking soda
- 1 egg
- 1/2 teaspoon vanilla
- 1 cup semisweet chocolate pieces
- 1/4 cup all-purpose flour

In a large bowl, beat peanut butter, granulated sugar, brown sugar and baking soda with an electric mixer on medium speed until combined, scraping sides of bowl occasionally. Beat in egg and vanilla until combined. Stir in chocolate pieces and flour.

Shape dough into 1 1/4-inch balls. Place 2 inches apart on an ungreased cookie sheet (do not use an insulated cookie sheet). Flatten slightly with your fingers.

Bake in a 325° oven about 10 minutes or until cookies are puffed and lightly browned around edges (centers will be soft). Cool on cookie sheet for 5 minutes. Transfer cookies to wire racks; cool completely. *Makes about 24 cookies.*

Note: To store, place cookies in layers separated by waxed paper in an airtight container; cover. Store at room temperature for up to 3 days or freeze for up to 3 months.

tastic: a charbroiled burger blanketed with melted Swiss cheese, bacon and mushrooms; Asian slaw, a vinaigrette creation made crunchy-good with Chinese noodles; and macho nachos, with the platter resembling Mount St. Helens in her active state.

The next morning, I find total satisfaction at the OK Café, a vestige of Hastings' railroad days, complete with a model train that clatters around the dining room at near-ceiling height every 27 minutes, with cars bearing messages from local merchants. I heartily devour three eggs, toast, bacon and sausage gravy over biscuits and then sample a monstrously big breakfast burrito packed with eggs, hash browns, sausage, onions and cheese—all swimming in a tasty, mild green chili sauce.

I've come to Hastings to learn about another Nebraska pioneer: entrepreneur extraordinaire Edwin Perkins, a farm boy who grew up in a sod house near Hendley and liked to experiment in the kitchen. Before long, he'd relocated to Hastings and had more than 100 inventions to his credit—toiletries, home remedies and an early stop-smoking aid—but his most famous product is Kool-Aid.

Sue Uerling, a staff member at Hastings' first-rate Museum of Natural and Cultural History, explains that Edwin's first take on the soft-drink mix was a concentrate called Fruit Smack, which he sold by mail. Then, inspired by Jell-O, he turned the liquid into a powder and started selling it for 10 cents a pack. When the Depression came along, he cut the price in half. America's financially pinched homemakers took to the novel drink mix as a low-cost treat for their families, and a success story unfolded.

As we walk through an impressive exhibit unveiled in 2002 to mark Kool-Aid's 75th anniversary, I learn that Edwin's genius resided as much in his promotional skills as in his product-development wizardry. He even printed his own flyers on a press in his home. On display is a boggling array of Kool-Aid merchandise: lunch boxes, canteens, kites, miniature toy cars and dolls, which have been hawked by characters including Captain Kangaroo, Bugs Bunny and, most indelibly, the smiley-faced Kool-Aid Man, who came along in 1975. As for the product, the formula is top secret (and now owned by Kraft). On average, 25 packages of Kool-Aid are sold every second. The tropical punch flavor rules, and there's even a new variation that won't stain when spilled. Edwin died a multimillionaire in 1961—by all accounts a kindly employer and loyal to his hometown to the end.

Another sweetly clever food entrepreneur also hails from Hastings: Eileen Harman, a former homemaker who became a cookie queen. As I turn onto Second Street, where Eileen's store is located, I'm reminded of what Midwest downtowns used to look like, before mega malls arrived on the scene: well-kept and busy. There's a jewelry store, a clothing store, a bookstore, a pet shop—and, under a big yellow-and-orange-striped awning, Eileen's Colossal Cookies.

I walk into the bright yellow interior and begin to order from the display case: lemon-lemon, sunflower, chocolate chip–walnut, sugar, snickerdoodle, monster oatmeal, peanut butter, oatmeal scotchie, white chocolate–macadamia nut, oatmeal-raisin, oatmeal–chocolate chip.

Eileen always considered herself a competent cookie baker (her mother was her inspiration and the source of many of her original recipes), but then she got serious and started the venture in her basement. These days, she owns three shops in Nebraska (the other two are in Kearney and Grand Island) and has nine franchisees elsewhere in the state as well as in

Colorado, Wyoming, Oklahoma and Montana. She's set her sights on conquering South Dakota and Arizona.

Eileen's secret? "Make 'em big and soft, with quality ingredients." The Hastings store alone sells about 200 dozen cookies a day and an Omaha franchisee sells double that number, including custom-decorated cookies as big as 16 inches across that help people mark special occasions.

All that gooey goodness requires a weekly supply of sixteen 500-pound bags of flour, ten 50-pound bags of sugar and eight 25-pound boxes of chocolate chips. Eileen even has a mega cookie decorated with a *Taste of the Midwest* logo while I watch! Stuffed and on an incredible sugar high, I leave to navigate the Nebraska prairies, clutching a sack full of Eileen's finest for the drive ahead.

More Fill 'Er Up Breakfasts

In my main Nebraska venue, Omaha (metro population 800,000), I eat two breakfasts that reveal contrasting aspects of the city's surprisingly diverse palate, as well as a common denominator: They're Nebraska-hearty! First, the 11 Worth Café downtown (on Leavenworth Street), a no-nonsense city diner in a gritty neighborhood and on the same block as the Lutheran Thrift Shop, Four Aces Snack and Tobacco and All Nations Grocery.

Historical photos of Omaha decorate this otherwise plain but spotless eatery, which serves a clientele of businesspeople, college students and a few denizens of the city's street scene. There's a lunch counter, and people can smoke in several rooms here. At a booth with a view, I order three fried eggs, bacon, toast, hash browns and biscuits with creamy sausage gravy (available to go by the quart and half gallon).

For another take on Omaha breakfast, I head "out west," as the locals like to say, to

CLOCKWISE, FROM ABOVE: (ALL TAKEN IN HASTINGS) FESTIVAL REMINDER AT A DOWNTOWN INTERSECTION. DAN AND A CUSTOM-DECORATED CREATION AT EILEEN'S COLOSSAL COOKIES. A FROSTY PITCHER OF HASTINGS' SIGNATURE REFRESHMENT.

KOOL-AID DAYS AUGUST 12TH–14TH

WheatFields, in a suburban office park just off Pacific Street. I'm bowled over by the extensive selections at this self-styled European bakery and restaurant. Founder Ron Popp grew up on hearty German farm food in nearby Dow City, Iowa, and is well known to Omaha-area diners for the erstwhile Garden Cafe chain he founded.

Like many Omahans, Ron's wife, Ruth Ann, settled here after a globe-trotting childhood in a military family (Offutt Air Force Base is in nearby Bellevue). For the WheatFields menu, she drew on memories of Europe and recipes contributed by loyal customers. I gaze upon a mouthwatering array of pastries inspired by bakers from Germany, Austria, Switzerland, Sweden, France—and even Liechtenstein and the Czech Republic: golden, buttery croissants; kolaches (yeast buns with fruit and other fillings); bismarcks (fruit-filled raised doughnuts); and pecan rolls.

Tons of cookies, bars and brownies and an astonishing array of pies and cakes make me feel as if I'm lost in a giant gingerbread house. The place is peppered with Teutonic trinkets and stencils of German proverbs such as *Essen und trinken halt lieb und seele suzzamen* ("Food and drink keep body and soul together").

My group's selections fill a tabletop: bountiful quiches, enormous omelets, breakfast strata casseroles, waffles (be sure to try the colorful fruit-crowned Grand Floridian), plus a few breakfast wraps. Oh, and rich breads and pastries; the orange caramel rolls are to die for. Ron tells me his staff aims to try a new recipe every day. By the time my friends and I finish, I believe we've sampled the entire year's quota at one delicious sitting!

Steak, Escargot and Carrot Cake

Omaha is the birthplace of the couch potato's culinary dream: the frozen TV dinner, introduced here by C.A. Swanson & Sons back in 1954. But today, metro-area residents leave their homes to dine in more than 1,000 eateries of various types, including several dozen that classify themselves strictly as steak houses and many more that highlight Nebraska steaks among varied specialties. International-cuisine options range from Vietnamese and Thai to Middle Eastern, Greek and Bohemian.

I plan to sample a variety of Omaha dining spots, but which ones? I'm not alone in my quandary: In the elevator of my hotel, I overhear two businessmen—one from Tampa and the other from Seattle—plotting which steak houses they'll patronize during their brief stay in beef heaven. I note that two on their list (Mr. C's and Caniglia's Venice Inn) are operated by the Caniglias, one of the Italian-American families whose surnames still mean "steak" in Omaha (one of the Caniglias also owns the 11 Worth Café, scene of my first breakfast).

I decide to start by having a little fun along with my filet at Brother Sebastian's

Steakhouse and Winery, a mildly kitschy suburban steak house on Omaha's west side. Back in 1977, University of Nebraska graduate Loren Koch (pronounced Cook) decided to open his own steak house. Loren knew he needed a gimmick to attract diners, so he chose the first name of actor Sebastian Cabot, who had played a TV detective in the 1960s, and a monastery–wine cellar decorative motif.

In homage to the hospitable, kind friars who dedicate their lives to the care of their fellow man, he outfitted his waiters as hooded monks and played somber chants on the speaker system outside. Brother Sebastian's was born! Very clever—but he also needed to "deliver the beef" in this steak-savvy town.

Loren's filets, sirloins and T-bones definitely pass muster, and he shares his secrets: For good grilling material, age beef until it's a grayish-pink color. Look for well-marbled cuts. Choose meat from a heifer (that's a young cow) rather than a tough old steer, and don't let anyone sell you steak from a dairy cow who's gotten her final notice. Never order a steak medium-well or well-done if you can help it: You're just letting all the goodness cook out.

Brother Sebastian's steaks are aged 21 days before they arrive here, then another seven to 10 days on the premises. The most popular cuts have remained the same through the years: filets, strip steaks and prime rib. In the kitchen, I watch a cook determine doneness strictly by feel—no clocks or thermometers required.

My next date is with a porterhouse fit for a king at Johnny's Café, right next to the old stockyards on L Street. If you saw *About Schmidt*, a 2002 movie starring Jack Nicholson as an emotionally moribund retiree, you saw Johnny's—it was the setting for Schmidt's retirement dinner. Co-owner Sally Kawa, granddaughter of founder Frank "Smiling Johnny" Kawa, even appeared on-screen during the movie as the restaurant hostess.

Johnny's started out as a tavern back in 1922 and prospered along with Omaha's meatpacking industry. Early menus on display include cafe selections not often seen these days: braised ox joints, stewed chicken and dumplings, corned beef and cabbage, calf's liver, sweetbread, Swiss steak. (Many of those entrées still are available as lunchtime specials.)

The place was patronized by cattlemen and cowboys who left their calling cards in the form of cow manure on the then-linoleum floors. South Omaha packing-house workers—Polish, Irish, Czech, German and Italian—also kept the place hopping from 6 a.m. to 1 a.m. daily. "There were so many cattle trucks lined up out on L Street back then, men would hop out and ask the driver ahead or behind to move their vehicle while they came in for a meal," Sally tells me.

Johnny's is a lot grander and tamer these days. Now rather isolated on an awkward traffic island, it's in a cavernous, 1970s-

Steak House Bread Pudding

Johnny's Café, Omaha

    2 eggs, slightly beaten
    2 cups whole milk
    1 cup sugar
  1/4 cup butter, melted
    1 tablespoon vanilla
 2 1/2 teaspoons ground cinnamon
    4 cups dry French bread cubes or regular
       bread cubes (6 to 7 slices bread)
  2/3 cup raisins
       Bread Pudding Glaze (recipe follows)

In a large bowl, beat together eggs, milk, sugar, melted butter, vanilla and cinnamon. In a greased 2-quart square baking dish, toss together bread cubes and raisins; pour egg mixture evenly over bread mixture. Press the mixture lightly with the back of a large spoon.

Bake, uncovered, in a 350° oven for 45 to 50 minutes or until puffed and set. Cool slightly. Cut hot bread pudding into 8 pieces; place each in a shallow dessert dish. Pour the warm Bread Pudding Glaze over the bread pudding. Serve immediately. *Makes 8 servings.*

Bread Pudding Glaze: In a medium saucepan, combine 1/2 of a 14-ounce (2/3 cup) can of sweetened condensed milk, one 5-ounce can evaporated milk and 3 egg yolks. Whisk mixture over medium heat for 6 to 8 minutes or until mixture slightly thickens and just begins to boil. Remove from heat. Stir in 3 tablespoons whiskey. Cover and keep warm.

style building with huge bronze doors depicting icons such as longhorn cattle and sandhill cranes. Inside, everything is red and black under steel structural beams that resemble T-bones. Historical stock-yard photos and various stuffed critters decorate the bar, but the real attraction is a mean-looking mounted longhorn whose orange eyes light up when the bartender pushes a button to activate a nasty bellow.

Sally and her co-owner and sister, Kari, are both hospitality graduates of the University of Nevada at Las Vegas. They give me a full tour and let me pick out my own 22-ounce porterhouse from the kitchen cooler. In minutes, I'm admiring a classic steak-house feast: Crackers and a home-made cottage-cheese-and-chive spread. A huge order of hand-cut and -battered onion rings. A salad with anchovies, crumbled blue cheese and vinaigrette that's a bit on the sweet side. Potatoes au gratin. And the real star—that home-run porter-house, with a wine-and-mushroom sauce on the side. For dessert there's gooey bread pudding with whiskey sauce.

I'd be doing Omaha a serious injustice if I limited myself to red meat here, so the day after my steak-house spree, I head back downtown for two elegant, early-afternoon lunches about a mile apart on historic Howard Street. The first is at the Flatiron Café, noteworthy for its setting and creative fare. The restaurant is in the four-story Flatiron Building, listed on the National Register of Historic Places and one of the gems that survived Omaha's wave of urban renewal. It's a smaller, terra-cotta-colored brick version of the much larger original, a pioneering New York sky-scraper completed in 1902. The cafe occupies the triangular prow of the street level, a once-neglected space rescued by husband-and-wife restaurateurs Steve and Kathleen Jamrozy (JAMrosy).

Kathleen is the spokesperson for this pair, who live with their three children close enough that Steve can ride his bicy-cle to work. "We're all about the new American cuisine," Kathleen tells me: an emphasis on fresh, often organically grown seasonal ingredients in creative interpreta-tions of classic dishes. "We have a man who comes to the kitchen door here with homegrown green beans in season, another with morels he finds in the woods," she says.

Reminding me that this is "just our lunch menu," Kathleen treats me to an impressive array of creative dishes: breast of free-range chicken seasoned with fen-nel and coriander, served on a green pea–potato risotto; a dazzling sauteed shrimp with sherry, tarragon, mustard and cream on a bed of purple "forbidden rice" and fava beans; pomegranate-glazed duck breast with a leek-garlic fondue. And for dessert? "The mixed-berry short-cake and, well, I think my carrot cake kills," Kathleen says with a purr. It really does, distinguished by several varieties of plump raisins and a yummy coconut-pecan filling.

My second lunch is at The French Café in downtown Omaha's compact Old Mar-ket district, which is seductive in a disheveled sort of way: wavy brick streets, flat metal awnings that shade sidewalk diners, potted flowers, vintage lampposts, slightly tipsy brick buildings that once housed produce wholesalers. It's Omaha's Greenwich Village, an old yet trendy shop-ping and dining area, popular with visitors and locals alike. Restaurants here run the gamut, from the family-friendly Spaghetti Works to more sophisticated spots such as V. Mertz (eclectic cuisine) and an interna-tional array of Indian, Persian, Chinese, Mongolian, German and Japanese eater-ies. And The French Café, where Julie and

I, as a couple of starry-eyed college students, had our first multicourse French meal—*with wine*. (I've promised to phone Julie to tell her whether the French onion soup is as wonderful now as it was then.)

Omaha may be one of the last places you'd expect to find bona fide French cuisine, so imagine what the locals must have thought back in 1969 when world-wise but Nebraska-friendly Tony Abbott and his landlord partners opened The French Café, boasting an elegantly understated, black-and-white dining room. The restaurant, with its green-glass lampshades hovering over each table and one huge wall dominated by images of Parisian street and market scenes, hasn't changed.

"I owe a lot to Julia Child," Tony says as we chat at a table outside under the sidewalk awning. "Her cookbooks and TV programs got people curious about French cooking and gave them the courage to try it here." When he opened the cafe, Tony says, Omaha was steak houses, Italian eateries and some Chinese fare.

"In those early days, we were classically French, in the style of Escoffier [the Paris chef who defined French cooking for decades at the Ritz Hotel—he died in 1929]. Our staff came from France. We spoke French. The menu was in French. Now, we're more relaxed, less stuffy. We want to make people feel comfortable. If you use the wrong fork, we'll replace it," Tony says with a laugh. Looking around me, I observe that the once-rigid dress code has relaxed as well; it's all about casual elegance these days.

Tony and Omaha-raised Executive Chef Brian Younglove still base their cuisine on those French classics made with buttery sauces and rich stocks—the de rigueur crusty baguettes and delicate croissants; French onion soup gratiné; garlicky and buttery *escargots bourguignonne*; Chateau-

CLOCKWISE, FROM TOP LEFT: (ALL TAKEN IN OMAHA) YELLOWFIN TUNA AT THE FLATIRON CAFÉ DOWNTOWN. KATHLEEN JAMROZY, CO-PROPRIETOR OF THE FLATIRON CAFÉ. ESCARGOT AT THE FRENCH CAFÉ. CHIC SIDEWALK SETTING AT THE FRENCH CAFÉ.

briand; *canard* (duck) *à l'orange*; *le carré d'agneau* (herb-encrusted rack of lamb); baked Brie; and *fromages du jour,* all complemented by a stellar selection of wines.

But there are other options and interpretations on the menu now as well: grilled salmon, grilled prawns, Dover sole, pepper steak, scallops, cheesecake, chocolate mousse—all of which I sample appreciatively. That French onion soup still is made with caramelized sweet onions combined with homemade beef and veal stock flavored with sherry and herbs, layered with oven-baked bread and topped with cheese. I'll definitely give Julie a glowing report.

Home on the Range

As much as I love Omaha's steak houses, I want to learn more about other links in the beef food chain here in Nebraska. So, I'm off to the headquarters of an internationally known mail-order purveyor of prime steaks and an honest-to-goodness beef ranch on the outskirts of the Sandhills.

My first stop is a contemporary test kitchen at the modern offices of Omaha Steaks, just off a freeway in sprawling southwestern Omaha. Here, I'll learn how to properly grill a steak from a master: Executive Chef Karl Marsh, who presides over the company's product development and recipe testing. (Our *Taste of the Midwest* public television crew is filming today, but Karl isn't bashful in front of a camera; he appears regularly on the Home Shopping Network.) "We're into value-added products," Karl informs me. "We sell about 20 marinades and rubs alone!"

When it comes to my grilling lesson, Karl is patient but quite precise. He's thawed two 6-ounce filets in cold water for about a half hour (they come frozen and last up to six months in your home freezer). We brush the steaks lightly with olive oil and sprinkle them with pepper and seasoned salt. Mean-

while, Karl has fired up the grill to almost 600 degrees. After searing the steaks on both sides to seal in their proverbial juices and "caramelize the protein on the outside," he explains the 60:40 method: "Cook the steak 60 percent of the time on one side and 40 percent on the second side." For these 1-inch-thick filets, that's six minutes and four minutes. Karl recommends calling it quits at medium-rare (about 135 degrees) and letting the meat rest for two or three minutes, which keeps the juices in the meat rather than on the plate. The result? Fork-tender, flavorful and quite juicy.

Omaha Steaks began with J.J. Simon and his son, B.A., Latvian immigrants who became meat wholesalers in Omaha's Old Market district back in 1917. As their business flourished, they added Union Pacific Railroad to their list of clients. Passengers who got a taste of Nebraska beef in the rail company's glorious dining cars wanted more. So, the Simons started wrapping their beef in butcher paper, packing it on ice and shipping it by rail to customers across the nation.

By the early 1950s, three developments set the stage for the company's phenomenal growth: improved parcel post service, the introduction of plastic-foam packaging and technology that enabled flash-freezing and vacuum-sealing. A few small ads in the *New Yorker* magazine, and Omaha Steaks International (now just Omaha Steaks) was on its way.

Today, this five-generation family business generates $400 million in annual sales; 90 percent of that is from filling consumer orders that come in via phone and Internet. The Simons also operate 70 retail stores in 16 states and supply many other fine-food retailers, as well as chains and independent restaurants. The huge Omaha Steaks call center is open 24/7, and the shipping center fires off 65,000 packages per day during peak holiday ordering season.

I stroll the 400 workstations in the call center, where friendly Omahans take orders from their clientele, many of whom are repeat customers who ask for the same order taker. The entire Omaha Steaks operation requires 1,800 employees, and double that during the holiday season!

Todd Simon, a great-great-grandson of J.J., tells me what the magic of the Omaha Steaks name is. "It's like Alaska salmon or Maine lobster; people just believe in that

The Omaha Steaks shipping center fires off 65,000 packages per day during peak holiday ordering season.

connection," Todd explains as we walk through a company retail store a few blocks away. The product line has expanded to include poultry and pork, fish and seafood, burgers and brats, seasonings and side dishes such as potatoes, pasta and salsa—all premium-quality products blessed by the golden Omaha Steaks brand. "People do consume less meat these days than they used to, and they want leaner cuts. But they want the very best—and this is it," Todd says, as he urges me to take home a bottle of chipotle seasoning to try when I apply my new-found grilling expertise back home.

Northwest of Omaha's busy freeways, cornfields gradually yield to a 20,000-square-mile ocean of windblown dunes held in place by a thin cloak of soil and short grasses. Here in the Sandhills, one county alone—Cherry—is larger than several small states and is inhabited by 6,100 people and 294,000 cattle and calves.

Despite high prices, low-fat diets, and mad cow disease scares, Americans love their beef. And why not? One modest 3-ounce portion is loaded with as much iron as three chicken breasts or three cups of spinach, plus oodles of protein, vitamins and minerals—not to mention juicy, satisfying flavor. Much of the latter lies in the meat's little white flecks of fat called marbling, which are most apparent in beef that's classified "prime" by the USDA, a little less so in the "choice" grade and even less in the leaner and less-expensive "select" grade. Of course, a lot also has to do with the breed of cattle, what those cattle are fed and how the meat is ultimately trimmed and aged.

About 10 miles northeast of tiny Bartlett (population 128), I sit on the front porch of a huge gray mansion, chatting with rancher John Olson. The imposing foursquare, worthy of a gothic novel, no longer is occupied. It was built in 1906 for Chicago tycoon Samuel W. Allerton, who knew a good deal when he saw one (he owned Chicago's Union Stockyards and First National Bank, along with vast landholdings throughout the nation); eventually he amassed a cattle-grazing empire in this area. Using sand from the Sandhills to help form blocks that resemble rough-cut stone, workers built Allerton a virtual palace, even though he never lived here permanently.

Allerton's successors sold the ranch around 1918, and the Olson family, who came to Nebraska from Sweden in the 1870s, purchased it in 1937. Thanks to them, the house remains in generally solid condition and is used for special family and community gatherings. The Olsons—John

CLOCKWISE, FROM TOP LEFT: TODD SIMON HELPING DAN STOCK UP AT AN OMAHA STEAKS RETAIL STORE, OMAHA. UP CLOSE AND PERSONAL AT THE OLSON RANCH, BARTLETT. HISTORIC ALLERTON MANSION, OLSON RANCH.

JOHN OLSON AT HIS RANCH.

and his wife, Chris, and his parents—live in more modern homes on the property.

John and I hop into a pickup truck to view more of the ranch, which encompasses 30,000 acres. I survey a soothing landscape comprising pastures, streams, cottonwoods, windmills (65 of them all told, to bring up groundwater for John's cattle)—and lots of blue sky. Some fields, naturally irrigated by the exceptionally high water table, yield corn and alfalfa hay that, along with grass, feed the Olsons' 2,000 Angus cow-calf pairs.

When they are about 18 months old and weigh about 1,300 pounds each, John's calves are sold to huge corporate packinghouses to be served up as prime beef at top restaurants and retailers. A brood cow typically spends 12 years on the ranch, giving birth to a calf each March after being bred each June. Then, her reproductive life over, the mom typically winds up as inexpensive hamburger.

How do you run a ranch this expansive? John has eight full-time employees,

including a foreman and four cowhands—plus part-timers and neighbors who help out when needed, such as when cattle are branded and vaccinated in spring. John and his cowboys still spend a lot of time in the saddle, but they also use about a dozen pickup trucks and 35 tractors, all serviced by a full-time mechanic. John is into computers, spreadsheets and other modern management stuff.

What challenges does he face? "Always, the weather: blizzards in winter, heat and drought in summer," he says. "And my costs keep increasing for fuel, fertilizer and equipment." (Despite all that, returns have been good in recent years.) During busy summer days, John is up at 5:30 a.m.—troubleshooting, checking on his cattle, mending barbed-wire fences and working on his computer until he turns in at about 11:30 p.m.

I ask about the big, numbered yellow ear tags John's beeves sport like a little girl's hair ribbons. "They're for identification and tracking purposes, such as health records," he says. "One day, I'll probably go to electronic tags." But, beware, all you rustlers: Cattle are still branded out here on the Sandhills. The Nebraska Brand Committee currently has nearly 37,000 brands on record statewide and a field force of 60 full-time brand inspectors.

I tell John he strikes me as a 21st-century rancher, following a way of life that's unchanged in many respects from frontier days, yet savvy about using computers and technology. "Well, I'm a 20th-century rancher, at least," he says with a chuckle. "I like this life. It's good to be outdoors, working with livestock." From what I've seen on my brief sortie around the Olson Ranch, I heartily concur: It's good to be here in the Sandhills once again, and it's good to have returned to Nebraska for an all-too-brief reprise taste of one of my home states.

Little Orange Caramel Rolls
WheatFields Eatery & Bakery, Omaha

    5 to 5½ cups all-purpose flour
    1 cup warm water or milk (105° to 115°)
    ⅔ cup sugar
    2 packages active dry yeast
    3 eggs
    1 teaspoon kosher salt or ½ teaspoon salt
    ½ cup butter, cut into small pieces and
        softened
    ⅓ cup butter, softened
    ⅓ cup sugar
        Orange Caramel Goo (recipe follows)

In a large mixing bowl, combine 1½ cups of the flour, the water, 1 tablespoon of the ⅔ cup sugar and the yeast. Beat with electric mixer on medium speed for 2 minutes or until smooth. (The mixture will be thick and sticky.) Cover with plastic wrap. Let stand at room temperature about 30 minutes or until mixture is bubbly.

Add the eggs, salt and the remainder of the ⅔ cup sugar to the flour mixture. Beat on medium speed about 2 minutes or until smooth. Add the ½ cup butter a few pieces at a time and beat until well combined. Using a wooden spoon, stir in as much of the remaining flour as you can.

Turn dough out onto a lightly floured surface. Knead in enough of the remaining flour to make a moderately soft dough that is smooth and elastic (3 to 5 minutes total). Shape dough into a ball. Butter a large bowl. Place the dough into bowl, turning once. Cover; let rise in a warm place until dough doubles in size (about 1 hour).

Punch dough down. Divide in half. Turn out onto a lightly floured surface. Cover; let rest for 10 minutes. Meanwhile, lightly grease two 13x9x2-inch baking pans; set aside. Divide and evenly spread the slightly warm Orange Caramel Goo in prepared pans.

Roll each half of the dough into a 12x8-inch rectangle. Divide and evenly

spread the 1/3 cup softened butter over dough rectangles; sprinkle with the 1/3 cup sugar. Roll up each rectangle starting from a long side. Seal seams. Slice each roll into 12 pieces. Place cut sides down in pans.

Cover dough loosely with plastic wrap, leaving room for rolls to rise. Chill for 2 to 24 hours. Uncover; let stand at room temperature for 30 minutes. (To bake rolls right away, don't chill dough. Cover dough loosely with plastic wrap; let rise in a warm place until nearly double in size, about 30 minutes.) Break any surface bubbles with a greased toothpick.

Bake in a 350° oven for 25 to 30 minutes or until light brown (if necessary, cover rolls with foil the last 5 minutes to prevent over-browning). Remove from oven. Let the rolls stand in the pans for 10 minutes. Carefully invert rolls onto serving trays. Serve warm. *Makes 24.*

Orange Caramel Goo: In a saucepan, combine 1 1/4 cups sugar, 1/3 cup butter, 1/3 cup whipping cream, 1 teaspoon finely shredded orange peel, 2 tablespoons orange juice, 1 teaspoon lemon juice, 1/4 teaspoon orange extract and 1/8 teaspoon salt. Cook and stir over medium-low heat for 5 minutes. Remove from heat; cool slightly.

Best-Ever Nebraska Burgers
Inspired by Nebraska beef

 1 egg, lightly beaten
 1/2 cup water
 1 1/2 teaspoons instant beef bouillon granules
 1/4 cup finely chopped onion, leek, shallot or green onion
 1/4 cup grated Parmesan, Romano or Asiago cheese
 2 tablespoons snipped fresh basil or parsley or 1 teaspoon dried basil or parsley, crushed
 2 tablespoons Worcestershire sauce or steak sauce
 1 teaspoon garlic powder
 1/2 teaspoon freshly ground black pepper
 1 pound lean ground beef
 1 pound ground pork
 8 onion buns, hamburger buns or kaiser rolls, split and toasted
   Mustard Sauce (recipe follows)
   Lettuce leaves (optional)
   Thin tomato slices (optional)
   Thin red onion slices (optional)
   Dill pickle spears (optional)

In a large bowl, thoroughly combine egg, water and bouillon granules. Stir in onion, cheese, basil, Worcestershire sauce, garlic powder and black pepper. Add ground beef and pork. Using clean hands, gently combine the egg mixture and ground meats. (Ingredients need to be evenly distributed. Use your hands to mix the meats and seasonings, but it is important to handle ground-meat mixture as little as possible for a more tender, moist burger.)

Shape the meat mixture into eight 3/4-inch-thick patties.

For a charcoal grill, grill patties on the greased rack of an uncovered grill directly over medium coals for 14 to 18 minutes or until meat is done (an instant-read thermometer inserted into burgers should register 160°), turning once halfway through grilling. (For a gas grill, lightly grease the grill rack; preheat grill. Reduce heat to medium. Place patties on grill rack over heat. Cover and grill burgers as above.)

Remove burgers from grill. Serve burgers on buns with Mustard Sauce. If you like, top burgers with lettuce, tomato and onion and serve with pickle spears. *Makes 8 servings.*

Mustard Sauce: In a small bowl, combine 1/3 cup stone-ground mustard, 2 tablespoons beer or apple juice, 1 tablespoon honey and 1/2 teaspoon Worcestershire sauce or steak sauce. *Makes about 1/2 cup.*

Apple Orchard Oatmeal
Lied Lodge and Conference Center, Nebraska City

 3 cups apple cider or apple juice
 1/4 teaspoon salt
 1 cup steel-cut oats
 1/2 cup apple pie filling or sweetened chunky applesauce
 1/2 teaspoon ground cinnamon (optional)
 2/3 cup milk
 1/2 cup raisins, dried cherries or dried cranberries (optional)
   Brown sugar (optional)

In a medium saucepan, bring apple cider and salt to boiling. Stir in oats. Simmer, covered, about 20 minutes or until oats are just tender and liquid is nearly absorbed. Stir in apple pie filling and, if you like, cinnamon. Serve with milk. If you like, sprinkle with raisins and/or brown sugar. Serve immediately. *Makes 6 (2/3 cup) servings.*

Travel Journal

More Information

Greater Omaha Convention & Visitors Bureau (866/937-6624, www.visit omaha.com). **Hastings/Adams County Convention & Visitors Bureau** (800/967-2189, www.visithastingsnebraska.com). **Nebraska City Chamber & Tourism** (800/514-9113, www.nebraskacity.com). **Red Cloud Chamber of Commerce** (402/746-2211, www.redcloud nebraska.com).

Featured Dining

Murphy's Wagon Wheel Hastings (402/463-3011).
OK Café Hastings (402/461-4663).
Timber Dining Room At the Lied Lodge and Conference Center, Nebraska City (402/873-8740).
Brother Sebastian's Steakhouse & Winery Omaha (402/330-0300).
11 Worth Café Omaha (402/346-6924).
Flatiron Café Omaha (402/334-3040).
The French Café Omaha (402/341-3547).
Johnny's Café Omaha (402/731-4774).
WheatFields Omaha (402/955-1485).

More Great Dining

The Embers Nebraska City. A local dining tradition for casual atmosphere and favorites such as prime rib, fried chicken and homemade soups (402/873-6416).
Bohemian Café Omaha. Open since 1924, this local favorite specializes in authentic Czech and Eastern European fare (402/342-9838).
Gorat's Steak House Omaha, southwest of downtown. A fixture since 1944, serving steaks, chicken, seafood and pasta in a family-friendly setting; live music in the lounge on weekends (402/551-3733).
Mister C's Steak House Omaha, north of downtown. An Italian steak house that began as a drive-in more than 50 years ago, featuring a full menu and specializing in prime beef and Italian favorites (402/451-1998).
V. Mertz Omaha. A classy restaurant and wine bar (some 370 selections) in the fruit cellar of an 1800s Old Market warehouse, with a changing menu of contemporary dishes such as mussel and shrimp soufflé (402/345-8980).

Featured Stops

Eileen's Colossal Cookies Hastings (402/462-2572).
Museum of Natural and Cultural History Hastings (800/508-4629).
Arbor Day Farm Nebraska City. Two hundred and sixty acres of lawns, orchards and an arboretum surrounding Lied Lodge and Conference Center and adjacent to the 52-room mansion of Arbor Day founder J. Sterling Morton. Check out the gift shop and the Tree Adventure program, providing access to miles of trails, the interactive Woodland Pavilion, the 50-foot-high Canopy Tree House and Lied Greenhouse (402/873-8717; 402/873-8710 for gift shop).
Kimmel Orchard Nebraska City. With 80 acres of apple trees and the Apple Barn, including a market, gift shop, lunch restaurant and cider/apple juice–processing operation (402/873-5293).
Omaha Steaks Omaha, with three retail stores (402/593-4223).
Willa Cather Pioneer Memorial & Educational Foundation Red Cloud. For guided tours of seven 1880s buildings, including the author's childhood home (402/746-2653).

More Great Stops

Omaha This vigorous city, Nebraska's largest, sports a downtown of sleek glass-and-steel skyscrapers neighboring the 12-square-block Old Market warehouse district of trendy restaurants, shops and nightspots. Besides the noted Joslyn Art Museum and Durham Western Heritage Museum, Omaha counts among its attractions a children's museum and Latino museum; botanical gardens; a world-class zoo; and Father Flanagan's Girls and Boys Town, a National Historic Landmark open for tours. Other attractions cluster 20 miles southwest of the city along I-80 (exit 426), including Eugene T. Mahoney State Park, a 690-acre preserve with outdoor recreation, cabins, a lodge and a dining room; a drive-through Wildlife Safari; and the soaring Strategic Air & Space Museum.
Nebraska City This hilly river town of wide streets and gracious homes lists more than 300 structures on the National Register of Historic Places—both downtown, with its specialty and antiques shops and factory-outlet stores, and in residential neighborhoods, where some homes are open for tours. Other attractions include the 1850s Mayhew Cabin (last stop on Nebraska's Underground Railroad) and Historical Village; Old Freighter's Museum, documenting the town's history as a transportation hub (open by appointment); and a major factory-outlet mall.

Dan's Lodgings

Comfort Inn Hastings ($$; 800/228-5150).
Hilton Garden Inn Downtown Omaha ($$$; 877/782-9444).
Lied Lodge and Conference Center Nebraska City ($$$; 800/546-5433).

More Great Lodgings

Sandhills Guest Ranch Brewster. A 5,000-acre working cattle spread about 90 miles northeast of North Platte, with guest lodgings in a red cedar barn and country cabin ($$), plus a bunkhouse ($). Activities include bird-watching, canoeing and joining in ranch chores (bring your own horse; 308/547-2460).
Double R Ranch Mullen, about 85 miles northwest of North Platte. A 5,000-acre working cattle spread established at the turn of the 19th century, with lodgings in three modern cabins ($). Activities include bird-watching, deer hunting, canoeing, fishing, trail rides and joining in ranch chores (horses provided; 866/217-2042).
Best Western Nebraska City Nebraska City. Across from the outlet mall just south of town ($; 800/937-8376).

WHEATFIELDS, OMAHA

Whispering Pines Bed and Breakfast Nebraska City. A restored Victorian home surrounded by more than six acres of trees and gardens just northeast of town ($$; 402/873-5850).

Downtown Courtyard by Marriott Omaha. In a renovated brick building near the Old Market district ($$$; 800/228-9290).

Hampton Inn Westroads Omaha. Across from the Westroads Mall, about 14 miles west of the Old Market downtown ($$$; 800/426-7866).

Peter Kiewit Lodge At Mahoney State Park, southwest of Omaha. With 40 lodge rooms ($) and 53 cabins ($$; 402/944-2523).

Food Events

Mennonite Central Committee Craft and Quilt Auction Aurora, first weekend in April—Plan to feast on home-cooked Russian-German fare when you come to bid on handmade quilts, furniture, toys and other wares that Mennonite churches auction for world relief. The *verenika* dinner gets everyone's bid: *verenika* (cottage cheese–egg pocket), ham and gravy, *pluma mos* (fruit soup) and *zwieback* (double-decker rolls). Food booths sell *zwieback*, canned meat, noodles, pies, smoked pork chops and pork sausage (402/947-8351, www.nebraskamccsale.org).

Cattlemen's Ball of Nebraska Location changes yearly, first weekend in June— Scoot your boots to a different ranch or feedlot each year for this fund-raiser for cancer research. Spend the afternoon at the casino tent, style show and live cattle displays, then follow the hungry herd to the big tents for a rib-sticking beef meal followed by an auction. You can two-step to the sounds of a live country band at the ball. Admission charged (800/421-5326, www.cattlemensball.com).

Celebrate Lincoln Ethnic Festival Lincoln, early June—Vendors spice up downtown with Greek gyros, Italian sausage, Eastern European pierogies, Cambodian egg rolls, Brazilian pastries and other ethnic eats. Get moving to the beat of African drummers, Greek belly dancers, Irish dancers and an array of other entertainers that perform on two stages. Merchants sell jewelry, wood carvings and clothing. Donation suggested (402/434-6902, www.celebratelincoln.org).

Central Nebraska Ethnic Festival Grand Island, last weekend in July—Graze your way around the world at food booths serving Indian tacos, baklava, Greek gyros, Vietnamese egg rolls, enchiladas and other ethnic treats. Scottish bagpipers, Native American and Irish dancers and other performers celebrate the region's cultural richness at this free fest. Shop crafts booths and boogie at street dances (800/658-3178, www.grand-island.com/ethnic).

Czech Festival Wilber, first full weekend in August—*Vitáme vás* ("We welcome you") to the self-proclaimed "Czech Capital of the Nation" for mouthwatering meals of liver dumpling soup, roast duck and pork, kraut, dumplings and kolaches (fruit-filled yeast buns) served by churches and other organizations. The town of 1,700 swells to 50,000 people for this weekend of polka music and dancing, three parades, the Miss Czech-Slovak USA Pageant and arts and crafts (888/494-5237, www.ci.wilber.ne.us).

Kool-Aid Days Hastings, second weekend in August—In the town where Edwin Perkins invented Kool-Aid in 1927, a $2 mug gets you all the Kool-Aid you can drink (14 flavors) at a 75-foot-long Kool-Aid stand, the world's largest. Enter the Kool-Aid-drinking contest and visit the Kool-Aid exhibit at the Hastings Museum. More than 250 classic cars roll into town for the Kool-Aid Cruise of America, just one of 30 separate events. Admission charged to museum (402/461-8405, www.kool-aiddays.com).

State Fair Lincoln, 10 days starting in late August and ending on Labor Day—Beef is always what's for dinner at the Nebraska State Fair. Chow down on prime rib, barbecued brisket or roast beef sandwiches at the Nebraska Cattlemen's Beef Pit, or vary your menu at booths selling all kinds of fare on a stick. Pineapple whip is sure to cool you off (402/474-5371, www.statefair.org).

AppleJack Festival Nebraska City, third weekend in September—In addition to AppleJack festivities at area orchards, the home of Arbor Day celebrates the apple harvest with a parade featuring more than 50 bands in a marching-band competition, an antique-car show, a crafts sale, dances, and pancake and barbecue feeds. Branch out to area orchards for tours, cider and just-picked fruit, along with other "core" festivities. Face painting, a mini train and crafts entertain kids at their own Apple Jam Fest (800/514-9113, www.nebraskacity.com).

Mail Order

Eileen's Colossal Cookies Big, soft and great-tasting cookies made daily from scratch using the finest-quality ingredients. Order a cookie care package with three dozen of your favorites. Twelve flavors are available by mail order; Dan loves monster oatmeal and peanut butter (800/353-8077, www.eileenscookies.com).

National Arbor Day Foundation The foundation offers 22 fruit trees, including apple (six varieties), apricot, cherry, peach, pear and plum and 146 other tree types (evergreens, flowering, nut, ornamental, shade and shrubs). Each is keyed to the U.S. climate map, with zone numbers to help you select trees best suited to your area (888/448-7337, www.arborday.org).

Omaha Steaks Grain-fed Midwest beef. Expertly hand-carved from the heart of the beef tenderloin, these tender steaks are 100 percent unconditionally guaranteed to be fresh and delicious. Choose your favorite cut or buy a combo. Gourmet seafood, veal, pork, lamb, poultry, smoked meats, desserts and appetizers also are available (800/228-9055, www.omahasteaks.com).

NORTH DAKOTA
Valley of the Good Earth

THIS PAGE: SUNFLOWERS DECORATE THE NORTH DAKOTA COUNTRY-
SIDE. OPPOSITE PAGE, LEFT TO RIGHT: TOMORROW'S FRENCH FRIES
AT KB FARMS, MILNOR. A HUGE PIVOT IRRIGATION UNIT MAKING ITS
POTATO-FIELD CIRCUIT, KB FARMS. RHUBARB, THE PRAIRIE DESSERT
STAPLE, GROWING AT FORT RANSOM.

The Red River Valley of the North fans out almost imperceptibly across eastern North Dakota and northwestern Minnesota and, ultimately, into Manitoba. It's 320 miles long and 50 miles wide, filled with alluvial soil deposits from a vast prehistoric glacial lake and flat, flat, flat.

That unrelenting but efficient-for-farming flatness; the valley's superb black, stone-free soil; and the area's abundant moisture make this one of the world's most fertile agricultural regions. Some call it America's Nile Valley. Where bluestem and other native prairie grasses once shot up to 6 feet tall, today's farmers harvest close-cropped, jumbo-size checkerboard fields of sugar beets, potatoes, corn, onions, wheat, sunflowers and more—all in spite of a relatively short but very sunny northern growing season.

Partly because it encounters no topographical barriers, the Red River subjects the region to calamitous floods every few years. Yet even these snowmelt submersions are more than compensated for by the valley's fecundity, the reason I'm spending the North Dakota interlude of my Midwest food journey here.

During the 1880s settlement boom, North Dakota was supposed to become another Iowa, in terms of both population and productivity. However, the state's brutal climatic extremes and off-the-beaten-path location (for most residents, the nearest large city is Winnipeg) got in the

way. Because it takes far fewer people to produce North Dakota's bumper crops than it once did, the sprawling state's population is relatively static at 634,000 residents. They live amid an uncluttered, largely pristine landscape that dazzles the eye, from spring's emerald green carpet to late summer's fields of gold to autumn's subtle palette of brown, taupe and beige.

I'm convinced that North Dakota's relative isolation and belated settlement, in Midwest terms, have kept it closer to its immigrant roots than any other state in the Heartland. Every Midwest state takes pride in its varied ethnic history, but in North Dakota, it's all still present tense.

For example, just drive into one of the seven shiny Kroll's diners around the state. Interspersed on the menu with hamburgers, shakes and fries, you'll find *knoephla* soup (little noodles swimming in milk and butter), borscht (a creamy variation of the cabbage classic) and *fleisch-kuechle* (a ground-meat patty fried in a doughy jacket)—culinary reminders of the state's significant German-Russian (largely Mennonite) community. Minot, a north-central community of 36,600,

annually hosts Norsk Hostfest (pronounced HAWSTfest), one of the nation's largest folk festivals and a veritable banquet for lovers of all flavors Scandinavian, from lutefisk and *lefse* to Swedish meatballs and rice pudding.

North Dakotans lead the nation in spring and durum wheat, sunflowers, pinto and navy beans, oats, flaxseed, honey, dry peas, barley and canola. They also perform quite respectably when it comes to soybeans, corn, rye, sugar beets and potatoes—and livestock in the form of cattle, hogs and sheep.

Wheat is the state's most important crop. Amazingly, North Dakota produces two-thirds of the nation's hard durum wheat, which is milled for pasta and pastry flour. That's enough for 10.6 million servings of spaghetti per year! One of the nation's largest pasta companies, Dakota Growers, is located in Carrington in the heart of east-central North Dakota's durum wheat country.

With so much *growing* here, it's a sure bet there's a lot *cooking* in eastern North Dakota as well. I'll experience both aspects as I eat and research my way from a historic "bonanza" wheat farm to modern-day sugar beet– and potato-growing operations and a gigantic vegetable-oil processing plant. Before concluding my Red River Valley epicurean sortie, I'll fittingly sample two of the area's more sublime offerings: delicate fruit wines at a small-town winery and a banquet of chocolate-coated delights at a classic candy shop.

Farming and Food Bonanzas

Among the first to mine North Dakota's agricultural mother lode in the 1880s were eastern speculators who invested millions of dollars in huge tracts of Red River Valley farmland that became available after the Northern Pacific Railroad went bankrupt. They called their vast holdings—more than 90 farms of up to 50,000 acres each—bonanza farms (from the Spanish word for "prosperity" and the Latin word for "good") and sent managers to oversee them. Today, these farms are only a memory, broken up into hundreds of operations that still would be considered quite large anywhere else.

I'm visiting what remains of one bonanza farm near Mooreton (population 200) in southeastern North Dakota.

Although this is no longer a working farm, the Bagg compound preserves 20-odd buildings on 15 acres of what was a 6,000-acre property. The place is a beehive of activity, because the farm is going to be named a National Historic Landmark this very day. While volunteers prepare for the speeches and reception to come, I tour outbuildings and the 21-bedroom structure that housed the owner-manager's family and some of the 125 men and 20 women who labored here.

Back downstairs, in the yellow and gray dining room next to the kitchen, I gaze upon a long covered table that seated up to 26 hungry workers at a time. I peek through the kitchen's "matchmaker window," so named because young female cooks who used it to monitor what needed replenishing also checked out the diners as future matrimonial prospects. Each day, breakfast was served at 5:30 a.m., dinner at noon and supper at 7 p.m. The noon dinners were carried to the field in huge trunklike dining boxes. The daily food bonanza consisted of an entire quarter of beef or pork, 20 dozen eggs, 1¾ bushels of potatoes, 40 loaves of bread and 18 pies! Plaques on the walls list the names of dozens who toiled here over the years.

The main house is attractively restored to its appearance in approximately 1915, when the farm was at its peak. Outside, I stroll around the neat, red-and-white-painted buildings that made this a self-sufficient village: blacksmith and harness shops; ice house; laundry; several granaries; mule, horse, sheep, hog and dairy barns; foreman's house; office and more. Several surviving pieces of vintage farm equipment once powered by dozens of mules and horses relate to photos of wheat harvesting I noted on the walls of the house. I now understand more fully how technology has revolutionized farming:

Tasks that once required scores of men (paid $1 per day!) now are accomplished by just one or two farmers and their awesome modern equipment.

Underground Treasures

For a more contemporary view of agriculture in North Dakota's Red River Valley, I visit two venues that specialize in the valley's underground bounty—sugar beets and potatoes. At the Mauch (pronounced Mock) farm near Mooreton, I meet something of a rarity in this state today: a young, single farmer. Luke Mauch runs a modern-day bonanza farm with his father, Bill, an uncle and a cousin. The property comprises 7,200 acres, more than the current average hereabouts of 3,000–5,000 acres.

The Mauchs grow some 1,000 acres of sugar beets in rotation with corn, soybeans and navy beans. We stand in a 160-acre field, discussing the 400,000 tons of sugar these beets yield per year. Grabbing onto the plants' tobaccolike tops, we pull up several of the jumbo-size beets, which are shaped like huge carrots. These monsters weigh up to 5 pounds each—and they're white, not red as I expected. Luke opens his pocketknife and offers me a slice. Very sweet!

Back in the farmyard, Luke introduces me to an array of equipment, including a "topper" and a "lifter" that harvest six rows of sugar beets at a time. "First, the topper knocks the green tops off in between the rows, and then we come back immediately and lift the beets into the truck and take them to town," he explains. Come late September and October, the Mauchs will harvest up to 2,500 tons of beets per acre—all destined to be processed into granulated sugar at a cooperative plant in nearby Wahpeton. One beet typically yields 5 ounces of pure sugar, with pro-

CLOCKWISE, FROM TOP LEFT: (ALL PHOTOS TAKEN NEAR MOORETON) REMINDER OF A BYGONE FARMING ERA, BAGG BONANZA FARM. DINING ROOM AT THE BAGG BONANZA FARM. SUGAR BEET FARMER LUKE MAUCH AND DAN INSPECT A FIELD. A JUMBO SUGAR BEET, ALMOST READY FOR HARVEST. OPPOSITE PAGE: VIGNETTE AT THE BAGG FARM.

cessing byproducts used to replenish the soil and feed livestock.

Next stop: a Red River Valley potato farm near tiny Milnor (population 710). A gift of the pre-Columbian Incan civilization in South America, potatoes grow in every state in the nation, but North Dakota leads the Midwest pack by a substantial margin. Each American consumes an average of 140 pounds of potatoes per year!

At a convenience store, I meet lifelong North Dakota farmer Joe Mathern and his wife, Linda, and follow their pickup a few miles to a 130-acre potato field, where we watch a 1,300-foot-long pivot-irrigation unit slowly creep counterclockwise—at the rate of one full rotation per 52 hours—to apply ½ inch of water.

The potatoes being watered in this rich, sandy soil are meaty, dense, golden Russet Burbanks, a popular variety that stores well and is considered the "workhorse of potatoes." Some will go to homes and restaurants as baking potatoes, but most will end up as french fries. Joe manages this 1,000-acre unit of the KB (Kosowski Brothers) Farms, with just two workers, increasing to 12 during harvest season in September and early October.

Joe tells me that milder weather in recent years has been a boon. Moisture is critical early in the growing season—potatoes are 80 percent water—but can be a problem if it comes late. The crop's enemies are blight and too-hot weather. One acre in this field will yield five hundred 100-pound sacks of potatoes. Joe plants cut potatoes, rather than seeds, on a rotation basis with corn, soybeans and other beans to avoid depleting nutrients and to curtail disease. We yank some potatoes out from the loamy, sandy soil before taking a short jaunt to a huge storage facility where temperature, humidity and ventilation are closely regulated. Each of Joe's

storage units holds 6 million pounds of potatoes—yet more evidence of the staggering productivity of these huge, flat Red River Valley fields.

Sweet Fruits of the Tundra

I didn't visit North Dakota expecting to gush about locally produced wines, but that is easy to do in Casselton (population 2,000), a main line of the BNSF (Burlington Northern Santa Fe) railroad. The town was settled back in the booming 1870s when the Northern Pacific line, one of 300 railways that eventually merged into today's BNSF, tried to cultivate cottonwood trees here for future use as railroad ties (the experiment failed). Now, Casselton is reminded of its railroading roots by the BNSF locomotives that frequently race through town, pulling freight cars

filled with wheat, coal and other goods.

I'm here to sample the exceptional vintages offered by the Maple River Winery, one of only two such businesses in the state. Greg Kempel and his wife, Susan, founded this fledgling operation in 2002. Greg formerly worked for the U.S. Postal Service, but he loved crafting homemade fruit wines for family, friends and neighbors. Now, he works at the winery 70 hours a week, aiming at a 2006 production goal of 2,500 cases of wine, as well as jams, jellies and fruit spreads.

Maple River products are made entirely from fruits cultivated or harvested in the wild in this area. More than 300 suppliers bring lots ranging from 50 to 500 pounds to the winery's back door; a Hutterite-

Mennonite father and son stop by with boxes of wild plums while I'm here. Greg walks me through the wine-making process and shows off his twelve 280-gallon fermentation vats. Maple River's fruit wines typically ferment for about 10 days and age 120–140 days. Unlike grape wines, which usually need no other ingredients, Greg's wines require sugar, water and yeast.

Greg explains that, regardless of whether it's deliberate or unintentional, most hobbyists wind up with far too much alcohol content or "legs," resulting in a bitter-tasting wine. How can you tell before you take a sip of your friend's finest? Swirl the contents and study the clear residue that remains on the sides of the glass; the more coating, the higher the alcohol content. Greg's wines are lighter than most fruit wines, about 10 percent

I confidently sniff, swirl and ingest seven fruity wines; Maple River's best seller is the ubiquitous rhubarb.

alcohol (grape wines typically range from 7 to 14 percent).

At the Red Baron Lounge and Pizza Pub next door, I join a local newspaperman, an attorney and a banker at a big round table for a wine tasting. Our selections are accompanied by a hearty pizza smorgasbord, including the Siberian Tundra special (Polish sausage, sauerkraut and black olives). I confidently sniff, swirl and ingest seven fruity wines. Some are dry (crabapple, wild plum and—surprise!—apple–jalapeño pepper), some middle of the road (apricot, chokecherry) and some sweet (rhubarb and raspberry). Greg says his favorite and the winery's best seller is the ubiquitous rhubarb, which tastes to me like a slice of perfect rhubarb pie. I vote for the amber-hued apricot and the apple–jalapeño pepper. The peppers aren't spicy hot; they just add a pleasant warmth to the delicate apple flavor. Other varieties include dandelion and elderberry. Greg has even developed a new apple-mint wine!

Maple River wines are sold in more than 100 North Dakota outlets, plus 30 states by mail, and have even won a following in California's Napa and Sonoma valleys. "It catches people off guard when you mention North Dakota wine," Greg says. "We use that to our advantage."

Chocolate Heaven

Time to nose into the heart of the Red River Valley and Grand Forks (population 51,000), about 100 skillet-flat interstate miles northeast of Casselton. It's a beautiful drive: Dense windbreaks—cottonwoods, American elms and Russian olives—appear on the landscape, and voracious combines march across wheat fields. Grand Forks almost floated away in 1997 during a disastrous flood. These days, things are looking a lot healthier downtown and just across the 1929 Sorlie Memorial Bridge in East Grand Forks, Minnesota.

I see the sign for my destination: Widman's Candy Company, a restored 1925 emporium on a tidy block facing a levee that now helps cosset the Red River. It's no secret that Americans love chocolate and will go to excessive lengths to experience its magical spell. Chocolate-covered treats are the reason I'm visiting this family business, which dates back to 1880s confectioners and bakers whose descendants gradually migrated from Dubuque, Iowa, to North Dakota via Minnesota.

Three generations later, the Widmans now tempt chocoholics at this Grand Forks flagship shop as well as in Fargo and Crookston, Minnesota. At 85, family

CLOCKWISE, FROM ABOVE: **RUSSET BURBANK POTATOES FRESH FROM THE SANDY SOIL AT KB FARMS, MILNOR. WINES MADE FROM LOCALLY HARVESTED FRUITS, MAPLE RIVER WINERY, CASSELTON. SELECTION OF DIPPED RIDGED-STYLE POTATO CHIPS, WIDMAN'S CANDY STORE, GRAND FORKS.**

patriarch George, a World War II Navy veteran, is the best candy salesman I've ever encountered. He's presided at the South Third Street location since 1955.

I browse the incredible array of temptations—nearly every kind of hard and soft candy you can imagine. Then I zero in on my target: the glass case by the cash register, filled with seductive-looking rows and rows of chocolate-covered "everythings"— pimiento-stuffed olives, corn and soy nuts, cranberries, sunflower seeds, hot jalapeños, dill pickle slices and, of course, ridged-style potato chips.

Widman's signature sweet-salty "chippers" are drenched in various coatings— milk, dark and white chocolate; almond bark; and peanut butter. What a great way to eat potato chips! The Widmans also have a passion for molded chocolates that replicate typewriters, trucks, cows (and those infamous cow pies), pigs, motorcycles, fish, frogs, cars and vans, tennis rackets, footballs—and ice skates and hockey sticks. (Ice hockey is another passion here; Grand Forks is the home of the University of North Dakota's $100 million, 400,000-square-foot Engelstad Arena, which boasts 11,000-plus leather-covered seats for spectators.)

As I make my selections for nibbling during the long drive ahead (the bag will be empty in a half hour), I ask about trends. "America used to be a milk-chocolate country, but that's changing; however, we still sell about three cases of milk chocolate to one case of dark these days. People think dark chocolate is healthier," George says. "You put chocolate on just about anything and people will want to eat it."

No Shortage of Oil—or Rhubarb

I seize the opportunity to drive an approximately 20-mile segment of the winding Sheyenne River Valley Scenic Byway that includes the tiny village of Fort Ransom (population 105). North Dakota isn't supposed to look like the view out my windshield this afternoon: a steep-sided (for this state, anyway) pastoral valley of woods and fields dotted with picturesque farmsteads that creases and wrinkles the otherwise flat prairie.

Leafy Fort Ransom itself is a revelation. Founded in 1867 as a military outpost and named for a Civil War general, it's become the hub of a popular year-round recreation area. Without a grain elevator or a rail line (two requisites for growth a century ago), the Norwegians of Fort Ransom never multiplied much, which accounts for the town's charm. I park at the side of the wraparound porch at Hartley's CupCakes Cafe, primed for some coffee and a piece of rhubarb pie. Humble rhubarb, or pie plant, is a dessert staple the pioneers brought with them to the Plains states (it originated in China). Although some classify it as a fruit because of the way it's used in cooking, rhubarb is a leafy green vegetable with a ruby-red stem; in this case, however, the leaves are inedible.

As I savor my pie (it's heavenly—just the right balance of sweet and tart), Shirley Hartley and I chat. She's a native of the area who migrated to South Florida to teach school and married Jim, a Miamian. After Hurricane Andrew hit in 1992, she convinced Jim that North Dakota winters aren't so bad after all. The couple resettled and bought a tavern, which they sold; they built this handsome facility in 2003.

I ask about all the cafe-branded coffee cups in the big antique hutch. "Those belong to our customers," Shirley explains. "You can buy one for $5 and use it anytime you come in." I wish I lived close by, so I could claim one as my own. I savor a few moments in Shirley's patio garden and stroll over a slightly swaying footbridge that crosses the gently flowing Sheyenne.

Minutes later I'm traveling back east toward the Red River Valley and Enderlin. Enderlin's boosters are justly proud of reaching a population milestone (more than 1,000 residents) that might get over-

looked anywhere but in rural North Dakota. Clearly this community got its requisite grain elevator and railroad line! Over dinner at a cafe—corn on the cob, steaks and a sweet cabbage slaw featuring sunflower seeds, a local signature ingredient—I consume my second and third pieces of rhubarb pie in six hours.

After a pleasant night at the spotless, 17-room Enderlin Inn, it's time for breakfast. Scones, cinnamon and caramel rolls and a perfectly brewed espresso await me at a sunny sidewalk table in front of Bless My Bloomin' Cookies, Inc. More evidence of small-town determination: Buddies and business partners Elise Nylander and Julie Ussatis were running a crafts enterprise when they decided to change career directions. Now they employ six local women and ship by mail cleverly hand-painted, frosted sugar-cookie bouquets and 42 varieties of designed gourmet cookies—sunflowers and buffalo are popular themes—from their coffee shop and bak-

ery in two-block-long downtown Enderlin. The unexpected espresso is the handiwork of John Nolan, a retired Air Force officer who returned to North Dakota after roaming 12 countries and earning his barista stripes in Europe.

Next, I drive about a mile east of Enderlin to the Archer Daniels Midland (ADM) plant to get down to business—the vegetable oil business, to be precise. After clearing security, I meet plant manager Richard Irish. Originally from South Africa, Richard and his family now live about 55 miles away, in Fargo. On a fast-paced tour of the huge ADM complex, Richard gives me the lowdown on one of North Dakota's top products: edible oils.

The two primary types processed here are sunflower and canola. The latter also is called rapeseed, a term derived from the Old English word for "turnip." Faced with obvious marketing challenges, growers chose "canola," a name inspired by the Western Canadian Oilseed Crushers

Association that helped develop it. North Dakota is the nation's top producer of both sunflower and canola seeds, and 75 percent of the nation's sunflower oil is processed in Enderlin. Forty to 60 tank cars of oil seed or meal are switched through the facility each day. Most of the oil produced is totally refined at this plant.

I learn that there are two types of sunflower seeds: the kind you eat at ball games, put on salads and pour into your bird feeder, and the kind that get crushed between huge steel rollers for the high oil content. Canola, the other yellow-flowered seed plant processed here at ADM, was used as a lubricant for steam engines until someone figured out how to make it palatable.

Today both oils, especially canola, are considered heart-healthy because they are high in monounsaturated and polyunsaturated fats and low in the current nutritional villains: hydrogenated trans fats, saturated fats, cholesterol and other bad guys that are thought to clog arteries and contribute to heart disease. Canola is touted for its high "smoke point," meaning it's good for frying.

Richard's 100 employees turn out another Red River Valley specialty, dehydrated beans—kidney, navy, pinto and black—as well as powdered organic soy milk. I ask Richard about global competition and am surprised to learn that China is emerging as a major soybean producer, along with Russia and Brazil. But rest assured: ADM, based in Decatur, Illinois, is a $36 billion global agribusiness colossus, with 250 plants, 25,000 employees and a roster of more than 1,000 food ingredients. Although the Red River Valley faces new competition, I suspect its fertile soil will long continue to make North Dakota one of America's and the world's agricultural powerhouses.

Taste of North Dakota

Chocolate-Covered Potato Chips

Inspired by Carol Widman's Candy Company, Grand Forks

- 1 cup semisweet chocolate pieces (6 ounces)
- 2 to 3 teaspoons shortening
- 5 ounces ridged potato chips

In a small heavy saucepan, melt the chocolate and shortening over low heat, stirring occasionally until the chocolate starts to melt. Immediately remove the chocolate from the heat and stir until smooth.

Dip a potato chip into the melted chocolate. (Handle carefully so chip doesn't break.) Holding chip over saucepan, allow excess chocolate to drip off. Place on a waxed-paper-lined baking sheet. Repeat with remaining chocolate and chips. Let stand at room temperature until chocolate sets. (Chocolate-dipped chips may be stored in an airtight container up to 24 hours.) *Makes 10 servings.*

Sunflower-Cracked Wheat Bread

Inspired by North Dakota whole grains, wheat and sunflower seeds

- 2 cups water
- 1/2 cup cracked wheat
- 1/4 cup butter
- 1/2 cup dark molasses
- 1 cup milk
- 2 packages active dry yeast
- 1/2 cup regular rolled oats
- 1/2 cup cornmeal
- 1/4 cup toasted wheat germ or unprocessed wheat bran
- 1 teaspoon salt
- 1 cup shelled salted sunflower seeds
- 2 1/2 cups whole wheat flour
- 3 to 3 1/2 cups all-purpose flour
- 1 egg white
- 1 tablespoon water
  Toasted wheat germ or unprocessed wheat bran

In a medium saucepan, bring water to boiling. Stir in cracked wheat. Reduce heat and simmer, covered, for 5 minutes. Stir in butter until melted. Stir in molasses and milk. Remove from heat. Let cool about 10 minutes or until lukewarm (110° to 115°). Add yeast, stirring until dissolved.

Add rolled oats, cornmeal, the 1/4 cup toasted wheat germ and the salt to the cracked wheat mixture. Stir in the sunflower seeds. Transfer mixture to an extra-large mixing bowl.

Using a wooden spoon, stir in the whole wheat flour. Stir in as much of the all-purpose flour as you can. On a lightly floured surface, knead in enough of the remaining all-purpose flour to make a moderately stiff dough that is smooth and elastic (6 to 8 minutes total). Shape into a ball. Place dough in a lightly greased bowl; turn once to grease surface. Cover and let rise in a warm place until double in size (about 1 hour).

Punch dough down. Turn dough out onto a lightly floured surface. Divide dough in half. Cover; let rest for 10 minutes. Meanwhile, lightly grease two 9x5x3-inch loaf pans. Shape into 2 loaves. Place in prepared loaf pans. Cover and let rise in a warm place until nearly double in size (30 to 40 minutes). Make 3 diagonal slashes across top of each loaf. Brush tops with mixture of egg white and water; sprinkle with additional toasted wheat germ.

Bake in a 375° oven for 40 to 45 minutes or until bread sounds hollow when you tap the top with your fingers. (If necessary, cover tops of loaves with foil during the last 15 minutes to prevent overbrowning.) Remove from pans. Cool on wire racks. *Makes 2 large loaves (32 servings).*

Travel Journal

More Information

For Casselton, Enderlin, Fort Ransom, Milnor and Mooreton: **North Dakota Tourism** (800/435-5663, www.ndtourism.com). **Fargo/Moorhead Convention & Visitors Bureau** (800/235-7654, www.fargo moorhead.org). **Greater Grand Forks Convention & Visitors Bureau** (800/866-4566, www.grandforkscvb.org). **Wahpeton Breckenridge Area Chamber of Commerce** (800/892-6673, www.wahpeton breckenridgechamber.com).

Featured Dining

Red Baron Lounge and Pizza Pub Casselton (701/347-4333). **Hartley's CupCakes Cafe** Fort Ransom (701/973-2140).

More Great Dining

Sanders 1907 Grand Forks. Fine dining downtown, featuring specialties with a North Dakota twist, such as king salmon with "prairie sauce" (701/746-8970). **Whitey's Cafe and Lounge** Grand Forks. A mainstay for more than 80 years, with a 1950s Art Deco interior, spacious bar areas and a full menu of steaks, seafood, salads and sandwiches downtown (218/773-1831).

Featured Stops

Maple River Winery Downtown Casselton (701/347-5900). **Bless My Bloomin' Cookies, Inc.** Enderlin (701/437-3778). **Carol Widman's Candy Company** Grand Forks (701/775-3480; 701/281-8664 and

218/281-1487 for the Fargo and Crookston stores, respectively). **Bagg Bonanza Farm** Outside Mooreton (701/274-8989).

More Great Stops

Grand Forks Grand Forks, North Dakota, and East Grand Forks, Minnesota, blend across the Red River. Home of the University of North Dakota and Grand Forks Air Force Base, this metro area of 97,500 features a newly restored downtown with antiques and specialty shops, a Cabela's sporting-goods store and the largest hobby-and-crafts-supply store between Minneapolis and Seattle. Other attractions include the North Dakota Museum of Art and Heritage Village, which documents northern Red River Valley history.

Dan's Lodgings

Enderlin Inn Enderlin ($; 866/416-2001). **Hospitality Inn & Suites** Wahpeton ($; 701/642-5000).

More Great Lodgings

Governors' Inn and Conference Center Casselton. A new 46-room hotel, family-dining restaurant, indoor water park and adjacent RV sites, all located 18 miles west of Fargo ($$; 888/847-4524). **511 Reeves** Grand Forks. A bed and breakfast in a 1901 Victorian with three individually decorated guest rooms; part of a historic district within walking distance of downtown ($$; 701/775-3585). **Hilton Garden Inn** Grand Forks. A newer 100-room, full-service hotel located next door to North Dakota University and the Engelstad Arena ($$; 877/782-9444).

Food Events

State Fair Minot, nine days in late July— The two-family-run Tubby's food stands dish out fresh-ground burgers, colossal onion rings and signature rib eyes served with sauteed onions on a kaiser roll (701/857-7620, www.ndstatefair.com). **Potato Bowl USA** Grand Forks, Tuesday through Saturday in early September—The Red River Valley touts its tubers with the world's biggest french fry feed, plus potato-

picking and recipe contests, a potato pancake breakfast and a potato chip giveaway. A parade and a tailgate party fire up visitors for a University of North Dakota football game. Admission charged to game (218/773-3633, www.potatobowl.org). **Sunflower Festival** Enderlin, third weekend in September—Reel in fish deep-fried in sunflower oil and served with sunflower slaw at this fest in the hometown of North America's largest sunflower-processing plant. Visitors can enter a seed-spitting contest and sunflower cook-off. More fun: 5K and 10K runs, a parade and midway rides (701/437-2000, www.enderlinnd.com). **Norsk Hostfest** Minot, Tuesday through Saturday in early October—North America's largest Scandinavian festival stars an array of ethnic foods, such as lutefisk, Danish *aebleskivers* (pancakes), Swedish meatballs, *rommegrot* (rich pudding) and Norwegian seafood chowder. Dancers and musical acts perform on six stages. Admission charged (701/852-2368, www.hostfest.com).

Mail Order

Bless My Bloomin' Cookies, Inc. Edible works of art on a stick. More than 42 varieties of gourmet cookies are available, along with hand-painted cookie bouquets and personalized designs (866/828-3778, www.blessmybloomincookies.com). **Carol Widman's Candy Company** Famous for chocolate-covered potato chips (chippers) and sunflower seeds. Other sweet treats include caramels, nougats, chocolates, toffee and hard candies (800/688-8351, www.carolwidmanscandyco.com). **Maple River Winery** Handcrafted wines made from native state fruits. Traditional flavors include chokecherry, elderberry, dandelion and rhubarb; more adventurous shoppers might try apple mint, honey apple and honey raspberry (701/347-5900, www.mapleriverwinery.com). **Pride of Dakota Mall** A multitude of North Dakota foodstuffs, including roasted sunflower seeds, soy nuts, wheat nuts, buffalo and elk, fruit wines, sunflower-seed butter and many more choices for good eating (701/788-4670, www.shopnd.com).

OHIO
A Garden of Hometown Favorites

An ominous thunderstorm looms as I slip into Toledo to begin my Ohio foray. Generally, the farther east or south you go in the Midwest, the wetter it gets. Cincinnati receives almost 42 inches of rain annually, while Scottsbluff, Nebraska, settles for a scant 16 inches.

That disparity explains a lot about the vegetation, the agriculture and the feel of the land I'm encountering on my journey—as well as the food specialties.

Ohio's moisture and fertile soil result in a state that resembles a huge, lush garden. It fairly explodes with tomatoes, bell peppers, onions, cucumbers, cabbages, strawberries, pumpkins and squash. It's the eastern anchor of the great Midwest Corn Belt, so corn and soybeans also abound, as well as the attendant livestock: hogs, cattle and dairy cows, plus enthusiastic laying hens who deliver nearly 8 billion eggs a year. Along the Lake Erie shore, orchards and vineyards yield grapes, apples and peaches.

Much of that bounty gets processed in Ohio, especially in the form of frozen foods. You'll find the nation's largest pizza plant in Wellston and the biggest canned-soup factory in Napoleon. Other Ohio food giants cook up a good share of our ketchup, yogurt and cheese, especially Swiss. The state's myriad food traditions reflect its multifaceted big-city/small-town personality, and vary from rural Amish themes in Holmes County to

Slavic, German and Italian influences in the big cities.

For this food tour, I cut a 210-mile swath through western Ohio, from Toledo to Cincinnati. Near the midway point, in Troy and Urbana, I tour two quite different farming operations—one specializing in fresh vegetables, the other in fish. My restaurant stops spotlight hometown classics, from Tony Packo's in Toledo to a tasty trio in my favorite Ohio food town, Cincinnati: Skyline Chili, LaRosa's Pizzeria and the Montgomery Inn. I also slip in some White Castle burgers and a few scoops of Graeter's ice cream. Bring it on, Ohio!

Paprika and Pickles

I'm waiting to place my order at Tony Packo's, not far from the minor-league baseball park where the hometown Mud Hens play. Most visitors to this corner eatery near the wide mouth of the Maumee River in East Toledo ask the same question: "Why on earth are all these hot dog buns mounted in acrylic cases?" I remember the story from my first visit here: Founder Tony Packo's daughter, Nancy, was so taken when actor Burt Reynolds came to dine

during a Toledo gig that she asked for an autograph. But the only signable thing at hand was a hot dog bun—fitting, because "Hungarian" hot dogs are what this place is famous for. Today hundreds of celebrities have their buns (ahem!) proudly displayed at Tony Packo's. (Don't tell, but the stars now sign plastic-foam replicas.)

Tony Packo, Sr., was a Hungarian-American factory worker who began selling hot dogs topped with a spicy chili sauce back in 1932. Trouble was, there weren't many takers for even 10-cent hot dogs in the depths of the Great Depression. So Tony sliced the dogs in half lengthwise and sold them for 5 cents apiece. A legend was born. The skinny wieners became known as Hungarian hot dogs, though I doubt if anybody in Budapest would know what that means. Today, the Packo Dog, a masterpiece when smothered with meat sauce, onions and mustard, costs $2.49.

Because this may be my only Hungarian dining experience on this trip, I go whole hog: handmade beef-, pork- and rice-stuffed cabbage roll; chicken *paprikas* smothered in a sour cream–paprika gravy with dumplings; kraut; mashed potatoes and more gravy; and flaky apple strudel for dessert. Oh, yes, and a few bites of a MOAD—at one pound, the "mother of all dogs." There's an array of Packo's pickles, of course: crunchy garlic dills, sweet-hots, hot peppers and the trademark "Hungarian" banana peppers. Many of the pickles come from Sechler's, an empire in nearby northeast Indiana that's been producing almost 40 mouth-puckering varieties since 1914. (Mrs. Frances Sechler happens to be the mother of longtime *Midwest Living*® senior food editor Diana McMillen.)

The whole restaurant has a very friendly, *Cheers*-type atmosphere; even the interior walls are painted a paprika-orange color. Most of the patrons sit at large tables under colorful Tiffany-style lamps. I stop at the old-fashioned bar for a moment on my way out. Over beers, a couple of fellows with tattoos and long ponytails follow a ball game on the big TV screen.

They're just part of the one-of-a-kind atmosphere and menu at Tony Packo's.

Eat Your (Ohio) Veggies!

I've never had a problem consuming my share of healthy vegetables, as an adult, anyway. From peas to parsnips, cucumbers to kohlrabi, I love 'em. I'm also a gardener, so I'm really looking forward to my visit to Fulton Farms on Old Troy Pike Road, just a few miles east of Troy's handsome roundabout. I arrive early so I can chat with the owners, Bill and Joyce Fulton, who grow an amazing 52 edible crops on 1,700 acres. Name most any Midwest vegetable or fruit, and they probably raise and sell it. Joyce also runs the bustling produce market and a small ice cream and coffee shop in the big retail barn.

Life here revolves around an endless parade of harvests. The season begins with rhubarb and asparagus, followed by peas and strawberries. By early July, it's

sweet corn, tomatoes, squash, peppers and green beans. August brings assorted melons. Autumn means pumpkins and hayrides, before the year ends with cut-your-own Christmas trees. Bill has been in this business almost all his adult life, and his family has farmed in the area more than 150 years. When he was a kid, Bill tells me, he and his dad would load their truck with produce at 2 a.m., arrive at a market in Dayton by 5 a.m. and head home by 8 a.m. Besides being sold in the Fultons' huge retail barn, lots of their produce goes to supermarkets in nearby Dayton and Columbus, as well as to restaurants, wholesale markets and food stands in the area.

The fertile soil of the Miami River Valley contributes to the farm's abundance—but even in water-rich Ohio, the Fultons irrigate much of their land because of the thirsty nature of their crops. We check a couple of fields before heading to the retail barn, which is soon packed on this Saturday morning. I walk in and immediately revel in the rich, sweet aromas. The sweet-corn tables are crowded, and melon thumpers are checking for ripeness. On an average day in season, the Fultons may sell up to 2,500 quarts of strawberries and 1,500 dozen ears of sweet corn! Come fall, 60 tons of fat pumpkins will go out the doors.

Joyce offers us fresh-vegetable snacks and a tasty veggie quiche. We crunch some yellow (yes, yellow) watermelon, which is as sweet and juicy as any I've tasted. Why do people flock here when they could drive just a few blocks to a supermarket for their produce? Bill echoes the theme I've heard again and again on my journey: These days, people want things raised close to home. Fresh. Grown locally. It makes them feel safer. Does Bill eat his veggies? "Everything but okra. I hate okra," he says with a laugh.

CLOCKWISE, FROM ABOVE: BILL FULTON AND DAN AMID A SEA OF SWEET CORN AT FULTON FARMS, TROY. SHOPPER WITH HELPER AND TOMATOES, BOTH AT FULTON FARMS. TOLEDO'S HUNGARIAN-DINING BASTION. OPPOSITE PAGE: BRING ON THE DOGS AND PICKLES AT TONY PACKO'S.

Trout with Captain's Stuffing

Freshwater Farms of Ohio, Urbana

6	8- to 10-ounce fresh or frozen whole trout, dressed
1	tablespoon olive oil
	Kosher salt or salt
	Coarsely ground black pepper
1	cup sliced celery
1/4	cup finely chopped onion
1/2	cup butter
1	8-ounce package fresh mushrooms, coarsely chopped
1	tablespoon snipped fresh sage or 1 teaspoon ground sage
1	tablespoon snipped fresh dill or 1 teaspoon dried dillweed
1/2	teaspoon kosher salt or 1/4 teaspoon salt
1/4	teaspoon coarsely ground black pepper
4	cups dry bread cubes or herb-seasoned stuffing mix
	Lemon wedges (optional)

Thaw fish, if frozen. Rinse fish; pat dry with paper towels. If you like, remove the heads of the trout. Rub both sides of fish lightly with olive oil. Lightly sprinkle each cavity with salt and black pepper. Set aside.

For stuffing: In a large skillet, cook celery and onion in hot butter over medium heat until tender. Stir in mushrooms, sage, dill, 1/2 teaspoon salt and 1/4 teaspoon black pepper. Cook and stir for 2 minutes more or until mushrooms are tender. Remove from heat.

In a large bowl, combine dry bread cubes and celery mixture. Spoon the stuffing into the cavity of each fish. (Stuffing will moisten during baking.) Tear off six 18-inch squares of heavy-duty foil. Place a stuffed fish in the center of each piece of foil. Bring up two opposite edges of foil and seal with a double fold. Fold ends to completely enclose fish, leaving space for steam to build. On two baking sheets, place packets seam sides up.

Place baking sheets on two separate oven racks. Bake in 375° oven for 25 to 30 minutes or until fish flakes easily with a fork, switching baking sheets halfway through baking. Transfer each packet to a serving plate. Open packets carefully to allow steam to escape. If you like, serve with lemon wedges. *Makes 6 servings.*

Catch of the Day

Sustainable fish aquaculture is an idea whose time has come, and the Midwest provides the perfect setting. Americans are devouring ocean fish at an alarming rate, but many of the waters that ocean and freshwater fish live in are dangerously polluted. One long-term answer is to raise freshwater fish the way we do cattle and hogs. Sound strange? Well, have you eaten any feral beef or wild pork chops lately? Both animals were domesticated ages ago.

I learned all this and more during an inspiring and informative visit to Freshwater Farms, just north of Urbana. On a five-acre site, it is the nation's largest indoor fish hatchery. The surrounding Mad River Valley countryside is lush and rolling and,

belies his academic smarts as a marine biologist, ecologist and nutritionist who studied at Ohio State, Louisiana State and the University of Wisconsin. "I get my R & D fix here," he says. Dave also consults on water-treatment and water-recycling issues, and he tells me all the water used in these tanks is recycled.

Fish mature here in about a year on average, shrimp in three months (a good thing, because shrimp wouldn't last the winter in the cold quarry waters). They all merrily fatten up on a grain-based diet of renewable food sources Dave and others pioneered: soybeans, corn and wheat. I toss the trout a few handfuls of the food from a bucket. In the barn, I join youngsters at the fish petting zoo, where a half-

Sturgeon have been around for more than 300 million years, predating dinosaurs.

fittingly, the clear, cool spring-fed Mad is one of Ohio's trout streams and rivers.

Nothing seems out of the ordinary as I approach the white farmhouse and outbuildings. But a closer look reveals several giant tanks containing more than 3,000 rainbow trout each. Inside the barn, even more tanks are filled with other species at various stages of life. Freshwater Farms raises and sells 50,000 pounds of trout and 8,000 pounds of yellow perch annually; much of that goes to restaurants in Dayton and Columbus. They also hatch or raise a marine menagerie of largemouth bass, bluegill, channel catfish and even prawn-size shrimp—the latter in several nearby abandoned gravel quarries.

The man behind all this is one of America's leading champions of freshwater fish farming, Dr. Dave Smith. Dave is a likable guy whose down-to-earth approachability

dozen dark, exotic-looking sturgeon zip about their tank. Despite the fact that they rather resemble sharks, without the bite, they are friendly. Perhaps that's because they know that as valuable breeding stock they aren't going to wind up on a dinner platter! Sturgeon—whose tiny eggs give us that quintessential gourmet delight, caviar—have been around for more than 300 million years, predating dinosaurs.

Dave's parents manage the retail shop, where nutritionist daughter Gretchen whips up specialties such as a delicious smoked-trout Mediterranean salad with capers and olives. (Other gourmet foods also are for sale, along with aquaculture supplies for home ponds.) Gretchen reminds me how nutritious fish are, especially species such as salmon and trout that are high in omega-3 fatty acids. Like the thousands of families who visit this place each year, I find I'm learning a lot about a new type of agriculture and having a whale of a good time—and that's no fish story.

Life in a Hamburger Castle

I shove off for Cincinnati, one of the Midwest's most historic and unique cities, justly proud of its memorable dining icons. This shabby-chic municipality has always enchanted me with its winding streets, wooded hills, distinctive old neighborhoods, slightly Southern air and great architectural bones. The panoramic view from atop Mount Adams is a classic cityscape: lush wooded hills on the Kentucky side, the busy Ohio River spanned by handsome old bridges, church steeples galore and downtown office towers beside vintage brick structures.

I head for my first stop, a White Castle hamburger outpost on Mitchell Avenue in the Avondale neighborhood. America's oldest surviving hamburger chain, White Castle was founded in Wichita, Kansas, in 1921, in a 15x10-foot building with $700 of borrowed money. Still owned by the Ingram family, it has been based in Columbus, Ohio, since 1934. The once 5-cent-hamburger enterprise now boasts almost 400 outlets and 12,000 employees. Annual sales exceed half a billion dollars, mostly in the Midwest states and in New York and New Jersey. You'll find 40 locations in the Cincinnati area alone, each one in a distinctive white building with crenellated rooflines and squat, medieval-looking towers.

It's an awesome food empire—all based on the original palm-size, individually boxed, 2½-inch-square patty steam-grilled on a bed of onions and served with a single dill pickle slice on a soft bun. People hereabouts get really fired up about their White Castles, also lovingly known as sliders and belly busters. The company

CLOCKWISE, FROM ABOVE: FISH FARMER DR. DAVE SMITH NETTING RAINBOW TROUT FROM A HUGE TANK AT FRESHWATER FARMS OF OHIO, URBANA. CLASSIC, ONION-SMOTHERED HAMBURGER "SLIDERS" AND A BUSY WHITE CASTLE DRIVE-THROUGH, BOTH IN CINCINNATI.

even sponsors a recipe contest each year. Ever considered making White Castle enchiladas or quiche? White Castle pâté? Or how about White Castle Burmese, with coconut milk, fish sauce, curry powder, ginger and other unexpected ingredients? I prefer mine straight up, thank you.

Nostalgic photos of people noshing White Castles in bygone days adorn the walls. Where did the castle design theme come from? I'm told it was inspired by Chicago's Old Water Tower on North Michigan Avenue, the only structure to endure the city's calamitous fire—a survivor, just like White Castle.

In this neighborhood, the restaurant is the equivalent of a small-town cafe. Manager Liz Merrill knows her regulars, what they order and precisely when they'll come in. One retired man, on a doctor-prescribed heart-healthy diet, drops off his wife at her office, then sneaks in for a White Castle fix on his way home. Liz understands. "I even come in for a cheese-burger on my day off. If I don't, I feel like I'm missing something in my diet."

Make My Chili "Five-Way"!

To outsiders, Cincinnatians may seem rather quirky when it comes to food. Just trail after them when they walk into their neighborhood "parlor" to dine on the dark, runny goo they call chili. With a few mumbled words such as "three-way" or "five," they wind up with a big plate of spaghetti (yup, spaghetti) blanketed by a combination of toppings. Greek immigrants brought the exotic sauce to town in the 1920s, and it caught on fast, first as a hot dog topping. Now chains and local chili parlors thrive here.

I zip through the leafy Clifton neighborhood, passing Catholic and Methodist churches and a handsome mosque on my way to the Skyline Chili shop at Clifton and Ludlow. It's the circa-1966 chain's oldest surviving chili parlor, located just across the street from a park with a lovely fountain. Skyline was founded in downtown Cincinnati by Greek immigrant Nicholas Lambrinides in 1949. His five sons took their dad's idea and made it a legend: Now there are 136 Skyline parlors and franchises, mostly in Ohio and Indiana, with 75 in the Cincy area. This one is operated by Pete and John Georgeton, brothers descended from one of the city's 400 or so Greek-American families.

The Skyline staff is mixing up a big, frothy cauldron in the back room, so I hop off my stool at the U-shaped counter and lend Pete a hand at stirring the huge pot—with a rowing oar. Back at my seat, a waitress takes my order and offers me a plastic bib. I watch a "five-way" rise on my oval platter: spaghetti, plus chili that's been cooked with ground meat, red kidney beans, diced raw onions and a huge mound of fluffy, finely shredded cheddar cheese—the works, and I don't pass up a bite. Of course, they've branched out here, serving baked potatoes, coney dogs, burritos and

LEFT TO RIGHT: (ALL TAKEN IN CINCINNATI) TO-GO FARE AND A HEAPING FIVE-WAY PLATE, BOTH AT A SKYLINE CHILI PARLOR. FOUNDER BUDDY LAROSA AND ONE OF HIS BEST-SELLING CHEESY CREATIONS AT LAROSA'S FLAGSHIP PIZZERIA.

even low-carb salads and wraps. But you can order most of the menu items with that heavenly chili sauce. I casually ask what's in it besides cinnamon.

"You have a good nose there, Danny, but I'm not telling," John says with a laugh. A couple of vacationing Tennesseans who attended college in Cincinnati chuckle. They stop whenever they're in town, just for old times' sake. "We know it's top-secret stuff, but we don't want to know the ingredients, anyway. That would ruin it for us!"

Meet the Pizza King

There have probably been as many fortunes made in the pizza business in the past 50 years as in Silicon Valley. Most of the pizzas we ravenously consume are descended from those of southern Italian immigrant ovens. But they didn't really catch on in the United States until GIs returned from World War II Italy. Now, there's a pizza variation for nearly every

preference imaginable, and the Midwest serves much of it. Did you know that Pizza Hut is based in Wichita, Kansas; Domino's in Ypsilanti, Michigan; Papa John's in Louisville, Kentucky; and Little Caesar's in Detroit, Michigan?

When you talk pizza in Cincinnati, you're talking LaRosa's. And that's because of one man: Buddy LaRosa, a musta-chioed ball of fire. Buddy has kindly met me at his namesake pizzeria on Boudinot in Westwood, flagship of a local chain, to share some of his favorites. A huge table with a lazy Susan in the middle is rapidly filling up with just about every kind of pizza imaginable, as well as focaccia-bread creations and cheesy stuffed calzone; savory lasagna, spaghetti and ziti pasta dishes; plus an array of Italian hoagie sandwiches bursting with ingredients. Have I died and awakened in some kind of an Italian food heaven? Buddy insists I sample his favorite pizza combo, the Buddy Topper: pepperoni, two types of

sausage, capocolla, banana peppers and extra provolone on Cincinnati's preferred thin crust. *Bene!*

Buddy is the real thing. He grew up in an Italian-American produce-peddling family in Cincinnati. After high school, he did a stint in the Navy, married and bounced around an assortment of jobs, winding up at the post office, where a big idea hit him like—well, like a pizza pie. He'd been helping out his mother and Aunt Dena at an annual festival in his old neighborhood when he realized the "Med-icans" (read that "Americans") were raving about the pasta sauce pizza he'd grown up eating at home. In the Navy, he'd seen how popular pizzas were in South Philly. It was Cincy's turn. Buddy raised $400 and found some partners, whom he later bought out, and started making pizzas—about 100 a week—in a storefront.

Today, there are 58 LaRosa's in the Cincy area, selling 100,000 pizzas a week chain-wide. Buddy's annual revenues are

Strawberry Daiquiri Shortcakes
Montgomery Inn at the Boathouse, Cincinnati

  4 cups strawberries, cut into quarters
  1 cup bottled Daily's Strawberry Daiquiri
     Mix or your favorite strawberry
     daiquiri mix
  3 tablespoons cold butter
2⅓ cups packaged biscuit mix
  ½ cup milk
  2 tablespoons sugar
  6 scoops high-quality vanilla ice cream
  1 cup whipping cream, whipped

For strawberry sauce: In a medium bowl,
combine strawberries and daiquiri mix.
Cover and chill at least 1 hour.

For shortcake: In a medium bowl, use a
pastry blender to cut butter into biscuit mix
until mixture resembles coarse crumbs.
Make a well in the center of the mixture.
Add milk all at once. Using a fork, stir just
until moistened. Drop dough into 6 mounds
on an ungreased baking sheet; flatten each
mound with the back of a spoon until about
¾ inch thick. Sprinkle with sugar. Bake in a
425° oven for 10 to 12 minutes or until
golden. Cool on a wire rack for 10 minutes.

To serve, cut shortcakes in half horizon-
tally. Place bottom layers in 6 shallow
dessert dishes. Top each with a scoop of
ice cream. Replace top layers. Top with
strawberry sauce and whipped cream.
Makes 6 servings.

$130 million, and his product line is avail-
able in area supermarkets and on the
Internet. He's still using his Aunt Dena's
sauce recipe, explaining that it's a bit
sweeter than the typical sauce; he insists
on a certain type of low-acid tomato with
just the right crimson color. Buddy also
uses a slightly smoky-flavored provolone
instead of mozzarella on his pizzas. He's
very picky. Although he's officially "strate-
gically retired," he says he still pops in to
"aggravate" the staff regularly.

Out front, Buddy is a celebrity, stopping
by tables and schmoozing. I trail behind as
he zips from table to table, chatting with
his customers; the place accommodates
400 and most tables are filled. The pizza
here certainly can't be beat, and neither
can the pizza man himself.

A Taste of Porkopolis

Back in the 1800s, when Cincinnati was
America's salt-pork packing hub, it was
known as Porkopolis. That's part of the
reason you'll find packaged-goods con-
glomerate Procter & Gamble (P&G)
ensconced here in its massive, postmod-
ern headquarters downtown. Pork fat
used to be a key ingredient in making soap
and candles, another early P&G mainstay.
The city pays tribute to that and other
aspects of its heritage at Sawyer Point, a
park tucked beside the Ohio River. A
whimsical bronze sculpture there portrays
winged pigs ascending to the heavens
from four steamboat smokestacks.

Cincinnatians pay homage to their
porcine past in another way: feasting on
pork-loin back ribs at the Montgomery
Inn. Of three locations, I choose the strik-
ing, round glass-and-concrete Boathouse
right beside the river, next door to Sawyer
Point. Ribs are one of those things I've
observed Midwesterners get really passionate about. Back home, I'm most

accustomed to Kansas City-style barbecue, with the smoky-good ribs a bit on the
dry side. Montgomery Inn ribs are a revelation to me: They're served very moist,
falling off the bone, drenched in a sweet
barbecue sauce.

Built in 1989, the restaurant is classy.
Inside, eyes feast on 180-degree views of
boats plying the Ohio against a backdrop
of the green Kentucky hills. After I order a
full slab of ribs from the wide-ranging
menu, a friendly server offers me a plastic
bib, just like at Skyline Chili. I find out
why when I start downing the sauce-
slathered ribs (which these days come
from my home state of Iowa), along with a
creamy baked sweet potato and thick,
hand-cut potato slices called Saratoga
chips. I don't expect to have the best
strawberry shortcake of my trip here, but
that turns out to be the case: homemade
shortcake biscuit, locally fabled Graeter's
vanilla ice cream, whipped cream and fat,
fresh strawberries on top. Oh, my!

I decide to finish the evening with a
view from the second-floor wraparound
balcony. On my way upstairs, I pass
mementos from local sports heroes as well
as a lot of Bob Hope memorabilia. My
host, Dean Gregory—son of the late
founder, Ted Gregory—reveals the connection. Hope loved Montgomery Inn ribs
and ate them whenever he performed in
Cincy. Soon, he and the cigar-chomping
Ted became fast friends, and the restaurant regularly shipped ribs to Hope in California. The comedian even had them
flown to Palm Springs when he entertained Her Royal Majesty, Queen Elizabeth II, and Prince Philip!

Where did this rib recipe come from?
Dean credits his mother, Matula, who
purchased a small restaurant with her
husband in suburban Montgomery back
in 1951. The original cook's offerings

were so bad that Matula brought supper, notably her barbecued ribs, to Ted and his friends. Soon, the cook vamoosed and Matula's ribs became the stuff of legend. That first Montgomery Inn expanded steadily over the years to encompass an entire block, with seating for 750, and it's still going strong.

Willy Wonka's Ice Cream

For years, people have been telling me that Graeter's Ice Cream, another Cincy food icon, is out of this world. I'm here to find out why at the firm's plant and retail store on Reading Road in the historic Mount Auburn neighborhood. It's July and National Ice Cream Month—what better way to celebrate?

The same German-American family has been concocting Graeter's ice cream since 1870—longer than any other family-run ice cream enterprise in the United States. Just after the Civil War, when ice cream still was a novelty, Graeter's kept its product frosty with ice cut during the winter from the nearby Ohio River. The family also sold oysters (the ice came in handy for that, too).

Richard Graeter, an affable, fourth-generation partner in the family business, explains the Graeter's mystique. The rich, custardy French-style ice cream is made in "French pots," resembling giant mixers, at the rate of 2½ gallons every 20 minutes, then chilled to 20 degrees below zero. Each batch contains one gallon of egg custard and nine gallons of a cream-and-sugar mixture. The butterfat content is 16–18 percent. All that makes Graeter's very dense, superior to what Richard witheringly calls "industrial ice cream that's really just frozen foam."

The plant is 25,000 square feet, sort of an ice cream version of Willy Wonka's chocolate-factory fantasyland. To keep up

CLOCKWISE, FROM ABOVE: (ALL TAKEN IN CINCINNATI) SUCCULENT BARBECUED PORK-LOIN BACK RIBS AND HOMEMADE SARATOGA CHIPS, MONTGOMERY INN BOATHOUSE. FASHIONING ICE CREAM MASTERPIECES AT GRAETER'S.

DEAN GREGORY (LEFT) AND DAN AT THE MONTGOMERY INN BOATHOUSE, CINCINNATI.

Chicken Paprikas

Tony Packo's Cafe, Toledo

2 1/2 to 3 pounds meaty chicken pieces (breast halves, thighs and drumsticks)
  2 tablespoons cooking oil or olive oil
     Kosher salt or salt
     Ground black pepper
  2 medium onions or 1 large onion, chopped (1 cup)
  1 tablespoon Hungarian paprika or paprika
1/2 cup chicken broth or water
  1 large tomato, peeled, seeded and coarsely chopped
1/2 teaspoon kosher salt or 1/4 teaspoon salt
1/2 cup dairy sour cream
1/4 cup whipping cream
  1 tablespoon all-purpose flour
  1 medium green sweet pepper, cut into thin, bite-size strips
     Hungarian Egg Dumplings (recipe follows) or 3 cups hot cooked wide noodles

Skin chicken. In a 12-inch skillet, cook chicken in hot oil over medium-high heat about 15 minutes or until light brown, turning to brown evenly. Sprinkle chicken with salt and black pepper. Remove chicken; set aside.

Add onion and paprika to skillet. Cook and stir until onion is tender. Return chicken to skillet, turning pieces to coat with paprika mixture. Add chicken broth, tomato and salt. Bring to boiling; reduce heat. Simmer, covered, for 25 minutes. Uncover; cook for 10 to 15 minutes more or until chicken is no longer pink (170° for breasts; 180° for thighs and drumsticks). Remove from heat. Transfer chicken to a serving platter, reserving pan juices. Loosely cover chicken with foil to keep warm.

For sauce: In a small bowl, stir together sour cream, whipping cream and flour;

with demand, ice cream is made 18 hours a day here. Graeter's has 12 stores and 26 franchises in the area, and they ship by mail (the product is packed in dry ice). During the winter holidays, the plant ships about 1,000 boxes a day containing 6–12 pints each. Hometown girl Sarah Jessica Parker is a mint chocolate chip fan (she's said to be high on Skyline Chili, too). Speaking of celebrities, somebody sent Oprah Winfrey a sample of Graeter's butter pecan a couple years ago, and she rated it the best ice cream she'd ever tasted. Now Richard says she's a regular mail-order customer.

I request an assortment of scoops, including Buckeye Blitz (a peanut butter and chocolate chip winner), coconut chip, toffee chip, butter pecan, vanilla, double chocolate chip, and the all-time best-selling black raspberry chocolate chip. Mmmm. I don't even care if I'm dripping on my shirt. Because Graeter's is loaded with milk and eggs, I'm getting a healthy breakfast—right? Richard tells me his favorite is the gold standard ice cream purists judge by: vanilla. He is proud of his family's calling. "Making ice cream is fun. People come in happy and they leave with even bigger smiles on their faces," he says.

gradually stir into pan juices. Return to heat. Cook and stir until thickened and bubbly. Add green pepper. Cook and stir for 1 to 2 minutes more or until green pepper is heated through.

To serve, spoon some of the sauce over chicken; pass remaining sauce. Serve with Hungarian Egg Dumplings or hot cooked noodles. *Makes 6 servings.*

Hungarian Egg Dumplings: For dumpling batter: In a large saucepan, combine 1 cup water, 1/2 cup butter and 1/2 teaspoon salt. Bring to boiling. Add 1 cup all-purpose flour all at once, stirring vigorously. Cook and stir until mixture forms a ball. Remove from heat. Cool for 10 minutes. Add 4 eggs, one at a time, beating well with a wooden spoon after each addition until mixture is shiny and smooth.

In a 4- to 5-quart Dutch oven, bring about 3 quarts lightly salted water to boiling; reduce heat. Carefully drop half of the dumpling dough by tablespoons into gently boiling water. Cook for 8 to 10 minutes or until dumplings are cooked through. Using a slotted spoon, drain on several layers of paper toweling. Repeat with remaining dough. Serve warm. *Makes 6 side-dish servings (about 24 dumplings).*

Cincinnati-Style Chili
Inspired by Skyline Chili, Cincinnati

    5 bay leaves
    1 teaspoon whole allspice
  1/2 teaspoon whole cloves
    2 pounds ground beef
    2 large onions, chopped (2 cups)
    2 cloves garlic, minced
    2 tablespoons chili powder
    1 teaspoon ground cinnamon
  1/2 to 3/4 teaspoon cayenne pepper
  1/8 to 1/4 teaspoon ground cardamom
    2 14-ounce cans beef broth or 3 1/2 cups
       water
    1 15- to 16-ounce can red kidney beans,
       rinsed and drained
    1 8-ounce can tomato sauce
    1 tablespoon vinegar
    1 teaspoon Worcestershire sauce
  1/2 teaspoon salt
       Hot cooked spaghetti
       Chopped onion (optional)
       Shredded cheddar cheese (optional)
       Oyster crackers (optional)

For spice bag: Place bay leaves, allspice and cloves in center of a 6-inch square of double-thickness, 100-percent-cotton cheesecloth. Tie into a bag with clean kitchen string; set aside.

For meat sauce: In a 5- to 6-quart Dutch oven, cook beef, the 2 cups onion and garlic until the meat is brown and onion is tender; drain well. Stir in chili powder, cinnamon, cayenne pepper and cardamom. Cook and stir for 1 minute. Stir in broth or water, beans, tomato sauce, vinegar, Worcestershire sauce and salt. Add spice bag. Bring to boiling; reduce heat. Simmer, covered, for 45 minutes. Uncover; simmer about 15 minutes more or until desired consistency. Remove spice bag; discard.

To serve, place hot cooked spaghetti onto dinner plates and make an indentation in the center. Top with meat sauce. If you like, sprinkle with additional chopped onion and/or shredded cheese and serve with oyster crackers. *Makes 6 to 8 servings.*

Fresh Sweet-Corn Salsa
Inspired by Fulton Farms, Troy

    4 large ears fresh corn or one 10-ounce
       package frozen whole kernel corn
    1 tablespoon cooking oil
    1 large onion, coarsely chopped (1 cup)
    1 large green or red sweet pepper,
       coarsely chopped (1 cup)
    1 fresh jalapeño pepper, seeded and
       finely chopped
    1 cup chopped, peeled tomatoes or
       one 14 1/2-ounce can diced tomatoes,
       drained
  1/4 cup lime juice
  1/2 teaspoon salt
  1/2 teaspoon ground cumin
  1/2 teaspoon freshly ground black pepper

Remove husks from fresh ears of corn; discard. Scrub with a stiff brush to remove silks; rinse. Cook, covered, in enough lightly salted boiling water to cover for 5 to 7 minutes or until tender; drain. Let cool. Cut kernels from cobs. Or, cook frozen corn according to package directions and drain.

In a large saucepan, heat oil over medium-high heat. Add onion, sweet pepper and jalapeño pepper. Cook until onion is tender but not brown. Stir in corn, tomatoes, lime juice, salt, cumin and black pepper. Cook and stir over medium heat until heated through. Let cool. Transfer to a storage container. Cover and chill for up to 1 week. Serve with pork, beef or poultry. *Makes about 4 cups.*

Travel Journal

More Information

Cincinnati USA Regional Tourism Network (800/344-3445, www.cincinnati USA.com). **Greater Toledo Convention & Visitors Bureau** (800/243-4667, www.dotoledo.org). For Troy, **Miami County Visitors & Convention Bureau** (800/348-8993, www.visitmiamicounty .org). For Urbana, **Champaign County Visitors Bureau** (877/873-5764, www.champaignohio.com).

Featured Dining

LaRosa's Pizzeria Cincinnati. Fifty-eight locations in the metro area (877/347-1111, ext. 2).
Montgomery Inn Boathouse Cincinnati. Three locations in the metro area (513/721-7427).
Skyline Chili Cincinnati. Many locations in the metro area (513/221-2142).
White Castle Cincinnati. Many locations in the metro area (513/559-0575).
Tony Packo's Café Toledo (419/691-6054).

More Great Dining

Primavista Cincinnati. In a hilltop high-rise apartment building on the western fringe of downtown, innovative northern Italian cuisine vies for your attention with the river view (513/251-6467).
Oliver House Complex Toledo. In the Warehouse District, this pre-Civil War landmark is the oldest building still standing downtown. It houses five restaurants, including Rockwell's, the city's premier steak house, and Maumee Bay Brewing Company & Restaurant (419/241-1253).

Featured Stops

Graeter's Ice Cream Cincinnati. Twelve stores and 26 franchises in the Cincinnati area (no plant tours; 800/721-3323).
Fulton Farms Troy (937/335-6983).
Freshwater Farms of Ohio Urbana (800/634-7434).

More Great Stops

Cincinnati City attractions range from the Museum Center in a 1933 Art Deco train station and the National Underground Railroad Freedom Center to the Cincinnati Zoo and Botanical Garden. Just across the river in Kentucky is Newport on the Levee, an entertainment and shopping district that includes the Newport Aquarium.
Findlay Market Cincinnati. In the Over-the-Rhine historic neighborhood minutes north of downtown, this year-round (Wednesdays–Sundays) indoor-outdoor marketplace has operated continuously since 1852 and is known for fresh produce, meats and ethnic foods (513/665-4839). Also the site of a seasonal farmers market.
Meier's Wine Cellars, Inc. Cincinnati. Just north of downtown, Meier's is Ohio's oldest and largest winery, with a tasting room and wine shop (800/346-2941).
Toledo Beside the Maumee River with Lake Erie at its doorstep, Ohio's fourth-largest city anchors the state's northwestern corner, attracting visitors with its zoo, COSI Science Center and art museum.
Erie Street Market Toledo. In the Warehouse District just southwest of downtown, you can shop and dine year-round at this fresh-food emporium filled with vendors' kiosks adjacent to a seasonal farmers market, the Libbey Glass Factory Outlet and Superior Antiques Mall (419/936-3743).
Robert Rothschild Farm Urbana. Three miles east of this county seat town are a market, cafe, gardens and production facility on a 170-acre pick-your-own raspberry farm that's evolved into a nationally known specialty food producer with a line of preserves, mustards, dips, salsas, sauces, dressings and toppings (800/356-8933).

Dan's Lodgings

Vernon Manor Hotel Cincinnati ($$$; 800/543-3999).
AmeriHost Inn St. Marys, about 50 miles northwest of Troy ($$; 800/434-5800).

More Great Lodgings

Cincinnatian Hotel Downtown Cincinnati. A 120-plus-year-old landmark ($$$$; 800/942-9000).
Hilton Cincinnati Netherland Plaza, Cincinnati. A 1930s Art Deco palace downtown ($$$$; 800/445-8667).
Mansion View Toledo. A seven-bedroom, 1887 Queen Anne bed and breakfast in the historic West End neighborhood ($$$; 419/244-5676).

Food Events

Tops Great American Rib Cook-Off and Music Festival Cleveland, Thursday through Monday of Memorial Day weekend—A dozen grilling gurus from eight states compete for prize money and the titles of "Greatest Ribs in America" and "Greatest Sauce in America." Sample their tantalizing ribs and fixin's, or save room for the rib-eating contest. Devour the saucy sounds of a different band each night. Admission charged (440/247-4386, www.cleveland .com/rib).
Taste of Cincinnati Cincinnati, Memorial Day weekend—At the city's official kickoff to summer, grazing gourmets fork into lamb shish kabobs, barbecued ribs, Creole gumbo and other delectable dishes served up by more than 40 area restaurants along four blocks of downtown's Central Parkway. The nation's longest-running culinary arts festival (since 1979) dishes out music, too, with acts on four stages (513/579-3124, www.taste-of-cincinnati.com).
Troy Strawberry Festival Troy, first full weekend in June—Berries rule down by the Miami River levee, where food vendors serve strawberry doughnuts, pies, fudge and even burritos. The party starts with a big Saturday parade and keeps rolling with a bike tour, Strawberry Stroll, 10K run, classic-car show, crafts and stage enter-

FOUNTAIN SQUARE, CINCINNATI.

tainment. Free family festival (937/339-7714, www.troyohiochamber.com).

Banana Split Festival Wilmington, second weekend in June—Split for the town where banana splits were created in 1907 and pile on the toppings at the build-your-own banana split booth. Add to your ice cream headache at the banana-split-eating contest. Nonfat temptations: 5K Go Bananas Run, a cruise-in of 350 classic cars, crafts and free 1950s and '60s concerts (877/428-4748, www.bananasplit festival.com).

State Fair Columbus, 12 days starting the first Wednesday in August—Pig out on pork loin sandwiches, milk shakes, rib-eye steaks, chicken dinners, corn fritters and gyros in the Ohio Food pavilion, where the state's meat, dairy and vegetable producers all serve their foods (888/646-3976, www.ohiostatefair.com).

Vintage Ohio Kirtland, first weekend in August—Twenty Ohio wineries join with regional restaurants to offer pierogies, seafood, strawberry crepes, gourmet cheeses and state-made wines. You can also attend cooking demonstrations and wine seminars. Also at Lake Farmpark:

jazz, reggae and oldies groups perform and fireworks dazzle on Friday night. Admission charged (800/227-6972, www.ohiowines.org).

Jackson County Apple Festival Jackson, third full week in September—It's fun to the core at the apple-peeling and apple-pie-baking contests, the car and crafts shows, and Saturday night's grand parade of lighted floats. Watch apple butter cooked daily, sip cider and buy a bushel of just-picked apples. Two stages of free entertainment offer gospel, country, oldies music and more (740/286-1339, www.jacksonapplefestival.com).

Ohio Fish and Shrimp Festival Urbana, third Saturday in September—Eat your limit of Ohio-raised seafood when vendors lure you with coconut-crusted shrimp, stuffed shrimp and orange-marinated trout. Reel in more fun at the shrimp-eating contest, crawfish races, sturgeon petting zoo and bluegrass festival. Also at the home of Ohio's largest fish hatchery, you can feed the trout and see the monster shrimp and koi display. Parking fee (800/634-7434, www.fwfarms.com).

Ohio Sauerkraut Festival Waynesville, second full weekend in October—Follow your nose downtown, where 30 food vendors dish up sauerkraut in many creative ways, or haul in your heads for the cabbage-growing contest. Approximately 500 crafts booths line the streets, and bands, singers and dancers entertain on stage (513/897-8855, www.sauerkraut festival.com).

Circleville Pumpkin Show Circleville, third Wednesday through Saturday in October—At Ohio's oldest (since 1903) and largest festival, pumpkins turn into everything except carriages: pizza, burgers, ice cream, chili and doughnuts. Witness the pumpkin weigh-in, where 1,000-pounders tip the scales; the pie-baking contest; art displays and stage shows. Seven parades pass by, including Saturday night's Parade of Queens, led by Miss Pumpkin Show (888/770-7425, www.pumpkinshow.com).

Mail Order

Freshwater Farms of Ohio Trout smoked to perfection with a blend of local hardwoods. Also smoked-trout mousse and smoked-trout cheese balls. Attractive gift boxes include Guggisberg Baby Swiss, old-fashioned piccalilly sauce and crackers (800/634-7434, www.fwfarms.com).

Graeter's Ice Cream Home of irresistible ice cream in an array of delicious flavors, all made in small batches with the freshest ingredients. Six- and 12-pint shipping coolers ensure safe arrival of your frozen order. Don't miss gift boxes of handmade chocolates (800/721-3323, www.graeters.com).

LaRosa's Mouthwatering pizza and other popular Italian selections made from LaRosa's Family Recipe Original Pasta Sauce. This Cincy eatery sells pizza kits, salad dressings, pasta sauce and lasagna-ravioli family dinner packs (877/246-2999, www.cincinnatifavorites.com).

Montgomery Inn Famous for sweet-sauced barbecued pork ribs. A wide range of specialties are available, including ribs, pulled smoked barbecue pork and chicken, barbecue sauce and, of course, bibs (800/872-7427, www.montgomeryinn.com).

Skyline Chili Skyline's sauce is notably thin in consistency and seasoned with a secret blend of spices. Skyline Crave Kit includes four cans of chili, a box of oyster crackers, hot sauce and peppermint patties. Or request Just Send Me the Chili, an eight-pack of 15-ounce cans (877/246-2999, www.cincinnatifavorites.com).

Tony Packo's Legendary Hungarian hot dogs. Known for Packo's Hot Dog Chili Sauce and a mouth-puckering assortment of outstanding pickles, including hot Hungarian banana peppers, chunky garlic dills and sweet-hot pickles (866/472-2567, www.tonypackos.com).

SOUTH DAKOTA
Wild Game, Buffalo and Native Legends

THIS PAGE: BUFFALO LUNCHING AT POSSIBILITY FARM, CARPENTER. OPPOSITE PAGE, LEFT TO RIGHT: PITCHFORK STEAKS, PRAIRIE SKY GUEST RANCH, VEBLEN. SUNSET IN THE HILLS NEAR VEBLEN. WES HANSEN, FLANDREAU SANTEE SIOUX RESERVATION, FLANDREAU.

In some respects, traveling the prairies of South Dakota is reminiscent of an exotic African safari. First, at 754,844 inhabitants, the uncrowded state ranks 46th in population among all the states. The once-wild, now-tamed Missouri River separates two distinct regions and landscapes.

Sure, eastern South Dakota has its familiar-looking towns and farms, as well as the prosperous city of Sioux Falls, but most of the state is wide-open spaces that belie the varied cooking traditions and dining options I'll soon experience.

Second, there's a substantial indigenous population here, with a rich and unique culture that somehow survived the often-brutal onslaught of European-American settlement. In fact, South Dakota is 8.3 percent Native American, mainly Lakota and Dakota Sioux, who reside on the nine reservations entirely or partly within the state—that's the third-highest percentage of Native Americans in the country. The great warriors Crazy Horse and Chief Sitting Bull are among the state's most revered native sons.

Third, South Dakota is the Noah's Ark of the Midwest when it comes to variety of fauna. Hunters and wildlife watchers alike are eagerly welcomed here for their dollars; tourism is the state's second-largest industry, after agriculture. The visitors revel in bagging or just viewing ring-necked pheasants, partridge, grouse, prairie chickens, ducks, geese, turkeys, quail, doves, deer, elk, mountain lions, bighorn sheep, coyotes, prairie dogs, red foxes and many more species.

Finally, there's the diverse land itself: more than 77,000 square miles comprising farmland, prairies, plains, buttes, vast man-made reservoirs on the Missouri River, eerie badlands and the forested, mountainlike Black Hills.

Wildlife and rural ways dominate most of the state; in fact, farms drive the state's economy to the tune of $4.5 billion per year in cattle, hogs, corn, soybeans, wheat, oats, sunflowers and other crops and livestock, including domesticated buffalo. Among Midwest states, South Dakota also produces an unusual number of sheep and lambs, raised primarily for meat in the eastern part of the state and premium wool in the western part. Overall, South Dakota farmers have benefited from new varieties of crops such as wheat, soybeans and corn adapted for the state's shorter growing season.

I've explored every corner of South Dakota during past visits, from Mount Rushmore in the southwest to the surprising prairie pothole lakes and *coteau* ridges of the hilly, glacier-created plateau in the northeast, but my route on this trip will take me through only the eastern part of the state. Still, traversing even a narrow swath yields plenty of open horizons, fresh air and diversity—epicurean and otherwise. I'll dine like a king in the heart of the state's largest city, forage and cook with Dakota Sioux, feast on the house specialty at a buffalo ranch and devour a unique dinner entrée: pitchfork steak. Let the safari begin!

Big Appetites, New Tastes

Among the first Europeans to feast on South Dakota's bounty were the 30-plus members of the Lewis and Clark Expedition, who traveled up and down the Missouri River on their 1804–06 round-trip sightseeing gig. Because the men (they didn't enlist Sacagawea as a translator-guide until they got to North Dakota) were paddling so intensely most of the time, their ravenous appetites can be forgiven—but hardly believed. Each person consumed up to 15,000 calories per day, mostly in the form of wild game: buffalo (an incredible 9 pounds of meat per day, when available), squirrel, opossum, bear, venison, antelope, elk, beaver, rabbit,

Pheasant Ravioli Appetizers
Minervas Restaurant & Bar, Sioux Falls

- 1 16-ounce package frozen pheasant ravioli or two 9-ounce packages refrigerated meat- or cheese-filled ravioli or one 16-ounce package frozen cheese-filled ravioli
- 2 tablespoons butter
- 1½ cups sliced and stemmed fresh shiitake mushrooms
- 2 cloves garlic, minced
- ½ of a 16-ounce jar Alfredo sauce or one 10-ounce container refrigerated Alfredo sauce
- ¾ cup chicken broth
- ½ cup freshly shredded Parmesan cheese
- ¼ cup snipped fresh parsley

Cook the ravioli according to package directions; drain. Set aside.

In a large skillet, melt butter over medium-high heat. Add mushrooms and garlic. Cook and stir about 5 minutes or until tender and most of the liquid has evaporated. Add Alfredo sauce and chicken broth. Bring to boiling; reduce heat. Add the ravioli. Simmer, covered, about 5 minutes or until heated through, stirring gently once or twice.

To serve, spoon the ravioli mixture into 8 small, shallow pasta plates or salad plates; sprinkle each with Parmesan cheese and parsley. *Makes 8 appetizer or 4 main-dish servings.*

Note: See page 173 for a pheasant ravioli mail-order source (Valley Game & Gourmet).

duck, goose, wild turkey and even an occasional wolf—all supplemented by wild berries, root vegetables and precious barrels of salt pork, dried corn, flour, sugar, beans and other provender.

Too bad the explorers arrived a couple hundred years too early to dine on the more refined wild-game creations now featured at many great restaurants throughout the state. At Minervas, on a corner of shady, mall-like South Phillips Avenue in prospering downtown Sioux Falls (population 144,000), for example, I enjoy pheasant ravioli served as an appetizer. The flagship of a five-state chain of restaurants and bars, Minervas is perhaps the state's best-known eatery.

The restaurant was founded as a *crêperie* in 1977, but head chef Don Anderson now tempts diners with a more extensive menu of steaks, fish, seafood, pasta, superb homemade French baguettes—the best of my entire journey—and a wondrous meal-in-itself salad bar. And then there's that pheasant ravioli, delicately flavored and moist (Don adds bits of bacon to the potentially dry pheasant breast meat), served with a shiitake mushroom cream sauce infused with hazelnut liqueur. Its sublime flavor proves just how much South Dakota cuisine has evolved since the Corps of Discovery trip.

Attractions with a Mission

I intersect with Lewis and Clark's route as I cross the bluff-lined Missouri on my way to Mitchell (population 14,600), about 90 miles west of Sioux Falls on I-90. I'm stopping here to pay my respects at the Corn Palace, the better known of two rather exotic food-related attractions on my itinerary. It's one of those places you have to see to believe.

Back in the late 1800s, boosters were having a hard time convincing settlers that South Dakota was a swell place to raise corn, which it eventually turned out to be in spite of seven-year droughts, arctic winters and grasshopper plagues. So, in 1892, the civic fathers kicked off a grand Corn Belt Exposition to promote the fertility of South Dakota soil. The centerpiece of that festival was the original (but temporary) Corn Palace building, which was replaced with a permanent concrete structure in 1921.

I'm here, among some of the 400,000 annual visitors, on a sunny morning trying to figure out how I'm going to explain this kitschy fantasy edifice. What otherwise would look rather like a typical, boxy municipal auditorium is copiously adorned with onion-shaped domes, minaretlike towers and murals fashioned from nine strains of corn—specially grown for their yellow, white, blue and red hues—as well as other grains and grasses. The perishable exterior artwork, which unappreciative birds see as one big banquet, gets replaced each summer by local carpenter-Michelangelos in time for an annual fall harvest festival. This year's images, designed by a local artist, illustrate a "Life on the Farm" theme.

The Corn Palace, which houses a busy gift shop in addition to agricultural and historic exhibits, is also a first-class entertainment and sports venue. Clearly, it has accomplished its original mission of promoting corn: Farmers in eastern South Dakota harvested almost 200 million bushels in 2004, worth more than $660 million. Back when the first Corn Palace was constructed, the average corn yield here was 4 bushels per acre—now, it's 130 bushels!

Further evidence of the state's exotic side is the lesser-known International Vinegar Museum in the tiny, pothole-lake country village of Roslyn (population 225), situated a long way from anywhere of size.

Housed in a small former community building, the museum is a revelation to me on several levels. From the exhibits inside, I learn that there's a whole lot more to pungent vinegar than meets the eye—or the nose! The sour liquid has a fascinating history, in terms of both culture (Cleopatra once dissolved a huge pearl in a glass of vinegar just to impress her new boyfriend, Marc Antony) and manufacturing (different nations have different techniques, but we can thank Louis Pasteur for developing the process most widely used today).

Then there are vinegar's extensive uses in cooking. The range of delicate flavors and aromas—from vanilla, pecan and nutmeg to saffron, tea and coriander—is amazing. It's also used medicinally, purportedly to remove freckles and soothe assorted nasty stings and bites, and as a cleaning aid. I get to sniff (at a distance) and sample (on a cotton swab) some of the more than 350 vinegar varieties on display, expertly guided by the museum's friendly and informative director, Lawrence Diggs.

Lawrence's story is the other reason I consider the vinegar museum a must-see. In a nutshell: He is a former San Francisco radio personality and Peace Corps veteran who became consumed by the subject of vinegar after writing a college paper about it. Soon, he was a globe-trotting consultant, advising eager clients about all aspects of vinegar making.

So how did Lawrence, a Buddhist and African American, wind up in Norwegian-Lutheran Roslyn? He simply wanted an affordable, off-the-beaten-path place to conduct his vinegar-development projects; he found his house in Roslyn via the Internet. The town welcomed its new citizen, and Lawrence in turn became involved in civic activities. When a local development committee asked him to

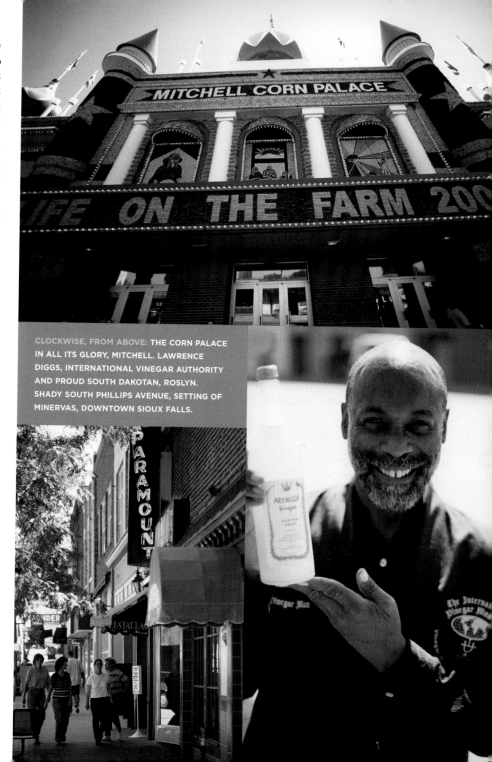

CLOCKWISE, FROM ABOVE: **THE CORN PALACE IN ALL ITS GLORY, MITCHELL. LAWRENCE DIGGS, INTERNATIONAL VINEGAR AUTHORITY AND PROUD SOUTH DAKOTAN, ROSLYN. SHADY SOUTH PHILLIPS AVENUE, SETTING OF MINERVAS, DOWNTOWN SIOUX FALLS.**

help create a tourism attraction, the International Vinegar Museum was born. It's a heartening story that attests to both the ingenuity of Great Plains communities struggling to survive and the mutual affection that developed between Lawrence Diggs and his adopted hometown.

When you visit Roslyn, be sure to stop by the local dairy drive-in to order a treat you probably won't find anywhere else: a strawberry-vinegar shake. It's made from the usual ingredients, plus a splash or two of strawberry vinegar (you can order other variations, too)—a subtly sweet-sour combination. It just proves that Lawrence has succeeded in his mission: "It goes beyond vinegar. I'm trying to get people to see their relationship to food and aromas in a new way."

You See Weeds; I See Food

My previous forays into South Dakota informed me somewhat about Native American culture, primarily that of the Lakota and Dakota Sioux, who ruled what's now the western part of the state. But I still have much to learn, especially in the food sense. That's why I'm delighted to tarry for a few hours in Flandreau (population 2,400) on the 2,500-acre Flandreau Santee Sioux Reservation.

Near I-29, about 45 miles northeast of Sioux Falls and 10 miles west of the Minnesota state line, it is South Dakota's smallest reservation, founded along the Big Sioux River back in the 1930s. I'm eager to interview two of the 470 tribe members who live here (out of 750 members total) about their food traditions.

Frankly, I'm surprised when I pull into the tidy town. I wasn't expecting tepees and campfires, but neither was I envisioning tree-lined streets, well-kept houses and a typical Midwest community. Flandreau is the home of the federal

government's 1871 Flandreau Indian School, attended by almost 400 Native American youths from around the nation who board here during their high-school years. That institution and the big Royal River Casino and Hotel, opened in 1990, have lifted Flandreau above the miasma of poverty that afflicts so many reservation communities.

The prosperity stems partially from a 1987 U.S. Supreme Court ruling that permits gaming on reservations, independent of state regulation. Casinos near urban centers, such as nearby Sioux Falls, can be highly profitable. Much of the money goes directly to tribe members in the form of stipends (each member of this tribe receives $1,000 per month), and a big share funds much-needed improvements in reservation services (medical, health, housing), infrastructure, tribal and non-tribal community projects, schools, and local and national charities.

In the vast casino kitchen, I'm introduced to my cooking instructor: Helena Thompson, whose Dakota name is Bear Woman, or *Mato Wiyan*. She's going to show me how to make fry bread, or *zeepzeepela*, a popular Native American treat that's eaten in a variety of ways. Helena grew up north of here on the larger Lake Traverse Reservation, where one of her sons now is a tribal director. That's where her grandmother and mother long ago taught her to make fry bread, along with other traditional foods, including roasted turtle. Helena says the turtles

went in the oven alive. "Once, my grandmother had me eat the heart raw, because it would make me brave," she tells me, adding that turtles are considered sacred by many tribes. (Personally, I'd rather remain a coward.)

Back to fry bread. Without any measuring cups or spoons, we mix flour, salt, baking powder, sugar, powdered milk and an egg in a bowl. Then, we add shortening and lukewarm water. The result resembles a biscuit mix. "Not too much flour there," Helena cautions me. "They'll be too heavy to fry properly." As I stir the dough, she explains the various ways she serves fry bread: plain, with jam and peanut butter, sprinkled with powdered sugar or in the shape of a bowl for "Indian tacos" consisting of seasoned hamburger, lettuce, cheese and onion.

Helena says her family ate a lot of game

The Sioux believe that each plant has its own song; they sing for the spirit of that plant while gathering it.

while she was growing up, including elk, pheasant, rabbit, skunk, opossum and muskrat (she claims the latter are rather sweet-tasting)—all roasted, boiled or stewed and usually unadorned. As for vegetables, she describes a specialty she still makes at home: corn soup. "I dry fresh corn, hanging it in a bag to dry a couple days when it's really hot outside. Then I make my soup with the dried corn, some wild turnips, potatoes and pinto beans, all seasoned with just salt and pepper."

Time to float the giant, platelike pillows of fry bread a few minutes in hot cooking oil until they turn golden brown on each side. For our second batch, Helena shows me how to fashion the fry-bread bowls used for taco salads. Then we sample our creations, some sugared, some filled with salad fixings.

My hands-on lesson completed, Helena introduces me to my next host, Wes Hansen, another Flandreau Santee Sioux. (The tribe's name in the Dakota language is *Mdewakantonwan,* which means "spirit lake people.") Wes tells me he's an Army veteran who studied social work and psychology in college, then held several positions at the Indian school and with the tribe until he became disabled by a painful back problem.

We leave the casino and cruise toward Wes' house, down a gravel road past a horse corral and a field where some of the tribe's 200 domesticated buffalo graze. "We take down about 10 of our buffalo a year to eat during our powwow in the summer," he says. "We also give the meat to senior citizens and to charities." Wes explains that his tribe migrated northwestward over the decades, often unwillingly, from its origins in the Southeast. Prior to a reservation uprising in the 1860s that resulted in their forcible relocation, Wes' seminomadic ancestors lived in what's now Minnesota's Twin Cities, fishing and hunting buffalo on the Plains during summer.

Eyes cast downward, we stroll Wes' large backyard, where he begins to demonstrate his incredible store of botanical knowledge, passed down orally through the generations. "Where you see weeds, I see food," he tells me, stopping every few yards to point out another plant with cooking, ceremonial or medicinal uses. Wes shows me some wild turnips, which he dries rock-hard and braids together like a garland of garlic bulbs or peppers, to be used a couple at a time in game stews. There's the arrowhead plant, with a tuber that's eaten like potatoes, and another Wes calls

CLOCKWISE, FROM ABOVE: (ALL TAKEN IN THE FLANDREAU AREA) WINDING COUNTRY ROAD NORTH OF TOWN. WES HANSEN HELPING DAN IDENTIFY USEFUL NATIVE PLANTS ON THE FLANDREAU SANTEE SIOUX RESERVATION. HELENA THOMPSON HOLDING HOT FRY BREAD.

LEFT TO RIGHT: **COMBINE AT WORK AT POSSIBILITY FARM, CARPENTER. SHREDDED BUFFALO SANDWICH AND CORN ON THE COB, POSSIBILITY FARM. A DESCENDANT OF THE ORIGINAL RESIDENTS OF THE GREAT PLAINS, POSSIBILITY FARM. RANCHER BRUCE PRINS (LEFT) PREPARING PITCHFORK STEAKS, PRAIRIE SKY GUEST RANCH, VEBLEN.**

the hog-peanut plant, a wild bean that field mice favor. "We always leave some for the mice. We never take all there is of anything. That's our way," he says.

Wes proceeds to some wild berries and talks of the many varieties: currant, chokeberry, strawberry, gooseberry, grape and elderberry. Then, our short stroll completed, we relax in lawn chairs in the shade of an elm tree, where Wes offers a fitting conclusion: "Whatever the food is, we always show our thankfulness. We pray for the spirit of the buffalo and other animals we hunt. Each plant has its own song, and we sing for the spirit of that plant while gathering it." I'm grateful for this profound reminder to always be thankful for what I eat.

All About Buffalo

My drive through eastern South Dakota's flat, fertile farm country is interspersed with eye-popping fields of bright yellow sunflowers and the squeaky call of the killdeer birds that seem to be winging all about me. I linger an hour in prosperous De Smet (population 1,200), about 42 miles west of the college town of Brookings. De Smet calls itself the "Little Town on the Prairie" because gifted storyteller Laura Ingalls Wilder lived here from 1879 to 1890. It was in this railroad outpost that stouthearted young Laura met and married equally hardworking Almanzo Wilder and bore their daughter, Rose, before the fledgling family relocated via covered wagon to the Missouri Ozarks.

After a quick tour of the well-preserved buildings at the popular Laura Ingalls Wilder Center, I drop in at the busy Oxbow Restaurant for coffee and a slice of cherry pie with ice cream. The menu features such marketing-savvy entrées as "Ingalls' Pork Chops" and a "Prairie Town Burger." I wonder what Laura would have thought of the Mexican Fiesta Special, mozzarella sticks, or the French vanilla and English toffee cappuccinos.

On to my date with a buffalo herd! At one time, anywhere from 30 to 60 million buffalo, or bison (*tatanka* to the Sioux), are thought to have roamed the Great Plains. The restive herds sometimes blanketed dozens of square miles at a time, generously sustaining the Plains Indians and their wandering lifestyle. But by 1890, in one of the most precipitous annihilations of a species in natural history, European Americans had reduced the numbers to just a few hundred. Now, husbandry has restored the buffalo population to about 230,000 nationally, most living in managed herds like the one I'm visiting.

Possibility Farm (the name was inspired by a Bible verse) is a 5,000-acre farm and bed and breakfast 10 miles from Carpenter (population 10). It's run by Darla Hofer Loewen, whose father founded the operation 60 years ago, and her husband Harold, an ordained Mennonite minister. Just a few miles from the farm are several Hutterite "colonies" of up to 120 mem-

bers each, in which followers of a Mennonite sect live the communal agrarian life that Darla's German-Russian immigrant forebears did.

The farmstead is typical of what I've seen throughout the area: neat, red-painted barns and outbuildings and an updated, 1950s ranch-style home with simple furnishings that include a few family antiques. At the large dining room table, we chat over coffee and a plate of Darla's homemade sticky rolls. Harvests have been good in this area in recent years, Harold tells me. Farmers are benefiting from hardy new varieties of wheat and other crops, and moisture has been plentiful.

In addition to a mix of crops, Harold and Darla raise herds of buffalo and Hereford-Angus cattle. The sphinx-faced, woolly brown buffalo, which the Loewens have bred for seven years, go to a kosher slaughterhouse when they reach about 26 months and 1,200 pounds, helping to satisfy the ever-increasing demand in

restaurants and markets across the nation.

Time to sample the specialty of the house. Harold invokes a blessing, then Darla serves up juicy, shredded buffalo atop yeasty buns she's baked from wheat grown on the farm combined with store-bought flour. My verdict? Buffalo tastes just like lean beef, perhaps a bit sweeter. "I cook it low and slow—that's the secret," Darla says. "We also serve our guests buffalo steaks, sliced roast buffalo and buffalo ribs."

Since opening their lodging operation in 1998, the Loewens have introduced summer guests from more than a dozen states to life on a South Dakota farm, and many hunters to abundant ring-necked pheasants, Hungarian partridge and grouse. After lunch, we hop into Harold's pickup to view buffalo of various sizes energetically milling about a large, fenced-in grazing area. "Buffalo are very intuitive, a lot smarter than cattle—and very active, which is why their meat is so lean," Harold

says. Though buffalo are known as the "lawn mowers of the Plains" because they eat just about anything that sprouts out of the soil, Harold adds some grain to his herd's menu to help fatten the animals. His "star" buffalo is all white, considered sacred by the Sioux.

Pitchfork Steaks

On to my last South Dakota stop, located in the rumpled hills and ridges of the state's northeastern corner, near the headwaters of the Red River and a continental divide that most of us have never heard of: Water flowing north of here winds up in the Red River and eventually in Canada's Hudson Bay and the Arctic Ocean, while water coursing south feeds via the Big Sioux into the Missouri and Mississippi rivers and, thence, the Gulf of Mexico and the Caribbean Sea.

Two-thousand-acre Prairie Sky, my destination, is another working ranch with cattle, buffalo and horses. Like the

Loewens' farm, it's also a guest ranch and hunting preserve, with a main lodge and four rustic-looking but very comfortable cabins. Guests also come for the summer horse camp and fishing and for snow-mobiling fun in winter. For the past six years, rancher Bruce Prins and his wife Corrine have run the property.

The signature food event here, and the reason for my visit, is the Prins' pitchfork steak fry (Wednesdays, June through August), a tradition sometimes referred to as "pitchfork fondue." I watch hungrily as Bruce and an assistant impale aged, 10-ounce prime sirloin filets—up to a dozen at a time—on pitchforks and immerse them in a 15-gallon container of 400-degree soybean oil. Precisely four minutes are needed for medium, three and a half for medium-rare.

The result: perfectly done beef, pleasantly crusty on the outside yet supremely juicy on the inside and not a bit greasy; the high temperature seals in the juices and keeps the oil out. As part of my novel South Dakota ranch feast, I devour some of talented Corrine's home-baked bread, potato and layered salads, baked beans and her unsurpassed rhubarb cobbler.

As we survey the glorious, early-evening "big sky" of the Prins' *coteau* ridges from the porch of the main lodge, Corrine tells me the couple has one daughter who lives in the area, as well as a daughter in Texas and a son in New York City. We laugh over a story: When Corrine visited her kitchen-less New York son, he requested that she bake a homemade cherry pie. "I just went to a deli in his neighborhood and asked if I could use their kitchen—and they let me!" It's yet more evidence of the typical resourcefulness and warmth I've experienced with everyone I've met on my food safari here in South Dakota.

Taste of South Dakota

Easy Indian Fry Bread

Inspired by Flandreau Santee Sioux Reservation, Flandreau

1 16-ounce package (12) frozen dinner rolls, thawed
  Cooking oil for shallow-fat frying
  Taco Meat Sauce (recipe follows)

On a lightly floured surface, roll out each dough ball into a 6-inch circle.

In a heavy skillet, heat about 1 inch of cooking oil over medium-high heat to 365°. Fry dough circles, 1 or 2 at a time, in hot oil about 1 minute or until bread circles are golden brown, turning once. Remove with tongs and drain on paper towels. Keep warm in a 300° oven while frying remaining circles.

To serve, top with Taco Meat Sauce. Serve immediately. *Makes 12.*

Taco Meat Sauce: In a large skillet, cook 2 pounds lean ground beef until meat is brown; drain fat. Stir in one 16-ounce can refried beans, 1 cup tomato juice, 1 cup water, 1/4 cup chopped onion, 1 tablespoon taco seasoning or chili seasoning and 1 teaspoon chili powder. Bring to boiling; reduce heat. Simmer, covered, about 30 minutes or until desired consistency. Spoon over warm fry bread. If you like, top with dairy sour cream, shredded cheddar cheese, shredded lettuce and chopped tomato.

Dakota Buffalo Taco Soup

Inspired by Possibility Farm, Carpenter

1 pound ground bison (buffalo) or lean ground beef
1 large onion, chopped (1 cup)
2 14 1/2-ounce cans diced tomatoes with onion and garlic, undrained
1 15-ounce can pinto beans or black-eyed peas, rinsed and drained
1 15-ounce can black beans, rinsed and drained
1 15-ounce can chili beans in chili gravy, undrained
1 15-ounce can hominy or whole kernel corn, undrained
1 cup water
1 4 1/2-ounce can diced green chili peppers, undrained
1 1.25-ounce package taco seasoning mix
1 1-ounce package ranch salad dressing mix
  Dairy sour cream (optional)
  Bottled salsa (optional)
  Crushed tortilla chips (optional)

In a 5- to 6-quart Dutch oven, cook meat and onion until meat is brown; drain. Add undrained tomatoes, pinto beans, black beans, chili beans, hominy, water and green chili peppers to meat mixture. Stir in taco seasoning mix and ranch salad dressing mix.

Bring soup mixture to boiling; reduce heat. Simmer, covered, for 30 to 35 minutes, stirring occasionally. If you like, top with sour cream, salsa and/or tortilla chips. *Makes 8 servings.*

Slow Cooker Method: Brown ground meat and onion as directed above. Drain and transfer meat mixture to a 4- to 5-quart slow cooker. Add undrained tomatoes, pinto beans, black beans, chili beans, hominy, water and green chili peppers to mixture. Stir in taco seasoning mix and ranch salad dressing mix. Cover and cook on low-heat setting for 6 to 8 hours or on high-heat setting for 3 to 4 hours. Serve as above.

Travel Journal

More Information

Black Hills, Badlands & Lakes Association (605/355-3600, www.blackhills badlands.com). For Flandreau: **Brookings Area Chamber of Commerce and Convention Bureau** (800/699-6125, www.brookingssd.com). For De Smet: **Southeast South Dakota Tourism Association** (888/353-7382, www.southeast southdakota.com). For Mitchell: **Corn Palace Convention & Visitors Bureau** (866/273-2676, www.cornpalace.com). For Roslyn and Veblen: **Glacial Lakes & Prairies Tourism Association** (800/244-8860, www.sdglaciallakes.com). **Sioux Falls Convention & Visitors Bureau** (800/333-2072, www.siouxfallscvb.com).

Featured Dining

Oxbow Restaurant US-14 in De Smet (605/854-9988).
Minervas Sioux Falls (605/334-0386).
Prairie Sky Guest & Game Ranch Veblen. Reservations required for Wednesday-night pitchfork steak fries. June through August only (800/587-2411).

Featured Stops

Ingalls Homestead De Smet. Featuring pioneer-type activities, an 1880s school session, interactive exhibits and replicas of homestead dwellings on Laura's prairie just southeast of town (800/776-3594). Laura Ingalls Wilder Memorial Society offers tours of the author's two homes in town (800/880-3383).
Corn Palace Mitchell (866/273-2676).

Ice Cream Shack Roslyn (605/486-4890).
International Vinegar Museum Roslyn (877/486-0075).

More Great Stops

Sioux Falls In this vital, growing city, which straddles the Big Sioux River near the Iowa state line, visitors can take self-guided tours of some 40 historic sites, including landmark St. Joseph's Cathedral and the home of one of the city's founding fathers, now a museum. Other attractions include a natural-history museum, tumbling waterfalls in Falls Park and a collection of vintage buildings made of locally quarried pink quartzite.

Dan's Lodgings

Royal River Casino & Hotel Flandreau ($; 800/833-8666).
Hampton Inn Mitchell ($$; 866/252-2900).

More Great Lodgings

Possibility Farm Carpenter. A working farm and ranch 10 miles northwest of Carpenter. Two bedrooms in the 1950s-style farmhouse open to guests ($$, including breakfast; 888/759-9615).
Prairie Sky Guest & Game Ranch Veblen. With rooms in the timber lodge ($$) and four comfortable cabins ($$$) on a working ranch nine miles southwest of Veblen (all meals extra; 800/587-2411).

Food Events

International Vinegar Festival Roslyn, Saturday of Father's Day weekend—In the hometown of the nation's only vinegar museum, party on at a vinegar tasting, cooking demonstrations, a Vinegar Queen contest and a parade. Be sure to tour the International Vinegar Museum. Music acts and kids' activities round out the day (877/486-0075, www.vinegarman.com).
Flandreau Santee Sioux Annual Wacipi Flandreau, third weekend in July—Native Americans from across the Great Plains rendezvous in full regalia at the powwow grounds on the Flandreau Santee Sioux Reservation for a celebration with dancing, drumming and singing. Eat at booths selling Indian tacos, buffalo burgers and corn

soup, and shop for traditional handicrafts (605/997-3891, www.santeesioux.com).
Great Plains Bison-tennial Dutch Oven Cook-Off Yankton, fourth weekend in August—In the territory where Lewis and Clark feasted on their very first buffalo, contestants enter bison entrées along with desserts and breads, all cooked in Dutch ovens over wood chips and coals. Eat your fill of bison burgers and brats all weekend. Free admission (605/664-5920, www.dutchovencookoff.com).
Corn Palace Festival Mitchell, Wednesday through Sunday, weekend before Labor Day weekend—The world's only Corn Palace celebrates the harvest with a fresh coat of corn on its exterior, fashioned into murals. Other fun includes a corn-eating contest, a corn cook-off and vendors selling corn fare. Visitors get an earful of live music (605/995-8427, www.cornpalace festival.com).
State Fair Huron, five days during the last week in August, ending on Labor Day—Try *chislic* (deep-fried lamb chunks served hot on a skewer), a South Dakota specialty that's little known outside the state, at J & W Concessions, where it's been served for nearly 30 years (800/529-0900, www.sdstatefair.com).

Mail Order

Valley Game & Gourmet Premium-quality wild-game meats, specialty meats and gourmet pantry foods. Choose from a variety of cuts of bison, elk, pheasant, quail and venison. Also available: pheasant, buffalo, rabbit, duck and lobster or wild boar ravioli (605/977-1234, www.valleygame.com).
Vinegar Connoisseurs International Gourmet vinegars at all price ranges, from $4 for 12 ounces of Steen's Cane Vinegar to $185 for 2.5 ounces of Malpighi's Traditionale Extra Vecchio (800/342-4519, www.vinegarman.com).
Wooden Knife Company Indian Fry Bread Mix, a ready-to-use mix for making authentic Indian tacos, is available in a 1-pound reusable jute bag, a 1.5-pound box or a 5-pound sack (800/303-2773, www.woodenknife.com).

WISCONSIN

Old-World Traditions,
New-World Food Artisans

THIS PAGE: SATURDAY FARMERS MARKET, MADISON.
OPPOSITE PAGE, LEFT TO RIGHT: CRANBERRIES ON
THE VINE, WARRENS. HOLSTEINS AT HINCHLEY
DAIRY FARM, CAMBRIDGE. SHEBOYGAN HARBOR.

More than any other state on my itinerary, Wisconsin epitomizes the rich tapestry of Midwest food traditions. Thank the state's old-world ethnic heritage and the infusion of new flavors from recent immigrants.

Then, there are the cooks and artisans who combine traditions and foodstuffs, including the state's celebrated triumvirate of cheese, beer and brats, in wonderful products and dishes.

The final ingredient in Wisconsin's food story is the awesome cornucopia of foods produced here: from mainstays such as milk, corn, potatoes and other vegetables to more unusual crops, including cranberries, ginseng—and rutabagas. (The latter provide the basis of a delightful breakfast I experience in the Midwest's rutabaga capital, Cumberland, a scenic community in Wisconsin's woodsy, lake-dotted northwest corner. Here, the giant, turniplike tubers are known as Swede turnips or "bageys." Local rutabaga boosters amaze me with an eye-opening repast of rutabaga scrambled eggs, rutabaga pancakes, rutabaga brats and rutabaga-potato hash browns. I'm only sorry I'm a month too early for more treats at the annual Rutabaga Festival!)

Despite all this caloric temptation, a recent national dietary survey reveals that Wisconsinites are the trimmest Midwesterners, having the region's lowest obesity rate (Michigan ranks highest on the Midwest chubbiness scale).

South-central Wisconsin is my base; specifically, the capital city of Madison, population about 218,000, with a metro area more than double that. Madison is a thriving, progressive, environmentally conscious community with lots of parks, two big lakes—Monona and Mendota—that define the landscape and a state university comprising 41,000 students. Everyone here seems to be running, bicycling, in-line skating or sailing on weekends—or shopping the farmers market at Capitol Square. In food terms, Madison is very with-it. "Organic," "sustainable" and "artisanal" are words you hear a lot. You could say that in Wisconsin's old-country sea of gravy and sauerkraut, Madison is an unexpected island of organic field greens.

Capital Flavor Sensations

Breakfast is the logical place to begin my Wisconsin food journal, and I have one of the best, right in the heart of Madison, just blocks from the capitol. Former Chicagoans Phillip Hurley and John Gadau are buddies and partners in the Marigold Kitchen, a popular breakfast and lunch spot. They moved to Madison with their families in 2000, attracted to the city's quality of life but also feeling they had something to add to the food scene. Their wives named the restaurant; they thought the bright feeling of the marigold flower suited their husbands' vision for the decor and food. Guitar music, contemporary interiors and artwork and a hustling, cheery waitstaff say it all.

But food is the real point here. Chile-flake-dusted poached eggs come with rosemary toast and prosciutto (Italian ham) and Spanish sheep's-milk manchego cheese on the side. The breakfast sandwich consists of applewood-smoked bacon and perfectly fried eggs with fresh tomato and French boursin cheese spread snuggled between two slices of chewy ciabatta. French toast that begins with eggy challah is served with pastry cream, maple syrup and four kinds of berries. There's homemade granola with dried fruit, and yogurt served with toasted walnuts, pecans, fruit and honey. If only I could stick around for the imaginative soups, salads and sandwiches served at lunchtime.

Just up the street is Wisconsin's unique cruciform-shaped capitol building, begun in 1906 and finished 11 years later. On Saturday mornings (seasonally; see page 195),

Capitol Square is the hub of fresh food rather than politics. There are more than 200 farmers markets in Wisconsin, packed with fruits, vegetables, meats and cheeses direct from producers. The Dane County Farmers' Market, with 160 vendors crowding every side of Capitol Square, is one of the nation's largest producer-only markets. When I pass by at 6 a.m., sleepy-eyed vendors are just setting up their stalls. A couple of hours later, 20,000 Madisonians proceed counterclockwise around the square in orderly fashion, bags overflowing with nearly every form of produce imaginable, plus flowers, baked goods and more.

I join the throng, scanning wares from tropical flowers to zucchini to awesome tomatoes and cherries to pickles, honey, herbs, cheese curds, jam, salsa and bread. You name it, it's likely here: smoked trout, even beef and buffalo. Vendors also sell some of the latest produce sensations, such as edamame, soybeans you eat fresh with salt; herbs, including pineapple sage

and opal basil; and new varieties of eggplant (they're not just purple anymore). This farmers market also provides a taste of yesteryear in the form of rediscovered heirloom veggies, usually not as pretty as today's hybrids but often more flavorful. A percentage of the offerings is certified as organically grown.

Larry Johnson, who has managed the market for three years, zips from corner to corner, walkie-talkie in one hand, cell phone in the other. I feel lucky to visit with him for a moment. "Every vendor here has to grow or produce what they sell, and they have to be from Wisconsin," he says. "It's a year-round market as well—we just move inside during the winter." Soon, like a rushing current, the crowd separates us. People greet friends and chat as they move about inspecting the produce, noshing on muffins or slurping coffee and making their purchases.

One intriguing stop is the Harmony Valley Farm booth, where I learn more about the growing CSA (community-supported

agriculture) movement. Harmony Valley, a family farm in western Wisconsin, raises about 70 organic crops on 75 acres. Members pay $640 annually to receive a share of the farm's bounty, which they can pick up here or at one of 12 other distribution points around town from May to December—30 boxes per year, all told. How much each receives depends on the growing season. They're all in this together—sort of like stockholders in a vegetable company. I peek in one box that Madisonian Buck Rhyne, a longtime member and booster of the concept, is picking up: beets, salad greens, onions, green beans and lots more—beautiful stuff.

At a nearby stall I meet Tricia Bross, owner and manager of Luna Circle Farms northeast of Madison. Tricia proudly tells me that although men work at Luna Circle, it is managed by women. "Farming tends to be a male-dominated industry. At one farm I worked, women weren't allowed to even drive the tractors," she

says. "We wanted women to be able to get the training they needed. My friends and I decided to start our own farm 16 years ago so women could have equal opportunities." The Boston lettuce I'm admiring, one of 50 crops grown here, is the most picture-perfect I've ever seen.

Time for a coffee break. Just a block from the farmers market is Ancora Coffee on King Street. It's a locally based operation founded by George and Sue Krug, who came to Madison from America's coffee capital, Seattle, in 1993. The place is packed and there's a line out the door. Director of Training Ryan Baughn, also from Seattle, kindly takes a break to answer a few coffee questions. He tells me that Ancora (meaning "anchor" in Italian) features more than 25 standard varieties and blends from around the globe: Ethiopia, Kenya, Indonesia, Mexico, Guatemala, Colombia, Costa Rica and other lands. Plain steamed-milk lattes are the most popular drink here, followed by mocha lattes.

I order an iced skinny (skim) clipper mocha latte—the "clipper" part is Ancora's nautical lingo for a large latte. Ryan emphasizes that Ancora's coffee is artisan roasted, which means it's finished in small batches of unique blends. It's also organic and "fair trade," meaning the producer gets a fair price and it's grown in an environmentally friendly way.

After more food stops in the area, I return to Capitol Square for dinner at L'Etoile—French for "the star," and indeed, it is—perhaps Madison's most famous dining spot. Food legend Odessa Piper, an American pioneer in purveying fresh, wholesome foods in creative, upscale dishes, founded L'Etoile in 1976. Although no longer the proprietor, Odessa is still part of the L'Etoile family. Her culinary heirs, siblings Tory and Traci Miller, who grew up in Racine, are adhering to her precepts and doing a splendid job. Traci is general manager and Tory is executive chef.

Tory is well-prepared for his role. He studied at the French Culinary Institute in New York and cooked at several noted Manhattan restaurants before returning here to study under Odessa. Early this morning, he pulled a wagon at the farmers market, as Odessa did for years before him, loading up on some of the flavors he would serve this evening: amazingly fresh squash blossoms, sweet onions, peas, mixed greens, fava beans, potatoes, asparagus and tomatoes. Many other ingredients, from spinach and mushrooms to eggs and beef, come directly from area farmers Tory takes pride in knowing personally. "We don't print our menu until 10 minutes before we open the doors," he says. "I like it that way."

My meal is a gustatory revelation. First, an appetizer of summer-squash ravioli, a squash blossom filled with chèvre cheese and baked. It's followed by a thick (two bones) locally raised pork chop that was brined for two days in sugar, salt, coriander, allspice, clove and bay leaf; a salad of frisee and sylvetta greens and cilantro-

Brined Pork Chops

L'Etoile, Madison

8	cups water
1/2	cup kosher salt or 1/4 cup table salt without iodine
1/4	cup granulated or packed brown sugar
1 1/2	teaspoons whole coriander seeds, coarsely crushed
1 1/2	teaspoons whole cloves, coarsely crushed
1 1/2	teaspoons whole allspice, coarsely crushed
1 1/2	teaspoons cracked black pepper
3	bay leaves
4	pork loin chops, cut 1 1/4 inches thick (about 4 pounds)

For brine: In a large saucepan, combine water, salt, sugar, coriander, cloves, allspice, pepper and bay leaves. Heat and stir until salt and sugar are dissolved. Cool to room temperature. Transfer to a 1-gallon plastic bag set in a deep bowl; seal bag. Chill brine for 4 to 6 hours or until completely chilled.

If you like, trim fat from chops. Add meat to brine in bag; seal bag. (The brine should completely cover the meat.) Cover and chill for no more than 4 hours, turning occasionally. Remove chops from brine; pat dry with paper towels.

For a charcoal grill, arrange medium-hot coals around a drip pan. Test for medium heat above drip pan. Place chops on the grill rack over drip pan. Cover and grill for 35 to 40 minutes or until done (160°), turning once halfway through grilling. (For a gas grill, preheat grill. Reduce heat to medium. Adjust for indirect cooking. Grill as above.) *Makes 4 servings.*

lime vinaigrette; cornmeal pancakes; and a dark-chocolate "mole" sauce. A plate of Wisconsin cheese is served with a glass of Semillon. Dessert is a puddinglike Chocolate Vesuvius creation with the perfect accompaniment, fresh raspberries. From my table in the simple, elegant second-floor dining room (L'Etoile's Café Soleil occupies the first floor), I gaze out a huge picture window, viewing the capitol grounds in the mellow early-evening light. What a perfect way to end my food adventures on Madison's one-of-a-kind Capitol Square.

Got Milk? You Bet—Cheese, Too!

Wisconsin calls itself America's Dairyland, and with ample justification. The state leads the nation in cheese production and now ranks second to California (thanks to the Golden State's abundant land, cheap labor and the alfalfa that dairy cows consume) in milk production, producing more than 22 billion pounds of milk annually. As a boy, I was lucky enough to spend part of several summers on an aunt and uncle's dairy farm where I hand-milked a big bovine for the barn kitties' breakfast. I'll relive that fond memory at Duane and Tina Hinchley's big red dairy barn near Cambridge, about a half hour east of Madison.

Duane and Tina own about 2,000 acres within a 60-mile radius of Cambridge. That may sound like a lot, but as Tina says, "It's how farming is these days. You have to be big to achieve the efficiencies you need." She's my tour guide as I greet some of the Hinchleys' 230 registered Holstein dairy cows, as well as assorted chickens, hogs, goats, geese, turkeys and a couple of cats and dogs. The Hinchleys also raise wheat, corn and pumpkins, plus soybeans and alfalfa to feed their dairy cows—oh, and four kids, ages 8 to 14. The farm has been in Duane's family since 1958.

A few years ago, when Tina wanted to earn a bit of extra income, a much-promoted concept called "agritourism" was her answer. It's a way for farmers to share their way of life and survive financially in a challenging economic climate. About 9,000 visitors annually—most of them schoolchildren—come to the Hinchleys' property to see a real working dairy farm, milk a cow, feed a calf and hear a rooster crow.

I poke around the big barn where 100 cattle await their afternoon milking session with modern tubes that deposit the milk in a 2,500-gallon tank. The liquid is emptied every other day and transported to a plant in Illinois, where it winds up as cheese, cottage cheese, yogurt, sour cream, ice cream and, oh yes—pasteurized milk.

A compliant, 1,600-pound Holstein named Jasmine is my challenge this afternoon. It's been a long time, but I do my best to make hand-milking comfortable for both of us. After a few futile squeezes, the technique comes back to me and I deliver enough milk to interest several kittens hovering nearby. Then it's back to that vacuum contraption, as Jasmine contributes the rest of her 10-gallon daily output and Tina tells me more about the farm. Low milk prices are a big issue in the dairying world these days, so efficiency counts more than ever. Tina spends much of her time keeping detailed computer records about each animal's intake and output.

Wisconsin accounted for more than a fourth of total U.S. cheese production in 2004 (a record-setting 2.36 billion pounds!). The varieties, textures, colors and flavors seem infinite: Colby (a Wisconsin original), Monterey Jack, Swiss, mozzarella, Muenster, Havarti, feta, Edam, even stinky Limburger. You know you're in Wisconsin when you see billboards touting the next cheese shop and

CLOCKWISE, FROM TOP LEFT: (ALL TAKEN AT HINCHLEY DAIRY FARM, CAMBRIDGE) HEALTHY SNACKING. DAN TRIES HIS MILKING HAND WITH JASMINE THE HOLSTEIN. MORE DAIRY-FARM DENIZENS. THE ORIGINAL DAIRY BARN.

those squeaky, rubbery treats known as fresh cheese curds. I've never enjoyed this quintessentially Wisconsin snack before, so now is the time and I know the perfect place: the Cedar Grove cheese factory just outside tiny Plain, Wisconsin (population 720), near the incredibly pretty Wisconsin River Valley.

Things are coming full circle in the world of cheese making. In the late 1800s, several thousand small Wisconsin farm-based cheese makers prided themselves on their unique products; 20 operated within a few miles of Plain alone. Then, huge corporations began turning out uniformly dependable—and some would say dull—cheese, edging out small producers.

Now, thanks to more discriminating consumers, a new generation of artisans is restoring the romance and flavor that have been lacking. Bob Wills and his wife, Beth Nachreiner, are two of those cheese makers, running an operation that employs 30, with a little help from their three kids. Cedar Grove was founded in 1878, and Bob and Beth purchased the place from Beth's parents in 1989.

Bob explains how the flavor of a given cheese can be affected by the type of dairy cow producing the milk and what it's been fed, the time of year and, of course, the processing. Goat's-milk cheese has more of a bite. Sheep's milk makes a sweet, rich cheese. Some cheeses are blends. "If you like sharp cheese, you know it's ready when you bite into the cheese and it bites you back!" Bob says. He's proud of the fact that every batch of cheese is different here. "It's all about chemistry, like with wine."

"Now is a really fun time to be a cheese maker," he says, thanks to all the interest in artisanal cheeses. At Cedar Grove cheese delights include butterkase, Havarti and marble Colby, created from nearly 140,000 pounds of milk daily from about 40 area dairy farms, none of which uses artificial growth hormones. "People are becoming much more educated about flavor differences. There's a lot more than cheddar out there," Bob says.

Nevertheless, cheddar remains Wisconsin's signature variety, and I watch the Cedar Grove staff make it in their immaculate factory. All cheese is basically the result of separating milk into solid curds and liquid whey, which is drained off. The process of "cheddaring" involves removing moisture from the curds to knit them together. Formed into 42-pound blocks, the cheddar goes to the aging room, where it might stay six months to seven years, for a mild or sharp flavor, respectively. Cheddar's distinctive yellow color comes from English cheese makers who simply wanted to distinguish their product; the natural coloring comes from the flavorless and odorless tropical annatto plant.

Of course, not all those rubbery little

curds get transformed into cheese. Cedar Grove turns out about 13 tons of cheese curds a week in such flavors as tomato and basil, onion and chive, garlic and dill, horseradish, jalapeño pepper and pizza.

My final stop is back in Madison, at Babcock Hall on the university campus, home of America's oldest dairy school, to sample another luscious result of Wisconsin's dairy abundance. Bill Klein is manager of the dairy plant and store, where students learn how to transform 10,000 pounds of milk each day into cheese, fluid milk products—and ice cream, the central attraction.

At any given time, Babcock Hall offers about 25 flavors from a repertoire of roughly 300, most created by students (who aren't above melting down someone else's product to analyze the ingredients). The two all-time headliners are cookie dough and butter pecan, but many kids go for cotton candy. I try banana-fudge marble, double butterscotch, peach melba, cranberry cheesecake and coffee and truffles. Then I depart, content that I've consumed my share of Wisconsin's amazing butterfat output.

Gemütlichkeit!

Beer is the liquid jewel in Wisconsin's culinary crown. No state is more identified with brewing what's basically an ancient recipe for fermented grain mush, thanks to the Germans who trekked here beginning in the mid-1800s and established small brewing operations that employed old-country techniques and standards. Then came the golden era of the state's megabreweries: Miller, Pabst, Old Milwaukee, Stroh's, Heileman, Blatz and Schlitz are giants in the Wisconsin brewing pantheon, but most of those big brands are history. Miller, the nation's second-largest producer, is the only survivor in Milwaukee.

The lagers of yore have been challenged by the diverse flavors of some wonderful regional beers and microbrews, including Wisconsin's own Huber, Leinenkugel, Sprecher, New Glarus, Capital, Lakefront, Stevens Point and Tyranena breweries. The state produces beers from light lagers to coffee-flavored stouts, and Oktoberfests are an annual event in communities large and small. Each autumn in La Crosse, 150,000 revelers listen to bands, eat German specialties and drink barrels of suds during a nine-day fest. Statewide, it's estimated Wisconsinites produce 220,448,000 cases of beer and consume about that amount annually. My choices for a sudsy day of research are the Huber plant in Monroe, a pleasant south-central Wisconsin town of almost 11,000 near the Illinois line, and Capital Brewery in Middleton, a Madison suburb.

Fittingly, Monroe's main industries are cheese and beer. Huber produces several richly flavored Berghoff beers, once associated with the historic downtown Chicago German eatery, as well as the Huber and Rhinelander labels. Founded in 1845, three years before Wisconsin became a state, Huber is the nation's second-oldest continuously operating brewery; near beer and soda pop kept it open during Prohibition.

The brewery had several owners through the years, and Joe Huber took over in 1940. My host is Director of Brewing Kristopher Kalav, an Armenian-Norwegian-Swede from Tucson, Arizona, with advanced degrees in biology and chemistry. He's been brewmaster here since 1997, helping formulate the contents of Huber's 180,000-barrel annual output.

Outside, the Huber plant is rather plain—two big, boxy buildings across the street from each other, one housing the brewing operation and offices, the other the bottling line. But what goes on inside is pure magic. Kris explains that the sci-

CLOCKWISE, FROM ABOVE: A CONVIVIAL BEER-GARDEN GATHERING AT CAPITAL BREWERY, MIDDLETON. HUBER AND BERGHOFF BEERS AND THE BOTTLING LINE AT JOSEPH HUBER BREWING, MONROE. OPPOSITE PAGE: A SELECTION FROM CEDAR GROVE CHEESE FACTORY, PLAIN.

Fork-Tender Pot Roast

Old Feed Mill, Mazomanie

- ½ cup all-purpose flour
- ½ teaspoon garlic powder
- ½ teaspoon ground white pepper
- ½ teaspoon dry mustard
- ½ teaspoon dried marjoram or basil, crushed
- ½ teaspoon dried thyme, crushed
- ½ teaspoon dried oregano, crushed
- ½ teaspoon dried parsley
- ½ teaspoon paprika
- ¼ teaspoon kosher salt or ⅛ teaspoon salt
- ¼ teaspoon ground black pepper
- 1 2½- to 3-pound boneless beef chuck pot roast
- ¼ cup butter
- 2 carrots, coarsely chopped
- 2 stalks celery, sliced into 1-inch pieces
- 1 large onion, coarsely chopped
- 1 clove garlic, minced
- 1 bay leaf
- ½ cup dry red wine
- 1 14-ounce can beef broth
- Beef broth (optional)

In a small bowl, combine flour, garlic powder, white pepper, mustard, marjoram, thyme, oregano, parsley, paprika, salt and black pepper. Trim fat from meat. Coat all sides of meat with flour mixture, reserving flour mixture that doesn't cling.

In a 4- to 6-quart Dutch oven, brown meat on all sides in 2 tablespoons of the hot butter. Remove meat; set aside. In same Dutch oven, cook carrots, celery, onion, garlic and bay leaf in the remaining 2 tablespoons butter, covered, for 10 minutes or until just beginning to brown, stirring occasionally. Stir in reserved flour mixture; mix well. Add wine, stirring and scraping up browned bits off the bottom of the pan. Add broth; cook and stir until slightly thickened and bubbly. Return meat to pan.

Bake, covered, in a 350° oven for 2½ to 3 hours or until meat is tender. Transfer meat to a platter; slice. Remove bay leaf; discard. If you like, thin gravy with a little additional beef broth to desired consistency. Serve gravy with meat. *Makes 6 to 8 servings.*

ence of making beer hasn't changed much since 1845 when a Mr. Bissinger started the business. Big copper kettles and tubs host 700 different chemical reactions among water, malted barley, yeast and hops. The beer ages (or lagers) a minimum of five weeks before being piped across the street for bottling or canning, labeling and shipping. Kris and I make the short journey. A mind-boggling 55 million bottles of beer annually chug through the clacking bottling line, which resembles a huge amusement-park ride. Each bottle is swiftly filled, capped, labeled and boxed—all by machine. After my tour, my fellow visitors and I head back across the street for a sample in the German-style Founder's Tap Room, where Kris and his associates work the taps.

Just outside Madison, in the affluent, tech-oriented suburb of Middleton (population 17,000), Capital Brewery has been hosting rousing beer-garden get-togethers since 1987. To me, this is the best of Wisconsin *gemütlichkeit*, which my dictionary translates from German as "warm friendliness and amicability." In Germany the tradition started with customers drinking still-cool beer in parklike surroundings under trees that shaded underground storage cellars. The whole point is relaxation and conviviality among friends and strangers. It's that way in Middleton on this Friday evening, one of several nights each week the brewery hosts this outdoor gathering.

Casually but nicely dressed adults, mostly in their 30s and 40s by all appearances, many with children, fill a huge courtyard adjoining the brewery, mingling or sitting at picnic tables munching food they've brought or had delivered. A local band is playing, and some guests dance in front of the stage. Across the street, kids perform stunts in a skateboard park.

Some nights the brewery shows outdoor movies; there's no admission, just the price of the beer. Youth and nondrinkers can enjoy root beer or other soft drinks at this establishment best known for its award-winning beers.

Wandering among 1,500 or so fellow quaffers, I chat with several *Midwest Living®* subscribers who've noticed the magazine's logo on my shirt. Bob Schmook and his wife, Nancy Graham, give me some advice about maintaining my figure on this eating journey. Other similarly friendly beer-garden denizens are just as willing to strike up a conversation, even offering me pizza and snacks. How wonderful that a great custom such as this crossed the Atlantic with the descendants of those who began the *biergarten* tradition generations ago in a far-off old-world homeland.

Solid Buildings, Solid Dining

Wisconsin is filled with venerable rough-cut limestone buildings: rock-solid churches, mills, shops, homes and restaurants. The dense, durable native stone contains a legacy of long-evaporated prehistoric seas, and the buildings evince the architecture and masonry skill of the German artisans who shaped them. That skill is evident in two historic restaurants I visit in the greater Madison area: the Old Feed Mill in Mazomanie and Quivey's Grove near Madison, each an enchanting step back in time in terms of setting and food.

The Old Feed Mill adjoins a largely abandoned railroad line on the edge of a farm town on the brink of suburbanization. I hope Mazomanie (population about 1,500) retains its identity here in the lush, bluff-lined Wisconsin River Valley just west of Madison. The town was founded as a railroad stop and named for a Native American chief. Since its construction in 1857, the durable mill has weathered a fire in the 1890s and damage from a train collision in 1907 to persevere as a local landmark.

Dan Viste was a hydrogeology consultant specializing in water-related environmental issues and his wife, Nancy, was a medical lab technician when they decided to trade in their fast-paced corporate world to settle in Mazomanie in 1995. Now they live just three miles from the restaurant they opened in an abandoned flour mill. On their "farmette" (small hobby farm), the Vistes grow much of the produce they serve—from zucchini, lettuce, beets, potatoes and cucumbers to dill and other herbs, such as basil and fennel. They also own several other historic properties in Mazomanie, but the Old Feed Mill is the jewel in their crown.

Clearly, this place has been restored with tender, loving care. Upstairs, a gallery showcases more than 100 quilts, some antiques for display and others for sale. Locally made gift items and crafts are available in the main-level shop. The furnishings are an artfully mismatched assortment of chairs and tables Nancy acquired at area farm sales and restored. "Sometimes customers come in and say, 'I recognize that piece! It was in my house as a child!'" she says. "That's fine with us. We want this place to be full of reminders."

But I'm here for some country cooking, and I'm not disappointed. The food matches the rustic setting: melt-in-your-mouth, fork-tender pot roast cooked for hours in its own rich brown gravy and a bit of red wine, along with carrots, potatoes and onions. Turkey and wild rice soup with dried cherries from Wisconsin's Door County. Various crunchy-fresh veggies and potatoes from the Vistes' garden mashed with garlic. Other starring entrées include cider-roast chicken, hickory-smoked pork and pan-seared walleye pike. I have a rich bread pudding for dessert and

ABOVE: FRIDAY FISH FRY ON THE PADDOCK LAWN AT QUIVEY'S GROVE, NEAR MADISON. BELOW: HISTORIC AMBIENCE AND GOOD FOOD AT THE OLD FEED MILL, MAZOMANIE.

sample my companions' apple dumpling with caramel sauce and double-chocolate turtle torte, all terrific.

The Vistes' chewy homemade rye bread is made with locally grown organic rye grain ground daily on the premises. Dan gives me a chance to grind some flour before I leave, emphasizing how important it is to include the germ (berry), for both nutrition and flavor. I get a brief lesson in the little flour milling room up front, equipped with both historic and modern equipment. It's been a long day, but this stop has restored me, taking me back to a time that wasn't so frantic in terms of dining and life in general.

The next evening I find myself admiring the black walnut, maple and elm trees outside another historic Madison-area eatery: Quivey's Grove on Verona Road, in Fitchburg, just south of Madison. This property sports two restaurants: the regal Stone House, an Italianate limestone farmhouse that dates back to 1855, and the Stable Grill, also built in 1855 and connected to the main house by an ancient-looking limestone tunnel and wine cellar, with handsome wrought-iron gates fashioned by an area blacksmith.

The 18-room Stone House was constructed by the pioneering Mann family from stone quarried just across the road. A restaurant since 1980, its architecture and tasteful interiors, which feature unstained hemlock floors, original wavy glass windows and converted oil-burning chandeliers, recall New England. Each themed room is decorated individually with stenciling, quilts, political cartoons and posters, maps or other memorabilia. Craig Kuenning, a member of the team that repurposed the property to its current use and took ownership in 1986, tells me the outside walls are 20 inches thick!

Courtly Craig is a Georgia native but

prides himself on serving traditional Midwest cuisine: lamb shanks, short ribs, beef rouladen, chicken-mushroom popovers, pretzel-crusted perch. My mouth is watering! However, this is Friday, and Fridays in Wisconsin mean one thing: fish. Craig serves beer-battered cod under a white tent on a huge side lawn called The Paddock. I'm mellowing out with more than 500 other diners, savoring the cod, a big parmesan potato cake (Craig credits his mother for the recipe) and a wonderful coleslaw. "Madisonians are partial to cod," Craig informs me. "In Milwaukee, people prefer whitefish, and up north, it's perch." But they all seem to want their fish fried on Friday nights.

We tour the rest of Quivey's Grove, which is listed on the National Register of Historic Places. The casual-dining Stable Grill boarded horses until the property became a restaurant. It was expanded with

authentic rough-hewn beams and trim recycled from three other area barns dating to the 1850s. Some of the tables are crafted from old wagon wheels; old saddle blankets, historic photos and sheet music adorn the walls. The atmosphere is open yet cozy—just as it is in the Stone House dining rooms. People seem to be everywhere on the grounds: families, couples, even a wedding party rehearsing on the shady, green front lawn. Quivey's Grove is more than a century and a half old, but I wonder if it's ever been more alive than on this balmy weekend evening.

Eat Your Dessert First!

Let me dispel a myth: Wisconsinites have a broader culinary repertoire than beer, cheese and bratwurst. They're also into pastries, candies and pies. I taste three of the state's most celebrated treats: a world-famous pastry in Racine, old-fashioned homemade candies and ice cream concoctions in Manitowoc and gooey-good pies in Osseo. With those sweet temptations and more almost everywhere you turn in Wisconsin, dentists must love this state!

Racine is a city of about 81,000 and the home of S.C. Johnson, maker of well-known household products—no wonder this town seems tidy. It's one of the many communities that hug the Lake Michigan shore between Milwaukee and Chicago. I easily find the bright, modern, 14,000-square-foot O&H Danish Bakery, with its Viking-ship logo and Scandinavian building design. Eric Olesen is one of the scions of Racine's premier baking dynasty. He's a third-generation descendant of Christian Olesen, who founded this 56-year-old enterprise (the Olesens bought out a Mr. Holtz, the "H" in O&H, early on), and he knows how to make pastry to die for. Kringle, to be specific.

Danes have been baking kringles in

Racine since the late 1800s, when they began settling the area. By the 1930s and '40s, the city was the hub of America's Danish community, and its bakery industry was thriving. Many of the bakers were drafted during World War II, however, and the pretzel shape of the classic almond-paste-filled kringle was judged too complicated for the shorthanded baking crews left behind. So they streamlined the design, and the legendary O-shaped kringle was born. Eric explains that the flat-as-a-pancake pastry is actually an amazing 32 layers of butter, flour, eggs, milk and sugar folded over and over during a three-day process (Viennese bakers on strike emigrated to Copenhagen and taught the art to the Danes about 1840).

As the years went by, O&H and other Racine kringle makers added fillings; pecan is the most popular, but you can order cherry, raspberry, apricot, cream cheese, chocolate and a whole bunch of other flavors, even turtle sundae and Key lime pie. Most O&H kringles are shipped to customers around the nation and the globe. You even can sign up for the Kringle of the Month Club. Other bakery items include breads, pies, cream puffs, cookies and a delectable Seven-Sister Coffee Cake of layered pastry, creamed-almond filling, custard and spiraled rolls. But kringle still rules.

Farther up the Lake Michigan shore is Manitowoc, home to Beerntsen's Confectionary, founded in 1932, with its white-and-red-striped awning and simple neon sign that reads "Fine Candies, Ice Cream." Glass cases packed with nearly every kind of homemade candy imaginable—125 varieties in all—seem to call out to me as soon as I walk in: light, crunchy sea foam; nonpareils; almond bark; hand-dipped clusters; caramel corn; brittles; suckers; ribbon candy; hard candy—even chocolate beer bottles! Hand-dipped chocolates

CLOCKWISE, FROM ABOVE: BEERNTSEN'S CONFECTIONARY, MANITOWOC. DANISH KRINGLES STAR AT O&H BAKERY, RACINE. COLORFUL JARS OF CANDIES TEMPT AT BEERNTSEN'S. OPPOSITE PAGE: SERVING UP BEER-BATTERED COD AT QUIVEY'S GROVE, NEAR MADISON.

made in copper kettles with wooden paddles are the specialty. But how can I tell what's inside without biting into them? My guide explains that different squiggles atop the confections denote particular flavors: An O means orange cream, M stands for maple cream, caramel cream (the favorite) bears an X and so on.

Feeling as if I've stepped into some kind of sugar time machine, I munch on a few pieces of almond bark and claim one of the dark-finished wood booths in back. I ask my server for something rich and gooey. She brings a delectable turtle sundae with marshmallow topping and nuts. You can create your own sundae here, so I ask about some of the strangest requests. How about Oreo ice cream with grape syrup or rock candy with chocolate ice cream, gummy bears and marshmallow topping? I order a sampler of each.

For decades, people have raved about the fantastic pie place across the state in Osseo, a farming community of 1,700, more than half of whom claim Norwegian ancestry. In this pie-oriented state, no venue is so famous for its pies as the Norske Nook, on quiet Seventh Street in Osseo, where the motto is "Pie so good, you'll want to eat dessert first!" And I do, I do! The restaurant resembles a European half-timbered cafe with its low-slung roof and little patio dining area at the side. Inside, coolers and glass display cases are packed with . . . pies, one of the dessert joys of my journey and my culinary life! Servers zip from kitchen to table and back with trays filled with lunch and . . . pies. A menu on the wall touts today's . . . pies.

Helen Myhre, who's now retired, founded Norske Nook across the street in 1973. She sold it to another Norwegian, Jerry Bechard of Hayward, in 1990. Now there are two other locations, one in Rice Lake, one in Hayward. But this quaint

and cozy place, where hundreds of pies are sold daily, is the flagship.

I decide to get the main course part of lunch out of the way quickly. I go past the usual sandwiches, salads and soups and the hot meat sandwiches served with mashed potatoes and gravy to a section labeled "lefse wraps." *Lefse* is a sort of Norwegian pancake or tortilla made of potatoes and flour. Here, it is used as a wrap for hearty fillings such as beef, pork, turkey and, in my case, Norwegian meatballs—all topped with gravy. These aren't your typical lettuce-and-air diet wraps. "Why should we serve the same food as everyone else?" says Debbie Zeller, general manager of the Osseo Norske Nook. "We're special!"

Now for the pie! Of the 36 flavors served here, banana cream is the No. 1 seller (it won the National Pie Championship in 2003), followed by sour cream raspberry, then fresh strawberry and fresh raspberry, both in season. In autumn the Norske Nook makes its own mincemeat. Helen's recipes are the core pies, but cooks have

added a few of their own. Sour cream apple-blueberry was the happy result of an ingredient mix-up.

My traveling companions and I poise our dessert forks and devour slices of blueberry crunch, peach, raspberry cream cheese, banana cream, chocolate mousse, sour cream raisin, chocolate peanut butter and fresh strawberry. The flaky, hand-rolled crusts—made with shortening, not lard—are as delectable as the fillings. I end my two hours in Osseo by waddling across the street to the Norske Nook's coffee shop and boutique, which is filled with Scandinavian crafts and imports. It's fun being a Wisconsin Norwegian for a couple hours. Especially if you love pie!

Best of Wisconsin's Wursts

Sausage—liverwurst, kielbasa, bologna—is one of our humblest gustatory delicacies. Devised to utilize otherwise undesirable bits of meat and offal, it becomes pure ambrosia when these trimmings are ground up, combined with salt and spices and stuffed into casings. Wisconsin is America's leading sausage state, and bratwursts—those crescent-shaped links with a distinctive spicy flavor—are its most famous sausage, indelibly linked with beer, cheddar and Green Bay Packers football. I'm in one of my favorite Great Lakes communities, Sheboygan (population 51,000). This beautiful midsize city on the Lake Michigan shore is next to the historic Village of Kohler, where you'll find plumbing giant Kohler Company and its golf-mecca American Club Resort as well as Johnsonville Sausage, a corporate giant that's riding America's bratwurst-grilling mania to superstardom.

I'm visiting a smaller hometown brat-making operation: Miesfeld's, just north of town off Interstate-43. Chuck Miesfeld, my host, is the descendant of Charles

CLOCKWISE, FROM TOP LEFT: (ALL TAKEN IN SHEBOYGAN)
DOWNTOWN. BRATWURST AS IT SHOULD BE SERVED,
MIESFELD'S. PLEASURE CRAFT IN THE SERENE LAKE
MICHIGAN HARBOR. OPPOSITE PAGE: CHOCOLATE MOUSSE
PIE AWAITING PATRONS AT NORSKE NOOK, OSSEO.

Miesfeld, a German-Russian who founded the Triangle Market in Sheboygan back in 1941. Chuck moved the business to this spiffy 18,000-square-foot plant and store in 1999. Forty assorted sausage stuffers and purveyors here focus on the science of bratwurst making, churning out 50 types, including Slovenian, Russian, Mexican and Irish as well as German wursts. Sheboyganites prize the fruits of their labors: A thousand people per day scarf down 2.5 tons of brats during the town's busiest holiday celebration, the Fourth of July, and 150 tons are sold per year! Miesfeld's brats are offered in dozens of supermarkets and restaurants in the Sheboygan area, as are the company's bologna, summer sausage, wieners, Irish potato sausage and Italian sausage. And they sell lots of ham, bacon and fresh-cut premium meats as well as cheese, beer and gourmet food items in this store.

But brats are king. Chuck guides me through storage coolers and meat-cutting and -grinding centers to a refrigerated retail case packed with some 16 brat varieties. While the traditional brat remains their best seller, Miesfeld's also offers a French apricot Dijon brat, a low-fat chicken-breast brat, a taco brat, a chili brat, a chicken *cordon bleu* brat (pork, ham, Swiss cheese, bread crumbs), a Cajun brat, a garlic-onion brat and others that incorporate Swiss cheese, mushroom, jalapeño and cheddar. Turkey. Beef. Pepper-coated summer sausage. Apple-pie bacon. "Some people want something a little different," Chuck says with a smirk.

On our tour of the immaculate plant, Chuck explains that bratwurst is a fresh meat product, not cured or smoked. It's made from ground pork shoulder and is relatively lean. Miesfeld's brats are seasoned with nutmeg, salt, pepper and a bunch of ingredients Chuck won't tell me

about (historically, the mix also can include garlic, ginger, coriander or caraway) and enclosed in a natural casing, which means the small intestine of a pig (don't think about it). Keys to a great brat, Chuck says, are how coarsely the meat is ground and the type of casing used. Miesfeld's must be doing something right: Their award-winning brats are shipped all over.

Chuck gets passionate when he addresses the topic of brat preparation and presentation. In Sheboygan, he says, brats are only to be fried or grilled. He should know: Besides devising, manufacturing and marketing brats, he cooks them at home several nights a week. First, he soaks the brats in cold water for five minutes to make the casings less likely to split and release precious juices during cooking. He then puts the brats on a white-ash-hot charcoal-fire grill (never gas), keeping a finger bowl

of icy water nearby; that's because you should turn brats only with your fingers (utensils might pierce the casings). When the brats feel hard to the touch, after about 15 minutes, they're ready to be paired two at a time on buttered hard rolls. No soft buns in Wisconsin, please! If you need to keep brats warm before serving, Chuck recommends putting them in a slurry of onions, butter and beer. After that, it's all frosting on the cake, so to speak: dill pickle slices, Düsseldorf-style German mustard and chopped onions. The master himself assembles a classic brat sandwich with all the fixings for me to taste.

Because mustard is practically an indispensable accompaniment for brats and other Wisconsin delights, I can't leave the state without a stop at the Mustard Museum in Mount Horeb, about 20 miles southwest of Madison. Tucked among the Scandinavian boutiques on Mount Horeb's troll-lined main street (Norwegians rule here) is an amazing collection of 4,500 jars, bottles and tubes filled with—mustard! All 50 states and 60 foreign nations are represented; a Slovenian variety is the proprietor's latest prize.

It's all the brainchild of Mustard Man Barry Levenson, a former prosecutor with the Wisconsin state attorney general's office who has devoted his life and livelihood to the yellow condiment for two decades. I'm agape at the panoply of mustard history, facts and products Barry has assembled in his yellow (of course) storefront location. The sampling counter reveals new sensations, including mustards teamed with flavors such as habanero, pineapple, horseradish, passion fruit, wasabi, praline, maple, ginger-pear and mango-cilantro.

Barry's zany humor permeates his beloved museum. Before leaving, I buy a T-shirt from his Poupon U collection of vaguely collegiate-looking sweatshirts, baseball caps and even baby bibs. Barry, here's wishing you the best of luck in your drive to have Mount Horeb named a ketchup-free zone!

Supper Club Prime Time

Rural and small-town supper clubs and roadhouses are a grand Wisconsin dining tradition. To find one, just keep your eye out for a big, lit-up sign at a crossroads in front of what once may have been a farmhouse or barn, with lots of cars in a parking lot seemingly drawn like moths to a flame (make that like steaks to charcoal). Half the adventure lies in simply finding your supper club destination.

Schwarz's, for example, is hidden about halfway between Lake Michigan and Lake Winnebago. A winding county road leads to the church-steeple-crowned village of St. Anna (population 150), a satellite community of greater Kiel (population 3,000), which is eight miles north of Elkhart Lake, known for resorts and auto road races. Lost yet? Elkhart Lake is about 22 miles northwest of Sheboygan. It's a pretty drive, but watch out for horse-drawn buggies as you near St. Anna—about 15 Amish families live in the area.

When you step inside Schwarz's, first order your dinner; then you can relax in the bar area with a beer, wine or preferably a brandy old-fashioned, Wisconsin's cocktail of choice. It comes garnished either sweet—maraschino cherry crowning orange and pineapple slices—or garden-style, with home-pickled mushroom, Brussels sprout and olive. You see, these efficient Wisconsin Germans have figured out that you can have a whole lot of fun imbibing and chatting in the lounge until you're called to the dining room to begin your meal (this procedure also means Schwarz's can serve more diners in the same time frame).

CLOCKWISE, FROM TOP LEFT: (ALL TAKEN AT SCHWARZ'S, ST. ANNA) JUICY PRIME RIB AND CRISP ONION RINGS. WARM WELCOMES AT THE COZY ENTRANCE. SUPPER CLUB BAR HUMOR. OPPOSITE PAGE: MUSTARD MAN BARRY LEVENSON, MOUNT HOREB.

If you have a reservation, you're in the wrong place.

Brandy Old-Fashioned Sweet

Schwarz's Supper Club, St. Anna

2   cubes sugar
1   teaspoon maraschino cherry juice
3   to 4 dashes aromatic bitters
6   ounces lemon-lime carbonated
      beverage, chilled (³/₄ cup)
    Ice cubes
2   ounces brandy (¹/₄ cup)
    Orange twist
    Maraschino cherry

In a 12-ounce highball glass, add sugar, maraschino cherry juice, aromatic bitters and a splash of lemon-lime carbonated beverage. Muddle mixture together using a spoon or a muddler (a rod with a flattened end). Fill glass with ice cubes. Add brandy. Fill space with the remaining lemon-lime carbonated beverage; gently stir to combine. Garnish drink with an orange twist and a maraschino cherry on a cocktail skewer. *Makes 1 serving.*

Schwarz's was founded as a modest country tavern by Ziggy and Evelyn Schwarz back in 1957. Word got around about Ziggy's terrific steaks, broasted chicken and Friday fish fry. Now run by Ziggy's son, John, and grandson, Charley, along with their wives, Lisa and Stephanie, the place is an institution hereabouts. John specializes in bartending and Charley is Schwarz's master meat cutter. Lisa and Stephanie orchestrate the seating and serving of guests in two large, country-style dining rooms that can accommodate up to 320 patrons total.

Beef—they serve up to 2 tons a week—is the house specialty here, along with walleye, scallops and other supper club standards. Charley offers to give me a meat-cutting lesson, so we put on laboratory-style white jackets and he expertly saws a huge loin into an assortment of beautifully marbled T-bones, sirloins and prized porterhouse steaks, explaining as he proceeds how the size of the tenderloin determines the type of steak he cuts. This could be dangerous work! (I surreptitiously count Charley's fingers. Yup, they're all still there.) Charley learned his craft from his late Aunt Millie, who worked here with Charley's parents and his Uncle Chief. "Aunt Millie was a small woman, but she could cut meat with the best of the big boys," Charley tells me.

In the adjoining kitchen, unique broiler devices Ziggy purchased in the 1950s sear and cook those juicy steaks to order. The Schwarzes better take good care of the huge toasterlike gizmos, because they're no longer manufactured.

It's my turn to be seated in one of the homey dining rooms. I've been hankering for the herb-rubbed prime rib ever since I ordered back in the bar. But first come some teasers: an old-fashioned veggie-and-pickle relish tray; homemade breadsticks;

my order of hand-dipped, lightly breaded "onion hearts"—they serve 1,000 pounds a week in the busy summer season; and a salad with creamy Roquefort dressing.

Then the main course arrives. At 16 ounces, the "Queen's Cut" looks daunting, but John tells me that each week several hardy diners manage to devour the I-dare-you, 32-ounce "Schwarz's Cut." A delicious twice-baked potato and fresh green beans from a local Amish garden accompany my serving. I slyly ask what's in the savory herb rub that flavors the rich outer crust on the prime rib, but to no avail: It's another one of those "family secrets" I keep coming across.

For dessert, I choose a homemade strawberry schaum torte, an airy meringue concoction with gobs of whipped cream that melts in my mouth. After more friendly banter with John in the now-crowded bar up front—it's Sunday afternoon, and the wait is an hour—I'm back on the road, a bigger fan than ever of Wisconsin's surprising supper clubs, especially the out-of-the-way (but definitely worth finding) Schwarz's of St. Anna.

Crazy About Cranberries

Many people associate cranberries with New England, but Wisconsin ranks as the No. 1 producer nationally. The first cranberry marshes in the west-central portion of the state were developed in the 1870s. Today, cranberries—which thrive in this water-rich area's climatic conditions and acidic soil—are Wisconsin's top fruit crop, as well as the core of its official juice. In fact, juice has become by far the most popular cranberry product, along with those dried, sweetened cranberries used for cooking, baking and snacking. The diverse uses of cranberries are partly a result of a herbicide scare that rendered the crop worthless back in 1959; I recall that cranberry-less Thanksgiving from my childhood. It was a blessing in disguise that spurred growers to develop year-round uses for the humble fruit.

Just east of Warrens (population 292), the southern anchor of central Wisconsin's cranberry-growing spine, I visit the Wetherby Cranberry Company. This 125-acre farm was founded in 1903; Nodji Van Wychen's German family took over in 1915, keeping the name. Nodji is married to Jim Van Wychen, a Dutchman who runs the business with her and one of her grown children; that makes five generations over the years!

Nodji knows cranberries. I pay close attention as we chat in a marsh where the delicately leafed, low perennial vine thrives on layers of peat and sand laced with irrigation pipes. I'm told that summer's tiny pink cranberry blossoms, which get pollinated by thousands of rented bees, resemble miniature sandhill cranes; hence, one theory about the origin of the name "cranberry."

The marsh is made up of neat, five-acre beds that need to be replanted only every 25 years or so. At harvesttime, the beds are flooded, and most of the berries are shaken off the vines by a special contraption called a water-reel beader. The berries then float to the surface, where they are corralled so they can be elevated to waiting trucks. During winter the beds are flooded to insulate the vines in ice. Nodji's beds yield the state average, around 200 barrels of cranberries per acre in a good year.

Most of the Wetherby crop winds up in juice on the shelves at retailers, even in a "white juice" made from cranberries harvested in late summer and early fall before the berries turn ruby red. The most perfect-looking Wetherby cranberries are sold fresh at markets, and some go to the farmers market in Madison or

CLOCKWISE, FROM ABOVE: (ALL TAKEN AT WARRENS) SIGNAGE PROCLAIMS THE AREA'S NO. 1 CROP. A CRANBERRY VINTAGE AND RIPENING BERRIES, BOTH AT THE WETHERBY CRANBERRY COMPANY.

FARMSCAPE IN THE MAZOMANIE AREA.

are purchased by customers directly from the marsh at Wetherby's during harvest-time in October. Nodji takes me into a big steel barn to explain cranberry processing and sorting, including the "bounce test." (Did you know that cranberries are also called bounceberries?) Each berry has to bounce above seven levels on a wooden device. The all-star shiny-red berries that pass the test get bagged and sold whole in all their glory.

Back in tiny Warrens, I pull my car over beside a handsome former cranberry warehouse that's been transformed into the Wisconsin Cranberry Discovery Center. In the basement museum, I learn even more from an excellent video about cranberries: how they're harvested and the history of cranberry farming. But it's the main level that holds me spellbound. So many cranberry products! Cranberry trail mix; cranberry-raspberry taffy; chocolate-covered cranberries; dried cranberries; cranberry honey (made by the busy bees that pollinate the crop); and cranberry jelly, preserves, salsa, jam, wine (a Wetherby vintage), syrup, ketchup, mustard, relish, grilling sauce, pie filling and jelly beans. There are even paintings of cranberries, a book called *The Joy of Cranberries* and, last but not least, cranberry

dental floss! Dental floss? Yes, thanks to the acidic berry's plaque-fighting properties. I stagger to the register, my arms loaded with cranberry delights. Then I detour to the old-fashioned, marble-slab soda-fountain counter for a cup of cranberry-flavored coffee to drink with my cranberry-walnut pie, cranberry-zucchini muffin, cranberry-fudge cookie and several kinds of cranberry ice cream. These people are doing an excellent job of dreaming up new uses for their crop!

Fittingly, I end my excursion in cranberry country—and Wisconsin—with a cranberry lunch at Burnstad's European Village Café in Tomah. It's quite a complex, combining a supermarket and apparel, gift and accessory shops with the cafe. I order the cranberry chicken sandwich, a chicken breast topped with cranberry-orange sauce and served on sourdough Craisin bread, and a piece of upside-down apple-walnut pie that has nothing to do with cranberries but which I can't resist.

So long, Wisconsinites! Your beautiful state rules when it comes to cranberries, pie, beer, cheese, brats and so many other Midwest food standouts. I just have to wonder: How do you folks manage to pack it all in and still wind up skinniest among the Heartland states?

Taste of Wisconsin

Fresh Peach Pie

Norske Nook, Osseo

- 1¼ to 1½ cups sugar
- ¼ cup all-purpose flour
- 2 tablespoons cornstarch
- 7 cups sliced, peeled peaches (about 12 medium) or frozen unsweetened peach slices
  Norske Nook's Basic Pie Pastry (recipe follows)
- 4 teaspoons cold butter, cut into thin slices
  Sugar

For filling: In a large bowl, combine the 1¼ to 1½ cups sugar, flour and cornstarch. Add peaches. Toss to coat peaches. (If using frozen peaches, let stand for 15 to 30 minutes or until peaches are partially thawed, but still icy.) Set aside.

For pastry: Divide dough in half. Form each half into a ball. On a lightly floured surface, use your hands to slightly flatten 1 dough ball. Roll dough from center to edge into a circle about 13 inches in diameter. To transfer pastry, wrap it around the rolling pin. Unroll pastry into a 10-inch pie plate or 9-inch deep-dish pie plate. Ease pastry into pie plate, being careful not to stretch pastry.

Stir peach mixture and transfer to pastry-lined pie plate. Dot filling with butter. Trim the bottom crust even with edge of pie plate. Roll remaining dough into a circle about 13 inches in diameter. Cut slits to allow steam to escape. Place remaining pastry on filling; trim pastry to ½ inch beyond edge of pie plate. Fold top pastry under bottom pastry. Crimp edge as desired.

Sprinkle top with additional sugar. Cover edge with foil to prevent overbrowning. Bake in a 375° oven for 25 minutes for fresh peaches or 50 minutes for partially thawed. Remove foil; bake for 20 to 25 minutes more or until golden. Cool about 4 hours before serving. *Makes 8 servings.*

Norske Nook's Basic Pie Pastry: In a large bowl, stir together 2 cups all-purpose flour and $1/2$ teaspoon salt. Using a pastry blender, cut in $2/3$ cup butter-flavored shortening until pieces are pea size. Sprinkle 1 tablespoon of cold water over part of the mixture; gently toss with a fork. Push moistened dough to the side of the bowl. Repeat moistening dough, using 1 tablespoon cold water at a time, until all the dough is moistened (7 to 8 tablespoons cold water total).

Cranberry-Zucchini Muffins

Wisconsin Cranberry Discovery Center, Warrens

2½ cups all-purpose flour
1¼ cups sugar
2 teaspoons baking soda
1½ teaspoons ground cinnamon
½ teaspoon salt
3 eggs, slightly beaten
1 8-ounce carton dairy sour cream
½ cup cooking oil
1 teaspoon vanilla
2 cups finely shredded, unpeeled zucchini
1 8-ounce can crushed pineapple (juice pack), drained
1 cup dried cranberries or dried cherries
2/3 cup chopped walnuts, toasted

Grease twenty-four 2½-inch muffin cups; set aside. In a large bowl, combine flour, sugar, baking soda, cinnamon and salt. Make a well in center of flour mixture; set aside.

In medium bowl, combine eggs, sour cream, oil and vanilla. Add egg mixture all at once to flour mixture. Stir just until moistened (batter should be lumpy). In same medium bowl, combine zucchini, drained pineapple, cranberries and walnuts. Fold zucchini mixture into batter.

Spoon batter into the prepared muffin cups, filling each two-thirds full. Bake in a 400° oven for 18 to 22 minutes or until golden and a wooden toothpick inserted in centers comes out clean. Cool in muffin cups on a wire rack for 5 minutes. Remove from cups; serve warm. *Makes 24 muffins.*

Rutabaga Pancakes

Inspired by Tower House, Cumberland

8 ounces rutabaga
1½ cups all-purpose flour
¼ cup packed brown sugar
2 teaspoons baking powder
½ teaspoon baking soda
½ teaspoon salt
2 slightly beaten eggs
1¼ cups milk
2 tablespoons melted butter or cooking oil
½ teaspoon vanilla

Wash and peel rutabaga; cut into ½-inch cubes. (You should have 1½ cups.) In a small saucepan, cook rutabaga, covered, in a small amount of boiling salted water for 30 to 35 minutes or until very tender. Drain well. In a medium bowl, mash rutabaga with a potato masher until smooth. (You should have 1 cup.) Set aside to cool.

In a bowl, stir together flour, brown sugar, baking powder, baking soda and salt. Make a well in center of flour mixture.

In another medium bowl, combine eggs, milk, mashed rutabaga, melted butter and vanilla. Add the milk mixture all at once to flour mixture. Stir just until moistened (batter should be lumpy). Add 2 to 4 tablespoons additional milk to thin batter, if necessary.

Heat a lightly greased griddle or heavy skillet over medium heat until a few drops of water dance across the surface. For each pancake, pour or spread about ¼ cup of the batter onto the hot griddle.

Cook over medium heat about 2 minutes on each side or until pancakes are golden brown, turning to second sides when pancakes have bubbly surfaces and edges are slightly dry. Serve immediately or keep warm in a loosely covered ovenproof dish in a 300° oven. *Makes 6 servings.*

Parmesan Potatoes

Quivey's Grove, Madison

¼ cup butter
1 medium onion, coarsely chopped
1½ cups half-and-half or light cream
1 30-ounce package frozen loose-pack, shredded hash brown potatoes, thawed
1 cup finely shredded Parmesan cheese (4 ounces)
¼ teaspoon salt
¼ teaspoon ground black pepper
¼ teaspoon paprika

In a 12-inch skillet, melt butter over medium heat. Add onion and cook until tender. Add half-and-half. Cook and stir for 2 minutes. Add potatoes. Cook and stir for 5 to 7 minutes or until liquid is absorbed. Sprinkle with half of the Parmesan cheese and all of the salt and black pepper; stir until melted.

Transfer mixture to a 9-inch square baking pan, spreading evenly over bottom of pan. Top with remaining Parmesan cheese. Sprinkle with paprika.

Bake, covered, in a 350° oven for 45 minutes. Uncover; place baking pan under broiler 4 to 5 inches from heat. Broil for 2 minutes. Let stand 5 minutes before serving. *Makes 9 servings.*

RUTABAGA FUN.

Travel Journal

More Information

Cambridge Chamber of Commerce (608/423-3780, www.cambridgewi.com). **Cumberland Chamber of Commerce** (715/822-3378, www.cumberland-wisconsin.com). **Greater Madison Convention & Visitors Bureau** (800/373-6376, www.visitmadison.com). **Manitowoc Area Visitor & Convention Bureau** (800/627-4896, www.manitowoc.org). **Monroe Chamber of Commerce** (608/325-7648, www.monroechamber.org). **Mount Horeb Area Chamber of Commerce** (888/765-5929, www.trollway.com). **Racine County Convention & Visitors Bureau** (800/205-0509, www.visitracine.org). **Sheboygan County Convention & Visitors Bureau** (800/457-9497, www.sheboygan.org).

Featured Dining

L'Etoile Madison (608/251-0500). **Marigold Kitchen** Madison (608/661-5559). **Quivey's Grove** Madison (608/273-4900). **Old Feed Mill** Mazomanie (888/345-4909). **Norske Nook** Osseo (800/294-6665); also in Hayward (715/634-4928) and Rice Lake (715/234-1733). **Schwarz's Supper Club** St. Anna (920/894-3598). **Burnstad's European Village Café** Tomah (608/372-5355, ext. 3).

More Great Dining

Tower House Cumberland. Home cooking in a refurbished Victorian; known for fresh-baked rolls (715/822-8457). **Ella's Deli & Ice Cream Parlor** Madison, east of downtown. Full-menu restaurant featuring kosher-style foods, salads and desserts (608/241-5291). **Smokey's Club** Madison. Casual, supper-club-type restaurant with quirky decor, serving great steaks (608/233-2120).

Featured Stops

Hinchley Dairy Farm Cambridge (608/764-5090). **Ancora Coffee Roasters** Madison (608/255-2900), with three other locations around the city. **Babcock Hall Dairy Store** Madison (608/262-3045). **Dane County Farmers' Market** Madison (608/455-1999). **Beerntsen's Confectionary, Inc**. Manitowoc (920/684-9616). **Capital Brewery, Inc**. Middleton (608/836-7100), with tours and retail sales. **Joseph Huber Brewing Company, Inc.** Monroe (608/325-3191), offering a Taster's Tour. **Mount Horeb Mustard Museum & Gourmet Foods Emporium** Mount Horeb (800/438-6878). **Cedar Grove Cheese, Inc.** Plain (800/200-6020), with tours and retail sales. **O&H Danish Bakery** Racine (866/637-8895), with three other locations around the city. **Miesfeld's Market** North of Sheboygan (920/565-6328). **Wetherby Marsh/Wetherby Cranberry Company** Warrens (608/378-4813), with in-season sales and public harvest-day tours the first Saturday in October. **Wisconsin Cranberry Discovery Center** Warrens (608/378-4878).

More Great Stops

American Club Resort Kohler (Sheboygan area; 800/344-2838). *Also see More Great Lodgings.* **Madison** The capitol dome soars above the skyline of Wisconsin's energetic capital city, which includes attractions such as the Monona Terrace Community and Convention Center, a dramatic Frank Lloyd Wright design (guided tours), and the State Street pedestrian mall, lined with trendy specialty shops, galleries and coffeehouses. **Lake Michigan Carferry Service** Manitowoc. Home port of the last Great Lakes car-carrying ferry, *S.S. Badger*, on which Dan shuttled across Lake Michigan to Ludington (800/841-4243). **Wisconsin Maritime Museum** Manitowoc. The largest maritime museum along the Great Lakes, with a World War II–era submarine (866/724-2356). **South-central Wisconsin** Amid emerald hills and river valleys, sample ethnic foods, admire architecture, join lively festivals and shop for artists' and crafters' works in communities such as Mount Horeb, New Glarus and Monroe, which remember their old-world roots. **Historic Cheesemaking Center/Welcome Center** Monroe. In a restored railway depot, exhibits and artifacts about the area's cheese-making industry and Swiss heritage (608/325-4636). **Cranberry Highway** Wisconsin Rapids/Woods County. Cranberry attractions, from marshes to restaurants serving cranberry specialties, on a 50-mile self-guided drive (free maps). Also guided tours and a 24-mile bicycle route (800/554-4484).

Dan's Lodgings

Best Western Arrowhead Lodge & Suites Black River Falls ($; 800/284-9471). **Cumberland Inn & Suites** Cumberland ($$; 715/822-5655). **Best Western Inn on the Park** Madison, just across the street from the capitol ($$; 800/279-8811). **Inn on Maritime Bay** Manitowoc ($$$; 800/654-5353). **AmeriHost Inn** Sun Prairie, northeast of Madison ($$; 608/834-9889).

More Great Lodgings

The American Club Kohler (Sheboygan area). A classic resort complex listed on the National Register of Historic Places, including world-class golf and a full-service spa ($$$$; 800/344-2838). Accommodations also available at the Inn on Woodlake on the resort property ($$$$; 800/344-2838).

Canterbury Inn Madison. Red-brick lodgings above a bookstore four blocks from the capitol ($$$$; 800/838-3850).

Mansion Hill Inn Madison. An elegant bed and breakfast located downtown ($$$$; 800/798-9070).

Food Events

Dane County Farmers' Market Madison, Saturdays and Wednesdays, late April through early November—Harvest a bumper crop of Wisconsin-grown vegetables, fruits, meats and flowers at this producer-only farmers market (held at Capitol Square on Saturdays; check website for Wednesday location). Stalls also brim with cheese, honey, pies, doughnuts and other goodies. The market continues indoors during the winter months (608/455-1999, www.dcfm.org).

Great Wisconsin Cheese Festival Little Chute, first weekend in June—Tickle your taste buds with the cheese-carving demonstration, Big Cheese Parade, cheese-curd-eating contest and cheesecake contest. You can also sample free cheese and fill up on omelets at the Sunday breakfast. Live music, crafts booths, carnival rides and children's entertainment round out the fun. Admission charged (920/788-7390, www.littlechutewi.org).

Dairyfest Marshfield, first weekend in June—Party till the cows come home when one of Wisconsin's top dairy-producing counties toasts its industry with a mayor's breakfast, an ice cream social and free milk. Other delights: the 5K and 10K Cheese Chase, a parade, 125 crafts booths, fireworks and church services in the world's largest round barn (800/422-4541, www.marshfieldchamber.com).

Milwaukee's Ethnic Festivals Milwaukee, June through September—Spend your summer savoring foods from around the globe. Whet your appetite at the Asian Moon Festival and Polish Fest in June, followed by Bastille Days, Festa Italiana and German Fest in July; African World Festival, Arab World Fest, Irish Fest and Mexi-

DANE CO. FARMERS' MARKET, MADISON.

can Fiesta in August; and the Indian Summer Festival in September. Ethnic foods and traditional music, dancing and arts span the gatherings, all held along the lakefront (except Bastille Days, held in downtown's East Town). Admission charged to all but Bastille Days (800/554-1448, www.visitmilwaukee.org).

State Fair West Allis, 11 days starting the first Thursday of August—Almost everyone who goes to this fair indulges in at least one cream puff—a light, flaky pastry stuffed with dairy-fresh whipped cream by the Wisconsin Bakers Association (414/266-7000, www.wistatefair.com).

Bratwurst Days Sheboygan, first Thursday through Saturday in August—Eat lots of brats (on a stick, or in jambalaya and egg rolls, for starters) at the food booths or stuff yourself at the brat-eating contest. Also in the "Bratwurst Capital of the World": four stages of entertainment, a parade, 4-mile Brat Trot, 2-mile walk and kids' activity area (800/689-0290, www.sheboyganjaycees.com).

Rutabaga Festival Cumberland, weekend before Labor Day—Located in what was once a top rutabaga-growing region, this town salutes its roots with 3- and 12-mile Rutabaga Runs, a 2-mile walk, live music, a crafts fair, a car show and a hot-pepper-eating contest. The underloved veggie also gets its due with a parade and food booths (715/822-3378, www.cumberland-wisconsin.com).

Warrens Cranberry Festival Warrens, last full weekend in September—At the world's

largest cranberry festival, seas of red will "bog"gle your mind on cranberry bog tours and at food booths selling cranberry cream puffs, pies and sundaes. Nearly 100,000 folks swarm wee Warrens (population 292) for the 1,200 booths of crafts, antiques and flea market items, a parade and the bumber crop of berries (608/378-4200, www.cranfest.com).

Mail Order

Ancora Coffee Roasters Wide variety of premium coffee beans artisan-roasted in small batches. Dan recommends a unique pack called Dessert & Coffee Pairings, which includes a fresh-made dessert from La Tarte Bakery (800/260-0217, www.ancora-coffee.com).

Beerntsen's Confectionary Hand-dipped assorted chocolates, as well as fresh-roasted nuts, caramel corn, brittle, caramels and fudge. Customized boxes of chocolates and molded novelty items available (888/771-5207, www.beerntsens.com).

Miesfeld's Market Home of grand champion bratwurst and award-winning sausages, in addition to ham and bacon smoked with selected hardwoods for mouthwatering flavor. Order fresh-cut premium meats, smoked meats, snack stixs, sauces and marinades (920/565-6328, www.miesfeldsmarket.com).

Mount Horeb Mustard Museum & Gourmet Foods Emporium Online store offers more than 800 different mustards, sauces and a wide range of gourmet food gift packs (800/438-6878, www.mustard web.com).

O&H Danish Bakery All items made by hand, using only premium ingredients. Kringles (O-shaped, butter-layered Danish pastries) are shipped worldwide daily. Coffee cakes, European-style breads, chocolate éclairs, bread puddings and celebration cakes also available (800/709-4009; www.ohdanishbakery.com).

Wisconsin Cranberry Discovery Center Delicious cranberry foodstuffs, from pancake mix and honey to candies and condiments (608/378-4878, www.discover cranberries.com).

More Midwest Recipes

APPETIZERS & SNACKS

Pierogies
Inspired by Zubrzycki's Warsaw Inn Polish American Smorgasbord, McHenry, IL

2¼ cups all-purpose flour
1 egg, slightly beaten
2 tablespoons dairy sour cream
1 tablespoon cooking oil
Dash salt
½ cup water
Onion-Mushroom Filling, Cottage Cheese Filling or Garlic-Potato Filling (recipes follow)
2 tablespoons butter or margarine

Place flour in a large bowl; make a well in center. Place egg, sour cream, oil and salt in well. Use a fork to stir together ingredients, gradually adding ½ cup water. On a lightly floured surface, knead until dough is smooth and elastic. Divide dough into fourths; cover with a towel.

On a lightly floured surface, roll a portion of dough to ¹/₁₆-inch thickness. Using a

2½-inch round cutter, cut into circles. Spoon 1 teaspoon of desired filling off center on each circle. Moisten edges of dough with water. Fold dough over filling to form a half-circle. Seal edges by pressing with tines of a fork. Lightly flour a baking sheet. Transfer pierogies to prepared baking sheet and cover loosely with a towel. Repeat with remaining dough and filling.

In a Dutch oven, bring 12 cups lightly salted water to boiling. Add about a third of pierogies. Cook for 3 to 5 minutes. Use a slotted spoon to transfer pierogies to a wire rack or paper towels to drain. Repeat with remaining pierogies.

To serve, in a 12-inch skillet, heat 1 tablespoon of butter. Cook half of drained pierogies for 3 to 4 minutes or until light brown, turning once. Repeat with remaining pierogies, adding butter as needed. If you like, sprinkle with snipped fresh parsley, paprika, nutmeg or coarsely ground pepper. *Makes 30 to 36 pierogies.*

Onion-Mushroom Filling: In a small skillet, cook ¼ cup chopped onion in 1 tablespoon hot butter until tender. Add 2 cups chopped mushrooms, ⅛ teaspoon salt and ⅛ teaspoon ground black pepper. Cook, uncovered, for 10 minutes, stirring occasionally. Remove from heat; cool slightly. Stir in 1 tablespoon fine dry bread crumbs, 1 tablespoon snipped fresh parsley and 1 slightly beaten egg yolk. Cool slightly before using. *Makes ³/₄ cup.*

Cottage Cheese Filling: In a food processor, cover and process ³/₄ cup drained cottage cheese or ³/₄ cup ricotta cheese until smooth. Add 1 egg yolk, ⅛ teaspoon salt and ⅛ teaspoon cayenne pepper. Cover and process just until combined. *Makes ³/₄ cup.*

Garlic-Potato Filling: In a covered medium saucepan, cook 6 ounces peeled potatoes (1 medium) and 2 cloves garlic in enough lightly salted boiling water to cover

for 20 to 25 minutes or until tender; drain. Mash with a potato masher or beat with an electric mixer on low speed. Add 1 tablespoon butter, ¼ teaspoon salt and ¼ teaspoon ground black pepper. Gradually beat in enough dairy sour cream or milk (1 to 2 tablespoons) to make mixture smooth and fluffy. Cool slightly. *Makes ³/₄ cup.*

KC Grilled Chicken Kabobs
Fiorella's Jack Stack Barbecue, Kansas City, MO

2 cups hickory wood chips (optional)
12 6-inch wooden skewers
Jack Stack's KC Spicy BBQ Sauce or Spicy Barbecue Sauce (recipe follows)
12 ounces skinless, boneless chicken breast halves or chicken tenders
2 teaspoons Cajun seasoning or steak seasoning
¼ cup shredded Monterey Jack cheese (1 ounce)
¼ cup shredded sharp cheddar cheese (1 ounce)

If you like, use wood chips. Soak chips in enough water to cover for at least 1 hour before grilling. Soak wooden skewers in water for 30 minutes before grilling. If using Spicy Barbecue Sauce, prepare sauce. Spoon ⅓ cup of Jack Stack's KC Spicy BBQ Sauce or homemade sauce into a small bowl; set aside.

If using chicken breast halves, cut chicken into long strips about ½-inch wide. Drain skewers. Thread 1 to 2 strips of chicken strips or chicken tenders accordion-style onto each skewer, leaving a ¼-inch space between pieces. Sprinkle all sides of chicken with Cajun seasoning.

For charcoal grill, drain wood chips, if using. Sprinkle chips over hot coals. Grill kabobs on greased rack of an uncovered grill directly over medium coals for 6 to

8 minutes or until chicken is no longer pink, turning to brown evenly and brushing all sides with 1/3 cup sauce for last 2 minutes of grilling. (For a gas grill, preheat grill. Follow manufacturer's directions for using wood chips, if using. Reduce heat to medium. Place kabobs on greased grill rack over heat, and grill as above.)

To serve, transfer kabobs to a serving platter. Sprinkle kabobs with cheeses. Serve with additional sauce. *Makes 12 appetizers.*

Spicy Barbecue Sauce: In a medium saucepan, combine 1 cup ketchup; 1/2 cup finely chopped green onion; 1/2 cup honey; one 4-ounce can diced green chile peppers, drained; 1/3 cup cider vinegar; 1/4 cup packed brown sugar; 2 tablespoons Dijon-style mustard; 2 teaspoons Worcestershire sauce; 2 to 3 cloves garlic, minced; 1 teaspoon ground cumin or chili powder and 1 teaspoon bottled hot pepper sauce. Bring to boiling; reduce heat. Simmer, uncovered, for 20 to 25 minutes or until mixture is thickened, stirring occasionally. *Makes about 2 cups.*

Smoked Fish Spread

Inspired by Lou's Fish House, Two Harbors, MN

- 3 ounces smoked trout, cod, arctic char or whitefish fillets, skinned, boned and flaked (about 1/2 cup)
- 3 ounces smoked salmon, sturgeon or mackerel, skinned, boned and flaked (about 1/2 cup)
- 1 8-ounce package cream cheese, softened
- 1 teaspoon finely shredded lemon peel
- 3 tablespoons lemon juice
- 1 tablespoon snipped fresh Italian (flat-leaf) parsley
- 1 tablespoon snipped fresh dill or 1 teaspoon dried dill weed
- 1 tablespoon finely chopped shallot
- 1/4 teaspoon coarsely ground black pepper
  Pita wedges, thinly sliced French bread and/or assorted crackers and vegetables

In a food processor or blender, add the smoked fish pieces, cream cheese, lemon peel and lemon juice. Cover; blend or process until almost smooth.

Transfer fish mixture to a serving container. Stir in parsley, 1 tablespoon dill, shallot and black pepper. Cover and chill in refrigerator for at least 4 hours.

To serve, let stand at room temperature for 15 minutes. If you like, garnish with additional fresh dill. Serve with pita wedges, bread or assorted crackers and vegetables. *Makes about 2 cups spread.*

Double Cranberry Crostini

Inspired by Wisconsin cranberries

  Fresh Cranberry-Ginger Chutney (recipe follows)
- 1/3 cup dried cranberries
- 2 3-ounce packages cream cheese, softened
- 2 tablespoons chopped pecans, toasted
- 1 teaspoon finely chopped, peeled fresh ginger
- 1 teaspoon lime juice
- 1 16-ounce loaf baguette-style French bread, cut into 1/2-inch slices
- 4 ounces thinly sliced smoked turkey or ham

Prepare Fresh Cranberry-Ginger Chutney; set aside to cool. In a small bowl, place dried cranberries; add enough boiling water to cover. Cover; let stand for 15 minutes. Drain well.

In a medium mixing bowl, beat cream cheese with an electric mixer until smooth. Beat in drained cranberries, pecans, ginger and lime juice; set aside.

Place bread slices on a large baking sheet (use 2 sheets if necessary to fit all of the slices in 1 layer). Bake in a 375° oven for 6 to 8 minutes or until edges just start to brown. Cool slightly.

Cut smoked turkey into about 30 pieces to fit on bread slices. Spread bread with cranberry-cheese mixture. Top each with a piece of turkey. Dollop with chutney. *Makes about 30 appetizers.*

Fresh Cranberry-Ginger Chutney: In a medium saucepan, combine 1 1/2 cups cranberries; 3/4 cup packed brown sugar; 1/3 cup dried apricot halves, chopped; 1/3 cup golden raisins; 2 tablespoons peeled and finely chopped fresh ginger; 2 tablespoons cranberry juice; 3/4 teaspoon ground cardamom and 1/4 teaspoon cayenne pepper. Cook and stir over medium heat until sugar is dissolved. Cook, uncovered, for 3 to 4 minutes more or until cranberries pop, stirring occasionally. Transfer to a medium bowl; let stand about 1 hour or until completely cool. *Makes about 2 cups.*

Vietnamese Spring Rolls

Inspired by Red Light, Chicago, IL

- 2 ounces dried rice vermicelli noodles
- 24 medium shrimp, peeled and deveined
- 2 cups shredded napa cabbage
- 1 cup shredded carrots
- 1/2 cup loosely packed fresh cilantro leaves
- 1/2 cup loosely packed fresh mint leaves
- 24 round rice-paper wrappers (8 1/2-inch diameter)
- 1/2 cup water
- 2 tablespoons sugar
- 2 tablespoons rice wine vinegar
- 1 tablespoon fish sauce (*nuoc nam* or *nam pla*)
- 1 tablespoon finely shredded carrot

In a medium saucepan, cook vermicelli in lightly salted boiling water for 3 minutes; drain. Rinse under cold water; drain well. Use kitchen shears to snip noodles into small pieces; set aside.

In a large saucepan, cook shrimp in lightly salted boiling water for 1 to 2 minutes or until opaque; drain. Rinse with cold water; drain again. Halve shrimp lengthwise; set aside.

In a large bowl, combine cooked vermicelli noodles, cabbage, 1 cup shredded carrots, cilantro and mint leaves; set aside.

Pour 1 cup warm water into a shallow dish. Dip rice papers, 1 at a time, into water; gently shake off excess water. Place rice papers between clean, damp, 100-percent-cotton kitchen towels; let stand for 10 minutes. Brush any dry edges with a little additional water. Place a well-rounded tablespoon of cabbage mixture across lower third of 1 softened rice paper (keep others covered). Fold bottom of rice paper over filling; arrange 2 shrimp halves across filling; fold in paper sides. Tightly roll up rice paper and filling. Place seam side down, on a large plate. Repeat with remaining rice paper, filling and shrimp. Cover and chill up to 6 hours.

For dipping sauce: In a small saucepan, combine 1/2 cup water and sugar. Bring to boiling over medium heat, stirring occasionally, until sugar is dissolved. Remove from heat and stir in rice wine vinegar, fish sauce and the 1 tablespoon shredded carrot.

Serve spring rolls with dipping sauce. *Makes 24 appetizers.*

Homemade Kettle-Style Popcorn

Inspired by Indiana's Amish popcorn producers

- 16 cups popped popcorn (about 2/3 cup unpopped)
- 1/4 cup light-colored corn syrup
- 1/4 cup butter
- Salt

Remove all unpopped kernels from popped corn. Put popcorn in a large roasting pan. In a small saucepan, heat and stir corn syrup and butter until butter is melted. Pour over popcorn mixture; stir gently to coat. Sprinkle lightly with salt; toss to coat.

Bake in a 300° oven for 30 minutes, stirring every 10 minutes. Cool mixture in pan. Break up any clusters before serving. (Cover and store any leftovers at room temperature in a tightly covered container for up to 1 week.) *Makes 16 cups (16 to 18 servings).*

BREAKFAST & BREADS

Dutch Letters

Jaarsma's Bakery, Pella, IA

- 4 1/2 cups all-purpose flour
- 1 teaspoon salt
- 2 cups cold butter (1 pound)
- 1 beaten egg
- 1 cup ice water
- 1 egg white
- 1 8-ounce can or tube almond paste
- 1/2 cup granulated sugar
- 1/2 cup packed brown sugar
- Granulated sugar

For dough: In a large mixing bowl, stir together flour and salt. Cut cold butter into 1/2-inch-thick slices (not cubes). Add butter slices to flour mixture; toss until slices are coated and separated.

In a small mixing bowl, stir together egg and ice water. Add all at once to flour mixture. Using a spoon, quickly mix (butter will remain in large pieces and flour will not be completely moistened).

Turn dough out onto a lightly floured pastry cloth. Knead dough 10 times by pressing and pushing dough together to form a rough-looking ball, lifting pastry cloth if necessary to press dough together. Shape dough into a rectangle (dough still will have some dry-looking areas). Make corners as square as possible. Slightly flatten dough. Working on a well-floured pastry cloth, roll dough into a 15x10-inch rectangle. Fold 2 short sides to meet in center; bring top edge down to meet bottom edge to form 4 layers each measuring (rectangle will now measure 7 1/2x5 inches).

Repeat rolling and folding process once more. Wrap dough with plastic wrap and chill for 20 minutes. Repeat rolling and folding process 2 more times. Chill dough for 20 minutes before using.

For filling: In a small bowl, stir together egg white, almond paste, 1/2 cup granulated sugar and brown sugar. Set aside.

Using a sharp knife, cut dough crosswise into 4 equal portions. Wrap 3 portions in plastic wrap and chill. On a well-floured surface, roll 1 portion into a 12 1/2x10-inch rectangle. Cut rectangle crosswise into five 10x2 1/2-inch strips.

Shape a slightly rounded tablespoon of filling into a 9-inch-long rope and place it down center of one strip. Roll up strip lengthwise. Brush edge and ends with water; pinch to seal. Place, seam side down, on an ungreased baking sheet, shaping strip into a letter (traditionally letter "S"). Brush with water and sprinkle with additional granulated sugar. Repeat with remaining dough strips and filling. Repeat with remaining dough portions and filling.

Bake in a 375° oven for 20 to 25 minutes or until golden. Remove from baking sheet. Cool on wire racks. *Makes 20 pastry letters.*

Tip: For best results, use an almond paste made without syrup or liquid glucose.

Wild Rice Quiche

Northern Lights, Beaver Bay, MN

- ½ of a 15-ounce package rolled refriger-ated unbaked piecrust (1 crust)
- 1 tablespoon Dijon-style mustard
- 4 eggs, lightly beaten
- 1 cup half-and-half, light cream or whole milk
- 1 teaspoon Worcestershire sauce
- ½ teaspoon salt
- ¼ teaspoon ground black pepper
- 1½ cups cooked wild rice
- 1 cup shredded Swiss cheese (4 ounces)
- ¼ cup sliced green onions (2)
- 1 cup finely chopped onion
- 6 slices bacon, crisp-cooked, drained and crumbled or 2 tablespoons cooked bacon pieces
- 2 tablespoons snipped fresh chives
- 2 tablespoons finely chopped pimiento

Let piecrust stand at room temperature for 15 minutes. Unroll piecrust. Ease piecrust into a 9-inch pie plate without stretching it. Crimp edge as desired. Line unpricked piecrust with a double thickness of foil. Bake in a 450° oven for 8 minutes. Remove foil. Bake for 4 to 5 minutes more or until piecrust is set and dry. Remove from oven. Reduce the oven temperature to 325°. Carefully brush mustard over the bottom of the hot baked piecrust; set aside.

In a medium bowl, stir together eggs, half-and-half, Worcestershire sauce, salt and

black pepper. Stir in wild rice, Swiss cheese, green onions, onion, bacon, chives and pimiento. Pour egg mixture into hot baked piecrust shell.

Bake in a 325° oven for 45 to 50 minutes or until a knife inserted near center comes out clean. If necessary, cover edge of crust with foil to prevent overbrowning. Let stand for 10 minutes before serving. *Makes 6 to 8 servings.*

Blueberry Surprise French-Toast Casserole

Inspired by the Blueberry Ranch, Mishawaka, IN

- 12 slices dry white bread, cut into ½-inch cubes (about 8 cups)
- 2 8-ounce packages cream cheese, cut into ¾-inch cubes
- 1 cup fresh or frozen blueberries
- 12 eggs
- 2 cups milk
- ½ cup maple syrup or maple-flavored syrup Blueberry-flavored, maple, or maple-flavored syrup

Place half of bread cubes over bottom of a well-buttered 13x9x2-inch baking dish (3-quart rectangular). Sprinkle cream cheese and blueberries over bread cubes. Top with remaining bread cubes.

In a large mixing bowl, beat eggs with a rotary beater; beat in milk and ½ cup syrup. Carefully pour egg mixture over bread mixture. Cover and chill in refrigerator for 2 to 24 hours.

Bake, covered, in a 375° for 25 minutes. Uncover and bake about 25 minutes more or until a knife inserted near center comes out clean, and topping is puffed and golden brown. Let stand for 10 minutes before serving. Serve warm with blueberry-flavored or maple syrup. *Makes 8 servings.*

Tip: To dry bread slices: Arrange bread in a single layer on a wire rack; cover loosely and let stand overnight. Or cut bread into ½-inch cubes; spread in a large baking pan. Bake, uncovered, in a 300° oven for 10 to 15 minutes or until dry, stirring twice; cool.

Morel Mushroom, Potato and Asparagus Frittata

Inspired by Michigan morels and asparagus

- 2 ounces fresh morel mushrooms or other fresh mushrooms
- 1 medium red or russet potato, coarsely chopped (about 1 cup)
- 1 cup water
- 4 ounces asparagus spears, trimmed and cut into 1-inch lengths (about ¾ cup)
- 6 eggs, slightly beaten
- ¼ cup milk
- 1 tablespoon snipped fresh Italian (flat-leaf) parsley
- 1 tablespoon snipped fresh dill
- ¼ teaspoon salt
- ¼ teaspoon ground black pepper
- 2 tablespoons butter
- ½ cup shredded Gruyère or Swiss cheese (2 ounces)
- 1 small tomato, seeded and chopped (½ cup)

To clean morels, place mushrooms in a bowl; add enough water to cover and ½ teaspoon salt. Let morels soak for 10 to 15 minutes. Drain off water, rinse and repeat 2 more times. Pat mushrooms dry.

Wash other mushrooms by gently wiping with a damp towel or paper towel. Trim ends of stems, if necessary. Slice mushrooms (should measure about ¾ cup). Set aside.

In a medium saucepan, combine potato and water. Bring to boiling; reduce heat. Simmer, covered, for 4 minutes. Add asparagus; return to simmering. Simmer, covered, for 3 to 4 minutes more or until vegetables are just tender. Drain vegetables well. Set aside.

In a small bowl, combine eggs, milk, parsley, dill, salt and black pepper. Set aside.

In a 10-inch broiler-proof skillet, melt butter over medium heat. Add mushrooms; cook over medium heat for 3 to 4 minutes or until mushrooms are tender. Stir in potatoes and asparagus.

Pour egg mixture over vegetable mixture. Cook, uncovered, over medium heat. As egg mixture begins to set, run a spatula around edge of skillet, lifting mixture so uncooked portion flows underneath. Continue until almost set. Remove from heat. Sprinkle with cheese.

Place broiler-proof skillet under broiler 4 to 5 inches from heat. Broil for 1 to 2 minutes or until top is just set. Sprinkle with tomato. Cut into wedges. *Makes 4 servings.*

Tip: If fresh morels aren't available, substitute 1/2 ounce dried morel mushrooms. In a small bowl, cover dried mushrooms with hot water. Let stand for 20 minutes. Rinse under warm running water; squeeze out excess moisture. Slice mushrooms.

Breakfast Burrito

Inspired by OK Café, Hastings, NE

- 6 eggs, lightly beaten
- 1/3 cup water
- 1/8 teaspoon salt
- 1/8 teaspoon ground black pepper
- 2 tablespoons butter
- 1 cup cubed cooked ham or cooked and crumbled sausage (6 ounces)
- 1/2 cup chopped green and/or red sweet pepper (1 small)
- 1/4 cup chopped onion
- 1/2 cup shredded cheddar cheese or Monterey Jack cheese (2 ounces)
- 6 8-inch tortillas, warmed
  Bottled green salsa

In a medium bowl, whisk together eggs, water, salt and black pepper; set aside. In a large nonstick skillet, melt butter over medium heat. Add ham, sweet pepper and onion. Cook and stir for 3 to 4 minutes or until vegetables are tender.

Pour egg mixture over ingredients in skillet. Cook, without stirring, until mixture begins to set on bottom and around edge. With a spatula, lift and fold partially cooked egg mixture so that uncooked portion flows underneath. Continue cooking over medium heat for 2 to 3 minutes or until egg mixture is cooked through but is still glossy and moist. Remove from heat.

To serve, divide egg mixture evenly among warmed tortillas. Sprinkle egg mixture evenly with cheese. Roll up tortillas. Serve with salsa. *Makes 6 servings.*

Tip: To warm tortillas, wrap them in foil. Heat in a 350° oven for 10 minutes.

Cherry-Oat Coffee Cake

Inspired by North Dakota sugar beets and grains

- 1 1/2 cups boiling water
- 1 cup regular rolled oats
  Streusel-Nut Topping (recipe follows)
- 1 1/2 cups all-purpose flour
- 1 1/2 teaspoons baking powder
- 1/2 teaspoon baking soda
- 1/2 teaspoon salt
- 1/2 teaspoon ground cardamom
- 1/2 cup butter, softened
- 1 cup packed brown sugar
- 2 eggs
- 1/2 cup dried cherries or finely snipped dried apricots

Grease bottom and 1/2 inch up sides of a 9x9x2-inch baking pan; set aside. In a small bowl, pour boiling water over 1 cup rolled oats; set aside. Prepare Streusel-Nut Topping; set aside. In a medium bowl, combine 1 1/2 cups flour, baking powder, baking soda, salt and cardamom.

In a large mixing bowl, beat the butter with an electric mixer on medium speed for 30 seconds. Add 1 cup brown sugar; beat on medium speed until well combined. Add eggs, one at a time, beating well after each addition. Alternately add flour mixture and oatmeal mixture to butter mixture, beating on low speed until just combined. Stir in dried cherries or apricots.

Spoon the coffee cake batter into the prepared pan. Sprinkle with topping. Bake in a 350° oven for 55 to 60 minutes or until a wooden pick inserted near center comes out clean. Cool on a wire rack. Serve warm. *Makes 9 to 12 servings.*

Streusel-Nut Topping: In a small bowl, stir together 1/2 cup rolled oats, 1/3 cup packed brown sugar and 1/4 teaspoon cup all-purpose flour. Using a pastry cutter, cut in 1/3 cup butter until mixture resembles coarse crumbs. Stir in 3/4 cup coarsely chopped walnuts.

Sweet Potato Pancakes

Inspired by Stafford's Bay View Inn, Petoskey, MI

- 1 1/4 cups all-purpose flour
- 2 tablespoons sugar
- 1 1/4 teaspoons baking powder
- 3/4 teaspoon salt
- 2 slightly beaten eggs
- 1 1/4 cups milk
- 1/2 cup mashed cooked sweet potatoes, cooled, or canned pumpkin
- 3 tablespoons butter or margarine, melted
  Apple butter or applesauce (optional)

In a medium bowl, combine flour, sugar, baking powder and salt. In a small bowl, combine eggs, milk, sweet potatoes and butter. Add egg mixture to flour mixture. Stir batter just until moistened (batter should be lumpy).

Heat a lightly greased griddle or heavy skillet over medium heat until a few drops of water dance across the surface. For each pancake, pour or spread about 1/4 cup of the batter onto the hot griddle.

Cook over medium heat about 2 minutes on each side or until pancakes are golden brown, turning to second sides when pancakes have bubbly surfaces and edges are slightly dry. Serve immediately or keep warm in a loosely covered ovenproof dish in a 300° oven. If you like, serve with apple butter. *Makes 8 servings.*

Four-Grain Rolls

Inspired by Kansas wheat and flour

> 1 cup warm water (105° to 115°)
> 2 packages active dry yeast
> 1 teaspoon sugar
> 1 cup warm water (105° to 115°)
> 1/2 cup sugar
> 1/2 cup cooking oil
> 2 eggs, slightly beaten
> 1 1/2 teaspoons salt
> 1 cup rye flour
> 1/2 cup regular rolled oats
> 1/2 cup whole bran cereal
> 4 1/4 to 4 3/4 cups all-purpose flour

In a large mixing bowl, combine 1 cup warm water, yeast and 1 teaspoon sugar. Let stand about 5 minutes or until yeast dissolves and mixture bubbles.

Stir 1 cup warm water, 1/2 cup sugar, oil, eggs and salt into yeast mixture. Add rye flour, oats and bran cereal; mix well. Let stand for 5 minutes.

Add 2 cups of all-purpose flour. Beat with an electric mixer on medium speed for 30 seconds, scraping bowl constantly. Beat on high speed for 3 minutes. Stir in as much of remaining all-purpose flour as you can.

Turn dough out onto a lightly floured surface. Knead in enough of remaining flour to make a moderately stiff dough that's smooth and elastic (8 to 10 minutes total). Dough may be sticky.

Shape dough into a ball. Place in a lightly greased bowl, turning once to grease surface. Cover and let dough rise in a warm place until dough nearly doubles in size (about 1 hour). Lightly grease twenty-four 2 1/2-inch muffin cups or 2 baking sheets.

Punch dough down. Turn out onto a lightly floured surface. Cover; let rest for 10 minutes. Shape into 24 rolls. Place in prepared muffin cups or 2 1/2 inches apart on prepared baking sheets. Cover; let rise in a warm place until nearly double in size (30 minutes).

Bake in a 375° oven about 12 minutes or until rolls sound hollow when lightly tapped. Immediately remove from cups. Cool on wire rack. *Makes 24 rolls.*

Fruit and Nut Granola

Café Patachou, Indianapolis, IN

> 1/2 cup butter
> 1/2 cup packed brown sugar
> 2 tablespoons honey
> 3 cups regular rolled oats
> 1 cup sliced almonds
> 1/2 cup raisins
> 1/2 cup dried cherries or dried cranberries

In a small saucepan, melt butter over medium-low heat. Add brown sugar and honey, stirring until combined. Remove from heat.

Meanwhile, in a large bowl, combine the oats and almonds. Drizzle butter mixture over oat mixture, tossing to combine. Spread evenly in a greased 15x10x1-inch baking pan.

Bake in a 325° oven for 15 minutes. Remove from oven; stir mixture well. Return to oven and bake for 10 to 15 minutes more or until lightly browned. Add raisins and cherries, tossing to combine.

Spread the granola in an even layer in the baking pan or transfer to a large piece of foil to cool. Break into smaller clumps, if needed. Store in an airtight container for up to 1 week. *Makes 6 cups (twelve 1/2-cup servings).*

MAIN DISHES & SOUPS

Michigan Cherry Salmon

Great Lakes Culinary Institute at Northwestern Michigan College, Traverse City, MI

> 6 5- to 6-ounce fresh or frozen salmon fillets or steaks, cut 1 inch thick
> 2 1/2 cups cherry juice
> 1 cup dried cherries
> 1/4 cup cherry liqueur (optional)
> 1/2 cup sugar
> 1/2 cup water
> 1 3-inch stick cinnamon
> 1/2 teaspoon vanilla
> 1 tablespoon tarragon-infused olive oil or any herb-infused olive oil
> Hot cooked wild rice

Thaw fish, if frozen. Rinse fish; pat dry.

In a medium saucepan, bring cherry juice to boiling; remove from heat. Add cherries; let stand about 10 minutes or until softened. Drain, reserving the cherry juice. Set the cherries aside.

For glaze: Return cherry juice to same saucepan. If you like, add cherry liqueur. Bring to boiling; reduce heat. Simmer, uncovered, until mixture measures 1/2 cup (this should take 25 to 30 minutes). Add sugar, water and stick cinnamon. Bring to boiling; reduce heat. Simmer, uncovered, for 10 minutes, stirring occasionally. Remove from heat; discard stick cinnamon. Stir in vanilla. Cool to room temperature. Set aside.

Brush oil over both sides of fish. Lightly sprinkle fish with salt and black pepper. For charcoal grill, grill fish on rack of an uncovered grill directly over medium coals for 8 to 12 minutes or until fish flakes easily when tested with a fork, gently turning once halfway through grilling. (For a gas grill, preheat grill. Reduce heat to medium. Place fish on rack over heat. Cover and grill as above.)

To serve, use a wide spatula to transfer fish to a serving platter. Drizzle cherry glaze over fish and top with cherries. Serve with hot cooked wild rice. *Makes 6 servings.*

Honey-Glazed Baked Ham

Inspired by the Keeter Center, College of the Ozarks, Point Lookout, MO

- 1 5- to 6- pound cooked ham (rump half or shank portion)
  Whole cloves (about 1 teaspoon)
- 1 cup packed brown sugar
- 1/2 cup honey
- 1/2 cup orange juice
- 2 tablespoons Dijon-style mustard

Score ham by making diagonal cuts in a diamond pattern. To stud ham with cloves, push in long end of a clove at diamond intersections. Place ham on a rack in a shallow roasting pan. Insert an oven-proof meat thermometer, making sure thermometer does not touch bone.

Bake ham in a 325° oven until meat thermometer registers 125°. For rump half, allow 1¼ to 1½ hours; for shank, allow 1¾ to 2 hours.

For glaze: In a medium saucepan, stir together brown sugar, honey, orange juice and mustard. Cook and stir over medium heat until sugar dissolves.

Brush about ¼ cup of glaze over ham. Bake, uncovered, for 20 to 30 minutes more or until meat thermometer registers 135°. Let ham stand for 15 minutes before carving. (Meat temperature will rise 5° during standing.) Reheat remaining glaze and serve with ham. *Makes 16 to 20 servings.*

Iron Range Porketta

Inspired by Minnesota Iron Range Italians

- 1/2 cup snipped fresh Italian (flat leaf) parsley or 1 tablespoon dried parsley flakes
- 2 to 3 cloves garlic, minced, or 1/2 teaspoon garlic powder
- 1½ teaspoons coarsely ground black pepper
- 1½ teaspoons fennel seeds, crushed
- 3/4 teaspoon salt
- 1 3- to 4-pound boneless pork shoulder blade roast, rolled and tied (also called Boston butt roast or butt roast)

In a bowl, combine parsley, garlic, black pepper, fennel seeds and salt; set aside.

Untie the pork roast and trim any fat from meat. Using a sharp knife, cut several 1-inch slits all over the roast. Using your fingers, press some of the parsley mixture into the slits. Sprinkle the remaining mixture evenly over the entire surface of the meat and rub in with your fingers. If necessary, tie the roast with 100-percent-cotton string to hold it together. Insert an ovenproof meat thermometer into the center of the meat.

For a charcoal grill, arrange medium-hot coals around a drip pan. Test for medium heat above pan. Place the meat on a grill rack over the drip pan. Cover and grill for 1½ to 2¼ hours or until the thermometer registers 155°. (For a gas grill, preheat grill. Reduce heat to medium-low. Adjust for indirect cooking. Place the meat on a rack in a roasting pan, place on grill rack and grill as above.)

Remove meat from grill; cover with foil and let stand for 15 minutes before carving. (Meat temperature will rise 5° during standing.)

To serve, thinly slice the cooked pork roast. Or, if you like, finely chop the meat and serve it on hard rolls spread with coarse-grain brown mustard. *Makes 10 to 12 servings.*

Cincinnati's Sacred Heart Meatballs

Sacred Heart Church and Italian Center, Cincinnati, OH

- 2 or 3 3/4-inch-thick slices Italian bread
- 1/4 cup water
- 1 egg
- 1/3 cup finely chopped onion
- 1/4 cup fine dry bread crumbs
- 1/4 cup grated Romano or Parmesan cheese (or a blend of both)
- 2 tablespoons water
- 2 tablespoons snipped fresh Italian (flat-leaf) parsley
- 2 teaspoons olive oil
- 1/2 teaspoon garlic salt
- 1/2 teaspoon Italian seasoning, crushed
- 1/4 teaspoon ground black pepper
- 1/4 teaspoon crushed red pepper
- 1 pound lean ground beef
- 8 ounces lean ground pork
- 1 tablespoon cooking oil
- 2 26-ounce jars LaRosa's Family Recipe Original Pasta Sauce or meatless pasta sauce (about 6²/₃ cups)
- 8 ounces dried spaghetti or linguine
  Finely shredded Romano or Parmesan cheese (optional)

In a medium bowl, soak bread slices in ¼ cup water for 5 minutes. Finely chop bread (you should have about ¾ cup).

In a large bowl, beat egg. Stir in chopped bread, onion, bread crumbs, ¼ cup cheese, 2 tablespoons water, parsley, olive oil, garlic salt, Italian seasoning, black pepper and red pepper. Add beef and pork to egg mixture; mix well.

Using a 2-ounce ice cream scoop or a ¼-cup measure, scoop meat mixture into 16 mounds. Wet hands; shape mounds into balls.

In a large skillet, heat cooking oil over medium heat. Cook half of meatballs at a time in hot oil for 8 to 10 minutes or until done (an instant-read thermometer inserted into meatballs should register 160°), turning to brown evenly. Remove meatballs from skillet; drain on paper towels. (Or, transfer meatballs to a 13x9x2-inch baking pan. Omit cooking oil. Bake meatballs in a 350° oven for 20 minutes; drain.)

In a 4-quart Dutch oven, bring pasta sauce to boiling; reduce heat. Add meatballs to pasta sauce. Simmer, covered, for 30 minutes, stirring occasionally.

Meanwhile, cook pasta according to package directions. Serve meatballs and sauce over hot cooked pasta. If you like, sprinkle with shredded Romano cheese. *Makes 4 servings.*

Greek Pastitsio

Inspired by New Hellas, Detroit, MI

- 8 ounces dried elbow or corkscrew macaroni
- 8 ounces ground lamb or lean ground beef
- 1 14-ounce jar spaghetti sauce with onion and garlic
- 1 teaspoon ground cinnamon
- 1/4 teaspoon fennel seeds, crushed
- 1 cup milk
- 1 1.8-ounce envelope white sauce mix
- 2 slightly beaten eggs
- 1/4 cup crumbled feta cheese (1 ounce)
- 1/2 teaspoon ground nutmeg
- 1/4 cup grated kasseri cheese or provolone cheese (1 ounce)

Cook pasta according to package directions; drain. Set aside. In large skillet, cook ground meat until brown. Drain off fat. Stir in spaghetti sauce, cinnamon and fennel seed; set aside.

In medium saucepan, slowly stir milk into white sauce mix. Cook and stir over medium heat until thickened and bubbly. Remove from heat. Gradually stir half of white sauce into eggs; return all of mixture to saucepan. Stir in feta cheese and nutmeg.

To assemble, layer half of cooked pasta in a greased 2-quart casserole dish. Spread meat mixture over pasta; top with remaining pasta. Evenly spread white sauce mixture over pasta. Sprinkle with kasseri cheese.

Bake in a 350° oven about 35 minutes or until set. Let stand for 10 minutes before serving. *Makes 6 servings.*

Stuffed Cabbage Rolls

Inspired by Sunrise Deli, Hibbing, MN

- 8 large cabbage leaves
- 12 ounces lean ground beef, ground pork, ground lamb or bulk pork sausage
- 1 medium onion, chopped (1/2 cup)
- 1 egg, slightly beaten
- 1 cup cooked long grain rice
- 2 tablespoons snipped fresh parsley
- 1/4 teaspoon salt
- 1 14-ounce can sauerkraut, rinsed and well drained
- 1 8-ounce can tomato sauce
- 2 tablespoons brown sugar
- 2 tablespoons water
- 2 teaspoons lemon juice
   Dash ground cloves
   Dash ground allspice

Fill a Dutch oven with water; bring to boiling. From the back side of the cabbage leaves, cut out large center vein in each cabbage leaf, keeping each leaf in one piece. Immerse leaves, 4 at a time, in the boiling water; cook for 2 to 4 minutes or just until leaves are just limp. Drain well.

For filling: In a large skillet, cook ground beef and onion until meat is brown; drain off fat. In a medium bowl, combine egg, rice, parsley, salt and meat mixture.

Lightly grease a 2-quart rectangular baking dish. Spoon sauerkraut into bottom of dish. Place about 1/3 cup of the ground beef mixture in the center of each cabbage leaf. Fold in sides. Starting at an unfolded edge, carefully roll up each leaf, making sure folded sides are tucked into the roll. Place cabbage rolls on sauerkraut in baking dish.

For sauce: In a small bowl, stir together tomato sauce, brown sugar, lemon juice, cloves and allspice; pour over cabbage rolls. Bake, covered, in a 350° oven for 30 to 35 minutes or until heated through. *Makes 4 servings.*

Bun-Buster Pork Tenderloin Sandwiches

Inspired by Joensy's, Solon, IA

- 1 3/4 pounds pork tenderloin
- 1/4 cup all-purpose flour
- 1/4 teaspoon onion powder or onion salt
- 1/4 teaspoon garlic powder or garlic salt
- 1/4 teaspoon ground black pepper
- 1 egg, slightly beaten
- 1 tablespoon milk
- 3/4 cup seasoned fine dry bread crumbs or 1 cup finely crushed rich round crackers (about 24)
- 2 tablespoons cooking oil
- 4 large hamburger buns or kaiser rolls, split and toasted
   Ketchup, mustard, onion slices and/or dill pickle slices

Trim fat from meat. Cut meat crosswise into 4 serving-size slices. Place each slice between 2 pieces of plastic wrap. Use the flat side of a meat mallet and work from center to lightly pound each slice to a 1/4-inch thickness. Remove the plastic wrap.

In a shallow bowl, combine flour, onion powder, garlic powder and black pepper. In another shallow bowl, combine egg and milk. In a third bowl, place bread crumbs. Dip meat into flour mixture to coat. Dip into egg mixture. Coat with bread crumbs.

In a 12-inch heavy skillet, cook 2 of the tenderloin slices in hot oil over medium heat for 6 to 8 minutes or until meat is slightly pink in center, turning once. Remove from skillet. Place on a baking sheet in a 300° oven to keep warm while cooking the remaining tenderloins. Repeat with remaining slices, adding more oil, if necessary.

Serve on warm buns. Pass the ketchup, mustard, onion slices and/or dill pickle slices. *Makes 4 servings.*

Indiana Roast Duckling

Inspired by Culver Duck, Middlebury, IN

- 1   4- to 5-pound domestic duckling or whole roasting chicken
- 6   quarts water
- 1   teaspoon kosher salt or salt
- 1   teaspoon coarsely ground black pepper
- 1   cup chopped mixed vegetables (celery, carrots and/or onions)
- 1   cup chopped mixed fruits (apples, pears and/or oranges)
- 1   tablespoon minced garlic
- 6   sprigs fresh rosemary
- 2   tablespoons Dijon-style mustard
- 1   tablespoon soy sauce
    Honey-Almond Sauce (recipe follows)
    Hot cooked wild rice (optional)

If using chicken, omit this step. Using a sharp knife, cut shallow slits every 2 inches across the duck's skin. In an 8- to 10-quart pot, bring water to boiling. Immerse duck into the boiling water; reduce heat. Gently boil, uncovered, for 15 minutes. Remove duck; drain well and discard water. Let duck stand until cool enough to handle (about 15 minutes).

Sprinkle cavity of duck with salt and black pepper. In a small bowl, combine chopped mixed vegetables, chopped mixed fruits, garlic and rosemary sprigs. Stuff cavity with mixture. Skewer neck skin to back of bird; tie legs to tail using 100-percent-cotton kitchen string. Twist wings under back. Place duck, breast side up, on a rack in a shallow roasting pan. Roast duck, uncovered, in a 450° oven for 1 1/4 hours. (For chicken, roast 45 minutes.) Remove duck from oven; reduce oven temperature to 350°.

In a small bowl, combine mustard and soy sauce. Spread mustard mixture over outside of duck. Insert an ovenproof meat thermometer into thigh. (Do not touch bone.) Return duck to oven; roast for 30 minutes or until thermometer registers 180°, drumsticks move easily in sockets, and juices run clear (roast 20 minutes for chicken). Discard hot fat as it accumulates.

Remove duck from oven; increase oven temperature to 500°. Let duck stand for 15 minutes. Spoon stuffing from cavity and transfer to a foil-lined baking sheet. Using paper towels to protect your hand from the heat, hold duck and use kitchen shears to halve duck lengthwise, cutting along backbone. Cut halves in half crosswise. Place duck quarters over stuffing on prepared baking sheet. Return duck to oven; roast for 8 to 10 minutes.

Pour Honey-Almond Sauce over duck. If you like, serve with hot cooked wild rice. *Makes 4 servings.*

Honey-Almond Sauce: In a small saucepan, melt 3 tablespoons butter over medium heat. Add 1/2 cup sliced almonds. Cook and stir about 5 minutes or until almonds turn a deep golden brown. Stir in 2 tablespoons honey; heat through. *Makes about 1/2 cup.*

Crispy Fried Chicken

Inspired by Chicken Annie's Original and Chicken Mary's, Pittsburg, KS

- 1/3 cup all-purpose flour
- 1 1/2 teaspoons poultry seasoning or paprika; dried basil or marjoram, crushed; or 1/2 teaspoon garlic powder or onion powder
- 1/2 teaspoon salt
- 1/4 teaspoon ground black pepper
- 2 1/2 to 3 pounds meaty chicken pieces (breast halves, thighs, and drumsticks)
    Cooking oil
    Creamy Gravy (recipe follows)
    Hot mashed potatoes (optional)

In a plastic bag, combine flour, poultry seasoning, salt and black pepper. Add chicken pieces, a few at a time, shaking to coat.

Add cooking oil to a 12-inch heavy skillet to a depth of 1/4 to 1/2 inch. Heat over medium-high heat until hot enough to sizzle a drop of water. Reduce heat. Add chicken to skillet. (Do not crowd chicken in skillet. If necessary, use 2 skillets.) Cook, uncovered, over medium heat for 15 minutes, turning to brown evenly. Reduce heat; cover tightly. Cook for 15 minutes. Uncover and cook for 5 to 10 minutes more or until chicken is no longer pink (170° for breasts; 180° for thighs and drumsticks). Drain on paper towels, reserving drippings for gravy.

Transfer chicken to a serving platter; keep warm. Serve with Creamy Gravy and, if you like, hot mashed potatoes. *Makes 6 servings.*

Creamy Gravy: Pour off drippings in skillet, reserving 2 tablespoons. Return reserved drippings to skillet. Add 2 tablespoons all-purpose flour; 1/8 teaspoon ground black pepper; and, if you like, 1 teaspoon instant chicken bouillon granules; stir until smooth. Add 1 2/3 cups milk all at once. Cook and stir over medium heat until thickened and bubbly. Cook and stir for 1 minute more. (If necessary, thin with a little additional milk.) *Makes 1 2/3 cups.*

Amish Bean Soup

Amish Acres, Nappanee, IN

- 1   pound dry navy or dry Great Northern beans (about 2 1/3 cups)
- 1   to 1 1/2 pounds meaty ham bone or smoked pork hocks
- 1   teaspoon dried thyme or sage, crushed (optional)
- 1   large onion, chopped (1 cup)
- 1/2 teaspoon seasoned salt
- 1/2 teaspoon celery salt
- 1/2 teaspoon ground black pepper
- 1/4 teaspoon garlic powder

Rinse beans. In a 4- to 6-quart Dutch oven, combine beans and 6 cups water. Bring to boiling; reduce heat. Simmer for 2 minutes. Remove from heat. Cover and let stand for 1 hour. (Or place beans in water in Dutch oven. Cover and let soak in a cool place for 6 to 8 hours or overnight.) Drain and rinse beans; set aside.

Add 6 cups fresh water and ham bone or pork hocks to same Dutch oven. Bring to boiling; reduce heat. Simmer, covered, for 1 hour.

Remove ham bone or pork hocks. When cool enough to handle, cut meat off bones; coarsely chop meat. Discard bones. Slightly mash beans in Dutch oven. If you like, add thyme or sage. Stir in onion, seasoned salt, celery salt, black pepper and garlic powder. Return to boiling; reduce heat. Simmer, covered, for 45 to 60 minutes more or until beans are tender, stirring occasionally. Stir in chopped meat; heat through. *Makes 6 servings.*

Three-Cheese Beer Soup
Inspired by Wisconsin cheese and beer

2 tablespoons butter
1 medium onion, finely chopped
1 medium carrot, finely chopped
1 stalk celery, finely chopped
2 green onions, thinly sliced
1/4 cup all-purpose flour
1/2 teaspoon dry mustard
4 cups chicken broth
1 cup beer or dark ale
1 cup whipping cream
2 medium potatoes, peeled and cut into
   1/2-inch cubes
1 cup shredded sharp cheddar cheese at
   room temperature (4 ounces)
1 cup shredded white cheddar cheese at
   room temperature (4 ounces)
1/4 cup grated Parmesan or Romano cheese
1/4 teaspoon bottled hot-pepper sauce
1/4 teaspoon Worcestershire sauce

In a 4-quart Dutch oven, melt butter over medium heat. Add onion, carrot, celery and green onions. Cook and stir 8 to 10 minutes or until onion is golden.

Stir in flour and mustard. Cook and stir 1 minute. Add broth; cook and stir until bubbly. Stir in beer and whipping cream. Add potatoes. Bring to boiling; reduce heat. Simmer, uncovered, for 10 to 12 minutes or until potatoes are tender.

Slowly add cheddar cheeses, whisking until cheeses are melted. Whisk in Parmesan or Romano cheese, hot-pepper sauce and Worcestershire sauce. *Makes 4 servings.*

SALADS & SIDE DISHES

Just Like Grandma's Potato Salad
Inspired by Prairie Sky Guest & Game Ranch, Veblen, SD

6 medium potatoes (2 pounds)
1/4 teaspoon salt
11/4 cups mayonnaise or salad dressing
1 tablespoon yellow mustard
1/2 teaspoon salt
1/4 teaspoon ground black pepper
1 cup thinly sliced celery (2 stalks)
1/3 cup chopped onion (1 small)
1/2 cup chopped sweet or dill pickles or
   sweet or dill pickle relish
6 hard-cooked eggs, coarsely chopped
   Lettuce leaves (optional)
   Paprika (optional)

In a medium saucepan, place potatoes, 1/4 teaspoon salt and enough water to cover. Bring to boiling; reduce heat. Simmer, covered, for 20 to 25 minutes or until just tender. Drain well; cool slightly. Peel and cube potatoes.

For dressing: In a large bowl, combine mayonnaise, mustard, 1/2 teaspoon salt and black pepper. Stir in celery, onion and pickles. Add potatoes and eggs. Toss lightly to coat. Cover and chill for 6 to 24 hours.

To serve, if you like, line a salad bowl with lettuce leaves. Transfer potato salad to bowl. If you like, sprinkle with paprika. *Makes 12 side-dish servings.*

Tip: Boiling potatoes in their skins prevents them from absorbing too much water during cooking and ensures firm potatoes for salad.

Crunchy Oriental Cabbage Slaw
Murphy's Wagon Wheel, Hastings, NE

1/3 cup salad oil
1/3 cup rice vinegar or vinegar
2 tablespoons sugar
2 teaspoons soy sauce
1/4 teaspoon ground black pepper or
   1/8 teaspoon crushed red pepper
1 3-ounce package chicken- or beef-
   flavored ramen noodles, broken
1/2 of a 16-ounce package shredded
   cabbage with carrot (coleslaw mix)
   (about 4 cups) or 3 cups shredded
   green cabbage and 1 cup shredded
   red cabbage
1/2 cup slivered almonds, toasted
1/4 cup sliced green onions
1/4 cup shelled sunflower seeds or
   2 tablespoons sesame seeds

For dressing: In a small bowl, whisk together oil, vinegar, sugar, soy sauce, black pepper and the contents of seasoning packet from ramen noodles. Set dressing aside.

In a large bowl, combine the broken dry ramen noodles, cabbage, almonds, green onions and sunflower seeds. Drizzle dressing over the cabbage mixture. Toss to coat. Serve immediately or cover and chill up to 1 hour before serving. *Makes 8 to 10 side-dish servings.*

Tabbouleh

Inspired by La Shish, Dearborn, MI

- ³/₄ cup bulgur
- 1 small cucumber, peeled, seeded and chopped (¹/₂ cup)
- ¹/₄ cup snipped fresh parsley
- 2 tablespoons snipped fresh mint or 2 teaspoons dried mint, crushed
- 2 tablespoons thinly sliced green onion
- ¹/₄ cup olive oil or salad oil
- 3 tablespoons lemon juice
- 2 tablespoons water
- ¹/₄ teaspoon salt
- ¹/₈ teaspoon ground black pepper
- ¹/₂ cup chopped, seeded tomato (1 small)

Place bulgur in a colander; rinse with cold water and drain. In a medium bowl, combine bulgur, cucumber, parsley, mint and green onion.

For dressing: In a screw-top jar, combine the oil, lemon juice, water, salt and black pepper. Cover and shake well. Pour dressing over bulgur mixture. Toss lightly to coat. Cover and chill for 4 to 24 hours. Bring to room temperature before serving. Stir tomato into bulgur mixture just before serving. *Makes 4 to 6 side-dish servings.*

Ohio Vegetable Medley

Inspired by Fulton Farms, Troy, OH

- 3 cups shredded cabbage
- 2 cups peeled and cubed eggplant
- 2 cups seeded and chopped tomatoes
- 1 cup sliced zucchini
- 1 cup sliced yellow summer squash
- 1 cup chopped onion
- ³/₄ cup chopped green or red sweet pepper
- 6 whole okra, sliced
- ¹/₄ cup snipped fresh Italian (flat-leaf) parsley
- 2 tablespoons snipped fresh basil or 2 teaspoons dried basil, crushed
- 2 cloves garlic, minced
- ³/₄ teaspoon kosher salt or ¹/₂ teaspoon salt
- ¹/₄ teaspoon freshly ground black pepper
- 2 tablespoons olive oil
  Finely shredded Romano or Parmesan cheese (optional)

In a large bowl, combine cabbage, eggplant, tomatoes, zucchini, summer squash, onion, sweet pepper, okra, parsley, basil, garlic, salt and black pepper. Toss to combine.

In a 12-inch skillet or 4- to 5-quart Dutch oven, heat olive oil over medium-high heat. Add vegetable mixture; reduce to medium heat. Cook and stir for 8 to 10 minutes or until crisp-tender. If you like, sprinkle with cheese. Serve immediately. *Makes 8 side-dish servings.*

Hickory Pit Beans

Fiorella's Jack Stack Barbecue, Kansas City, MO

- 1 31-ounce can pork and beans in tomato sauce, drained
- 1 cup Jack Stack's KC Original BBQ Sauce or your favorite purchased barbecue sauce
- 1 cup chopped purchased or leftover cooked beef brisket
- ¹/₂ cup water
- ¹/₄ cup ketchup
- ¹/₄ cup packed brown sugar
- 1 teaspoon liquid smoke

In a large saucepan, combine drained beans, barbecue sauce, brisket, water, ketchup, brown sugar and liquid smoke. Bring to boiling; reduce heat. Simmer, uncovered, for 20 to 30 minutes or until desired consistency, stirring occasionally. Serve hot. *Makes 10 to 12 servings.*

Mint-Buttered Soybeans

Inspired by Green City Market, Chicago, IL

2 teaspoons butter or margarine
3 cups shelled fresh or frozen (thawed) sweet soybeans (edamame)
3 tablespoons fresh small mint leaves
1 tablespoon snipped fresh basil
1/4 teaspoon salt

In a medium skillet, melt butter over medium heat. Add soybeans to skillet. Cook and stir about 5 minutes or until tender. Stir in mint, snipped basil and salt. If you like, garnish with basil sprigs. *Makes 6 side-dish servings.*

DESSERTS & PIES

Persimmon Pudding

Inspired by Indiana persimmons

2 teaspoons butter, melted
1 cup all-purpose flour
1 teaspoon baking powder
Dash ground cinnamon
1/2 cup half-and-half or light cream
1/2 cup buttermilk
1/2 teaspoon baking soda
1 egg, slightly beaten
1 cup persimmon pulp
1 cup sugar
1/2 teaspoon finely shredded orange peel
2 tablespoons butter, melted
3/4 cup whipped cream

Grease an 8x8x2-inch baking pan with 2 teaspoons melted butter. Set aside.

In a small bowl, stir together flour, baking powder and cinnamon. Set aside. In another small bowl, combine half-and-half, buttermilk and baking soda. Set aside.

In a medium bowl, combine egg, persimmon pulp, sugar and orange peel. Add flour mixture and buttermilk mixture alternately to persimmon mixture, stirring well after each addition. Stir in 2 tablespoons melted butter. Pour batter into prepared pan.

Bake in a 325° oven for 35 to 40 minutes or until a knife inserted off-center comes out clean. Cut into squares. Serve warm with whipped cream. *Makes 6 to 8 servings.*

Strawberry Schaum Torte

Schwarz's Supper Club, St. Anna, WI

4 egg whites
Sugar
1 teaspoon vanilla
1/2 teaspoon vinegar
1/4 teaspoon salt
1 cup sugar
2 cups sliced strawberries
1 cup whipping cream
2 tablespoons sugar
1/2 teaspoon vanilla

Allow egg whites to stand in a large mixing bowl for 30 minutes. Meanwhile, butter a 2-quart square baking dish. Dust bottom and sides with sugar; set dish aside.

For meringue: Add 1 teaspoon vanilla, vinegar and salt to egg whites. Beat with an electric mixer on medium speed until soft peaks form (tips curl). Gradually add 1 cup sugar, 1 tablespoon at a time, beating about 4 minutes on high speed until stiff peaks form (tips stand straight) and sugar is almost dissolved.

Spread meringue into prepared baking dish (do not build up sides). Bake in a 300° oven for 35 minutes. Turn oven off. Let meringue dry in oven, with door closed, for 1 hour. (Do not open oven door while drying.)

For filling: Chill a medium mixing bowl and beaters of an electric mixer. Pat strawberry slices dry with paper towel. In chilled bowl, beat whipping cream, 2 tablespoons sugar and 1/2 teaspoon vanilla on medium speed until soft peaks form. Fold in strawberries. Evenly spread whipped cream mixture over meringue. Cover loosely; chill for 6 to 12 hours.

To serve, cut into squares with a wet knife. If you like, garnish with strawberry halves. *Makes 6 to 8 servings.*

Raisin-Walnut Bread Pudding

Old Feed Mill, Mazomanie, WI

2 1/4 cups milk
3/4 cup sugar
2 slightly beaten eggs
1/4 cup butter, melted
1 tablespoon vanilla
3/4 teaspoon ground cinnamon
1/4 teaspoon ground nutmeg
4 cups dry French bread cubes or dry regular bread cubes
1/2 cup raisins, dried cherries or dried cranberries
1/2 cup chopped pecans, toasted
1/3 cup flaked coconut, toasted

In a large bowl, whisk together milk, sugar, eggs, melted butter, vanilla, cinnamon and nutmeg. In an ungreased 2-quart square baking dish, place bread cubes. Sprinkle with raisins, pecans and coconut; pour egg mixture evenly over bread mixture. Press mixture lightly with back of a large spoon.

Bake, uncovered, in a 350° oven about 50 minutes or until top is evenly puffed. Cool for 30 to 45 minutes. Serve warm. *Makes 6 to 8 servings.*

Maple-Oatmeal Drops

Inspired by Casier Maple Syrup,
Empire, MI

- 1/2 cup shortening
- 1 1/2 cups all-purpose flour
- 1 cup pure maple syrup
- 1 egg
- 1/4 cup milk
- 2 teaspoons baking powder
- 1/2 teaspoon kosher salt or 1/4 teaspoon salt
- 1 1/2 cups quick-cooking rolled oats
- 1/2 cup dried cherries or raisins
- 1/2 cup chopped walnuts or pecans

Lightly grease cookie sheets; set aside. In a large mixing bowl, beat shortening with an electric mixer on medium to high speed for 30 seconds. Beat in 3/4 cup of flour. Add maple syrup, egg, milk, baking powder and salt. Beat until combined. Stir in remaining 3/4 cup flour and rolled oats with a wooden spoon. Stir in dried cherries and walnuts (dough will be soft).

Drop dough by heaping teaspoons 2 inches apart onto prepared cookie sheets. Bake in a 350° oven about 13 minutes or until edges are lightly browned. Cool on cookie sheets for 1 minute. Transfer cookies to wire racks and cool completely. *Makes about 40 cookies.*

Swedish Sandbakkelse

Inspired by Minnesota Scandinavians

- 1/2 cup butter, softened
- 1/2 cup sugar
- 1 egg
- 1/2 teaspoon almond extract
- 1/4 cup ground almonds
- 1 1/2 cups all-purpose flour
  Loganberry jam or orange marmalade (optional)

Season 2 1/2-inch sandbakkelse molds, if necessary. (To season brand-new sand-bakkelse molds, grease insides of molds with shortening. Heat in a 300° oven for 30 minutes. Cool. Wipe out excess shortening. (After use, rinse with water and wipe with paper towels. You won't need to season the molds again.)

In a large mixing bowl, beat butter with an electric mixer on medium to high speed for 30 seconds. Gradually add sugar, beating on medium speed until well combined and scraping sides of bowl. Add egg and almond extract, beating until combined. Beat in ground almonds. Beat in as much of the flour as you can with the mixer. Using a wooden spoon, stir in any remaining flour. Cover and chill dough about 1 hour or until easy to handle.

Place 2 to 2 1/2 teaspoons of the dough in the center of each seasoned sandbakkelse mold. Press dough in an even, very thin layer along the bottom and up the sides, making sure no dough extends over edges of the molds. Place molds on a cookie sheet. (Or, press dough into 1 3/4-inch tart pans or muffin cups.)

Bake in a 350° oven for 10 to 12 minutes or until edges are firm and very light brown. Remove from oven. Turn over each mold; cool tarts upside down in molds on cookie sheet for 5 minutes. Gently tap bottom of the molds; carefully remove tarts. (Or, cool cookies in tart pans or muffin cups for 5 minutes; remove cookies.) Cool on wire racks. If you like, fill with loganberry jam or orange marmalade. *Makes about 36 sandbakkelse.*

Norwegian Kringla

Inspired by Minnesota Scandinavians

- 3 3/4 cups all-purpose flour
- 2 teaspoons baking powder
- 1/2 teaspoon baking soda
- 1/2 teaspoon salt
- 3 egg yolks, slightly beaten
- 1 1/4 cups granulated sugar
- 1/2 cup milk
- 1/4 cup dairy sour cream
- 1 tablespoon butter, melted
- 1/4 teaspoon anise extract or 1/2 teaspoon vanilla
  Coarse and/or fine decorating sugar (optional)

Lightly grease a cookie sheet; set aside. In a medium bowl, stir together flour, baking powder, baking soda and salt; set aside.

In a large bowl, combine egg yolks, granulated sugar, milk, sour cream, melted butter and anise extract. Using a wooden spoon, stir flour mixture into egg mixture until combined. Dough will be stiff and sticky.

On a well-floured surface, drop 1 rounded tablespoon of the dough. Roll dough into a 5- or 8-inch-long rope. On the prepared cookie sheet, shape a 5-inch rope into a ring, crossing it over itself about 1 inch from ends. Or fold an 8-inch rope in half and twist 3 times; seal ends with egg-white mixture. Repeat with remaining dough, placing shapes 2 inches apart on prepared cookie sheet. Brush with egg-white mixture. If you like, sprinkle with decorating sugar.

Bake in a 350° oven for 8 to 10 minutes or until lightly golden brown. Cool on a wire rack. *Makes 48 cookies.*

Green-Tomato and Apple Pie

Bagg Bonanza Farm Historic Preservation
Society, Mooreton, ND

- 1 15-ounce package rolled refrigerated unbaked piecrusts (2 crusts)
- 3 cups thinly sliced green tomatoes (about 1 pound)
- 3 cups thinly sliced, peeled cooking apples (about 1 pound)
- ½ cup granulated sugar
- ½ cup packed brown sugar
- ¼ cup all-purpose flour
- 2 teaspoons finely shredded lemon peel
- 3 tablespoons lemon juice
- 2 tablespoons butter, melted
- 1 teaspoon ground cinnamon
- ¼ teaspoon salt
- ¼ teaspoon ground nutmeg
- ¼ teaspoon ground allspice

For pie pastry: Let piecrusts stand at room temperature for 15 minutes. Unroll piecrusts. Ease 1 of piecrusts into a 9-inch pie plate without stretching it. Set aside.

For filling: In a large bowl, place green tomatoes. Pour boiling water over tomatoes to cover; let stand about 20 minutes or until slightly cooled. Drain well. Stir apples into tomatoes.

In a small bowl, combine granulated sugar, brown sugar, flour, lemon peel and juice, 2 tablespoons melted butter, cinnamon, salt, nutmeg and allspice. Add flour mixture to tomato-apple mixture; stir to combine.

Transfer filling to pastry-lined pie plate. Trim bottom piecrust to edge of pie plate. Cut slits in remaining piecrust; place on filling and seal. Crimp edge as desired. If you like, brush top piecrust with a little additional melted butter or milk. To prevent overbrowning, cover edge of pie with foil.

Bake in a 450° oven for 10 minutes. Reduce heat to 375° and bake for 30 minutes. Remove foil. Bake about 20 minutes more or until fruit is tender and filling is bubbly. Cool on a wire rack. *Makes 8 servings.*

Peppermint-Fudge Ice Cream Pie

Graeter's Ice Cream, Cincinnati, OH

- 2 pints (4 cups) Graeter's peppermint ice cream or high-quality peppermint ice cream, softened slightly at room temperature
- 1 9-inch purchased chocolate-flavored crumb pie shell
- 1 12-ounce jar chocolate fudge ice cream topping
  Whipped Cream (recipe follows)
  Mini candy canes and/or red- and green-colored sprinkles

In a large bowl, soften peppermint ice cream using a wooden spoon to stir and press ice cream against side of bowl. Stir until soft but not melted.

Quickly spoon softened ice cream into pie shell. Use back of spoon to gently push ice cream, building up edges slightly. Cover and freeze for 1 hour or until firm. Spread fudge topping over ice cream to evenly cover. Cover and freeze for 1 hour more.

Prepare Whipped Cream; place in a pas-

try bag fitted with a star tip and pipe in mounds on top of pie. Cover and freeze pie for several hours or overnight until firm.

To serve, remove pie from freezer. Let stand 10 to 15 minutes before serving. Decorate top with mini candy canes and/or red- and green-colored sprinkles. Use a large heavy-duty chef's knife to cut pie into wedges. *Makes 8 servings.*

Whipped Cream: Chill a medium mixing bowl and beaters of an electric mixer. In chilled bowl, beat 1 cup whipping cream, 2 tablespoons sugar and ½ teaspoon vanilla with an electric mixer on medium speed until soft peaks form. *Makes 2 cups.*

Sweet Potato Pie

Inspired by Army & Lou's Restaurant, Chicago, IL

- 2 medium sweet potatoes (about 1 pound), peeled and cubed
- 1¼ cups all-purpose flour
- ¼ teaspoon salt
- ⅓ cup shortening
- 4 to 5 tablespoons cold water
- ¼ cup butter or margarine
- ¾ to 1 cup packed brown sugar
- 1½ teaspoons ground cinnamon
- ¼ teaspoon ground nutmeg
  Dash salt
- 3 eggs, slightly beaten
- 1 12-ounce can (1½ cups) evaporated milk

In a large saucepan, cook sweet potatoes, covered, in boiling water about 15 minutes or until tender.

Meanwhile, in a medium bowl, combine flour and ¼ teaspoon salt. Using a pastry blender, cut in shortening until pieces are pea-size. Sprinkle cold water, 1 tablespoon at a time, over part of mixture. Gently toss with fork just until all dough is moistened. Form dough into ball.

On a lightly floured surface, roll dough from center to edge into a 12-inch circle. Transfer pastry to a 10-inch deep-dish pie plate. Trim pastry to ½ inch beyond edge of plate. Fold under extra pastry; crimp edge as desired. Line unpricked pastry shell with a double thickness of foil. Bake in a 450° oven for 8 minutes. Remove foil;

bake for 4 to 5 minutes more or until set and dry. Set aside. Reduce oven temperature to 400°.

Drain potatoes. In a large mixer bowl, combine potatoes and butter. Beat with electric mixer until smooth. Add brown sugar, cinnamon, nutmeg and dash salt. Beat until combined. Add eggs. Beat on low speed just until combined. Gradually stir in evaporated milk.

Carefully pour filling into prepared pastry shell. To prevent overbrowning, cover edge of pie with foil. Bake in a 400° oven for 10 minutes. Reduce heat to 350° and bake for 40 to 50 minutes more or until knife inserted in enter comes out clean. Cool on a wire rack for 1 hour. Serve warm. (Or, cover and refrigerate after 2 hours.) If you like, serve with whipped cream sprinkled with ground nutmeg. *Makes 8 servings.*

Rhubarb-Apple-Cheese Pizza Pie

Inspired by Red Baron Lounge and Pizza Pub, Casselton, ND

Pizza Pie Pastry or Sugar Cookie Pizza Crust (recipes follow)
- 2/3 cup sugar
- 2 tablespoons cornstarch
- 1 teaspoon ground cinnamon
- 1/4 teaspoon salt
- 1/2 cup apple juice
- 2 cups sliced fresh rhubarb or frozen unsweetened sliced rhubarb
- 2 cups thinly sliced, peeled Braeburn and/or Granny Smith apples
- 1 tablespoon butter
- 1 8-ounce package cream cheese, softened
- 1/2 cup sugar
- 2 eggs
- 1 teaspoon vanilla
- 1/2 cup chopped pecans or walnuts, toasted
  Unsweetened whipped cream

Prepare Pizza Pie Pastry or Sugar Cookie Pizza Crust.

For topping: In a large saucepan, combine 2/3 cup sugar, cornstarch, cinnamon and 1/4 teaspoon salt. Add apple juice. Cook and stir over medium heat until thickened

and bubbly. Stir in rhubarb and apples. Cook over medium-low heat for 8 to 10 minutes more or until fruit is tender, stirring occasionally. Remove from heat. Stir in 1 tablespoon butter. Let cool slightly.

For filling: In a medium bowl, beat cream cheese with an electric mixer on medium to high speed for 30 seconds. Add 1/2 cup sugar, eggs and vanilla. Beat until combined, scraping sides of bowl occasionally. Stir in pecans. Pour cheese mixture into crust.

Bake in a 350° oven for 15 to 20 minutes or until set. Spread topping over cheese layer. Cool slightly and serve warm. (Or, cover and chill before serving.)

To serve, garnish top with small dollops of whipped cream around edges. Spoon whipped cream in center; insert pastry cutouts. Cut into wedges. *Makes 8 to 10 servings.*

Pizza Pie Pastry: In a medium bowl, stir together 1 3/4 cups all-purpose flour and 1/2 teaspoon salt. Using a pastry blender, cut in 1/2 cup butter and 3 tablespoons shortening until pieces are pea-size. In a small bowl, combine 1 beaten egg yolk and 3 table-

spoons ice water. Sprinkle 1 tablespoon of egg mixture over part of flour mixture; gently toss with a fork. Push moistened dough to side of bowl. Repeat moistening flour mixture, using 1 tablespoon of egg mixture at a time, until all flour mixture is moistened. Using fingers, knead lightly to form a ball. Cover; chill pastry for 30 to 60 minutes or until dough is easy to handle.

On a floured surface, use your hands to slightly flatten dough. Roll dough from center to edges into a circle 14 inches in diameter. To transfer pastry, wrap it around rolling pin. Unroll pastry into a 13-inch pizza pan. Ease pastry into pizza pan without stretching it. Trim pastry to 1/2 inch beyond edge of pizza pan. Fold under extra pastry. Crimp edge as desired. Prick pastry with tines of a fork. Bake in a 350° oven for 15 to 18 minutes or until golden. Cool on a wire rack.

Meanwhile, reroll pastry trimmings to 1/8-inch thickness. Cut into desired shapes with small cookie cutter. Place cutouts on ungreased baking sheet. Bake in a 350° oven for 8 to 10 minutes or until golden. Cool on a wire rack; set aside.

Sugar Cookie Pizza Crust: Cut one 18-ounce roll refrigerated sugar cookie dough into 1/4-inch-thick slices. Press cookie dough slices into a greased 13-inch pizza pan. Bake in a 350° oven about 15 to 20 minutes or until golden. Cool on a wire rack; set aside.

Spiced Apple-Ginger Pie

Inspired by Historic Kimmel Orchard, Nebraska City, NE

- 1/2 of a 15-ounce package rolled refrigerated unbaked piecrust (1 crust)
  Coconut-Almond Crumb Topping (recipe follows)
- 3/4 cup sugar
- 3 tablespoons all-purpose flour
- 2 tablespoons finely chopped crystallized ginger
- 1 teaspoon ground cinnamon or apple pie spice
- 6 cups peeled, sliced Granny Smith apples or tart cooking apples (6 apples)

For pie pastry: Let piecrust stand at room temperature for 15 minutes. Unroll piecrust. Roll dough from center to edges into a circle 13 inches in diameter. To transfer pastry, wrap it around the rolling pin. Unroll pastry into a 10-inch pie plate. Ease pastry into pie plate, being careful not to stretch pastry. Fold under extra pastry. Crimp edge as desired. Do not prick pastry. Set aside.

For topping: Prepare the Coconut-Almond Crumb Topping. Set aside.

For filling: In a very large bowl, combine sugar, flour, crystallized ginger and cinnamon. Add the apples; gently toss to coat. Transfer apple mixture to pastry-lined pie plate. Sprinkle evenly with the Coconut-Almond Crumb Topping, pressing down as necessary. Cover top of pie loosely with foil.

Place pie on the middle rack of oven. Place a baking sheet on the rack below the pie plate to catch any juices that bubble over. Bake in a 375° oven for 40 minutes. Remove foil. Bake for 20 to 30 minutes more or until fruit is tender and filling is bubbly. Cool on a wire rack for at least 2 hours before serving. If you like, serve with scoops of vanilla ice cream. *Makes 10 servings.*

Coconut-Almond Crumb Topping: In a small bowl, combine 1/3 cup finely crushed gingersnaps, 1/3 cup finely crushed vanilla wafers (or 2/3 cup of either), 1/2 cup chopped almonds or pecans, 1/3 cup flaked coconut and 3 tablespoons butter, melted. Toss to coat.

Michigan Cherry-Berry Pie
Inspired by Jesperson's Restaurant, Petoskey, MI

- 3 cups frozen unsweetened pitted tart red cherries
- 1 cup frozen red raspberries
  Cherry juice or cranberry juice
- 1 15-ounce package rolled refrigerated unbaked piecrust (2 crusts)
- 2 teaspoons butter, melted
- 1¼ cups sugar
- 3 tablespoons cornstarch
- 1 tablespoon quick-cooking tapioca
- ¼ teaspoon salt
- ¼ teaspoon ground nutmeg
- 2 tablespoons butter, cut up
- 1 tablespoon lemon juice
  Vanilla ice cream (optional)

Thaw frozen cherries and raspberries in a colander over a medium bowl, reserving juice. Add enough cherry juice to measure 1¼ cups.

For pie pastry: Let piecrusts stand at room temperature for 15 minutes. Unroll piecrusts. Ease 1 piecrust into a 9-inch pie plate without stretching it. Do not prick pastry. Brush piecrust bottom and sides with 2 teaspoons melted butter. Set aside.

For filling: In a medium saucepan, combine sugar, cornstarch, tapioca, salt and nutmeg. Add the 1¼ cups reserved juice. Cook and stir until thickened and bubbly. Remove from heat. Stir in 2 tablespoons butter, lemon juice and thawed cherries and raspberries.

Transfer filling to the pastry-lined pie plate. Trim bottom piecrust to edge of pie plate. Cut slits in remaining piecrust; place on filling and seal. Crimp edge as desired. If you like, brush top of piecrust with a little milk and sprinkle with additional sugar. To prevent overbrowning, cover edge of pie with foil.

Bake in a 375° oven for 30 minutes. Remove foil. Bake for 30 to 35 minutes more or until filling is bubbly and piecrust is golden. Cool on a wire rack for at least 2 hours before serving. If you like, serve with scoops of vanilla ice cream. *Makes 8 servings.*

KIMMEL ORCHARD

←ENTRANCE

Location Index

Recipe Index

Contributors

Dan Kaercher

Dan Kaercher has been a writer and editor with Meredith Corporation in Des Moines, Iowa, since 1972 and editor-in-chief of *Midwest Living*® since its founding in 1987. He has lived in the Midwest almost his entire life, primarily in Nebraska and Iowa, and he currently resides in the Des Moines suburb of Urbandale with his wife, Julie. Dan describes himself as an eager but thoroughly amateur cook and outdoor griller who never met a meal he didn't like.

Bob Stefko

Bob Stefko's photography talents are showcased throughout this book. In addition to *Midwest Living,* his wide-ranging work has appeared in many national magazines, from *Gourmet* to *Forbes,* and his fine-art images are exhibited in several permanent collections. A native of Ohio, Bob now lives in Evanston, Illinois, with his wife, Holly, who accompanied him on part of the *Taste of the Midwest* journey. Before choosing a photography career, Bob aspired to be a chef.

Sandra Mapes Granseth

Sandra Granseth vetted, adapted, and/or developed all the recipes that appear in this book. A lifelong Midwesterner, she won numerous blue ribbons for food entries at her county and state fair while growing up on an Iowa farm. Today, Sandra is a food writer, a cookbook editor and co-owner of Spectrum Communication Services in Des Moines, where she lives with her husband, George. At home, she enjoys sharing new dishes with family and friends.

Joan Lynch Luckett

A native of Independence, Missouri, *Midwest Living* Editorial Project Manager Joan Luckett served as project coordinator for the trip itself and for this book, planning each day's itinerary and subsequently managing the editorial production and fact-checking. Joan is a former speech clinician, audiologist and entrepreneur. Before moving to Des Moines, she lived in the Kansas City, Louisville, St. Louis and Cincinnati areas.

Paul Hickey

Paul Hickey, who accompanied Dan throughout his journey on behalf of Iowa Public Television, was impressed by the generosity of the cooks he met on the trip. Paul is a freelance videographer, a director of photography, and a lighting designer for commercials, documentaries and corporate productions nationally. A native of Ontario, Canada, he attended the University of Iowa and now lives with his wife, Leslie, in Des Moines.